St. Helens Libraries

Please return / renew this item ~~by~~ ~~~~ items
may be renewed by phone and ~~internet~~.

Telephone: (01744) 676954 or 677822
Email: centrallibrary@sthelens.gov.uk
Online: sthelens.gov.uk/librarycatalogue

STHLibraries   sthlibrariesandarts   STHLibraries

IN OUR TIME

Celebrating Twenty Years
of Essential Conversation

MELVYN BRAGG
& SIMON TILLOTSON

IN OUR
TIME

CELEBRATING TWENTY YEARS
OF ESSENTIAL CONVERSATION

SIMON &
SCHUSTER

London · New York · Sydney · Toronto · New Delhi

A CBS COMPANY

MMXVIII

First published in Great Britain by Simon & Schuster UK Ltd, 2018
A CBS COMPANY

1 3 5 7 9 10 8 6 4 2

Simon & Schuster UK Ltd
1st Floor
222 Gray's Inn Road
London WC1X 8HB

www.simonandschuster.co.uk
www.simonandschuster.com.au
www.simonandschuster.co.in

Simon & Schuster Australia, Sydney
Simon & Schuster India, New Delhi

Interior images © Getty Images
Photograph opposite © Amanda Benson/BBC

A CIP catalogue record for this book is available from the British Library

Publishing Director: Iain MacGregor
Project Editor: Melissa Bond
Desk Editor/picture research: Kaiya Shang
Design: Keith Williams, sprout.uk.com
Production: Karin Seifried

The publishers would like to thank Ruth Gardiner, John Goudie and all the
many academics who have given their time to record the many episodes of the
series across two decades.

Hardback ISBN: 978-1-4711-7448-3
eBook ISBN: 978-1-4711-7450-6

Printed in Italy

CONTENTS

PHILOSOPHY

CULTURE

RELIGION

A Note on the Text

My thanks to Melvyn's guests whose ideas and expertise appear in the following pages. All original thoughts and research are theirs, all errors and omissions are mine, made as I condensed the live, unscripted discussions into these chapters.

Listeners often tell us which programmes they enjoy most and this collection represents a selection of their favourites. We could have filled this book several times over. My thanks also go to the thousands of guests who have taken part in the past twenty years and who are not represented in the book. I urge you to listen to the *In Our Time* archive to appreciate just how much we have missed out.

The introductions to each chapter are the words Melvyn spoke at 9.02 a.m. in Studio 50F at BBC Broadcasting House on the relevant Thursdays. Some of his guests' professional titles have changed since then and are printed as they are today. I have aimed to capture the shape and energy of the broadcasts, all unrehearsed, where Melvyn's guests speak to each other informally as colleagues, rather than formally for publication. All quotations are identified, and the sentences before or after are likely to be brief paraphrases of that same speaker's words.

I hope this brings new listeners to *In Our Time* and BBC Radio 4, as well as inspiring interest in the topics under discussion. We often hear teachers and students recommending the programme and that brings us a lot of joy. You may find some chapters useful, but all offer recreational learning for its own sake, as part of what it is to be human.

Simon Tillotson

INTRODUCTION

In 1998, BBC Radio 4 offered me the 'Death Slot' – how could I refuse?

I had been fired from *Start the Week*: the powers that be thought it had been contaminated by my acceptance of an offer made by Tony Blair's government of a seat in the House of Lords. The idea was to expand arts subsidies and it was felt that the House of Lords' Labour benches needed beefing up. David Puttnam went in, as did Genista McIntosh and others. Despite evidence that *Start the Week* had never been politically biased under my watch, I had to be seen to be as pure as Caesar's wife.

I had enjoyed the ten years of Monday morning's talk programme. With the producer Marina Salandy-Brown, we had changed it from predominantly show business to overwhelmingly science, history, literature and philosophy. For instance, when I went to *Start the Week*, 1 per cent of contributors were scientists; ten years later, the percentage was in the high thirties. And, counter-intuitively, the audiences had grown.

The Thursday morning Death Slot – a title widely and cheerfully brandished by the BBC – had somehow become stuck in the mire: it had bruised or sunk reputations, gathered obstinately low audiences and there was a deep sense of purposelessness. It was way below the profile and audience of *Start the Week*. So it was a chance to do something from scratch as I had tried to do on BBC One with the book programme *Read All About It* and on ITV with *The South Bank Show*. James Boyle, the Radio 4 controller, gave me a free hand, a six-month contract and the wonderfully inappropriate title.

I knew what I did not want. Good though *Start the Week* could be, I saw a chance to stop discussing books of the day, to concentrate on one subject and not four and, above all, to devote the programme to academics who, over the years, I had come to respect and enjoy as excellent broadcasters. Olivia Seligman, who had produced *Start the Week*, came alongside and we dived in. Neither of us expected it to last more than the six months.

We were lucky to get a few early positive reviews. We were also lucky that the casting of subjects was eclectic. I was determined to cover the territory – all the territory. From 'The Gin Craze' to 'The Palaeocene–Eocene Thermal Maximum', from 'Zeno's Paradoxes' to 'Icelandic Sagas', from 'Rabindranath Tagore' to 'Confucius', from 'Maimonides' to 'Hildegard of Bingen', from 'Ada Lovelace' to 'Dark Matter, – I loved the idea of taking the listeners by surprise with unlikely juxtapositions, which, in the long run (though I did not work this out at the time), would fall into an encyclopaedia. I loved the exhilarating feeling of infinitely varied knowledge. I have an autodidactic streak, which was now unleashed!

As this book is published, there have been 815 editions of *In Our Time*. It has become the BBC's most downloaded weekly podcast worldwide (and, on the level of individual episodes, the most downloaded of any). It is now a – free – massive archive. We get over 2 million listeners for the live broadcast on Thursday mornings and another 300,000 to 400,000 for the cut-down evening repeat. These podcasts take about 3 million copies of the programmes into forty-eight countries each month and, as importantly, to people – judging from the reactions – as widely varied as could be imagined: university graduates, workers in factories and on shop floors, men on oil rigs, people of all backgrounds catching up on their education.

That, I think, is the key. My first attempt to get a job after university was at the WEA – the Workers' Educational Association. I was turned down. The reason I went to university at all and did not leave school at fifteen like all my best friends was because my history teacher, Mr James, went to see my parents on three separate occasions to persuade them to let me stay at school (something I was not aware of until I was seventy-four). I like learning. I like listening to scholars. I could never have been an academic but their knowledge and turn of mind has always impressed and even seduced me. *In Our Time* has given me an education I could not have dreamt of at school or university.

The strength of the programme is in the contributors. Many of them have little radio experience, some none. But because we try to concentrate on those who teach as well as research, they have no problems. Partly this is because they have listened to some of the programmes and know how it all works. The composition of the contributors has changed. It is now at least fifty/fifty male and female and has been for some time. As it happens, over the past year it was fifty-eight female/forty-two male.

The original programme lasted thirty minutes. Helen Boaden, when controller of Radio 4, gave us an extra fifteen minutes. I had been struggling to make it work at thirty minutes. Forty-five meant that we could have three mini acts: the proposition, the discussion, the conclusion – all in forty-three minutes 'live'.

Sometimes – holiday times – we record the programmes, but 'live', I think, gives all of us an edge. I meet the contributors at about 8.55 a.m., take them through the structure (but not the questions) and, after a two-minute news bulletin, we are on air. We have what might be called rules – for instance, we are never knowingly relevant – and therefore, for example, if we are discussing a Middle Eastern country from past centuries, we keep off the current crises. There are ways in which we structure the programme to help it flow through the three acts, and I have been accused of over-urgency when trying to reach our conclusions before 9.45 a.m. After the programme finishes, we continue to talk for about five to ten minutes – a recent addition – which is added on to the podcast. Then we have a cup of tea and leave the studio at 10 a.m. prompt. The current controller of Radio 4, Gwyneth Williams, couldn't be more supportive. Before her, Mark Damazer as controller was always available and intellectually rich. The producer, Simon Tillotson (who has helped put together this book), is the successor in a line of fine producers. Together with Victoria Brignell, they make up the staff. I get the notes six days before the programme – they have now become my chief 'non-fiction' reading. They come with a structure from Simon on which I work right up to the last couple of minutes on the Thursday morning.

Above all, I am so very pleased that students have found it and find it useful and, equally, that those who missed out on education feel that *In Our Time* gives them the chance to catch up. I have been in broadcasting for fifty-six years and have never had such a warm and widespread response to a programme.

HISTORY

+━━●━━+

Every six weeks, Simon draws up a list of possible subjects. There are about ten in each of the sections we work to. Ideas come from Simon himself, from me, from previous contributors and from enthusiasts who write in, and, over a thrifty cup of coffee and for rarely more than three-quarters of an hour, we pick the 'team' for the next six programmes. Usually we have two programmes in hand, so, effectively we work two months ahead. Then Simon casts the programmes at the highest level available.

The fun is in the culture clash. As I write this, George Eliot's *Middlemarch* has been followed by a programme on the proton and the week afterwards we shall be in eleventh- and twelfth-century Islamic Spain.

At university in the late 1950s, I read modern history. This consisted of: British history from 412 to 1832; a slab of European history (say, 1492 to 1715); and a 'special subject' (in my case, the Italian Renaissance, which entailed learning Italian, a paper on Latin legal documents and, finally, a paper in Latin – to be translated into and out of the language and at least one other foreign tongue).

A lot was left out. Worlds and civilisations were left untouched. As one of the secret ambitions and pleasures of this series is to fill out an education, I have taken every opportunity to depart from the university syllabus.

In this selection, Simon has taken the reader into Roman history, with Romulus and Remus to the Picts, Ashoka the Great, Hatshepsut and the Lancashire Cotton Famine. The death of Elizabeth I was a chance to burrow deeply into a narrow but profound moment in domestic history. Similarly with the death of Charles I. The Gin Craze was a way to use social history to illuminate the more shocking and sensational aspect of that eighteenth-century debauched society.

In each case, the task for the academics (which they made seem simple) was to condense a lifetime's learning into a few minutes of broadcasting, which would not only hold onto their integrity but also reach out to a large audience whose appetite was keen but whose knowledge on the subject was often meagre. Time after time they did it. Perhaps this came from years of addressing students, but I think that they quickly mastered what was required of them – simply by listening – and prepared accordingly. When you listen back or read the transcripts (usually about 8,000 words), it is quite remarkable how much and how actively they covered the waterfront. The 'extra time' on the podcast now gives them room to finalise arguments made 'in the heat'. But, in my view, the 'live' imperative can not only accelerate thought but also sharpen it.

I am always impressed by how they combine two aspects of the subjects. The first is to give a rapid and accurate survey of the matter, citing the latest and best modern scholarship. The second is to find the space to differ courteously with each other on what are, at times, the thorniest areas of research.

Most important of all, I think, they are unafraid to refer to events, people and past commentators, among much else, that will be known only to a small percentage of the audience but are accepted and, I believe, understood by a larger audience in the general sweep of the discussion. These colloquies can be, at their very best, mini marvels of scholarly dialogue that operate on at least two levels simultaneously.

Of course, I am biased.

THE GIN CRAZE

The Gin Craze gripped Britain in the eighteenth century, when the government feared that poor people were drinking far too much cheap gin, damaging their own health and the safety and well-being of all. The roots of the craze could be traced to William of Orange, whose Dutch gin became the drink of choice for loyal Protestants. His new laws made beer expensive and let anyone distil and sell gin very cheaply at home; it was said that soon you could 'get drunk for a penny, dead drunk for twopence'. Hogarth later highlighted the horrors of alcohol in his Gin Lane, *made as tougher and tougher laws were being imposed to end what was seen as a dangerous overconsumption by the masses.*

With Melvyn to discuss the Gin Craze were: Angela McShane, head of research at the Wellcome Collection; Judith Hawley, professor of eighteenth-century literature at Royal Holloway, University of London; and Emma Major, senior lecturer in English at the University of York.

The one fundamental fact laid down by Judith Hawley was that everybody drank alcohol in the seventeenth century, across all age ranges, both men and women, while there was a glass of small beer for the children at breakfast. Beer was thought to be good for you, while water was muddy or contaminated. Drinking was socially stratified, with ale houses run for the poor by the poor, while taverns were run for the better off and gentry and served wine, but the really strong spirits weren't drunk regularly in Britain until William of Orange brought them over in 1688. With the support of leading Protestants, he had been invited to Britain to displace his Catholic father-in-law, James II, in what was known as the Glorious Revolution. Until then, people were drinking spirits but not in very large quantities, because they weren't made in large quantities.

MELVYN BRAGG: *Was there an impression that this island was a sort of rocking boat of drunkenness?*

JUDITH HAWLEY: *Yes, but also the British referred to the Dutch as drunks; everybody called everybody else a drunk.*

The drinking of alcohol was already embedded in society by the swearing of loyal toasts to kings and queens, but Angela McShane was clear that William changed drinking culture in Britain. Firstly, in 1690, he brought in an act to encourage the distilling of liquors in Britain, without regulation, to counteract the fact that he was banning the import of French brandy. He was at war with France and wanted to damage it economically. By the 1730s, there were 1,500 distillers in London, of whom 1,200 or so were small scale and 100 had really big stills, producing hard liquor, with medium-sized ones in between. Secondly, he brought from the Netherlands

A 1751 print by William Hogarth, entitled Gin Lane, depicts the evils of gin-drinking.

a vast number of Dutch sailors who were used to drinking gin and other spirits, which were much easier to drink on board ship than beer or wine. Gin was thought of as fortifying. Thirdly, since a lot of male sailors and soldiers were pouring into Britain, and into London in particular, women followed them and were drawn into this new drinking culture.

MELVYN BRAGG: *Can you just develop the idea of it being a Protestant drink?*

ANGELA MCSHANE: *It is Protestant because, when William comes in, he is the great Protestant deliverer, going to war both against James II and the Catholics in Ireland and against the Catholics in Europe. You could be thinking about gin as a Protestant drink, in that it is feeding your armies, it is deliberately anti-French.*

Dutch gin was available, but the British were now distilling more and more of their own in place of French brandy. Gin became intertwined with the British personality, Emma Major said, and was known as 'Madam Geneva', from the Dutch word for the juniper in gin, *jenever*, which gives us the English word 'gin'. Madam Geneva fired up the sailors and soldiers fighting for the Protestant cause, proving that God had chosen Britain as his favourite nation by providing it so generously with gin. To its proponents, there was no end to the benefits, even reviving 'marital bliss in the home by firing up tired husbands and rendering aged, fed-up wives into young, teenage, desirous and desirable beings'. It was sold as a medicine to ward off other perceived harms.

EMMA MAJOR: *There is a sense that it must be good for you because it counters the evil effects of too much tea drinking. So, if you drink too much tea, you are made ill by your tea addiction, and you can turn to gin to make you better.*

As well as the social changes, there were real economic forces underpinning this consumption. Judith Hawley pointed to William's desire to improve the British farming industry, where the chief grains were wheat, barley and rye. Wheat was crucial for bread, the staple of the masses, and barley was planted between the wheat sowings as part of crop rotation to maintain the health of the soil. The trouble was there was little demand for barley other than for brewing spirits.

JUDITH HAWLEY: *Producing spirits in large quantities was a way of keeping farming going, to keep the wheat producing, so it also then proved very important for keeping landowners on side, and they provided a very powerful lobby to keep the distilling industry going.*

It was a virtuous circle of supply and demand. And the demand kept growing, as the drinking of flavoured gins became more fashionable. There had always been high levels of drinking in the seventeenth century, but the difference now was the number of women who were drinking as excessively as men. There was an element of performance to this, and drinking gin became something that was done ostentatiously.

ANGELA MCSHANE: *You get this lovely little glass to drink from, you haven't got this massive great pewter thing, and everybody is keen to show themselves off, including people who we think of as the working poor.*

The adoption of gin by women and the poorer people gave the legislators a shock. The perception grew that there was a craze, and that gin was being not so much used as abused by the poorer classes, particularly women, reducing productivity while giving them ideas above their station, enjoying luxuries to which they were not entitled. This unease became a driving force behind the growth in regulation. Stories spread of terrible cases such as a drunken nursemaid mistaking her baby for a log and throwing it on the fire, and a mother murdering her child and selling the clothes to buy gin. Little matter that people were getting drunk from other kinds of alcohol, or taking desperate measures for other reasons – gin was becoming notorious.

According to Judith Hawley, people started to petition parliament and, from 1729 to 1751, there were eight separate legal instruments to try to control gin. These controls faced opposition from landed interests and from the larger distillers, so the regulations affected the smallest producers the most and they, Emma Major told us, became very creative about dodging the legislation. Her favourite evasion was a kind of vending machine, the 'Puss and Mew' machine, as a secret way of selling gin. Next to a building, fronting onto the street, there was a model of a cat, larger than life ...

EMMA MAJOR: *Its tail was a pipe, so you would go up to the cat and say: 'Puss, I would like some gin.' And if the seller had some gin, it would say, 'Mew' – and you would put your money into the mouth of the cat and some gin would come out of the tail.*

Customers could drink straight from the tail, for discretion, or collect the liquid in a glass. Still, pressure on the smaller distillers grew, as did concern that gin was indistinguishable from mob rule and criminality. The 1736 act raised the price of a distilling licence to £50, beyond the reach of all but the big distillers, though not everyone agreed to pay it. This attempt to control gin failed, as informers were beaten up. Even when the evidence of wrongdoing was there, it was hard for the authorities to secure convictions as juries were sympathetic to the culture of making and drinking gin.

JUDITH HAWLEY: *There were street riots and one of the cries that came out again and again was, 'No gin, no king; no gin, no king.'*

MELVYN BRAGG: *Because the English man or woman reserved the right to be drunk if they wanted to?*

JUDITH HAWLEY: *Yes, it is a sign that we are not French; we can get completely intoxicated when we want to.*

EMMA MAJOR: *Absolutely, and the reformers tried to spin that and say: no, this is not liberty, you are not really free if you are addicted to gin, and the true British liberty is abstinence – which, of course, is much duller.*

*After the accession of William of
Orange, it became an act of loyalty
to drink Protestant gin.*

Besides, the poorer people did not recognise themselves as suffering
from gin's corruption in the way that anxious legislators did. Angela
McShane emphasised that gin could be drunk in moderation, and
there was a pleasure in the sociability that went with it. Hogarth's
Gin Lane is often taken now as representation of what really
happened, all the time, but it was propaganda. It was a bringing-
together of all that was said to be bad about gin where, among all the
horrors, the most telling is the woman who is taking snuff from a box
as gentry did. This contrasted with the companion image, *Beer Street*,
in which tobacco was being consumed in a way appropriate to the
poor, by being smoked in a pipe. The message, she said, was that the
poor who were drinking gin were out of place, 'so desirous of their
luxuries that they are ignoring the things that they ought to be doing,
which is producing children to fill the factories, to work, and to make
the army strong'.

This came to a head from 1748, as soldiers were returning from
the War of the Austrian Succession without work or money and
some were turning to crime. The perception was that there was a
crime wave, that it was linked to gin and that it was time to draw a

line. The first act to make a difference was in 1751, which required that gin could only be sold from licensed premises. Judith Hawley explained that this almost wiped out the smaller providers, so that now gin came mainly from the traditional premises mentioned at the start, the ale houses, taverns and inns, which were already licensed and could afford to pay. Moreover, some of the factors behind the Gin Craze were starting to change. The harvests had been worsening since the height of the craze, there were wars taking soldiers abroad, beer was a little cheaper and, with the economy struggling, there was less money to spend on gin. At the end of the 1750s, there was so little grain, even barley, that the government banned distilling from grain altogether for four or five years.

So why was there so much anxiety over gin in this period that it was labelled a craze? Judith Hawley and Angela McShane suggested that much was to do with the fear of the new metropolitan life and what went on there. Some of the legislation was aimed at turning back the clock to before urbanisation, as if that were possible. Gin became the focus of this, Emma Major added, as the drunkenness in cities was more visible than in the countryside, because 80 per cent of gin consumption took place in London.

Afterwards, in the studio, everyone returned to the idea that the small distilleries were often run by women, who sold the gin to other women, and it was this feminine side to the production that alarmed the legislators. Melvyn recalled his childhood in Wigton and the pot houses run by 'an old lady, sitting in her front room with a couple of barrels, with three or four customers, and they were very cosy little places. You could go to places like that and one of the reasons you went, of course, was because there was a fire. The centre of this town was like a slum, it was pulled down, damp places, cold places, and in the pub there was a big fire.'

That prompted one final example of the scare stories told in the Gin Craze, before we had to give up the studio.

EMMA MAJOR: *Combustion! We have to have spontaneous combustion.*

MELVYN BRAGG: *Tell us about spontaneous combustion.*

EMMA MAJOR: *During the eighteenth century, part of the anti-women drinking gin campaign featured cautionary tales of women who drank so much gin that they spontaneously combusted.*

THE PICTS

The Picts, according to Bede writing in the eighth century, were one of four peoples of Britain, along with the Scots, the Anglo-Saxons and the Britons. In the tenth century, those last three still existed but the Picts did not. They left stone monuments carved with astonishing artistry and intricacy and other peoples wrote about them. But where was Pictland, what language did the Picts speak and why did they disappear as a distinct group? As we marked the start of our twentieth season in autumn 2017, we discussed this before an audience of students in the Memorial Chapel at the University of Glasgow, many of them studying the subject and some, as it later transpired by inference, with Pictish ancestors.

⊹⊱•⊰⊹

With Melvyn to discuss the Picts were: Katherine Forsyth, reader in the department of Celtic and Gaelic at the University of Glasgow; Alex Woolf, senior lecturer in Dark Age studies at the University of St Andrews; and Gordon Noble, reader in archaeology at the University of Aberdeen.

The first mention of people described as Picts, Katherine Forsyth said, was in a poem in AD 297 praising the Roman emperor Constantius Chlorus. To the Romans, these Picts appeared as the iconic enemies – bloodthirsty savages who ran around without clothing and covered in tattoos, the hostile barbarians living in the north. The word *picti*, on the face of it, means 'painted people' in

Bull motif on Pictish incised stone from Burghead, Scotland.

Latin and that seems the most obvious root for the name. However, there is a chance it was a native Celtic word, not a Latin word, as there was a Pictones tribe in Gaul, which was the origin of Poitiers and Poitou. The Picts were perceived as an important enemy on the fringes.

KATHERINE FORSYTH: *There's a wonderful little dice box that was used for playing games, from the empire, from the frontier near Cologne, and it's been carved with an inscription that says, 'The Picts are defeated, play in safety'.*

At the time of Constantine in the early fourth century, the enemies to the north were described as the 'Caledonians and other Picts', suggesting that 'Picts' was then used as an umbrella term for a range of tribal groups in the north of Britain. Earlier, Tacitus (AD C. 55–C. 120) had written about Roman military incursions that had come to a head at the Battle of Mons Graupius, six or seven generations before the first use of the word Picts, and there he called the people 'the Britons of Caledonia'. To him, they were noble heroic savages, untainted by the decadence of civilisation, 'the last of the free', as he called them, so something hardened between the time of Tacitus and the perception of the people as Picts in AD 297.

Alex Woolf pointed to the period of Roman occupation, where the Britons within the frontier gradually became Romans; they become provincial citizens and the name 'Briton' was still attached to them. There were the civilised, Romanised Britons, and there was the Roman provincial nation, which ultimately became the land of the Welsh, and then there were the others, the painted Britons north of the wall who continued as barbarians.

ALEX WOOLF: *Within Britain itself, even within the province of Britain, the levels of Romanisation varied enormously and, we might imagine, although here it has to be speculation, that for people living in the south-east, where there were lots of villas and fully developed towns, perhaps even people in Yorkshire might have been thought of as a bit Pictish … a pejorative term of the uncivilised.*

The challenge for those wanting clarity on the emergence of the term 'Picts' is that there are no surviving written records from the Picts themselves, though there were later accounts of them from the Romans, the Irish and, in the time of Bede (AD C. 672–735), the English. That makes it harder to know when these people, who others described as Picts, began to use the term for themselves or if they ever did.

ALEX WOOLF: *We don't know whether, even at that late period, the people who we call Picts would have used that word themselves. The likely thing is that they adopt that terminology perhaps in the seventh century when they become Christian and they start engaging with classical material; they may think, 'Oh, yes, that's us, we're the Picts.'*

On apparently firmer ground, Melvyn turned to Bede, 'our father of British history, one of the world's great historians', and invited Gordon Noble to relate what Bede made of the Picts. Bede was writing in Northumbria, one of the southern neighbours of the Picts and he, as Melvyn mentioned in his introduction, made a very famous statement that there were four peoples of Britain and five languages, where Latin was the language that united them. From that point, Bede went on to give an account of the origin myth of the Picts, saying that they came from Scythia, between eastern Europe and central Eurasia. These people sailed all the way to Ireland initially but Ireland was full, so the Irish said, 'Why don't you head over to the next island, Britain, and settle there?'

GORDON NOBLE: *But they don't have any wives so they ask the Irish for wives and the Irish give them wives and the Irish say that if there was ever a doubt in the succession of the Pictish royal line then you should favour the maternal line. This is where we get the idea that the Picts had matrilineal succession.*

MELVYN BRAGG: *Do you give credence to any of that?*

GORDON NOBLE: *No.*
   Gordon Noble added that all peoples have fantastical origin myths, and the Scots have similar myths about coming from Scythia. While Bede was not strong on the origins of the Picts, he was aware of the balance of power in his own lifetime and the century before. He knew that in the seventh century there was a period when the Anglo-Saxons and Northumbrians had an over-kingship of the Picts and that this over-kingship ended in AD 685 with the Battle of Nechtansmere. As for the region inhabited by the Picts, the abbot Adomnán, who was writing his *Life of Columba* in the seventh century, said the Picts occupied the area east of Druim Alban, the ridge of Britain, which placed them somewhere east of the highlands of Scotland. Bede wrote of them occupying the area north of the Forth, north of modern-day Edinburgh, and there are suggestions that they occupied an area from Fife up to Caithness, possibly having an over-kingship of the Orkneys at some stage, perhaps even over the Western Isles.
   The reference to Bede's mention of the four peoples being united by Latin, the language of the Church, led the conversation to the Picts and Christianity. Katherine Forsyth remarked on the stained-glass windows of Ninian and Columba in the Memorial Chapel where the discussion was taking place, who, in Bede's account, were the evangelists of the Picts. That, she said, tied in with the popular narrative of great men and heroic missionaries, but the evidence does not back up their claim to significance. It seems that the Picts were first exposed to Christianity through their contact with the Roman Empire, when there was a lot of interaction between the people to the north of the frontier and the Roman world.

KATHERINE FORSYTH: *We have a reference. St Patrick in the fifth century writes a letter to the British king, Coroticus, to complain about his slave raiding in Ireland in company with apostate Picts, implying that they were already Christian Picts who had reneged on their faith.*

That reference provides evidence of Christianity in Pictland from the fifth century onwards, which was the century before Columba. There are references to Columba preaching to the tribes of Tay, but not converting them, though he was also supposed to have seen the Loch Ness monster.

Earlier, Gordon Noble mentioned the Battle of Nechtansmere and Melvyn returned to this now, describing it as the great moment in Pictish history and a great moment in British history. This was when Ecgfrith, king of Northumbria, who was on course to unite almost the whole of Great Britain, went far north to meet the Picts and, completely unexpectedly after winning battles for thirty years, was not only defeated but killed, and so were his top henchmen. Nechtansmere changed everything, he said.

ALEX WOOLF: *It is one of the defining battles of British history and what Bede says, who was actually about twelve years old when it happened, is that from that time the strength and power of the English ebbed away. And 100 years later, the Welsh author of the* Historia Brittonum, *the history of the Britons, chose to end his history at that point because he saw that as the end of history, in a rather Francis Fukuyama way.*

In the sixth and seventh centuries, he added, it seemed as though the whole of Great Britain were to be controlled by the Northumbrians, it was just a matter of time. But in AD 685, the inevitable was stopped. It seems that Ecgfrith had previously invaded Pictland at the beginning of his reign, and Bridei, who was Ecgfrith's cousin, may well have been put on the throne of the Picts by Ecgfrith. There were references in the run-up to Nechtansmere that Bridei was spreading his wings, 'deleting' the Orkneys in AD 682. Ecgfrith went north, expecting presumably that Bridei would kowtow, but that did not happen. At some place somewhere in the north of Scotland, his army was wiped out.

MELVYN BRAGG: *How come they took on this man who had never lost a battle in thirty years, Ecgfrith?*

ALEX WOOLF: *I suspect he was overconfident, he probably also thought that Bridei was ultimately his friend: he was his cousin, they'd worked together for over a decade. He probably thought, 'I've just got to read him the riot act.'*

The years after the battle were probably when Bridei, technically the king of the northern Pictish kingdom Fortriu, based around the Moray Firth and Inverness, expanded south into areas that had likely been more tightly controlled by the Northumbrian overlordship, around the River Tay, Perth, Dundee and perhaps Fife. That is when there was probably a firm Pictish overlordship stretching from Fife to Caithness.

Gordon Noble explained that one of the main advances in the understanding of the Picts in the past twenty years had come from archaeology. Professor Martin Carver at the University of York carried out work at Portmahomack on the Tarbat Peninsula in Easter

Ross, north of Inverness. Excavations by Professor Martin Carver and his team from 1994 to 2007 uncovered an amazing wealth of evidence. He found a roadway leading up to the church with huge amounts of traces of metalworking for reliquaries and other objects, and great quantities of sculpture, cross slabs, parts of shrines, corbels and finials from a stone church, all of them signs of an incredibly wealthy monastic foundation.

GORDON NOBLE: *Some of the most exciting evidence – it doesn't sound that exciting – are bone pegs they found, and an amazing piece of detective work [showed] that these are actually from wooden frameworks to stretch calf skin to make vellum. So they were actually producing books at Portmahomack.*

These discoveries indicated that the Picts did write and they were perhaps producing illuminated manuscripts at Portmahomack. Martin Carver's excavations uncovered this fantastically wealthy settlement and it seems to have come to an end sometime in the ninth century, when it looks as though it was sacked by the Vikings.

This idea of a literate, skilled people runs counter to that of the hairy savages portrayed elsewhere. Katherine Forsyth noted that the stereotype established in the Roman period was remarkably enduring and is one of the aspects that draws people to the Picts, adding, tongue in cheek: 'If you just call them sort of arty Christian farmers it doesn't have the same glamour. But really that's probably more accurate.'

The most prominent surviving artefacts of these 'arty Christian farmers' are the stone monuments. Where the Irish and Northumbrian high crosses were, unsurprisingly, in the shape of crosses, the Picts chose giant slabs and cut their crosses onto them, leaving rectangles in the corners that could be decorated.

KATHERINE FORSYTH: *These are 6, 7, 8ft tall, beautifully decorated with very, very intricate geometric patterns, interlaced patterns. Some of the most complex and virtuoso displays of geometry are on Pictish stones. But also weird monsters attacking humans, which are probably quite sophisticated meditations on evil and death and Christian salvation and so on.*

There were also a lot of depictions of apparently secular scenes, with Pictish men and women in contemporary dress and on horseback. And, while Katherine Forsyth emphasised how similar the Picts were to

The Aberlemno Kirkyard cross-slab is one of five Pictish stones found in, or around, the village of Aberlemno in Scotland.

other peoples in Europe, she noted that they did have a unique system of symbols that they carved on stones. Alex Woolf suggested there were thirty or forty of these, some of them very naturalistic with images such as bulls, wolves and eagles, and others with geometric patterns, which people sometimes speculate may be ordinary objects viewed from unusual angles.

ALEX WOOLF: *The most likely thing is that they're some sort of label, possibly a personal name, although it's not writing in any normal sense. But they recur across the whole range of Pictland in this same very standardised format, with very little variation. My own view is that, unless we get some sort of Rosetta Stone text, we're not going to ever know exactly.*

There are a number of reasons we don't have surviving texts in Pictish, he added. One is that the Pictish territory was much smaller than the other nations. Another is that writing in vernacular languages was really only beginning to take off at about the time the Picts were disappearing, and most of the books produced at places like Portmahomack would probably have been in Latin. We may still have some of these books. There is a St John's gospel book in Corpus Christi College, Cambridge, that has an image of an eagle on it that looks exactly like the eagles from the Pictish symbols, so that book was probably a Latin gospel book made in a Pictish monastery. Alex Woolf suggested that, if we examine that book and one or two other books like that with image-enhancing technology, we might see little glosses in Pictish of a hard word explained or something similar.

If ever there is to be more insight into the language of the Picts, it may emerge from excavations. At Rhynie, Gordon Noble has been digging at a site that was known to have Pictish symbol stones, and one was still standing in its original place, the Craw Stane, which has a salmon and a Pictish beast on it, a pair of symbols. In the 1970s, there was the discovery of the Rhynie Man, a full-length figure with big pointed teeth who was carrying an axe over his shoulder and was probably some kind of pagan god. Excavations from 2011 have shown that the stones were in a high-status settlement of the fourth to sixth centuries AD, with the unearthing of artefacts from the eastern Mediterranean, glass from western France, glass and metalwork from Anglo-Saxon England and objects that have even been depicted on the stones. For example, among the finds is an iron axe pin that is about 5 inches high and shows a little axe with a serpent biting on to it, very much like the sacrificial axe that the Rhynie Man holds.

Moving on towards the ninth century, Melvyn looked for evidence for the demise of the Picts, asking whether the Vikings had a role.

ALEX WOOLF: *There's a sustained series of military campaigns, major battles, the most important of which happens in 839 when the king of the Picts, his brother, and the king of the Gaels of Dalriada in Argyll are all killed, along with innumerable others. And this precipitates a major political upheaval in the kingship of the Picts.*

There were extensive Viking settlements in Pictland, in the Northern Isles, Caithness, Sutherland, the Western Isles and the western coast. These incursions had a knock-on effect, increasing the Gaelic influence moving from the west into Pictland. Gordon Noble referred to the archaeological records that show that promontory forts emerged in the third and fourth centuries that match the accounts of the activities of the Picts in that same late Roman period. By the end of the first millennium AD, many of these forts were being destroyed, and somehow the Pictish language also disappeared. In the Northern Isles, the Hebrides, and the north of the mainland, everyone seemed to be speaking Norse by the twelfth century. It is unclear how much of that was cultural mixing and how much was genocide, but, in the bulk of the Pictish territories, it was the Gaelic language that replaced Pictish. In the areas where Norse took over, no Pictish place names remain, whereas many of the settlement names of Gaelic Scotland were inherited through Pictish or from the Pictish times.

ALEX WOOLF: *The easiest ones to spot are the ones that begin with the word 'aber', which is the old British word for a river mouth, like you get in Aberystwyth in Wales, but you also get Aberdeen, Aberfeldy, Abernethy and so on. These names have survived Gaelicisation and that suggests there was much more interaction, there was much more continuity between the Pictish kingdom and the later kings of Scotland.*

The Picts were missed, after a while. Katherine Forsyth said that Henry of Huntingdon, writing in the eleventh century, read Bede and noticed the reference to Picts and asked where they had gone. In the same period, the writer of the history of the Norwegians, the *Historia Norvegiae*, noticed the souterrains or underground structures and surmised that these used to be where the Picts lived – they came out at night to build big towers and hid in the day.

KATHERINE FORSYTH: *They're wondering about them and speculating and this is where we get these myths about the Picts as little people hiding away in their underground dwellings.*

GORDON NOBLE: *In the sixteenth century, there are these fantastic etchings of the Picts by John White. And he's depicting the Picts as these incredible savages and he's basically saying to the Elizabethan court that we shouldn't be scared of the Native Americans because in our past we've got even more savage communities.*

Steadily, though, Melvyn's guests said, there is more evidence coming forward about the Picts to replace the myths. There has always been interest in the Picts, Gordon Noble added, but now the scholarship is really beginning to help illuminate this period of Scottish history.

As the live programme came to an end, to the unusual sound of audience applause, Melvyn took questions from the students there who were carrying out their own research into the Picts, which may lead to new revelations. These questions ranged from where Melvyn's guests thought the investigations would be going (archaeology was the answer), whether Argyll was a Pict territory (there was a lot of going back and forth to Ireland from Argyll, hard to separate them),

whether the recent discovery of a stone engraved with a Pictish naked
man was connected to Rhynie (very similar, and the butt of the spear
was similar to that described by Roman writers, which was helpful),
why the term Pict stopped being used (maybe it was not a vernacular
word and went out of use as Latin did), where the Picts were from
if not Scythia (being a Pict was an identity not a people, like the
Victorians were not a people distinct from the Georgians), what
genetics tell us (we don't really know enough, but so far the people
tested in former Pictland have the same genetic signature as would be
found in Iron Age Scotland and Britain), what the Picts thought of
being described by their tattoos (these tattoos were cultural attributes
that lots of barbarians had, but, over time, the Picts were the ones
who were left still doing it), what we know of their everyday life (not
enough, more excavations please), what new, big excavations might
reveal (Dunkeld, which Bede said was the centre of the southern Picts,
is already very promising – and we should excavate places adjacent
to the big collections of the Christian stone sculptures), whether the
sculptures are religious artefacts or artistic expressions (both – these
are not exclusive terms), and what relationship the Picts had with the
rest of Scotland (some shared kingships and artistic motifs, plus links
to Anglo-Saxons, including requests for Northumbrian stonemasons).
Then, after more applause, Melvyn and his guests slipped quietly off
for tea, an hour after they had started this live discussion in front
of an audience at the Memorial Chapel, taking the chaplain, Stuart
MacQuarrie, with them.

THE TRIAL OF CHARLES I

In defending the killing of a king, the poet and republican John Milton declared:

> *If men within themselves would be governed by reason, and not generally give up their understanding to a double-tyranny: of custom from without, and blind affections from within; they would discern better what it is to favour and uphold a tyrant of a nation.*

Milton's tyrant was Charles I, executed for treason in 1649. The events of his trial saw a drama of ideas about kingship, parliament, law and power, set amid political confusion and the bloody aftermath and rupture of civil war. And despite Milton's claims, whether Charles was justly killed or the victim of a messy coup is still debated 370 years after his death.

⊢─◼─⊣

With Melvyn to discuss the trial of Charles I were: Justin Champion, professor of the history of early modern ideas and honorary fellow at Royal Holloway, University of London; Diane Purkiss, professor of English literature at the University of Oxford; and David Wootton, professor of history at the University of York.

A painting depicting King Charles I of England being led to his execution.

The trial started on 20 January 1649, when Charles I was brought into Westminster Hall under armed guard to face his accusers. He had fought and lost in civil wars with parliamentary forces, first from 1642 to 1645 and then in 1648, with royalists at Pontefract Castle holding out until March 1649. Justin Champion set the scene – a bustling public space ordinarily full of shops and booths but cleared out for this event. There was a real anxiety that Charles would try to escape, or that there would be a military attack by his supporters. The prosecutors had been thinking about the ceremony that would accompany the lord president, John Bradshaw, as he walked in, and whether he would have a mace or a sword of state. Charles was not given special prominence and was almost hidden in a crowd of 4,000 to 5,000 onlookers, some shouting 'God save the king' and others 'Justice, justice'.

JUSTIN CHAMPION: *[Charles] is only allowed to come in with three servants, he doesn't have any legal counsel; he has his back to the audience. He is very, very, confused. This is somebody who is used to being treated with regal majesty. In front of him there are sixty-seven commissioners; many of them he won't recognise at all.*

Many of the legal officers are lost to history. As well as John Bradshaw, there were John Cook, a lawyer, Isaac Dorislaus, who was a Dutch historian, and a man called John Ask, about whom nothing is known. The charges were based on the premise that the House of Commons had represented the sovereignty of the people and that Charles I was a tyrant, a traitor and a murderer.

JUSTIN CHAMPION: *He is a 'public enemy' – a wonderful phrase – to the Commonwealth of England. And, in essence, he is put on trial both for war crimes and for treason against the people. He has, in again their own phrase, 'exercised unlimited tyrannous will, against the liberties and privileges of the people'.*

The commissioners were spending a lot of time trying to work out what the precise charge would be, improvising as they went along. Charles, meanwhile, was asking why they were trying him and in whose name, calling them 'a rump'. As Diane Purkiss explained, he called them a rump because of Colonel Pride's purge the previous autumn of every MP who was liable to want to continue to try to talk with Charles, to try to reach a negotiated deal with him. After the Restoration, they would be known as the Rump Parliament, closely associated with Cromwell's New Model Army, which was the driver behind the will to try the king at all, and particularly the will to find him guilty as a murderer and traitor.

DIANE PURKISS: *Not everybody on the radical fringe actually wanted Charles tried. John Lilburne, the leading Leveller, didn't want Charles tried; he really wanted to save Charles. There is a lot of bobbing and weaving to try to come up with something that will stick and will work and will pay off what the army has come to see as this enormous blood price that has to be laid at somebody's door. The mentality is not unlike the post-First World War wish to hang the Kaiser.*

Those who had been purged included those who had stood up to Charles before but now represented moderate Protestant opinion. There was Denzil Holles, who was one of those who tried to arrest Charles in parliament in 1642; there was John Clotworthy, a violent Presbyterian iconoclast. William Prynne was another, famous for having his ears cut off in the pillory, and Robert Harley, the man who actually cancelled Christmas. They were strongly Protestant, but were now seen as too moderate, and the trial was proceeding without unanimity.

DIANE PURKISS: *Royalists, and there are still many of those, are unenthusiastic, but there is no sense that the will of the people of England is being either expressed or thwarted by the trial. There isn't a single will by this stage, there are factions, there are divisions. And you can't really resolve that into 'everybody is against the trial, everybody is for it'.*

Melvyn asked whether there was, effectively, a military junta here, and David Wootton agreed. It was a show trial. When Lady Fairfax, disguised, called out in protest, for shame, the troops levelled their muskets at her and their officer threatened to fire. It was a very intimidating presence, and the troops were there to quell the spectators as well as to ensure that Charles didn't escape. This was nothing like a normal English trial, which enforced the king's justice in front of a jury on the basis of the known law of the land. The charges were improvised, but we might be forgiven for thinking there was an inevitability to the process.

DAVID WOOTTON: *This is something historians currently disagree about. My view of this is straightforward: if you put someone on trial for treason, and that's one of the charges, there is only one known outcome to a treason trial. Anybody who goes in front of a court charged with treason ends up dead.*

Injecting some doubt, Justin Champion cautioned that we do not really know the inside workings of the trial process, only the public side. Within the Painted Chamber, part of the medieval Palace of Westminster between the House of Lords and the River Thames, where the commissioners worked out their plans, different people turned up every day, making different pitches for what they should do the following day. Any plan was compromised by Charles's refusal to plead, challenging the authority of the court, and the rump, head on.

JUSTIN CHAMPION: *They are claiming that they represent popular sovereignty and Charles is claiming that he represents the liberty of every single man in the land.*

MELVYN BRAGG: *Because he says: 'If you can do this to me, you can do this to anybody. So I am representing the people of England.'*

JUSTIN CHAMPION: *Absolutely. It is a wonderful performance, and even though there is some evidence that the lord commissioners thought about what they would do if Charles refused to acknowledge their authority, they are thrown into chaos.*

Ordinarily in trials, there was a contingency for those who refused to plead, and that was to be crushed between two stones until the accused changed his mind. Where the likely sentence was death, the advantage of withholding a plea was that there was no finding of guilt and so the accused's children could inherit.

DAVID WOOTTON: *Properly, under English law, Charles, by refusing to plea, should be crushed to death. They don't want to torture the king in public, that's the last thing they want to do, so they are constantly scurrying back to their room saying: 'What are we going to do now?'*

That may have been the legal conundrum, but there was an alternative purpose to the trial, as Diane Purkiss argued. This was to represent the House of Commons as the voice of the people, allowing the depositions of twenty-three people about the atrocities committed by royalist forces, putting those grievances before Charles. While denying the authority of the court, Charles did not address the question of whether he was the enemy of the people.

DIANE PURKISS: *They are trying to lay down that it's they, the House of Commons, who are sovereign; and Charles says, 'Okay, I'm not going to answer your charges, because you are just a rump, but if you reconvene a proper parliament, I will answer to that proper parliament.' And that really is very intelligent, because it sees off their representational campaign, which, to them, I think, is the nub of the matter.*

It was difficult to establish that the royalists had carried out any atrocities on the king's orders, so the weightiest claim was that Charles had declared war on his own people. Justin Champion added that Charles was presented as a man of blood, who drove war on, and that the routine violence was the king's fault, even if there were relatively few atrocities compared to the wars that had been raging across Europe or the conflicts that would follow in Ireland or Scotland.

MELVYN BRAGG: *Diane, you were shaking your head, violently.*

DIANE PURKISS: *I was, because I don't think people knew that at the time; they had all been reading the newspapers, and every single newspaper that comes out in London, parliamentarian, or royalist, from Oxford is all about atrocities. I don't think the people in London in 1649 knew that atrocities were uncommon, I think they thought that they were incredibly common.*

The commissioners were unsure how to underpin the charges. As David Wootton said, the real charge against Charles was that he was responsible for plotting the second civil war while he was under army captivity, arranging for the Scots to invade England, but they chose to try him for the first civil war as well, and debated whether to try him for killing his father, something he had not actually done.

MELVYN BRAGG: *Can we just clear this up? The first civil war we are talking about, 1642–6, and they thought that was the end of it, a lot of people, and they have gone and negotiated peace; and the thing*

The frontispiece of Eikon Basilike
portrays Charles I as Christ,
kneeling with a crown of thorns.

that really triggered the [trial] was the second civil war of 1648–9,
which they laid squarely, and Diane thinks fairly and squarely, at the
door of Charles I, don't you?

DIANE PURKISS: *Well, I think it is impossible not to lay that at*
the door of Charles I. He was offered fairly good deals by Cromwell
and Ireton, [which] certainly would have saved his life, would have
ensured the continuation of the monarchy. And that was what
everyone had been aiming for in the first civil war, anyway.

Yet there he had been, before the second civil war, apparently
holding out the hand of friendship to people like Oliver Cromwell
and his son-in-law Henry Ireton whom he was negotiating with while
plotting their destruction, which naturally alienated them. David
Wootton suspected that, for many of the military figures, it became
fairly apparent that the only way they were going to stop Charles
was to kill him. It seems, too, that Charles feared he would be
assassinated while in captivity. Usually he was immaculate, but Justin
Champion had an explanation for his comparatively dishevelled state
at the trial and for his fuller beard: he had not wanted anyone to
shave him in case they cut his throat.

JUSTIN CHAMPION: *It is enormously difficult for us to recognise: Charles does believe he is appointed by God. He is almost bemused, especially in the court, when nobody will help him. You know the tip of his silver cane is meant to have fallen off. 'Help me?' Nobody does. It is almost that he is incapable, but that, I think, gives him the stubborn authority to challenge the court.*

Looking around the room, Charles despised the commissioners ranged before him. He only recognised two or three faces, according to David Wootton, and thought that the rest were nobodies put up to try him, whose presence was a form of contempt for him, and that may have contributed to his misjudgement of the situation.

DAVID WOOTTON: *He has always been treated with respect and he cannot imagine an England without a king. And that's why he thinks parliament in the end must do a deal with him. Right up until the beginning of the trial, he is convinced they must do a deal with him, because there is no alternative king, and England without a king is unimaginable. He thinks he has a veto on any settlement.*

There was disagreement in the studio over how smart Charles was in his assessment of the threats he faced. Diane Purkiss suggested he was great at plotting but that, in the end, this did him no good. It was what her grandmother would have called 'silly cunning'. He was within an ace of being summarily murdered, as other rulers had been, and yet he could not see the bigger picture.

MELVYN BRAGG: *What was the bigger picture?*

DIANE PURKISS: *The bigger picture was the fact that it had become possible for everybody else in the country to imagine the country without a king, to imagine a country ruled by the army grandees rather than by himself, and that, indeed, is what happened.*

MELVYN BRAGG: *Is that true? At that time, in 1649, do you think it was possible for people in the country to imagine that?*

DIANE PURKISS: *Yes, I think it was. I don't think it was possible for every single person, but I think it was possible for the people in charge of him to imagine that, and that was what he resolutely refused to see.*

Since assassination was always an option, the action of the commissioners was all the more remarkable. They were breaking with all custom by putting a king on trial, and they had to believe that providence was on their side or else, as Justin Champion put it, they were 'blowing it big time'. The commissioners thought they were doing God's will, while Charles thought he was divinely appointed. For people like Cromwell, God was clearly supporting the side of parliament as it had defeated Charles twice in the wars. They were still so worried, though, Diane Purkiss said, that they interviewed a prophetess, Elizabeth Poole of Abingdon, who told them she had had a divine revelation saying parliament had every right to try Charles, but not to hurt him.

JUSTIN CHAMPION: *Those radical puritans are constantly anxious that they have got it wrong. If we look at Cromwell's meditations and letters at this time, he is constantly going back to bits of the Old Testament and looking at the parallels. 'Have I got it right? Is this a time of necessity? Is this a time of providence? Or what happens if I've got it wrong?' So these people are anxious not that they are making a mistake, in a civil or a legal way, but that they are doing the Antichrist's work.*

This was, effectively, the first attempt to try a monarch for war crimes and it was not done furtively but in public. This action in the open light of day was something that David Wootton found to admire, even though he did not have much sympathy for the way in which Cromwell and his associates conducted the trial otherwise.

DIANE PURKISS: *One reason that they felt themselves capable of dethroning and executing a king was because [some] were expecting to be ruled by Christ the King any day now. People actually say things like, 'We have identified Charles as one of the ten horns of the beast from the Book of Revelations.'*

Others believed that the blood of the dead was actually crying out from the ground. The perception of the dead as murder victims, and the atrocities in the battles, meant that some actually felt a sense of obligation to lay those bones to rest. All the while, Charles refused to enter a plea and, by 27 January, the court had heard all the evidence it wanted and retired to the Painted Chamber to consider the sentence. Lord Bradshaw returned to declare to the court why Charles was guilty and this, Justin Champion said, was when Charles suddenly realised they were going to sentence him to death. He had a moment in which he uttered 'either a haughty "huh", as in "what do I care?", or an agonised "haw", as if he has suddenly got the view', two interpretations on which royalists and parliamentarians were divided. Then, denounced as a tyrant, Charles was taken away.

There was a delay while parliament made preparations for the execution, choosing the location in front of the Banqueting House, erecting the platform and passing the legislation permitting the killing. Charles had shown composure and restraint throughout the trial, but parliament was still concerned that he would break loose on the platform and struggle. On Tuesday 30 January 1649, he was led out.

DAVID WOOTTON: *They have put staples where they can chain him down if he tries to struggle and they have put up a block that is only 10 inches high. Normally a gentleman would kneel and the block would be about 2ft high, and would fit neatly under his neck. And they ask Charles to put his head on the block, and he knows he is going to have to lie down to do this, and he says, 'Why can't the block be higher?' The reason the block can't be higher is that they are afraid of him struggling.*

Charles spoke to those around him, and his words were recorded. He spoke with great dignity, and then he put his head down on the block, and raised his hair under his hat so that the executioner could get a good blow. David Wootton added that the executioner and his assistant were wearing fake moustaches and fake hair as a disguise, frightened of being murdered in reprisal, something that was to happen to Isaac Dorislaus a few months later at the hands of royalist agents. And Charles died what might be called a noble death, in what some soon called a martyrdom. Justin Champion mentioned a work probably written by Charles's chaplain, *Eikon Basilike* (the king's image), but attributed to Charles himself, which came out soon after the death, presenting Charles as Christ, kneeling with a crown of thorns.

As for the regicides, there was some peace until Charles II was restored to the throne in 1660. At first, he said he would show mercy to those who fought against him. Soon, though, a royalist parliament was elected and the regicides were under threat. Some were already dead, some fled, many were tried and sentenced to life imprisonment. Several were hanged, drawn and quartered. Some were executed posthumously.

DIANE PURKISS: *They actually dig up the bodies of Cromwell and Ireton, and hang them on a gibbet at Tyburn. It is important not to underestimate how vindictive the Restoration regime is and, though Charles II does come in saying he is not going to do anything nasty and he is going to be a very peaceful kind of figure, it doesn't turn out that way at all.*

In the view of Justin Champion, the trial of Charles I resonated not only through English history but also through European and global history, becoming the model for subsequent revolutions, whether the Americans in 1776, the French in 1789 or Fidel Castro in the 1950s. This first political trial of a head of state for crimes against the people, however inaccurate a charge that may have been, became an icon in itself. And, for all that, the trial showed it is 'almost still too complicated, even with our ability to forget the past, to imagine carrying an axe and killing a king'.

*The Capitoline Wolf is a bronze
statue of the mythical she-wolf
suckling Romulus and Remus.*

ROMULUS AND REMUS

*The Capitoline Museums in Rome contain a small but magnificent
room known as the 'chamber of the she-wolf'. Its marble walls are
covered in Latin inscriptions and colourful murals, and its floor
has an elaborate mosaic, but the centrepiece is a bronze statue of a
wolf suckling two human infants, an image revered by Romans as
a symbol of their city. A similar object was described by Cicero as
adorning the Roman Forum more than 2,000 years ago. The statue
depicts the most celebrated of Rome's foundation myths: the children
are the twins Romulus and Remus who, according to tradition,
having been left to die, were discovered and fed by the wolf and
miraculously survived. Romulus went on to give his name to Rome,
the city he founded. Remus was killed. It is a powerful story and
one that encapsulates many of the peculiarities of ancient Rome, its
society and people.*

┼━━●━┼

With Melvyn to discuss Romulus and Remus were: Dame Mary
Beard, professor of classics at the University of Cambridge; Peter
Wiseman, emeritus professor of classics and ancient history at the

University of Exeter; and Tim Cornell, emeritus professor of ancient history at the University of Manchester.

At the heart of this discussion were three questions: what stories did Romans tell about their foundation and why, and when did the stories originate? Melvyn called on Mary Beard for a basic outline of the Romulus and Remus story and, noting that there were lots of different versions, she offered a composite. This started in Alba Longa, a small town outside the future site of Rome, where the brothers Numitor and Amulius were rival kings. Amulius deposed Numitor, the rightful ruler, before disposing of Numitor's male family and making his daughter a virgin priestess so that she would not have children to challenge him.

MARY BEARD: *But he doesn't manage that because the daughter, who is called Rhea Silvia, gets pregnant; she says the father is the god Mars. In some versions she says he appeared from the flame of her temple fire in the form of a phallus. So she is pregnant. It turns out to be divine twins, if Rhea Silvia's story is true.*

Amulius asked his servants to get rid of the twins, and they were left in baskets by the Tiber where they were found not by humans but by a she-wolf who suckled the twins and kept them alive long enough for a shepherd to find them. This shepherd was Faustulus, who took the twins to be raised by his wife Acca Larentia. Once they are adults, they are reunited with the deposed Numitor and reinstate him on the throne of Alba Longa.

MARY BEARD: *They would like to have a city themselves. They think they are going to have to wait a very, very long time if they have to wait until Numitor has finished his rule at Alba Longa, so off they go to a nearby place, which is going to be Rome, and decide to establish a city there.*

Romulus and Remus then had a contest in which they asked the gods to help them decide which of them should rule the city and name it. Looking for signs from the heavens, Remus saw six vultures and claimed victory, only for Romulus suddenly to see twelve and claim that victory was his. He started to build a rampart, but the quarrel continued and Romulus killed his twin and took command of what would be Rome.

Following that summary, Melvyn turned to Peter Wiseman who took up the question of why it was said the twins were suckled by a wolf, and why they had been left out to die. The exposure story, he said, was found in the Bible with Moses and the bulrushes, as it was in the Oedipus myth, where it was used as a way of showing how someone, who appeared to come from nowhere, did in fact have a significant background. These children were always the product of pregnancies that someone did not want.

PETER WISEMAN: *Sometimes it is because the queen herself is pregnant but has a dream or some oracle that tells that her offspring is going to have a disastrous career, so they try to frustrate the will of the gods by destroying the child; and that kind of story shows that* *you can't do that, and eventually the gods will make sure the child survives and comes back.*

Often in these stories there was the exposure, but the suckling by a wild animal was rarer. Peter Wiseman told of exceptions such as Paris, prince of Troy, who was son of Priam and Hecuba, and Hecuba had a dream that he would be responsible for the fall of Troy and he was exposed to die, only to be suckled by a she-bear. Then there was an Arcadian called Telephus, who was exposed to die on Mount Parthenion and was suckled by a doe, and he went on to become a hero. Cyrus, the king of the Persians, was reputedly suckled by a bitch.

Noting that Mary Beard had said there were different versions of Rome's foundation story, Melvyn asked Peter Wiseman to offer examples, and he offered those in which Remus was not killed, or in which he and Romulus ruled together. Virgil's version in *The Aeneid* has no quarrel and no fratricide.

PETER WISEMAN: *In a way, the Beard version is the one we all know, because it is in the great authors, Levy and Plutarch. This is, if you like, the privileged version but, [if] you root around in the more obscure corners of classical literature, you can find references to all kinds of different versions.*

In some versions, Remus is killed not by Romulus but by a man called Celer, who was building the rampart and took offence when Remus leapt over it, striking him dead with a shovel. Sometimes Celer hits him instinctively and sometimes on the orders of Romulus, who is then given the momentous words, 'So perish all who cross my walls.' There is another version in which Remus is killed as a sacrifice to make the wall stronger.

Melvyn turned to Tim Cornell for what happened after the building of the physical city, which was the issuing of an invitation for more men to join him and his few friends at Rome.

TIM CORNELL: *The first thing Romulus does is to create an asylum, and he founds this space on the Capitoline Hill where anyone is welcome to come along: political exiles, asylum seekers and runaways and runaway slaves, criminals and more all gather there. These are the first Romans.*

This asylum aspect of the story is discussed below, but first Tim Cornell turned to what these men supposedly did to ensure their settlement had a future. At first, Romulus apparently asked neighbouring cities if they would allow intermarriage, but this was turned down as his men were not respectable. He then arranged a festival and invited the neighbours, among them the Sabines, who were living in hills to the north-east of Rome and who brought their daughters with them. It was a trap and, at a signal, all the young Romans grabbed a woman, which became known as the abduction of the Sabine women, also dubbed the rape, from the Latin *rapere*, which means 'to seize'; it was the 'seizure' of the Sabine women, as well as rape in the conventional sense. This act led to outrage and war, and the Sabines, under Titus Tatius, came to Rome. They set up camp on the Quirinal Hill on the north-east side and captured the

Capitoline, and there was then a great battle in the valley between the hills on the ground that later became the Forum.

TIM CORNELL: *This battle in the Forum takes place and, while it is raging, the women themselves intervene and urge the men to stop fighting each other, so that husbands and fathers must stop, pull themselves together and come to some agreement. The result is a joint community in which the Sabines decide to stay on, and Romulus and Titus Tatius actually become joint kings of the new double community.*

According to legend, Romulus then created the constitution, the senate and other institutions, fought wars and helped Rome become very prosperous. Titus Tatius disappeared in mysterious circumstances, in which Romulus was sometimes implicated, and, in time, Romulus himself disappeared, with some versions of the story saying that he was taken up to heaven.

Melvyn asked Mary Beard if she could give the earliest references for this foundation story and say how valid the story was. She answered with one word: 'No.' All the most detailed accounts are really from the first century BC and later, so the game with this story has been to trace that point between the first century BC and the eighth, at which the story originated, using all kinds of conjectures and guesses.

MARY BEARD: *Many people, me included, would point to a fourth-century Etruscan mirror, which has on it ... I can see already Peter shaking his head ... which has on it a very clear picture of an animal, that is a plausible wolf, and two kids underneath it, probably about 325 BC, perhaps 350 BC. For many people, that is a clear sign that you have a wolf and twins story, i.e. Romulus and Remus, in the fourth century BC.*

She acknowledged that there were other stories about animals and babies being suckled, and that this mirror was not unquestionably Romulus and Remus. Later, there was a clear literary reference in the work of Livy (*c.* 59 BC–*c.* AD 17) to a statue of twins and a wolf being put up in the centre of Rome in 296 bc. Peter Wiseman disputed the evidence of the mirror, saying that one of the other characters on the mirror was recognisably the god Hermes, or Mercury, which to him suggested that either the mirror depicted a totally different version of the Romulus and Remus story in which Mercury was involved, or that Mercury was involved because the twins were not Romulus and Remus but rather the Lares, guardian deities with whom Mercury was associated.

PETER WISEMAN: *I don't think that the story of Romulus and Remus goes much back beyond 300 BC; the story that Tim was telling, the Sabine women's story, the outcome of that is a joint community of Romans and Sabines and that is actually what happened in the early third century when the Romans conquered the Sabines in the 290s and they incorporated the whole area into the Roman stage, and they called the joint Roman state 'Quirites'.*

The Romans were still the dominant force under that state but, in theory, it was a joint enterprise. Peter Wiseman observed that this idea was put forward by the great historian Theodor Mommsen (1817–1903), and has never been refuted, and this context suggested that the story was created at some point after 320 BC. That did not satisfy Tim Cornell, for whom the foundation myth was not the kind of story that was created to fit with political circumstances.

TIM CORNELL: *It strikes me that if you were going to invent a nice patriotic story about your city's origins, you wouldn't invent one that involved fratricide and rape and so on. These are things that are rooted in the sort of folklore character of it. It seems to me it is much more likely to be an older story. I would like it to be fifth/sixth century. I think that is perfectly reasonable.*

MELVYN BRAGG: *Mary, you are wanting to get in?*

MARY BEARD: *Yes, because I think this is not just a disagreement about evidence, and about whether the twins are Romulus and Remus, and what on earth Mercury is doing there. What underlies this kind of disagreement is really a bigger question about what we think these Roman stories were for.*

In defence of the early third century BC as the origin of the legend, Peter Wiseman argued that every story was once told for the first time and that it was perfectly reasonable to ask when, why, in what circumstances and for what purpose the story was created. He added that stories don't simply appear out of nowhere – they are created, they are told to an audience.

MELVYN BRAGG: *I have to point out to listeners that there is deeply puzzled disagreement on behalf of the others; not puzzled, but agitated.*

Tim Cornell preferred an explanation more like the Grimm fairy tales, where the Brothers Grimm went around collecting stories that were already being told, which were much older folk tales. For this, he had some support in the studio.

MARY BEARD: *I don't buy [the] idea that myth is like a piston engine and somebody has invented it, and here we are: one day we don't have the story of Romulus and Remus and this clever old sausage invents it and now we have got it. I think myth is a conversation that people are having, an imaginary conversation, and it is a dynamic way of thinking about yourself in relation to the world.*

Romulus and Remus depicted on a Roman silver coin.

Unpersuaded, Peter Wiseman distinguished between myth as an abstract noun, which he said fitted with Mary Beard's perspective, and myths that were separate stories.

PETER WISEMAN: *I may be wrong about when it was created, why it was created, but it was created, somebody dreamt up the story of the twins and the she-wolf at some point in history, pre-history, God knows when. My suggestions are about 300, Tim's is maybe 600 or something before that. There could be a million other ways of doing it, but, at some point, somebody created the story.*

Tim Cornell countered that stories are not as convenient as that, and that the Romans were always extremely embarrassed by their origin myth. The Romans tried to get around the fratricide, or the role of the she-wolf, since wolves were notorious predators and the enemies of Rome later were able to say, 'Well, these Romans are beastly imperialists, [they are] children of wolves.'

TIM CORNELL: *Roman historians are terribly upset about this, and they found ways around this, and they said: 'Well, actually it didn't happen like that, what happened was that the shepherd Faustulus who was supposed to expose the children and so on, didn't do so, he took them home to his wife to bring up, and it so turned out that his wife was actually a prostitute for which the Latin word is* lupa, *a slang word meaning prostitute.'*

According to this later rationalisation, it was preferable to say that Romulus and Remus weren't really the sons of a wolf (*lupus*), they were the sons of a prostitute. To Mary Beard, that kind of shift is what makes it so complicated to analyse these stories.

MARY BEARD: *Roman writers are as puzzled as we are by them, and so what we are reading is both some kind of oral primitive folk tale, or whatever, and somebody's attempt to make sense of it, and the Roman writers are as busy making sense of this the whole time as we are.*

The fratricide was as troubling to Roman writers as whether the suckling was by a wolf or a prostitute. What was particularly puzzling, for Tim Cornell, was why there were twins at all. Usually, stories with twins explain something, as was the case in Sparta, where it was said there were two kings on account of their twin ancestors. In this vein, there are ways in which it could be said that Rome was a double community, with both Romans and Sabines, and with the two consuls, chief magistrates who succeeded the kings from the late sixth century, and either of these aspects of their story could be presaged by the twins. The trouble with that approach is that, very early in the foundation story, one of the twins is eliminated.

For Mary Beard, it is almost impossible to say why the Romans had the fratricide story, but it is quite easy to see what the Romans did with the story they had.

MARY BEARD: *It becomes absolutely central in Roman political thought about themselves that they are a community that is destined to fratricide and civil war. You know that Romans…*

MELVYN BRAGG: *We have a shaking of the head on my left …*

MARY BEARD: *He is nodding his head, of course he is, he always does when I say this. The point about Rome is it was absolutely destined to tear itself apart, brother versus brother.*

Following this up, Peter Wiseman referred to a poem by Horace (65–8 BC) in which the writer imagined himself asking the Romans why they were at war with themselves *again*, and answered his own question by saying it was because of the killing of Remus.
The foundation story was flexible, though.

PETER WISEMAN: *Rome was ruled by two consuls. Why? Because there was a historic compromise between so-called Patricians and the so-called Plebeians in the fourth century BC, which is a very good context for the creation of twin founders, in order to illustrate a double community. What mattered to that community varied enormously from the fourth century BC, when twins mattered most to the first century BC, when fratricide mattered most.*

TIM CORNELL: *Well, that would be all right if the Patricians had killed all the Plebeians, that would be a good reason to have a brother killing a brother, but the civil war is rather interesting because, on your view, Peter, the origin of the fratricide story ought to be the civil wars – that was the time when they had to invent this – but we actually know that the fratricide was in much earlier historians, writing in 200 BC.*

Peter Wiseman countered that there were the alternative foundation stories already alluded to, such as those in which Remus accepted Romulus's victory in the augury contest with the vultures and the twins ruled together. He cited Virgil's account of the founding of Rome in the *Aeneid*, written in first century BC, only for Tim Cornell to suggest that this was very, very tenuous support.

MARY BEARD: *I think we perhaps ought to explain to listeners that there is no primary contemporary evidence for that whatsoever, it is all in your head.*

PETER WISEMAN: *It is a hypothesis, a historical hypothesis, which depends on evidence and argument, and the evidence, as you rightly say, is utterly inadequate.*

ALL: *{laughter}*

Whatever its origin, the foundation story of the wolf-suckled twins was used for the emblem of Rome from early times. Tim Cornell mentioned the first set of silver coins that the city of Rome produced, which are said to date from 270 or 269 BC and have the wolf, the twins and *Romano* on the reverse. Looking at the myth again, though, he was particularly interested in another ideological aspect of it: the part where Romulus created an asylum for all those who wanted to settle there.

TIM CORNELL: *Rome is a community that is open to outsiders, that accepts people, even if they are criminals and runaways and so on, because Rome was, throughout its history, a society that expanded and incorporated – first of all, its neighbours through conquest and through intermarriage and then through the institution of slavery, where they brought outsiders into Rome as slaves, and then freed them, and then freed slaves in Rome automatically obtained the Roman citizenship, which is a very remarkable fact.*

By the first century BC, when many versions of the foundation stories were being written, the population of Rome very largely consisted of people who were either outsiders themselves and had become citizens or who were descended one or two generations back from non-Romans, from outsiders. To Mary Beard, too, that was probably the most important thing about the myth, as Rome had constantly been saying that its people originated elsewhere, with migrants, and that it was an asylum, which was very different from any known foundation stories of other cities. Conversely, the Athenians and Spartans thought of themselves as autochthonous, springing from their own ground. In the same vein, Tim Cornell said there was nothing that was intrinsically Roman, it was all borrowed. That idea of the asylum was described admiringly by some authors, but not all.

PETER WISEMAN: *Many authors refer to the asylum in a shocked tone. Not only do you have the community proud of being welcoming to incomers, you also have forces within that community who resist it and are furious about it.*

Finally, Mary Beard noted the gender aspect of the foundation story, where the rape of the Sabines was later seen as the first Roman marriage, an institution that was conceived in terms of abduction, rape, seizure and was then buried deep inside Roman views of domestic life, the family and the role of women.

Thinking about the discussion later, for the newsletter he dictated in those years, Melvyn was frustrated by the fact that written history was introduced so late in civilisation. One of the things he most enjoyed about the Romulus and Remus discussion was that there were serious disagreements between the three academics and that they were developed in a seriously polite and courteous way. That's one of the things he likes about the programme, he said. 'These people have put their entire lives to the service of scholarship and very often to a theory, or a few theories, about the field to which they have dedicated themselves. When challenged head on, they don't scream and shout – like politicians – or bicker and squeal – like crypto-politicians – they slightly raise the temperature of their tone but bat it back with great courtesy. It's terrific.'

1816, THE YEAR
WITHOUT A SUMMER

*In April 1815, the volcano Mount Tambora erupted on the island of
Sumbawa in what we now call Indonesia. It was one of the largest
eruptions in the past 80,000 years, killing more people than any
other volcano and releasing millions of tonnes of sulphur dioxide
into the stratosphere. The effect on the immediate area was clear
and devastating. What was less well known, until now, is the effect
Tambora had on global weather and arguably global events. The
following year, 1816, became known as 'the year without a summer'
across Europe and eastern America. June and July storms and frosts
inspired creative imaginations but devastated crops and brought more
hunger to a Europe short of food and work as it struggled to recover
from the Napoleonic Wars.*

◆

With Melvyn to discuss Tambora and the year without a summer
were: Clive Oppenheimer, professor of volcanology at the University
of Cambridge; Jane Stabler, professor in Romantic literature at the
University of St Andrews; and Lawrence Goldman, professor of
history at the Institute of Historical Research, University of London,
and a senior research fellow of St Peter's College. Oxford.

CLIVE OPPENHEIMER: *Volcanologists have a technical term for
eruptions of this scale and size. It's 'colossal'. It was a huge, huge
event, larger than anything we've seen in the modern period.*

The size of the eruption was hard to imagine, but Clive
Oppenheimer was doing his best to help us with that. We heard that
volcanologists have a scale similar to the Richter scale for earthquakes,
which measures the thermal energy released by eruptions by estimating
the mass of pumice, lava and ash that are ejected. The eruption of
Tambora in 1815 measured 7, which reflects the assessment that it
produced something like 150 cubic km of volcanic debris, which is
enough to cover the whole of Great Britain knee-deep.

CLIVE OPPENHEIMER: *It's something like 100 times larger than the eruption of Mount St Helens in 1980, it's more than ten times greater than the Pinatubo eruption in 1991, it's 1,000 times bigger than the eruption in Iceland in 2010 of Eyjafjallajökull, which caused so much disruption to aviation.*

There was some unrest at Tambora from about 1812, though no one recognised what was in store. Then, in April 1815, the explosions were so loud that they were heard for 1,000km across Indonesia and wherever people heard them they thought they were coming from nearby, from somewhere they could not yet see, perhaps from cannons being fired out at sea. Soon there were huge quantities of ash and pumice climbing into the atmosphere, up to 20 or 30km in the air, two or three times higher than commercial aviation today. Then, at around 7 p.m. on 10 April, the eruption was so violent and there was so much material coming out that it did not really become airborne but devastated all the settlements within a radius of 20km or so. This was the deadliest known eruption in human history.

That human and environmental catastrophe happened in the tropics, in the southern hemisphere, where the destruction was clearly and directly linked to the eruption. As Melvyn's guests went on to explore, there were unexpected, damaging events on the other side of the world, in Europe and North America, which are only now being linked to Tambora.

Lawrence Goldman explained how vulnerable Europe was to sudden shocks. There had been more than twenty years of war, first the French Revolutionary Wars and then the Napoleonic Wars, which were about to end with Waterloo in June 1815. The continent was depleted. Systems had long been set up to support the fighting rather than the domestic world; trade had broken down and there was high unemployment. There were political tensions within countries and, as new alliances formed, between countries, too. Then, while there was a relatively good harvest in 1815, there was cold and rain throughout the spring of 1816, the growing season was much reduced, there were very late frosts and there was snow.

LAWRENCE GOLDMAN: *Through June and July and August there is snow in the middle of summer ... when you find snow falling in central Europe in June of 1816 coloured sort of orange and brown, we can extrapolate that this is the ash from some remarkable volcanic event and there's every reason to believe that it's Tambora spreading its gases and ash through the global wind system.*

In Britain, lower harvests meant that, from 1817 to 1818, the price of bread more or less doubled over the course of twelve months. There was not only urban political unrest but also riots in the towns and the countryside. To Lawrence Goldman, these shortages help explain why the years from Waterloo to Peterloo, the famous massacre at St Peter's Field in Manchester in 1819, are unified by unrest and government repression. With the poorer harvests, food was in even shorter supply in central Europe where there was a subsistence crisis. With its sea trade, Britain was at least able to import some of what it lacked and, in that year of price rises, it imported more foodstuffs than in any other year up to that point in its history. But in central Europe, away from the coasts, particularly in Germany, the transport was much more rudimentary, food was harder to distribute and the impact of the poor harvest was much worse.

Meanwhile, there were other witnesses to the unusual weather who have left us literary reminders of that time. In the summer of 1816, Lord Byron, his personal physician John Polidori, Percy Bysshe Shelley, Mary Shelley and her stepsister Claire Clairmont had all gathered on the shores of Lake Geneva to get away from what they saw as London and winter. When the Shelley party had crossed France, they were told that the spring had been much delayed and that there was much more snow than normal, and they had to hire ten men and four horses to get their carriage over the mountains to Geneva. Percy Shelley noticed that, when they visited the Arve ravine, the cornfields were under water.

When they first arrived in Geneva the weather was fine and sunny, but, soon afterwards, the weather changed and they were confined indoors.

JANE STABLER: *And the causality here is quite clear. Mary Shelley states that, because they're confined indoors, they have to fall back on telling ghost stories and then eventually writing their own stories, and that's the genesis of* Frankenstein.

She had been thinking of the story of the scientist Victor Frankenstein and the monster he created for a while, and the storms were what prompted her to develop them in Geneva. The book was published in 1818.

Lawrence Goldman had mentioned the discoloured snow and suggested a correlation with the eruption that had happened a year before, on the other side of the world. Melvyn asked Clive Oppenheimer what evidence there was to link Tambora and Europe's weather. He said it used to be thought that the ash, spread across the atmosphere, was what altered the climate but, more recently, it has been realised that sulphur was the key agent.

CLIVE OPPENHEIMER: *The sulphur gas makes its way up into the stratosphere and it oxidises to generate tiny particles of sulphuric acid, and they're above the weather systems, they don't get washed out rapidly. And, in an eruption in the tropics, the way the atmosphere works, this sulphurous dust can be dispersed into both hemispheres and form a veil over the whole planet.*

Once the sulphurous dust is above the weather system, it takes five or six years for the levels to drop back to their previous state. These particles intercept some of the incoming sunlight and the net effect is a cooling at the surface of the planet. Since the eruption in 1991 of Mount Pinatubo in the Philippines, we have a fairly clear picture of what happens when a lot of sulphur is released, especially if it is in the tropics.

CLIVE OPPENHEIMER: *We see a significant summer cooling in the continental regions of the northern hemisphere, so parts of Europe, Scandinavia, parts of North America. If we average the effect over the planet over a year, it might be about half a degree of cooling, but if you look at the regional scale, you see that the cooling, compared with average temperatures, is more like 3–4°C. These are significant in terms of harvests.*

People in these parts of Europe and North America were not to know of the veil of sulphurous ash cooling their climates, but they did notice the change. News of the eruption had reached London at the end of 1815 and America the following year, before the harvests. Nobody made the connection being made now, but Lawrence Goldman said there was a mass of evidence that people had observed the dramatic change in the weather.

LAWRENCE GOLDMAN: *In the summer of 1816, The Times is full of discussion of what it means, and even talks about fears of God's wrath, providential explanations of this and that. It's noticed by many that, in Britain and France, more people are going to church and chapel in the summer of 1816 as it becomes clear that the harvest is being ruined.*

There were many observations of the change in temperature, collected by amateur meteorologists. People noted that harvests were bad, that the price of food was going up, that there were economic problems and social disturbances. The impact of Tambora was not known, but Lawrence Goldman believed we now had the evidence that allowed historians to begin to say, 'Here is a further causal problem in this period.'

The unusual weather was an inspiration to the poets around Lake Geneva, and Jane Stabler told us that this aspect of the natural world was the base rock of the poetry of the period. The poets were attuned to the sublime, supposedly the strongest emotion that the mind was capable of feeling, according to Edmund Burke, emotions that were dependent on terror and the experience of vastness, infinity, obscurity, darkness, loudness, everything that a thunderstorm was. Byron's manuscript of *Childe Harold* (Canto III) was punctuated with exact observations of what was going on along the shores of Lake Geneva.

*Villa Diodati, near Geneva, which Bryon
and Polidori rented. Percy Shelley and
Mary Godwin, later Mary Shelley, stayed
nearby and were frequent visitors.*

JANE STABLER: *He'll say something like, '2 June, this was written in
the eye of Mont Blanc, which even at this distance dazzles mine.' Or,
'13 June, the storm in these lines took place at midnight on 13 June.'
The poetry is almost akin to diaries in that it keeps a close record of
exactly what was happening in the atmosphere of the time.*

When looking more widely at poets' diaries, Jane Stabler added,
the experience of the summer of 1816 was very varied. Some
people talk about the weather a lot and other people seem wholly
preoccupied with other things, with political matters. William
Wordsworth, for example, did not mention the weather much in
1816, although Dorothy, his sister, did.

There may have been other factors that made Tambora so
significant. From discoveries in the polar ice cores, it appears there
was another substantial eruption in 1809, perhaps similar to the

1883 eruption of Krakatoa. Volcanologists have no idea where it took place other than somewhere in the tropics, deduced from the distribution of the ash and sulphur at both poles. As this unidentified eruption was within about seven years of Tambora, there may still have been a memory of it in the climate system when Tambora hit.

Clive Oppenheimer: *One of the things that we find is that multiple events can lead to more prolonged impact on the global climate system. And there's even an idea that the little Ice Age might have been triggered by machine-gun detonations of volcanoes in the mid-thirteenth century.*

Lawrence Goldman commented that the decade 1810–20 was one of the coldest in the past 200 years or so, and the years before Tambora were cold in the northern hemisphere, especially in North America, so perhaps that earlier eruption had an impact there in particular. The year 1816 was especially bad and, in response, more people than before migrated westwards, both from Europe to America and from the east coast of America inland. Listeners could walk around parts of Massachusetts today and find homesteads that were abandoned at that time. The evidence that this followed the change in climate is not foolproof, he said, but it is there.

Arguably, the movement westwards within America brought a new fusion of people. From the coasts of New England there was migration into western New York state and Ohio and the area bordering the Great Lakes, what was known as the burned-over district as it had been burnt over so many times by religious revivalism. This was a combustible area, with social movements emerging alongside the religious ones.

Lawrence Oppenheimer: *They bring from New England, these people going west, a profound and already established anti-slavery commitment, making this area the kind of epicentre of abolitionist politics in America thenceforth. And there is this suggestion, but one can't be much stronger than [this], that what you've got is the combination of factors that explains why anti-slavery takes root here and then spreads.*

Melvyn left that thought there and crossed the Atlantic back to the writers in Geneva who were encapsulating the unusual weather in their verse, and he remembered the poem 'Darkness', which Byron wrote in July 1816, and which starts:

> I had a dream, which was not all a dream.
> The bright sun was extinguish'd, and the stars
> Did wander darkling in the eternal space,
> Rayless, and pathless, and the icy earth
> Swung blind and blackening in the moonless air …

Melvyn described this as a terrible dystopian vision that Bryon had, from a day he had lived through. It transpired it may also have alluded to a prophecy.

JANE STABLER: *It's a day he records as being one where the fowls all went to roost at noon and candles had to be lit as at midnight. I think it's also been suggested that it comes from apocalyptic suggestions at the time that the world was about to end. There was something called the Bologna Prophecy in 1816 where an Italian stargazer had predicted that the sun would be extinguished and the world would end on 18 July.*

MELVYN BRAGG: *And he turned out to be right!*

JANE STABLER: *The sun actually rose on the eighteenth, as it did on many of the other days on which the end of the world was predicted in this period …*

These prophecies were very much a flavour of the time, with anxiety about the end of the world being bound up with the tumultuous world events and the very unsettling weather.

Turning to disease, Clive Oppenheimer noted that, while people in this period were not connecting the poor harvests with the volcano, they were connecting the malnutrition from the poor harvests to the illnesses that were spreading and the living conditions that went with poverty and hunger.

CLIVE OPPENHEIMER: *There's a doctor at a fever hospital in Belfast who writes in 1818, that the reason for this typhus outbreak is because of the poor harvest. So many people have been demobbed from the Napoleonic Wars and are out of work and are vagrant and gathering in soup kitchens where the disease is spread because it's so contagious.*

Lawrence Goldman looked at other phenomena at that time that affected health and resulted from poor weather. One of the theories was that epidemics of cholera, which affected the whole world across the nineteenth century, emerged first in the Bay of Bengal as a consequence of the weather disruption, namely drought followed by an inundatory monsoon in 1817 and 1818. Another tempting but unproven link with Tambora looked at Yunnan Province in the far south-west of China, a rice-growing area where the crops were wiped out by cold conditions in 1816–18. When the climate improved, the peasants planted not rice but a cash crop of opium poppies, so Yunnan became the main source of opium in the nineteenth century. Clive Oppenheimer cautioned that the causal links between an eruption and monsoons were more tenuous than those discussed earlier, and, with that, Melvyn had to thank his guests and end.

Hatshepsut

In the early fifteenth century BC, a woman came to power in ancient Egypt. Her name was Hatshepsut and she remained the longest-reigning female pharaoh until Cleopatra 1,400 years later. She was remarkable for ruling in a society normally controlled by men, and she ruled for about fifteen years. But that is far from the most remarkable thing about her. Many scholars regard her as one of the most influential pharaohs of the New Kingdom period of Egyptian history. She for ever changed the public image of the pharaoh, embarked on a far-reaching building programme and increased Egypt's prosperity by expanding its trade network. Yet at some point after her death, it seems that a systematic attempt was made to erase her memory from the records and her image was removed from many of her monuments.

— ✦ —

With Melvyn to discuss Hatshepsut's life and legacy were: Elizabeth Frood, associate professor of Egyptology at the University of Oxford; Kate Spence, senior lecturer in Egyptian archaeology in the Department of Archaeology, University of Cambridge; and Campbell Price, curator of Egypt and Sudan at the Manchester Museum.

This was a programme where Melvyn and his guests were sifting through the evidence like Egyptian sand, and he started with Elizabeth Frood, who placed Hatshepsut historically at around 1500 BC after a period of turmoil in Egyptian history. The throne had only been stable for about seventy years, or three full generations, and, before that, the kingdom had been split.

The head of a statue of Queen Hatshepsut.

ELIZABETH FROOD: *In the north, you have what we call the Hyksos rulers and these are rulers who probably were of Canaanite origin, so from Syria, Palestine. To the south, and North Sudan, you have the Kingdom of Kush, which was a major African kingdom based in the site of Kerma, which is just south of the Third Cataract.*

There were some less powerful Egyptian dynasties squeezed between these peoples, and, among them, the Theban kingdom of Egypt was the one that drove the reascendence of Egypt – it was to this dynasty that Hatshepsut belonged. The Thebans pushed their borders back, enlarging their Egypt.

Hatshepsut was not the first powerful woman in Egypt, as Campbell Price explained, but none was described as *pharaoh* before Hatshepsut. Usually these powerful women would be regents who had outlived their husbands and ruled until their young sons were old enough.

CAMPBELL PRICE: *Immediately before Hatshepsut comes to the throne there's this warlike dynasty, the seventeenth dynasty, and they comprise again several regents, powerful women. There's one woman in particular, Queen Ahhotep, for whom we've got a nice text describing her bashing up foreigners and mustering the troops. And there's a sense that she's a kind of Amazonian queen.*

A queen was not a pharaoh, though, and there was no word for queen in the Egyptian language in the sense of ruler rather than spouse of the ruler. For example, Ahhotep was a king's mother who acted for her young son, while there was another woman, Ahmose-Nefertari, who was regent and was worshipped as a goddess and was so long-lived that Hatshepsut may have met her.

CAMPBELL PRICE: *So there's this precedent for strong female characters with real ability in a world where you don't live for very long; maybe women have a greater life expectancy ...*

MELVYN BRAGG: *The average is early thirties?*

CAMPBELL PRICE: *Even less than that.*

It appears that there was a close royal group who would intermarry. When connecting the events together, though, to try to understand what happened when or even to whom, Melvyn's guests emphasised that there are many difficulties. Even for the royal families, there were no family trees in this period, and people were generally described according to their relationship with a king without identifying the king in question.

The period under discussion is described as that of the eighteenth dynasty, where the dynasties were a series of rulers over a more or less united Egypt, each with one common ancestor. There were thirty-one dynasties, with the first thought to have started in the thirty-second century BC and the last ending with Alexander the Great's conquest in 332 BC.

Kate Spence pieced together Hatshepsut's claim to power. She was the daughter of Thutmose I, who was a general (probably) and who seemed to have become heir when Amenhotep I didn't produce any children. The dates are disputed, but Ahmenhotep may have ruled 1525–1504 BC and Thutmose I 1504–1493 BC. His wife Ahmose was the great wife, the chief of many wives within the harem, and Hatshepsut seems to have been her eldest daughter. When Thutmose I died, there was no adult male heir so the throne passed to Thutmose II, who may have been a small child at that point, the son of a minor wife, but old enough to marry Hatshepsut who might have been his half-sister.

KATE SPENCE: *Egyptians generally don't seem to have practised brother–sister marriages but this does occur within the royal family and seems to be particularly strong in the early eighteenth dynasty. The idea seems to have been that this is modelled to some degree on divine precedent but, primarily, probably to keep wealth and power within one family.*

As if the flurry of unfamiliar names were not bewildering enough so early in the discussion, Melvyn found himself calling Campbell Price 'Graham' for reasons explained later.

With the death of Thutmose I and the youth of his successor, Hatshepsut was in an extremely strong position, perhaps rivalled only by her mother, Ahmose. One of the most important Egyptian gods was Amun, often called King of the Gods, and Hatshepsut was celebrated with the important title of God's Wife of Amun.

CAMPBELL PRICE: *With this title of God's Wife of Amun, there's a link, a direct link, between the woman fulfilling that role and the god and it's a quasi-sexual role that's not quite clear to us. It's interesting, after Hatshepsut, that the title of God's Wife of Amun is dropped for several centuries, perhaps out of fear that women with that title had become too powerful.*

Still, Hatshepsut was not yet pharaoh, even if she came to be depicted more and more like one. That started to change once Thutmose II was dead, probably after only three years on the throne although that, as with so many other aspects of this period, is disputed. He may have been in his early teens, old enough to father Hatshepsut's daughter Neferure. The succession passed to Thutmose III who may have barely learnt to walk by that time, and whose mother seems to have been another minor wife in the harem. His mother did not become regent, as might have been expected from precedent, but instead Hatshepsut had herself appointed.

KATE SPENCE: *She is ruling the country effectively for a toddler, even though she's probably fairly young still herself, maybe sort of late teens, possibly even into the early twenties. She already is ruling the country for this child and trying to hold the dynasty together.*

She was in power, but not yet pharaoh. There are inscriptions showing Hatshepsut doing things that were usually reserved for kingship, and it appears that slowly she moved from carrying out the tasks of a king to actually declaring herself king and taking a full royal set of titles.

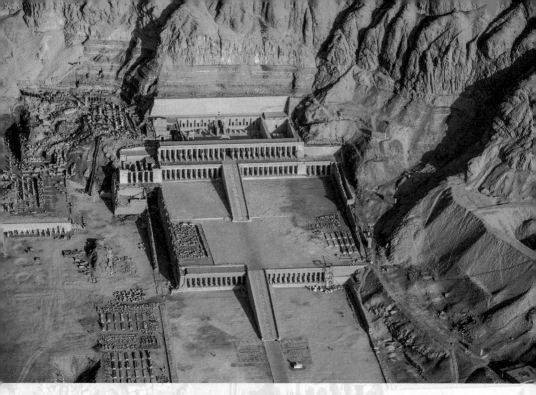

*The Mortuary Temple
of Hatshepsut.*

A lot of our understanding of this time comes from well-informed speculation, but it appears that Hatshepsut was not ruthlessly seeking power. It may have been, as Elizabeth Frood suggested, that her principal concern was to maintain the dynasty, and a sudden grab for power could have destabilised the wider court, a base of advisers that was needed to support the rulers who might otherwise have been too young to be as strong as their role required. That accretion of power over years would have been normal, even unremarkable.

ELIZABETH FROOD: *You have a very stable court, very stable family group and so [Hatshepsut] does what is expected: she steps in as queen regent. It's what happens next that is extraordinary.*

It is not possible to put precise dates on many of these events, something that Melvyn put to the test only, as he said, to see a kind of glaze on his guests' eyes as he tried to press them. Campbell Price identified one significant piece of evidence for Hatshepsut's transition, which is the so-called Red Chapel that housed a key part of Egyptian temple ritual – the barque in which the statue of the deity would be transported.

CAMPBELL PRICE: *In this [chapel], Hatshepsut takes the opportunity to depict herself and her supposed co-regent, Thutmose III, but she shows herself and Thutmose III both as men, but she takes the precedent. She is the leading figure in these scenes and, in one text, she says the god Amun speaks to her and says, 'You are my chosen king.'*

That depiction is taken as the acknowledgement that Hatshepsut had seized power and was now pharaoh, not only the regent.

She went on to make her mark by creating monumental buildings, establishing trade and excelling in diplomacy. Beside her own tomb and temple carved into the rock overlooking the vast temple complex of Karnak, she established a mortuary cult for her father, Thutmose I, and it seems she even moved her father's body and buried it in her tomb.

KATE SPENCE: *It was constructed as the culmination point of a big festival called the Beautiful Festival of the Valley, which was a Theban festival of the dead when the cult statue of the god and moon was taken from Karnak Temple, across the river and spent the night in this temple as part of these celebrations of the dead.*

Monuments were an essential way of shaping the influence of the dynasty, and she was doing this more than previous kings, changing the whole temple landscape with a range of new routes for rituals.

There was also a new trading culture developing in this period, which it appears Hatshepsut advanced. Elizabeth Frood drew attention to an expedition to what was known as the Land of Punt, a semi-mythical place that may have been by the Red Sea, or in Somalia, or perhaps somewhere else – it may even have been a trading destination that moved around. This was an ancient trading route but one that had fallen into disuse, and it seems Hatshepsut was opening it up again, asserting her connection with traditions. Again, Melvyn was keen to test the strength of the evidence.

ELIZABETH FROOD: *She sends an expedition to this strange and fantastic land to bring back all sorts of exotic goods. The key things, which she makes a big deal of in the scenes and texts that narrate this journey, are myrrh trees.*

MELVYN BRAGG: *I ask this with due tentativity – have we real evidence that she expanded trade in the Near East, as we now call it, in Africa, as we now call it, as well as Punt? I mean is there … ?*

ELIZABETH FROOD: *We have archaeological material, material culture of oils and things, new things, products, new musical instruments, new military weapons that are coming into Egypt. And she would have been a driver for that, certainly.*

While Hatshepsut was an exceptional person in ancient Egypt, she was supported, to some extent, by someone for whom there is a relatively high level of biographical material. This was Senenmut, who, it appears, rose from a modest background to become tutor to Hatshepsut's daughter Neferure, and he is sometimes depicted in statues (including one on display at the British Museum) enveloping her in his cloak, something that Campbell Price described as 'unheard of, royal people don't touch non-royal people, let alone be shown in a statue form like this'. Moreover, he was not married, which was unusual for an elite man.

CAMPBELL PRICE: *This has led to speculation that he may be Hatshepsut's lover and there's one particularly controversial graffito that seems to show some sexual act between a man and a woman, which some have interpreted as Hatshepsut and Senenmut. Now I don't think the evidence is strong for that, I don't think any of us here think, but ...*

MELVYN BRAGG: *There are two shaking heads on your left.*

CAMPBELL PRICE: *... but this illustrates the thing about Hatshepsut. The story is so attractive, people like to speculate.*

Senenmut also created what Kate Spence described as 'incredible cryptographic inscriptions with hieroglyphs, friezes around the mortuary temple, which are representations of Hatshepsut's name'.

KATE SPENCE: *They say Hatshepsut's name but they represent part of her as a cobra goddess with sort of uplifted ka arms and sun discs. They're beautiful, beautiful things.*

Senenmut added images of himself praying, something that, we heard, ordinary Egyptians would have found very, very problematic, so it appears he had the confidence to take such liberties with his position. In Kate Spence's view, he was an extraordinarily talented individual, whose talent was recognised by a very talented female ruler who needed someone like that to help her create the monuments, the ideas, all the new things she was coming up with, since the level of innovation in her reign was extraordinary. As the surviving inscriptions show, she changed the way in which pharaohs were depicted in relation to gods, or at least the extent to which that relationship was emphasised.

KATE SPENCE: *Hatshepsut is represented as the bodily son of the god Amun. The god Amun is said to come to her mother in her bedchamber in the form of the king ... but she knows that it isn't really her husband because he smells nice, he smells of the scent of Punt and all the myrrh that is being brought back is to create the scents of Amun's home and background.*

For all her achievements, nothing is known of Hatshepsut's decline or death. What is known is that, within a few years, perhaps two decades, her name started to be erased from records, something on which all of Melvyn's guests had theories. Campbell Price looked at Hatshepsut's long period in power, around fifteen years, which suggested she had support at court, and he pointed to the relatively long time before her name disappeared. Thutmose III, once her co-ruler, was the sole pharaoh by then. Egyptologists used to speculate that he erased her name as an act of revenge or aggression, but if that were the case he might have done this earlier. Kate Spence suggested that succession may have been an issue, and that her name disappeared as she represented a competing family line. Elizabeth Frood identified some elements of her name and image being removed soon after she disappeared from history, but this erasing then petered out until later in the reign of Thutmose III when it was taken up again, presenting a more complex process. That writing out of history was not only Hatshepsut's fate, as Senenmut's name was erased as well. And, with that, the programme ended.

In the studio immediately afterwards, there was some regret that Hatshepsut's diplomacy had not been discussed, or her legacy. But there was more discussion of the graffito, supposedly of Hatshepsut and Senenmut, although the date and the identities are not clear and people have tended to see what they wanted to see.

ELIZABETH FROOD: *But you have a pharaoh – a woman in a pharaonic headdress – being in a sexual position with a man.*

KATE SPENCE: *Except I don't think it's a headdress, I think it's a representation of a wig.*

CAMPBELL PRICE: *A wig.*

KATE SPENCE: *It's just a woman and a man engaging in a sexual act and there is some graffiti in the cave that is of a similar date.*

For Elizabeth Frood, the discussions around the graffito tell us much about how Egyptologists have changed their approach to gender. In the early twentieth century, Hatshepsut was viewed as a woman who was being manipulated by Senenmut, who supposedly had a torrid relationship with him and was influenced by men in the court. Now she is seen as a powerful woman in her own right. And that mention of powerful women may have prompted Campbell Price to remember something he had meant to say in the programme. He had read a newspaper column in the mid-1990s in which Tina Turner claimed she was a reincarnation of Hatshepsut, and that inspired the first track of her album *Private Dancer*, 'I Might Have Been Queen'.

And Melvyn explained why he had called Campbell Price 'Graham'.

MELVYN BRAGG: *I know a Graham Price, he was a big friend of mine when I was a kid. My mother's best friend was Mary Price and her son, my age, was Graham.*

All roads lead to Wigton!

THE BERLIN CONFERENCE

On 15 November 1884, the representatives of fourteen world powers arrived at the Berlin palace of the German chancellor, Otto von Bismarck, for an international summit. For the next three months, they sat locked in negotiation in a grand ballroom, dominated by a 16ft-high map of Africa. Officially the summit was known as the Conference on West African Affairs; in practice, the delegates were discussing the future of the entire continent and how to carve it up. European powers had been setting up colonies in Africa for decades, now they decided which parts of the continent they would each be allowed to treat as their own. The conference was part of the process known as 'the scramble for Africa' and the decisions reached at it had effects that have lasted to the present day. Not a single African took part in the summit and only two of the diplomats involved in these crucial negotiations had ever set foot there.

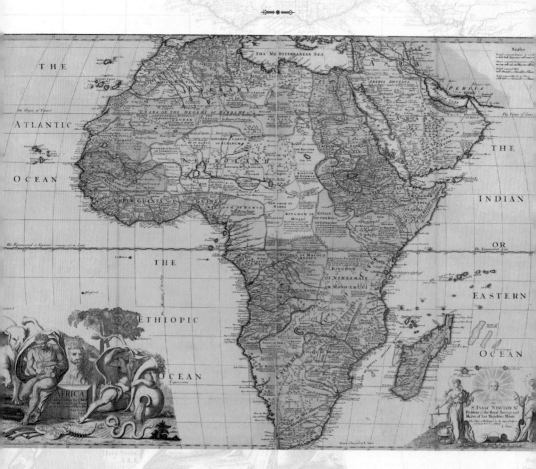

With Melvyn to discuss the Berlin Conference and the scramble for Africa were: Richard Drayton, Rhodes professor of imperial history at King's College London; Richard Rathbone, emeritus professor of African history at SOAS, University of London; and Joanna Lewis, associate professor at the London School of Economics.

Before the discussion turned to the late nineteenth century and the conference, Richard Drayton traced the origins of those European interests in Africa. In early modern times, by their Treaty of Tordesillas of 1494, Spain and Portugal claimed to divide the world between them, with Spain taking the Americas and Portugal taking Africa, though other European powers disputed that carve-up. Within 200 years, Africa had become a critical part of the European global economy, with African slaves essential for the production of all commodities in the New World, and, between 1500 and 1800, more Africans than Europeans crossed the Atlantic. This trade was also a central part of the processing of profits for the Europeans' East India trading companies. For example, they traded a product, such as Indian cloth, for African slaves, who were then sold in America for money. Before the nineteenth century, there was already considerable imperial competition for Africa underway.

RICHARD DRAYTON: *We can see there both a kind of scramble to explore Africa between France and Britain, but, most clearly, also a scramble to acquire particular secured trading enclaves.*

On the west coast of Africa, more easily reached by sea, Britain claimed the mouth of the Gambia River and controlled some areas such as Sierra Leone, which became a formal colony by the end of the eighteenth century, while the French placed themselves at Senegal. The Dutch had been in the Cape from the seventeenth century, and the Portuguese still claimed large parts of Africa. Mostly the interests were on the coasts, accessible by sea, but the Industrial Revolution introduced new transport technologies and new means of waging war.

MELVYN BRAGG: *Transport and arms?*

RICHARD DRAYTON: *Transport and arms, I think, are probably the two most significant technological revolutions. The breech loader, smokeless powder, the rifle, the machine gun ...*

MELVYN BRAGG: *The repeater rifle.*

RICHARD DRAYTON: *The repeater rifle by the late nineteenth century is generating a significant arms gap between Europeans and non-Europeans.*

The building of steamboats that could go up rivers, the completion of the Suez Canal in 1869 with its links to east Africa, and the construction of railways combined to make Europeans look at the interior of Africa as

Map of Africa before the continent was carved up by European empires in the scramble for Africa.

somewhere that might be profitable. For example, Gabon had been a French stronghold from the eighteenth century and it was by travelling up the River Ogooué in Gabon that an Italian-born French explorer, Pietro di Brazzà, reached the hinterland of the Congo and began to negotiate with King Makoko to establish a French claim to the vast interior.

RICHARD RATHBONE: *I think the key thing to grab hold of is getting the image of Africa as very, very gigantic; it is an absolutely enormous continent and much, much bigger than Mercator maps presented.*

Europeans were nibbling around the edges on the west coast, Omani Arabs on the east coast, but the interior was untouched. Meanwhile, in the north, the Ottoman Empire was collapsing and that spurred on the Europeans.

RICHARD RATHBONE: *It's not just technology but it's also the fact that, by the late nineteenth century, it's clear that the Ottoman Empire's on its knees. Hence the French have taken Algeria in 1830, the Italians have got their eyes on what will become Libya, the British are already trying to control Egypt. This is a fantastic transformation in terms of balance of power.*

France and Britain were the two major European players in Africa before the Berlin Conference. France was expanding up the Senegal River and across the shores of the Sahara and then into the Sahara itself, conquering by military force from almost the westerly point of Africa across to Lake Chad and then down to the Congo River and up to the Mediterranean. The British had parts of the Gold Coast, the mouth of the Niger, the Gambia and Sierra Leone, the latter an enclave for freed slaves by that point. The Portuguese held Angola and Mozambique and had done so for a long time. Cape Town was chiefly a port for the Dutch East India Company and then a coaling station for the East India Company. Arab traders from places like Oman came to dominate Zanzibar, interested in the ivory trade and the slave trade. In the Horn of Africa was the independent empire of Ethiopia, which had been resisting invasion attempts for centuries.

Into this came King Leopold II of the Belgians, who wanted a large piece of Africa for himself. He had taken power in 1865 over a small and new kingdom that had seceded from the Netherlands in 1830.

JOANNA LEWIS: *He's definitely got kingdom envy, empire envy. His first cousin is Queen Victoria, about to be made Empress of India, and there he is with virtually no territory overseas at all. He tries to do something about it, he actually tries to buy the Philippines, but that didn't work.*

Leopold II, we heard, wanted to have some imperial real estate, to take his seat alongside all his cousins in the other royal families in Europe, and he did this in a way that was ruthless, brilliant and deadly. He had long been fascinated by the explorers in Africa such as David Livingstone and Henry Morton Stanley and by the proceedings of the Royal Geographical Society. He learned that none of the major powers was yet that interested in central Africa, and he noticed that there was a lot of support for organisations going into Africa with the aim of stopping slavery. He was one of the first to congratulate Stanley on his return after mapping the Congo, and tried to buy his services. In 1876, Leopold set up a front for his goal of dominating the Congo, which was the African International Association, or Association Internationale Africaine.

MELVYN BRAGG: *[Purportedly] the aim of the [asssociation] was to civilise, [it was] humanitarian. He was doing this for unblemished motives. In fact, he was buying it for himself.*

JOANNA LEWIS: *He said he was doing it from the heart, he was putting his own money behind the institute. He got philanthropist anti-slavers to support it. And he gets Stanley to go back to Africa and start making treaties with chiefs up the Congo River.*

Leopold II then had his agent go to America and get the Americans to recognise that his association had sovereignty over an area of 1.3 million square miles. From that, the French supported the association if they could have some first rights themselves. The crisis came when Britain recognised Portuguese control over a region near the mouth of the Congo, and Germany refused to ratify that. It was perceived that Britain was in a position of decline and looking slightly vulnerable, so could be challenged.

For the roots of the Berlin Conference, Richard Drayton noted the role of the Ottoman question and Bismarck's diplomacy, as the Reich's chancellor wanted to maintain Germany's place within the European state system. He was concerned about France, which wanted to recover Alsace-Lorraine, and about the extent to which Britain wanted a commercial monopoly.

RICHARD DRAYTON: *But the real roots of the conference actually lie in Franco-British competition. That's actually the nub of the matter. And the ways in which free-trading Britain had locked up bits of the palm oil trade along the Niger through a cunning device called the 'trust', which restricted Africans' ability to trade freely with Europeans …*

MELVYN BRAGG: *There're always these weasel words, aren't there? Trust – all that stuff.*

RICHARD DRAYTON: *And the French, of course, were doing exactly the same, using tolls and tariffs and other forms of protective contracts.*

Once Britain had endorsed Portugal's claims, Bismarck very quickly recognised one of his adventurers, Adolf Lüderitz, who had created a small trading port in Namibia at Angra Pequena in 1883. As the tempo increased, Bismarck gave a grand speech about why there should be a conference in Berlin, and it opened in November 1884 with all the European powers rather than only the major ones, as Bismarck wanted to play them off against each other and to act as a counterweight to Britain and France.

At that point, Britain was still the major maritime power in the world, with Germany challenging.

RICHARD RATHBONE: *In the case of Britain and Germany, it's certainly the case that, as the palm oil trade in west Africa grows, for example, one of the major beneficiaries of that is Hamburg, and it's the Hamburg merchant shipping companies carrying a great deal of these very valuable cargoes back. So there's real competition for goods, but also competition for access to ports.*

The British Foreign Office was a tiny agency in all of this. The secretary of state for the colonies was a minor post and the colonial office was a 'tiny little instrument in Whitehall', at least until the discovery of gold in South Africa in the 1880s when the potential reward from the empires became much greater. Until then, the trade was in commodities.

RICHARD RATHBONE: *Here is a world of pressure-group politics in which major ports like Liverpool, London, Hamburg, Marseilles and Bordeaux are playing big roles in pushing their governments to, sometimes, I think, rather unwillingly, go along with it. Bismarck has to follow the Hamburg line because they're crucially important to his electoral politics.*

One of the considerations at the conference was the doctrine of effective occupation. Joanna Lewis explained that European powers such as Leopold II argued that, as they had treaties with chiefs who had handed over their rights to trade and to the waterways, these powers, in effect, were going to be in charge of everything and were the recognised government. Leopold had taken the advice of an Oxford scholar called Sir Travers Twists, who told him how to convert his association into being recognised as a formal state by following certain steps.

JOANNA LEWIS: *This is why he gets Stanley to up the ante with making treaties with the chiefs and the treaties are quite shocking. For example, two chiefs are told that they will get a piece of cloth every month if they hand over all the rights to their kingdoms and will always give labour for various projects when they're asked for it.*

MELVYN BRAGG: *For a piece of cloth every month?*

JOANNA LEWIS: *Yes.*

Richard Drayton added that the principle of effective occupation, where proof of sovereignty would be found in government, had emerged already by the seventeenth century and was the basis on which the French, British and Dutch claimed their colonial spaces.

RICHARD DRAYTON: *It draws on the Roman law. It certainly is something that the French are pushing particularly hard and we see the ambassador of France write to Jules Ferry in December 1884 saying this has got to be our strong card and we must occupy and prove that we occupy and are in a position not only to keep what we claim, but to administer or at least to govern the country.*

To this, Richard Rathbone added that effective occupation permitted a colonial world in which there were very powerful capital

The Berlin Conference of 1884–5 was a meeting of the major European powers to negotiate and formalise their claims to territory in Africa.

cities, from where rule was conducted, and then incredibly weak peripheries, something that is still visible on maps on which very little detail appears for the hinterland.

The commercial interests were all around the fringes of the conference, lobbying for influence, expecting representation. Nearly all of the territories under consideration were being administered not by the European states, but by those carrying out work that had been put out to relatively small companies as part of purportedly benign missions. Nowhere, though, were there any delegates from the continent that was being carved up.

Richard Rathbone: *The paternalism that lurks behind this is a very, very powerful bit of nineteenth-century reasoning. This was good for Africans, Africans were going to be saved from themselves, saved from the darkness by the combination of Christianity, commerce and civilisation, as it was seen.*

Leopold's association was to deliver those aims in the Congo, and Bismarck applauded him for having such principles. Leopold, personally, came out of the conference owning land that was seventy-eight times the size of his own kingdom in Europe. On this land, he was to become responsible for one of the major humanitarian disasters of the modern age, in which millions died. Melvyn wondered why he was praised by Bismarck, when previously he had called him a swindler and a fantasist.

JOANNA LEWIS: *Maybe they think it'll be all right on the night, but actually they don't know the extent of what's going to happen. He has huge support from abolitionists, from Baroness Burdett-Coutts, he is the toast of all humanitarians virtually, although there is just some scepticism.*

Not all the European countries emerged with what they wanted. Portugal had hoped for more. Britain had protected its interests and had stopped France from getting the Congo even if that meant Leopold had it instead.

Within days of the conference settlement in early 1885, Richard Drayton said, the Germans claimed a protectorate over east Africa, the area covered by Tanzania today. The British soon tried to enforce their control over the Niger, sending King Jaja of Opobo, for example, away on a gunboat to the West Indies because he had interfered with British trade in the Niger. In the Congo, Leopold decreed very quickly that all vacant lands belonged to his territory and he created a private army, the Force Publique, to ensure there was a supply of forced labour.

While gold in South Africa transformed the profitability of the colonies from the 1880s, an industrial development in Europe was felt in the Congo from the 1890s.

JOANNA LEWIS: *One significant discovery, which affects the Congo dramatically and increases the enslavement of peoples that's going on there, ironically under the banner of getting rid of slavery, is the development of the inflatable tyre by Joseph Dunlop in the late 1880s. So that means that Leopold has got another lease of life in order to try to clear his debts.*

For these inflatable tyres, Leopold turned his attention to the rubber vines in the forests and that led to conditions that inspired the story Joseph Conrad eventually told in *Heart of Darkness* after Conrad had sailed up the Congo. Some say he based the character of Kurtz on a Belgian officer in the Force Publique, Captain Léon Rom.

Richard Rathbone wanted to stress the extent to which Africans were agents in the nineteenth century, not simply passive recipients of whatever Europeans did. There were existing issues, such as those leading from the importation of modern firearms, which gave rise to serious warlordry in central Africa, and the breakdown of law and order, which helped the slave trade internally and across the Indian Ocean. There were civil wars within African kingdoms and, for many of those parties, the arrival of Europeans on the ground meant potential allies.

Picking up on this, Richard Drayton noted that, by the end of the nineteenth century, there were attempts by Europeans throughout the continent to transform what had previously been forms of collaborative relationships into ones in which Africans were more clearly subordinate. To him, many contemporary understandings of European imperialism essentially involve a retrospective application to the early nineteenth century of a kind of white dominance that didn't really exist in the earlier period.

RICHARD DRAYTON: *We could see the scramble for Africa, from another perspective, as having to do with what we might call the crisis of the middlemen states, which had emerged in the eighteenth and nineteenth centuries on the coast of west Africa and had actually become quite strong and wealthy, dealing in slaves first of all and then later on in palm oil and gum and other commodities.*

Richard Rathbone pondered what might have happened if there had been no scramble for Africa, and whether there would have been more examples like that given by Ethiopia, which had retained control of its destiny to some extent. Richard Drayton noted the Europeans' disproportionate, violent command of the world's resources, and the impact it had on the forms of modernity that appeared in Ethiopia and, under American protection, in Liberia. Following on from that, when looking at the kinds of possibilities for decolonisation that emerged later on, the options were all extremely constrained by the structures set in place under empire.

MELVYN BRAGG: *What would you say is the legacy, Joanna Lewis?*

JOANNA LEWIS: *The legacy of the scramble for Africa is that Africa gets divided up by countries who produce states that are too greedy, too rushed and too racist to live up to any of the humanitarian ideals that were on the books in the Brussels Conference in 1889 on anti-slavery and empire, and in Berlin. And so, at independence, they were then passed-over states and not nations.*

As the programme closed, Melvyn apologised for rushing through, with so much to say in a live discussion of forty-two minutes. He picked up some of the themes in the newsletter he dictated in these years to Ingrid, the production assistant who has worked on *In Our Time* since the first episode. 'After the programme ends, we have approximately thirteen minutes in the studio. Then a World Service programme moves in. In those thirteen minutes, we grab a cup of tea and a bit of fruit and generally talk through the programme. In this instance, the three contributors talked as fast, as enthusiastically and as intensely as they had done on the programme itself.' They told him that North America, China and western Europe would fit into Africa. Joanna Lewis said that her favourite film was *Anchorman* and she managed to see it in full, twice, while flying over the Democratic Republic of Congo. On the question of the Congo, Mark Twain wrote a very long poem about called 'King Leopold's Soliloquy' and, according to Melvyn's guests, Twain 'got him'. While the programme had left Melvyn almost winded with information, as he described it, and in the guilty knowledge that so much had not been said, he left the building. 'Outside on the pavement – blow me down – the three contributors were standing together, intently continuing, with no sign of concluding, the discussion they'd had so vividly in studio 50F a few minutes ago.'

ASHOKA THE GREAT

*In 1837, a young British administrator in Calcutta, James Prinsep,
succeeded in deciphering a series of mysterious and ancient
inscriptions. These had been discovered on rocks and stone pillars
all over India. Prinsep proved that they were relics of the reign of an
ancient king called Ashoka, who had lived in the third century* BC.
*Ashoka ruled most of the Indian subcontinent for almost forty years,
creating one of the largest empires the region had ever seen through
ruthless military endeavours. But he later renounced violence and
converted to Buddhism. In a series of edicts carved into monuments
all over his territories, he depicted himself as a benevolent and kindly
leader intent on the welfare of his subjects. Today it is believed that
his influence was of critical importance in the development and
spread of Buddhism.*

With Melvyn to discuss Ashoka the Great were: Dr Jessica Frazier,
research lecturer at the University of Oxford and the Oxford Centre
for Hindu Studies; Richard Gombrich, founder and academic
director of the Oxford Centre for Buddhist Studies and emeritus

*The Great Stupa built by
Ashoka the Great at Sanchi,
Madhya Pradesh, India.*

professor of Sanskrit at the University of Oxford; and Naomi Appleton, senior lecturer in Asian religions at the School of Divinity, University of Edinburgh.

Ashoka was a member of the Maurya dynasty, which came to power in India in the fourth century BC. Jessica Frazier compared the nature of that power to other examples in the world at that time, in the Mediterranean, in China and in northern India, in which there were many different states, kingdoms, city states and administrative units that were thriving and could be linked but were not yet unified.

JESSICA FRAZIER: *Alexander the Great had almost unified this region when he came in and tried to take north India, but he retreated, he failed, probably best for India. But this had left a power vacuum of different dynasties and it is into this context that the Mauryans are going to come into power.*

She mentioned the stories, of uncertain accuracy, that tell of a political adviser named Kautilya, who is often credited as the author of the *Arthashastra*, a work that explains how to rule. These stories place Kautilya in that period, and say that he was insulted by one of the most important of the earlier dynasties, the Nandas, in the vibrant kingdom of Magadha. Looking for a champion to overthrow that dynasty, he put forward someone called Chandragupta Maurya, who succeeded in fomenting dissent within Magadha and took over the throne in 321 BC, establishing an extraordinarily successful empire.

JESSICA FRAZIER: *There was great diversity – it was really not just an empire of states, it was an empire of ideas. And, among the most important of these, we get a real pluralistic range of religions. There's the ritual Brahminic culture that later becomes Hinduism, but there's also a swathe of atheist ethical philosophies.*

This world included the Jains, who had a monastic culture and focused on non-violence, the Charvakas, who were early atheist materialists, and the Buddhists, who also had a monastic culture and a very strong ethical tradition that was going to be influential on Ashoka later on.

On top of the uncertainties hinted at by Jessica Frazier, Naomi Appleton recommended caution over the quality of the evidence about Ashoka's life. There are later Buddhist biographies of Ashoka, for example, but not contemporary.

NAOMI APPLETON: *We do hear that he was not the natural heir, according to some accounts he was very ugly, his father didn't like him, he sent him off to quell an uprising but without any weapons, we're told, so a clear indication that he didn't think he was the chosen one. Some accounts tell us that he tricked his father into crowning him on his deathbed because his brother was away, and, when his brother came back, he tricked his brother into falling into a pit of live coals.*

There are other stories that he killed ninety-nine brothers, half-brothers by the king's many wives, and he was depicted as a violent character and not the natural successor. Naomi Appleton suggested that the violence of his pre-conversion life was exaggerated in order to make his conversion seem more remarkable.

NAOMI APPLETON: *He's said, for example, to have tested the obedience of his ministers by telling them to dig up all the flowering and fruiting trees and leave only the trees that had thorns in them. And his ministers queried this as a bit of a strange command, and in the end he got so impatient with them he's said to have had them all beheaded.*

Richard Gombrich emphasised the uncertainty even further, with the only contemporary evidence for Ashoka being his inscriptions. The Buddhist texts come from many hundreds of years later and it is typical of hagiography that if you want to say someone became a great saint, then you say he was a terrific sinner before.

MELVYN BRAGG: *So you're casting dispute on everything that's been said so far?*

RICHARD GOMBRICH: *Absolutely, yes.*

MELVYN BRAGG: *Well, at least we know where we are.*

Ashoka, though, was rather unique in leaving thirty-three inscriptions, which Richard Gombrich said were the first examples of writing in India. The inscriptions are all over India: some are on rocks, others are on pillars. In this way, Ashoka recounted that, when he was in the eighth year of his reign, he fought against the people of Kalinga, which is in modern Orissa, in eastern India. He was terribly distressed, he said, by the fact that 150,000 people were captured and enslaved, that 100,000 were slain and many times that number died after.

RICHARD GOMBRICH: *He certainly modelled himself on the Persian habit of putting up great inscriptions, and Darius had put up great inscriptions saying that he killed hundreds of thousands of people, enslaved hundreds of thousands of people and so on. And this is a counter-statement, so to speak: 'I do it differently.' And he then says how he's terribly upset and this caused him, really, a complete change of heart, and he converted to Buddhism.*

Ashoka wrote at some length, he added, about how terribly people suffered when their relatives were killed, when all the people they respected were scattered, and Ashoka described it as an awful thing that changed his mind and made him into a Buddhist. There was another, later story that told how he was converted by a Buddhist monk on the road, but there is no surviving contemporary evidence for that.

RICHARD GOMBRICH: *This is probably, I think, unique in the history of the world. He renounces war completely and says he will never again wage war and he hopes that none of his descendants will ever wage war, and that he will only reserve the right to defend himself if attacked. And I don't know of any king, any great king, who has ever put up such a statement before or since.*

Following his success at Kalinga, for which he felt such remorse, Ashoka commanded a huge area from Bengal to Afghanistan and almost to the tip of India, and he started to communicate his message across it. Jessica Frazier argued that Ashoka had to hold that region not by force but by ideas, and that was where the pillar and rock inscriptions came in. There was no paper for publishing, and there were too many villages to send out criers from a central point. According to Richard Gombrich, people gathered around the inscriptions and officials explained their meaning.

JESSICA FRAZIER: *On the one hand, he has the pillars, quarried near Varanasi, sent up and down the Ganges, and they talk about his philosophy of life, his philosophy of politics and the kind of state that he hopes to reign over. He also has rock edicts inscribed much further afield, often on routes that are taking people outwards towards the Mediterranean, up into the Himalayas, down into the south.*

These were messages not only to his own people but also to the people at the borders, written in Prakrit, an Indian language, but there were also some in Aramaic and Greek, and Ashoka talked about links with kings as far afield as Egypt and north Africa, as well as in Macedonia. He was saying that he was the kind of ruler people wanted, that he was not like other rulers. Naomi Appleton added that some of the messages on the practical steps that Ashoka took, such as digging wells, planting trees and finding herbs to cure diseases, were all proclaimed on the main routes across his enormous empire. Richard Gombrich mentioned another, where Ashoka said he should always be active for the welfare of his people and strictly commanded that anything that needed doing must be reported to him: even if he was in his bedroom, even if he was with his women, even if he was on the toilet, he must be informed, because he was the father of his people and he felt responsible for everything.

MELVYN BRAGG: *And I think the big question that we all want to know is: was this mere propaganda or a bit of propaganda or not propaganda at all?*

RICHARD GOMBRICH: *I'm convinced that it was absolutely sincere. Why would you go to this immense trouble of talking about spreading your doctrine? He used the Buddhist term* dharma *and he actually says in these words: 'What is* dharma? *Dharma is having few vices and many virtues, compassion, generosity, truthfulness and purity.'*

Melvyn sought some further clarification of what Ashoka meant by *dharma*. Jessica Frazier explained that there are different spellings, from different languages, and the meaning for Buddhists was also multi-faceted, including things like the truth of reality, an ethical way of life and, specifically, compassion, which she described as the most impractical and yet one of the most idealistic of virtues.

When Ashoka translated these ideas into Greek in his inscriptions, he used the word *eusebeia*, a kind of piety, the good way of right conduct. The implication was that behaving in the right way was natural, and that it was easy to be ruled in an empire where Ashoka was in charge.

RICHARD GOMBRICH: *He says: 'Don't rely on silly rituals. What you've got to do is to be kind to your servants, obedient to your parents, respect your religious teachers, be generous and give money wherever it is needed. And should these things not bring you good results in this life, at least you won't have lost anything and they will certainly bring you good results in the next life.'*

These inscriptions were created during Ashoka's reign, and are significant for how he is understood today. It can be hard to reconcile the Ashoka of the inscriptions with the Ashoka of the later Buddhist texts, though, the earliest of which date from the first or second century AD.

NAOMI APPLETON: *The textual sources provide a very different account and they don't seem to show any awareness of the Ashoka of the edicts at all. So, for example, the Kalinga conversion is not mentioned, he's said to have been converted simply by a charismatic monk.*

In the later texts, there are two main sets of legends about Ashoka. One is from north India, the early one mentioned above with Kautilya, and the other is from Sri Lanka and is concerned with the history of Buddhism there. These hold Ashoka personally responsible for sending missionaries to Sri Lanka, including his son Mahendra, also known as Mahinda. Naomi Appleton suggested that some of the perception that Ashoka sent out Buddhist missionaries, rather than envoys, may have been coloured by these later texts. Whatever the case with those envoys or missionaries, Richard Gombrich was clear that Ashoka listed a number of Buddhist texts by title on one of his inscriptions, and recommended that his people should study them.

Did Ashoka rule as he promised? On the evidence available, Jessica Frazier found that very difficult to assess. There were earlier reports from Greek travellers that indicated there were already sophisticated societies in India before Ashoka, well run, just as there were after, and it is very hard to find evidence for the difference he made.

JESSICA FRAZIER: *People sometimes are sceptical because a lot of his most idealistic edicts are found furthest away from the territories he's actually ruling. So, for instance, his remorse about Kalinga is expressed away from Kalinga. But, when he gets actually to the edicts that are in Kalinga, he doesn't say, 'Guys, I'm really sorry', he says, 'I'm just going to try to rule you well from now on.'*

Her own feeling is that his success may be reflected in what happened in succeeding centuries, as Indian culture after Ashoka and the Maurya was very impressive, and also in the spread of Buddhism and Ashoka's ideals. Richard Gombrich argued that the evidence for sophisticated societies, before and after Ashoka, was written down too late for it to relate reliably to his period. Notably, he said, many of Ashoka's views ran counter to those of the later Hindu rulers.

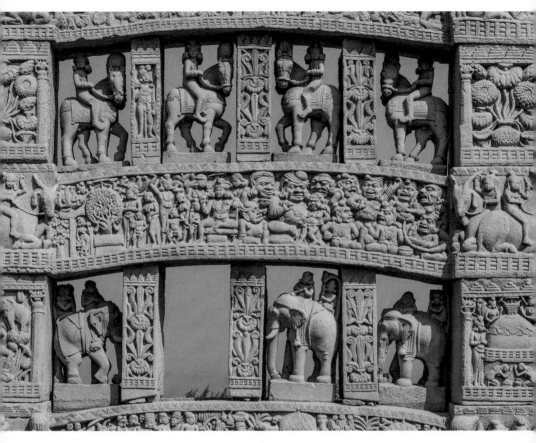

*A detail of the Northern Gate
of the Great Stupa at Sanchi.*

RICHARD GOMBRICH: *Ashoka, for instance, doesn't mention
the caste system; he doesn't support the caste system because he's a
Buddhist. He also forbids blood sacrifices; he also denigrates, in very
strong language, the rituals that are being carried on. In other words,
in just one word, he's anti-Brahmin, he's anti-Hindu.*

Richard Gombrich emphasised how crucial the caste system was
in India at the time. It was the very essence of society and the job of
a king was normally to support the caste system, and somebody who
did not do that, or did not support Brahmin priests in their sacrifices,
was going to be cataclysmic in India. He added that, while there
were many Buddhist kings and kingdoms in India in the 300–400
years after Ashoka, he was not celebrated by the Brahmins and he is
generally known in India now as a Hindu king.

Over time, Ashoka's inscriptions were forgotten and even
Buddhists remembered him differently.

NAOMI APPLETON: *They remembered him as a king who set up
stupas or shrines, who established pilgrimage to the sites associated*

with the Buddhist life, who patronised the Buddhist community, supported the monastic community very highly with great gifts, very, very elaborate gifts. He's said to have given everything away. Right up unto his deathbed, he gave away his last belonging, which was half a piece of fruit.

The way of life that was described by later Buddhists, with Ashoka's support for monastic communities, created a model of kingship that was followed by kings throughout the Buddhist world in subsequent centuries. It appears Ashoka also insisted on religious tolerance.

RICHARD GOMBRICH: *He says it is very bad to praise your own religion and denigrate other people's religion. You must inform your neighbours and you must inform each other about your religions and he repeats, 'Do not praise your own religion and don't denigrate other people's', you will only suffer demerit for doing wrong for that. And he says, 'It is very difficult to do good and easy to do evil, but it is most difficult to do good if you're high up in society.'*

In Jessica Frazier's estimation, what Ashoka did was to see that it was practical to pursue his ideals and ethics, to create an empire that was based on compassionate welfare, on the principles of virtue that made communities self-sustaining. He was sincere and pragmatic, and his great genius was to see that both worked well together.

The tomb of Elizabeth I in Westminster Abbey, London.

THE DEATH OF ELIZABETH I

In February 1603, Queen Elizabeth I began to complain of insomnia and loss of appetite. She had been on the throne for forty-four years. It was clear that she would leave no heir, and her death had been long expected; but when its imminence became apparent, and there were widespread fears of insurrection, a complex, highly staked series of manoeuvres followed, and there were devils in the details. To some, Elizabeth's passing and the arrival of a younger, male monarch, James I, with wife and children, seemed as much a liberation as a loss; and yet in death she became a mythic figure and remained all too present as her Scottish successor began his troubled reign in England.

━━◆━━

With Melvyn to discuss the death of Elizabeth I were: John Guy, fellow of Clare College, Cambridge; Clare Jackson, lecturer and director of studies in history at Trinity Hall, Cambridge; and Helen Hackett, professor of English literature at University College London.

The discussion began in February 1603, when Elizabeth fell ill and people were not expecting her to recover. John Guy spoke of how there was a fear of disorder as she had made no provision for succession, an omission that he characterised as quite irresponsible. There was a lot to take into account, including the need to bring Catholics back into the system after their years of alienation.

JOHN GUY: *How will the succession be handled? People are, of course, expecting that James will be an important candidate, but he is 400 miles away. He is a Scot – that is a matter of great concern.*

It was noticed that Elizabeth had reacted badly to the death of her friend and cousin Catherine Howard, Countess of Nottingham, on 24 February and she had lost her appetite and her ability to sleep. There were rumours of Elizabeth's death even while she was still alive.

There was a risk of everything falling apart, and the man who was trying to hold everything together was Sir Robert Cecil, the queen's chief minister. He had taken on his rival Robert Devereux, 2nd Earl of Essex, and had him executed in 1601, and Cecil was powerful but vulnerable to a sudden change. He had been writing to James in Scotland and to the Earl of Northumberland to make plans.

MELVYN BRAGG: *And these are potentially treasonous activities, aren't they?*

JOHN GUY: *They are potentially treasonous. And, of course, he had to pretend to Elizabeth that he wasn't doing it. And, of course, she knew that he probably was, but she chose to turn a blind eye.*

There was a broader sense of unease. Clare Jackson mentioned the harvest failures, with prices going up, wages falling and the population rising, and, in the towns, there had been plague and influenza, decimating communities. These strains on Elizabeth's subjects were exacerbated by the wars that Elizabeth had been pursuing in the 1590s after a period of non-intervention.

CLARE JACKSON: *There is rising xenophobia and war-weariness in the 1590s. There are criminally inclined deserters, troops being billeted on the populations, there is a rise in crime and vagrancy. A lot of that is met with quite harsh, repressive authoritarianism. So there is a real sense that there might be an undercurrent of trouble.*

There was a fear that England could, at any point, be encircled by superior counter-reformation forces. Spain had invaded Ireland in 1601 unsuccessfully, but there was always a worry that Ireland might be a side door into England for Catholic armies.

Despite the uncertainty over her succession, Elizabeth had resisted all attempts to persuade her to name someone. She did not want an alternative constituency around her and, Clare Jackson said, from the beginning of her reign, Elizabeth expressed her view that 'people will look to the rising [rather] than to the setting sun'. She had been aware during Mary's reign that those who were opposed to Mary were looking to her, and she did not want to create an alternative power base. That reticence may have solved one issue, but it created others. As early as 1593, a puritan MP, Peter Wentworth, urged her to declare her succession and he was put in the Tower for refusing to keep silent about that.

CLARE JACKSON: *He makes the argument that, if she doesn't declare her successor, she will remain unburied at her death, because all of her courtiers and all of her officials will only have their posts for as long as her reign continues. Elizabeth tries to get around this by saying that she is not to be disembowelled, so the court indicates rapidly that she will have to be buried.*

As with so many programmes, the evidence for what happened at this time had to be teased from different sources. Helen Hackett looked at the literature written when Elizabeth's death was in prospect. There was poetry that proclaimed she had conquered time, was ever young and immortal, although this protestation of immortality seemed, to Helen Hackett, rather to reflect consciousness of her mortality. There were other, more cynical verses, such as those spoken by Theseus in *A Midsummer Night's Dream*, alluding to Elizabeth with the image of the moon, which had often stood in for her in poetry: 'How slow / This old moon wanes! She lingers my desires / Like to a stepdame or a dowager / Long withering out a young man's revenue.'

HELEN HACKETT: *We can quite plausibly read into that impatience among the young men of the nation about this old woman lingering and a feeling of stagnation that's coming with that.*

As for what happened in the weeks leading up to Elizabeth's death, there is an incomplete and inevitably unreliable picture. There was the evidence of Sir John Harington, a favoured godson, who talked of visiting her in November 1602 and finding her melancholy, walking around her chamber stabbing the arras with her sword in case there were interlopers and treasonous plotters there. Others talked about her suffering from fever and sleeplessness, with swelling in her throat and increasing difficulty in speaking. She spent the last three days of her life in private, with three or so ladies-in-waiting. One of these was Lady Southwell, who later talked of Elizabeth being haunted by visions of her own wasted body.

HELEN HACKETT: *She talks about how a playing card of the queen of hearts, with a nail through its head, was found on the bottom of Elizabeth's chair, and, after Elizabeth's death, she says that her corpse was so full of noxious vapours that it exploded in the coffin. Now she is the only one who gives us these details, so they are perhaps not entirely reliable ...*

John Guy told how Elizabeth, in her illness, refused to go to bed as she would never get out of it. He thought she knew that her number was up and was just waiting.

JOHN GUY: *You see, one has to get a sense of what Elizabeth is actually like.*

MELVYN BRAGG: *That's what I want to get.*

JOHN GUY: *At that time ... I mean, she is bald, she wears a wig; her breath stinks, her teeth are bad because she had a fad for sugar much*

*On 24 March 1603, Queen Elizabeth I died
and King James VI of Scotland succeeded
to the English throne as James I, uniting
the Scottish and English crowns.*

*earlier in her life. She puts a silk perfumed handkerchief in her mouth
when she receives any visitors, and she won't appear without her
make-up; and to look beneath her make-up would essentially require
an archaeological dig. There are quite a lot of people who would like
to see the back of her.*

Clare Jackson brought up what she called a very poignant moment
about a month before Elizabeth's death, where her ring, which had
been her sign of her marriage to the state as opposed to any man
who might have produced an heir, had to be cut from her finger as it
had grown into the flesh, which a lot of people took to be an omen
that her contract with her country was now broken. That prompted

John Guy to say that there is a different version of the story, which emphasised again how much is unknown or unproveable. He sets some weight by a later account of Robert Carey, who said the Privy Council had an audience with Elizabeth on 23 March, the day before her death.

JOHN GUY: *And when James's name was mentioned, she raised her hand to her head, as it were, in a gesture. Now, if that were true, and, actually I personally believe that it is true, if that were true, then, by the law of wills, the testamentary law, that could be construed as a nuncupative will. You could make a will on your deathbed in front of witnesses.*

Yet, with her death, there would be an interregnum and the authority of the state officials, of the court, would cease. To prepare for that, Robert Cecil used a device that his father, Lord Burghley, had invented when Elizabeth had recovered from smallpox in 1562 to guard against this risk should it arise again. This device called for the Privy Council to reinforce itself with the great nobility, to be called the 'Great Council', and this drew on a tradition going back to the Middle Ages that allowed the Great Council to summon parliament in its own name in the absence or incapacity of the monarch.

JOHN GUY: *And, in fact, the actual course of events after Elizabeth's death (if we now cut or scroll back to 3 o'clock in the morning of 24 March, when Elizabeth dies), what happens is that immediately, Cecil gets as many of the counsellors as he can together; and he sends for the Earl of Northumberland, he sends for the Earl of Shrewsbury. It is all done by 6 a.m.*

They were agreed on what had to be done, which was for James to succeed, and this succession was proclaimed at the gates of Whitehall and again in the City of London. A student at the Inns of Court at that time, John Manningham, wrote a very vivid account of how the people of London heard the proclamation in silence. He said there was no shouting, nothing happened, and he gave a very vivid sense of London existing in a sort of suspended animation. In the evening, an air of celebration broke out, of relief that it had all been achieved peaceably.

Helen Hackett argued that Cecil's plans were buoyed up by popular support for James. There were elegies published for Elizabeth's death, but not that many. A lot of the poets wrote about how other poets were not writing, 'but the ones that do appear say things like: "Eliza's dead, that rends my heart in twain: and James proclaim'd, that makes me well again!"'

While London knew about the succession, no one had yet told James. Robert Carey wanted to be the first to do this. He slipped out of Whitehall after Cecil, who wanted to control the order of events, and ordered the gates to be barred so that no one could leave. Carey made it from London to James in three days.

HELEN HACKETT: *He had made plans, he had written letters and made plans well ahead. He rides at full tilt. He does have an accident on the way – he falls off his horse part of the way there and is kicked in the head by his horse – but continues and makes it to James at nightfall on 26 March, which is rather extraordinary.*

CLARE JACKSON: *When the poor bleeding Carey arrives, James has already gone to bed, and he falls at his feet and acclaims him King of Scotland, England, Ireland and, somewhat euphemistically, France as well, the moment James has been waiting for. James later says: 'Is there anything I can do for you?' And Carey says, 'I would like to be a gentleman of the bed chamber.' And James says, 'That's fine.'*

Before he came to England, James sent a book he had written, *Basilikon Doron*, an informal handbook of kingship and the king's duties before God. It sold 16,000 copies at a time when the population of London was tiny. Many of the surviving copies are in good condition, suggesting that they were not read thoroughly, if at all.

CLARE JACKSON: *But actually, had people read it and engaged with it, if you like, it would have given quite a good indication of the type of monarchy that James intended to operate and practise. A lot of people see it as a kind of Jacobean equivalent of a coronation mug – people bought it more to cherish than to actually read.*

James made it clear that he did not want to arrive in London until after the funeral, which did not take place until 28 April. That was a huge procession and included even the most lowly members of the royal household, such as the maker of spice bags, the wine porters and the scullery maids. Thomas Dekker, the dramatist, described the hearse as like an island in an ocean of tears. Yet, as Clare Jackson added, James was in no hurry to reach London.

CLARE JACKSON: *He is a passionate hunter, this is the one thing that James is absolutely passionate about, and he once heard that every English gentleman kept his country park well stocked. And he intended to hunt his way down the A1, basically.*

James left his Scottish subjects, setting off from Edinburgh on 5 April and promising to return often, though, in fact, he returned only once. He suffered some hunting injuries but, more significantly, had someone hanged without trial on the way, which might have given his courtiers pause for thought.

JOHN GUY: *When he does get down to London, it isn't that long before he issues proclamations without consulting parliament, and possibly without even consulting the Privy Council in a formal sense, that he should be King of Great Britain, that there should be an integrated coinage, that there should be a British flag ...*

The coronation was on 25 July 1603. The plague was at its height, but James needed to get crowned because plots were hatching and some of the plotters were arguing that it was no treason to plot against an uncrowned king. Owing to the plague, the triumphal entry of James I was postponed until the following March, which meant that he progressed through London with all the assurance of a reigning monarch, rather than a monarch on his way to the crown.

THE LANCASHIRE COTTON FAMINE

In 1863, in the middle of the American Civil War, President Lincoln wrote: 'I know and deeply deplore the sufferings which the working men of Manchester, and in all Europe, are called to endure in this crisis. I cannot but regard your decisive utterances upon the question as an instance of sublime Christian heroism, which has not been surpassed in any age, or in any country.' He was replying to a letter from Manchester citizens, who had urged him to fight the Confederates, abolish slavery and continue the blockade of the cotton trade that had closed mills in northern England, and left hundreds of thousands of workers unemployed. The blockade had led to what is called the 'Lancashire Cotton Famine', a defining episode in world trade and British social history.

Cartoon from Punch, 1862, depicting
Britannia banishing starvation
by collecting private charity for
unemployed mill workers.

With Melvyn to discuss the Lancashire Cotton Famine were:
Lawrence Goldman, professor of history at the Institute of Historical
Research, University of London, and senior research fellow of St
Peter's College, Oxford; Emma Griffin, professor of history at the
University of East Anglia; and David Brown, senior lecturer in
American studies at the University of Manchester.

By the outbreak of the American Civil War in 1861, the textile
industry had become very important in Britain indeed. According
to Lawrence Goldman, there were 2,500 cotton mills in Lancashire
employing 430,000 hands and a majority of these were women. With
related trades, it was estimated that 4 million people in England and
Wales depended on the cotton trade for their livelihood. Manchester
was the centre of this.

LAWRENCE GOLDMAN: *It was known as 'Cottonopolis'; it was the
shock city of the Industrial Revolution, but it was the Athens of the
north as well.*

Roughly 75 per cent of all the raw cotton that was turned into cotton
textiles in Lancashire came from America, and this was the very best
cotton, the Sea Island cotton, as it was called, with plantations
spreading out across the southern states as Alabama, Mississippi and
Louisiana were turned over to cotton. While the mills were using new
industrial technology, the plantations used slave labour, and about
1.8 million slaves were engaged in the production of cotton in
America, almost half the total number of slaves in the American
south in 1860. At first, the slavery was not a significant concern in
Lancashire, but, as it became better known, it became one.

Since the majority of the population of the mill towns worked in
or around the mills, a new way of life had grown up in Lancashire.
This was skilled work for which mill workers were valued, and Emma
Griffin said that this was particularly true for the women. In rural
areas of Great Britain, there would be few ways for children to earn
money, but, in and around Manchester, children could start working
from age nine doing menial tasks, progressing in their teens to
operating machinery, which made wage earners of the whole family.
This incentive helped drive the move to mill towns from the rural
communities in which often only the adults had a chance to earn.

EMMA GRIFFIN: *Instead of people dovetailing working at home
with managing a cottage garden or something, now they are going
into the factories. And it is the beginning of the modern working
patterns that we are familiar with, where we are, effectively, paid for
our time, rather than what we manage to get done.*

The newly independent work force was built on the import of
cotton produced by slaves, a situation that was brought into sharp
perspective once America was at war with itself. British campaigners
had achieved great successes with the abolition of the Atlantic slave
trade in 1807, if not slavery itself, though this was followed by
emancipation in the West Indies from 1833. Now the focus was
on slavery in the American south. David Brown pointed to the
popularity of works by writers such as Harriet Beecher Stowe, which

had a huge impact in Great Britain, and to African-American speakers such as Frederick Douglass, who regularly toured Britain in the 1840s and 1850s. There was even Henry 'Box' Brown, a slave who mailed himself to freedom in a parcel from Richmond to Philadelphia – he would arrive in the lecture halls in a box and emerge after about five minutes to present his account of his time as a slave.

MELVYN BRAGG: *What knowledge would you say there was in this country about the slave trade in the south of America, about the Confederates?*

DAVID BROWN: *Most Britons got their knowledge from sources such as* Uncle Tom's Cabin, *from reports in the press that emphasised the break-up of slave families, the long working hours, the terrible conditions that slaves endured.*

This knowledge of slavery might have been superficial in some respects, but it certainly emphasised the worst aspects of cotton slavery. When the Confederate south wanted to secede from the Union, it trusted that British reliance on cotton would win out over other considerations, and it calculated that, if they were to withhold cotton exports from Europe, their independence would be recognised.

MELVYN BRAGG: *Why was the Confederate south so confident that Britain would crumble, it would cry: 'Oh, let's support the Confederates so we can have the cotton back'?*

LAWRENCE GOLDMAN: *There is a phrase that they used in the 1850s: 'king cotton' or 'cotton is king'. It goes back to a number of speeches made by a South Carolinian, a senator, James Henry Hammond, who said that, cotton is king, and Britain could not, as a civilisation, continue if the cotton supply across the Atlantic stopped.*

The Confederates did not reckon on the diversity of the British economy, nor on the way in which workers in Lancashire responded to the embargo on cotton. They also lost some of the control of the embargo, which started with them withholding exports, but eventually the Union navy blockaded ports to prevent cotton crossing the Atlantic, so that it could not be exported even if the Confederates wanted it to be. Cotton bales were left to rot on the quaysides of the American south.

Ahead of the war, Lancashire mill owners had stockpiled cotton so the problems were not very acute in 1861, but then the next year's harvest failed to make it out of the south.

EMMA GRIFFIN: *That's when the problems really start to emerge. All through 1862, well into 1863, not nearly enough cotton is entering the district and that's when the factories start to go onto short-time work, and eventually many, many people are made unemployed.*

Relief funds were set up, and workers looked to the local help under the Poor Laws, but there was not enough room in the workhouses or enough of the usual menial work schemes such as rock-breaking.

DAVID BROWN: *It is a difficult time, there is a large literature in press, there are songs, there are poems written about the distress in Lancashire, one wonders what these people are going to do in such terrible circumstances, but there does seem to be an underlying moral commitment that, while negotiations with the Confederacy might be advantageous on one hand in bringing cotton back and reopening the mills, on the other hand, most mill workers, most working folk in Lancashire, are not going to align themselves with a slave power.*

Local authorities had to find new ways of helping with unemployment, borrowing money for work-creation schemes such as building sewers or setting out parks. This was a time of great suffering yet, at a meeting in the Free Trade Hall between Christmas and New Year 1862–3, it was resolved to send a message of support to President Lincoln from the citizens of Manchester, praising his stand on emancipation, saying, 'The vast progress you have made ... fills us with hope that every stain on your freedom will shortly be removed, and that the erasure of that foul blot on civilisation and Christianity – chattel slavery – will cause the name of Abraham Lincoln to be honoured and revered by posterity.' This was the letter to which Lincoln replied on 19 January, mentioned in Melvyn's introduction, in which the president added, 'It has been often and studiously represented that the attempt to overthrow this government, which was built on the foundation of human rights, and to substitute for it one that should rest exclusively on the basis of slavery was likely to obtain the favour of Europe. Through the action of disloyal citizens, the working people of Europe have been subjected to a severe trial for the purpose of forcing their sanction to that event.' These working people, though, were not giving in to the embargo.

For David Brown, that was an extraordinary move by Lincoln at one of the busiest periods of his presidency, particularly as emancipation was extremely unpopular in the United States generally and, even in the northern states, there were many who did not support his policy.

DAVID BROWN: *I suspect that he was writing back to the folks in Manchester in order to galvanise that support. Certainly American newspaper editorials suggested that, if the workers of Lancashire and Manchester – particularly at a time of immense distress and suffering – can support emancipation for good moral reasons, then so should the rest of the United States.*

The skilled workers were supported by the mill owners, who tended to be independent-minded Unitarians or Congregationalists, Lawrence Goldman added. One of them, John Bright, put up a quarter of the costs of purchasing Frederick Douglass's freedom from his legal owner when he was in Britain and feared recapture. The Confederates could clearly not count on the mill workers to lobby parliament to recognise them.

In parliament, there was a lot of sympathy for the Confederate cause, particularly among the land owners, but even they knew they had to be careful not to intervene and risk supporting the losing side. The

Mill operatives at the time of the Lancashire Cotton Famine.

battles at Antietam (1862) and Gettysburg (1863) had not gone the Confederate way, which gave pause for thought. Pragmatically, it looked as though it was better to wait and see, at the very least. Even Lancashire was divided over the question of who to support. David Brown pointed to the Southern Independence Association, which was the main pro-Confederate group and had a lot of support among the Liverpool importers, and the Union and Emancipation Society of Manchester. These battled it out, trying to sway public opinion.

While the Union argument had found support in Manchester, the City of London also had reason to be wary of the Confederates. London was one of the largest investors in the industry and railroads in the north.

LAWRENCE GOLDMAN: *And their fear, their very considerable fear, is that if Britain were to come in on the side of the Confederacy, then the loans would be lost, there would be defaults on the loans, the federal government would instruct all its agencies to break with Britain, private businesses likewise, and millions would be lost.*

As if that were not enough, something like 30 or 40 per cent of the grain coming into Britain was from the wheat lands of the north, which weighed heavily against the value of the cotton from the south.

EMMA GRIFFIN: *Britain has other industries: we have ammunition, we have gun-making in Birmingham and the Black Country, we have shipbuilding in the north-west and we also have a very developed merchant marine. There are all sorts of other ways in which industries in other parts of Britain are benefiting from the civil war.*

With so much at stake, it was argued that the Confederates were misguided in thinking that their embargo and the Lancashire Cotton Famine would force Britain to recognise them. By the time their leaders realised that they needed the proceeds of cotton to buy ammunition and other supplies from Britain, it was too late. Lincoln's blockade was beginning to bite. To David Brown, the embargo policy was naïve, if not foolish.

Matters took a further turn for the worse for the Confederates. As the Union forces spread across the south, plantations fell into disarray, slaves fled and the southern economy fell apart. Meanwhile, with the embargo, it had been the survival of the fittest in Manchester. Emma Griffin suggested that several hundred mills closed during the Cotton Famine, never to reopen, and that the newer, streamlined ones tended to survive.

There were other changes. As the Lancashire mill owners had been trying to find new sources of cotton to replace the bales coming from the south, their search led to large acreages being planted in Egypt, Brazil and, most notably, India. With so much production, the price of cotton went down and undermined the south even further.

The public support offered by the citizens of Manchester to Lincoln had further repercussions. According to Emma Griffin, historians have suggested that the way the working people of Manchester conducted themselves, putting the interests of emancipation above their own well-being, was taken as a sign that they were mature enough to be allowed to vote.

DAVID BROWN: *William Gladstone in 1866 specifically mentions the stoic behaviour of Lancashire workers as strong evidence that they are reliable and should be given the vote.*

It may well be that the Cotton Famine was an important stepping stone to the Third Reform Act in 1884, which extended the franchise.

After the programme, Melvyn and his guests discussed how the Poor Laws were hated by the proud, independent mill workers. There were collections in London for the people of Manchester, and there was some solidarity from the Union in America, beyond Lincoln's letter, with ships crossing the Atlantic to bring flour, bacon and other food supplies for the unemployed in Lancashire. And his guests were concerned to check that they had conveyed the nuances of this period, particularly that not everyone in Lancashire supported Lincoln and that there was a strong Confederacy presence in the ports. Of that, Melvyn was in no doubt. 'We avoid being relevant in this programme, but [there was] the trivial thing that began to emerge, the deep-seated rivalry between Liverpool and Manchester ... '

SCIENCE

+)━●━(+

Science is a particular pleasure because I know so little about it. I gave up physics and chemistry at fourteen, struggled with biology and failed it in what were then called O Levels, and enjoyed maths only to be barred from doing it in the sixth form. The excuse was that, being a very small school, they could not accommodate it in the timetable. The darker reason, I suspected later, was that Mr James, the history teacher, had already set his sights on my attempting to do history at university, in which case, in those days, I would need A Level Latin. I hated Latin. I am certain that the reason for this was that the teacher couldn't abide me. She was a brilliant taunter of young boys and all it did for me was to make me learn lessons in resentment. Or maybe I had neither the knack nor the intelligence to assimilate that great dead language. I regret the terrible waste of time when I could have been enjoying maths but, yes, I needed it to get into university and, worse, through the three years at university, I also needed it! Some teachers can be destructive – probably without being aware of it. But that was long ago and in another country.

So first *Start the Week* and then *In Our Time* were to make up for all that. It felt rather subversive at times. Using the good offices of the BBC to further an education *and,* along the way, being paid for it. Still, there were, it seemed, many people 'out there' who felt as I did, that science had been the neglected area in their youth, too, and, like me, they had arrived in adulthood faced with the unprecedented advances in science ill equipped to keep up. On certain programmes, I'm convinced that the key to making everything work is to follow your own instincts and hope there are enough others who also want to take it on.

Some of those programmes – once again, Simon has picked ten out of more than 100 – were dazzling. They took us into new worlds, with new words and new ways of thinking. And there was a recklessness about it. What did I really know about Gauss, the greatest mathematician of his time or, arguably, of all time? Little. Like most of the listeners. My job was to use the documents supplied by Simon to be sufficiently prepared to enable the trio of contributors to unleash their best.

It helped that Gauss's own story was sensational – from poverty in late eighteenth-century Brunswick, through royal patronage, to predicting where to find asteroids, challenging Euclid and laying the foundations for Einstein's theory of relativity. What was going on in that mind? How did that mind get to be that mind? As his achievements were meticulously tabulated by the outstanding mathematicians at the microphone, I held on for dear life.

But, whenever I have discussed a subject about which, six days before take-off, I have known near zilch, I have confessed this to the attendant scholars and told them that I was relying on their generosity and knew just about enough to steer, but no more than that, they have extended a helping mind.

The result is that, on Gauss, on P vs NP, on Pauli's exclusion principle, on absolute zero and much else, audiences have been served information that, judging by the response, has satisfied and often whetted their appetites. And often, to my surprise, I find that I, too, especially during the discussion itself, feel a dawning of understanding, even a grasp of the subject.

Some were easier. Dark matter, photosynthesis, Ada Lovelace – yet, on reviewing these programmes, the level of interest and excitement seemed much the same as the harder topics. It was excitement that swept me along. These scientists were masters of the new universe and their explanations not only replaced new news for old, often as they were uncovering previously unthought thoughts. I imagine that surfers feel as I felt when a particularly colossal wave comes their way and they can ride it.

And simple mysteries were explored. The programme on Bird Migration was not only an explanation of a common phenomenon but a story of heroism, survival, mental brilliance, scarcely fathomable sensory perceptions. A world was revealed in many ways higher than our own – from the obvious to what is still unknowable to *Homo sapiens*.

Moreover, in these programmes, as well as in all the others, the BBC has built a tremendous website of cross-references – in short, a broadcasting university course freely available, as are the podcasts.

What I think I discovered early on about these programmes on science was that at least two languages were being spoken. One was that of general understanding in plain-enough English, which outlined the ideas and could even describe concepts. That was the level on which most of the discussions operated. The second language was the vocabulary of the initiates; to outsiders, a dense jargon of terms only a few of which could be grasped without several years of grind. These, too, were part of the programme but, early on, the scientists in a collective unconscious decision appear to have strengthened the presence of language number one (plain) and, by some alchemy, simplified (without dumbing down) the essential structure of language number two.

And, as we can see from the cascade of erudite but readable books that have recently arrived from so many first-class scientists, they are effortlessly bilingual.

BIRD MIGRATION

For millennia, bird migration was a complete mystery to humans. Today, while what we know is remarkable, much of that mystery remains. There was an idea in ancient Greece that birds turned into fish when no one was around. In later folklore, some were thought to turn into barnacles, others to hibernate in cliffs or at the bottom of lakes. And perhaps those ideas are less extraordinary than what we now know: for example, that birds weighing less than a cup of water can fly across oceans non-stop from New Zealand to Alaska, breed and return. How birds know where they're going is not yet fully understood, but may include some combination of internal clocks, some ways of detecting magnetic fields and a heightened sense of smell.

With Melvyn to discuss bird migration were: Barbara Helm, professor for biological rhythms of natural organisms at the University of Groningen, and visiting professor at the University of Glasgow; Tim Guilford, professor of animal behaviour and tutorial fellow of zoology at Merton College, Oxford; and Richard Holland, senior lecturer in zoology (animal behaviour) at the University of Bangor.

First, Melvyn turned to Tim Guilford for an overview of migration. While it means different things to different people, there is a classical definition in which something such as a bird or a turtle makes a very long journey, repeatedly, from one season to the next, between a breeding site in one location to an overwintering site somewhere else on earth.

TIM GUILFORD: *That is the iconic definition of migration. But, of course, people do refer to migration of plankton and fish on a daily basis in the marine water column, up towards the surface at night and down deeper during the day, and some people would regard that as migration.*

There is always this cyclical movement, even within these different meanings.

Long before modern tracking techniques, naturalists have shown a lot of interest in migration across the centuries. One of those mentioned was Gilbert White (1720–93), vicar of Selborne in Hampshire, who made repeated observations, but the first methodical approach to working out where birds went when they disappeared was in Denmark in the early twentieth century. There, Hans Christian Cornelius Mortensen (1856–1921) started to place little metal bands around the legs of birds before they disappeared for the winter. When birds appeared in the spring, he could tell if his birds were among them and had returned, as they carried the same unique identity number on the metal ring.

MELVYN BRAGG: *Did he know where they'd been?*

TIM GUILFORD: *The rings don't tell you, until, of course, somebody spots or catches or finds a dead bird somewhere else on the globe, and it's the reports of these individually numbered rings found on a dead bird, say in Senegal, which will tell you that this is the same individual that is at one time breeding in Denmark, the next it is found dead on migration in Africa.*

While many birds were ringed, Mortensen only needed one documented example of the same individual, ringed in a breeding site in northern Europe and later spotted alive or dead in Spain, to know that migration must be something to do with long-distance movement. Besides, as Melvyn said, the Europeans exploring Africa in the nineteenth century were finding birds that looked very much like ones they had seen in Europe, and that piqued their curiosity.

The puzzlement about where birds went was one part of the debate, Barbara Helm said, but there were quite a few people who had never believed stories about birds turning into fish and who had learnt from what they had seen of wild birds and caged birds. From the early 1700s onwards, just when wild birds would migrate, bird fanciers reported that there was an odd change in the behaviour of caged birds if the same migrating species.

BARBARA HELM: *These birds become really activated and restless, they also become plump, they put on a lot of extra weight for that time, and then they change their behaviour from active in the daytime to being really, really active in the night-time, to the extent that the birds would hit their heads, because they would fly against the cages at night.*

The owners talked about things like 'instinct' as they realised that the birds were showing this behaviour when inside a house not just when they were in an aviary outside and could see birds of the same species flying away.

This prompted Melvyn to recall 'a defining and magnificent, extraordinary illustration' he had seen, a photograph of a stork that had been captured in Germany in the 1820s with a long Bantu arrow or spear piercing its neck. That, we heard, helped with ideas a lot.

BARBARA HELM: *One example already proves the point in some ways. That Bantu spear in 1822 was establishing that. And then there were actually, in Germany alone, twenty-five occurrences of storks coming back with spears. It's amazing that they could actually carry out that long migration carrying a spear …*

MELVYN BRAGG: *Yes, it's a big spear, isn't it?*

BARBARA HELM: *Through the neck. And that one famous, in some ways game-changing, stork then, of course, met its sad fate when it returned to the breeding grounds. It was shot because it was such an oddity and it is now visible for inspection as a preparation in a museum.*

Why, though, do some birds migrate, when others do not? The classical explanation, Richard Holland said, was that there was competition for food in their home areas, and some birds would try to escape this competition and discover new sources.

RICHARD HOLLAND: *If you've ever been to Finland, then you'll experience a lot of mosquitoes, a lot of small biting insects, but, for birds, this was fantastic. There was this very intense emergence of food resources that allowed them to move north, exploit these resources, breed very successfully, feed their chicks very rapidly, and their chicks could grow very quickly and then retreat back down to the tropics as the winters came in.*

In biology, though, he cautioned, nothing is ever quite as simple as that classical explanation. In Britain, the robin is an iconic winter bird but, in Europe, many robins migrate. Even within some species, some individuals from the same population migrate and others do not. It could be a matter of body size, where larger animals can fast through winter so don't have to find new food sources, or where older and more dominant ones stay and the younger migrate, as with lesser black-backed gulls. Another argument is called the arrival-time hypothesis. In that category, examples can be found in small songbirds that require a breeding territory, and the males defend their territory in the summer to attract females and defend resources.

RICHARD HOLLAND: *There's an argument that birds would arrive earlier and earlier to get the best territories, to the point where some would never leave. If you think about it, that's quite similar to the phenomenon we see at Spanish holiday resorts around the pool, battling for sunbeds, getting there earlier and earlier to defend that.*

Sometimes there is potentially a *choice* about whether to stay or go, for some birds in a species, depending on age, size or dominance. Sometimes, though, the environment, so full of insects in summer, becomes too harsh to stay over winter and, while it is impossible to stay, it is also risky to leave. The northern wheatear, Tim Guilford said, was one of his favourites, a small songbird that weighs about the same as a bag of crisps. These breed all across the northern hemisphere but, in North America, there are populations breeding in Alaska and populations breeding in eastern Canada – for example, Baffin Island – but then both populations migrate to sub-Saharan Africa, and they do that by following opposite routes around the globe.

TIM GUILFORD: *An eastern Canadian breeding northern wheatear will head on a 7,500km journey across Greenland, 2,500km across the open ocean (this thing weighs 20g), all the way down to sub-Saharan Africa and back to breed again.*

An Alaskan bird will go the other way, which is twice as far but less risky and requires less fuel stored up as it feeds on the way. A wheatear migrating from Canada will need to double its mass before it heads out on that migration in order to fuel that flapping flight. In the case of the northern wheatear, nearly half of the year is spent on migration and, given the time spent and the risk of flight, that is probably where the greatest number of mortalities occur. For a shearwater, migrating between the Welsh coast and South America, it is a much less costly journey. For some of the pelagic seabirds, such as shearwaters and albatrosses, these long-distance movements can be almost effortless.

MELVYN BRAGG: *Yes, there's a wonderful albatross – scarcely flapped its wings in his whole existence, isn't it amazing? Just soaring around, it's wonderful, isn't it? No wonder Coleridge got intoxicated by it.*

TIM GUILFORD: *Well, it's not clear that it was an albatross actually, it might have been a giant petrel.*

MELVYN BRAGG: *We're not here to discuss that.*

One of the great wonders of migration, said Barbara Helm, is one that people have long observed. This is that some birds return to their breeding grounds so punctually and regularly that they could be used as an agricultural calendar, as in Borneo, when seeds would be sown as the brown shrike arrived. While that was a reliable event, other birds go more by the weather, which led to a distinction between calendar birds and weather birds.

Barbara Helm: *The calendar birds carry some sort of an endogenous clock, an internal clock that tells them when it's time to come back. Imagine, a bird crosses the equator and winters in sub-Saharan or southern Africa, for example, [where] days are actually increasing, birds down there are starting to breed, and yet, instead of just staying and breeding along with them, they just take off.*

The longer the distance they have to fly to their breeding grounds, the more these birds have to rely on their internal clocks. An Arctic breeder has just a few weeks, and then summer is gone and, with it, the chance to breed. We still do not know how this clock works or where it is located in the brain, but it kicks off a cascade of events that prepare that bird to go, transforming it into an athlete, facilitating the fast use of oxygen and conversion of fat, and the accumulation of the right levels of fat.

Melvyn Bragg: *And parts of their bodies shrivel away – the liver, the reproductive organs, they shrivel right down.*

Barbara Helm: *Yes, exactly. They turn into a different bird in many ways, and that takes preparation. Some birds renew their flight feathers for migration, that can take up to a month, so they have to anticipate the time of breeding a long time in advance.*

Preparation is essential, but there is then the question of how the birds choose their destinations.

Richard Holland suggested there are two ways in which birds could do this, as far as we think. One is that a lot of large birds, the storks, swans, geese and other large waterfowl, often migrate in groups, sometimes as family groups, where the young birds who haven't been to their winter destinations before follow the experienced ones. That, though, is not the case for a lot of songbirds.

Kittiwakes fly over the frozen Chukchi Sea in Alaska.

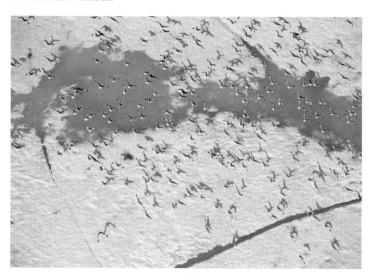

RICHARD HOLLAND: *Songbird adults usually leave the breeding area before their offspring, so the birds that were born in the breeding grounds that year are having to head to somewhere they've never been to before, and we don't think that they follow other birds, we think that they're heading there of their own volition.*

The ones that survive these journeys and make it back have made it to a place where they can survive the winter, which is usually the place that the adults have returned to. It appears that these juveniles have an inherited compass direction and a way of judging the distance they have flown, perhaps through a clock or even, some suggest, the number of wing flaps. Barbara Helm mentioned experiments where birds were cross-bred, with some that usually went north-west mating with some that went south-west, and the resulting hybrid birds would take an intermediate course between north-west and south-west. Some experiments with homing pigeons have suggested that sense of smell may have a role. There is, though, a certain amount of chance.

RICHARD HOLLAND: *There're actually a few studies suggesting that juveniles are much more likely to die on migration. There's even [one suggesting] as much as 80–90 per cent of mortality happening to juveniles on migration. We're not 100 per cent sure if that's always true, but it shows that juveniles are at the greatest risk.*

Enough of them get *somewhere* to survive the winter and come back and, having made it there once, they can then return to that same location time and time again in subsequent years. Tim Guilford said that these birds would need some sort of map sense and another compass sense. The compass might be based on the sun, a visual prompt for direction, except that, from the perspective of the earth, the sun moves during the day.

TIM GUILFORD: *It's useless unless you have a clock, and clocks are important not just in determining the timing of migration, but in compensating for the sun's movement across the sky during the day. And it's astonishing just how accurately birds can compensate for the sun's movement during the day, using a clock in order to maintain a compass direction based upon the sun's position.*

First time out, whether a bird knows when to land may be a matter of having an expectation of the right temperature or how much daylight there is or what kind of food is available. On subsequent flights, though, the birds will stop in the same place, so they must have learnt something about their destination, and the role of memory is another thing that is being studied. The earth's magnetic field is an important cue in the long-distance movements of birds in particular, but the birds appear to have an inclination compass rather than a polarity compass, which means that they can tell the difference between going polewards and going equatorwards, but not the difference between north and south.

Birds can do some things to mitigate the risks of migration, such as flying at night to avoid predators or to avoid the turbulence of daytime. The decision to fly may not coincide with the best weather conditions, though, and Barbara Helm recalled being on an island in the Baltic watching calendar birds take off into storms.

BARBARA HELM: *If you go very far, there is relatively limited scope to modify because, if you need to go from the southern hemisphere to your Arctic breeding grounds, you should not be late by a few days. You cannot really sit out bad weather conditions. There is a problem now with changes to seasonal timing across the world, because birds may just get it wrong.*

Melvyn asked his guests to end with an assessment of something that fascinated him when he was preparing for the programme, which was the complexity of the technology available to birds.

MELVYN BRAGG: *Does it amaze you or am I the only one in this quartet amazed?*

TIM GUILFORD: *No, every few months you read an article that has come out in a journal and you think, 'Oh, I'd loved to have discovered that.'*

As for whether the technology really was complex, Tim Guilford thought that the migratory phenomenon was varied and complex but that there were simple principles running through it. Barbara Helm, answering in the short time left, said she was on Melvyn's side and that migration was dauntingly complex and measured up to Silicon Valley, which pleased Melvyn very much.

In the studio afterwards, Melvyn's guests talked about the visual cues that the birds may use, particularly the long-distance birds, such as the albatross, that navigate across the ocean. The surface of the water may offer more clues than we appreciate. It may also be that the cues need only be approximate when the bird is far from the destination, but that a different set of cues comes in as the bird senses that it is getting closer until eventually the bird can come back to the same tree where it landed the year before. It may be that a sense of smell comes into play, although on that, as with so much besides, more research is needed.

TIM GUILFORD: *The challenge for us as scientists really is to understand how you can use relatively simple machinery to solve such a staggeringly complex task. And I think that this sort of hierarchical approach to the solution is part of that resolution. Nature has this way of finding relatively simple solutions to problems that look unbelievably complex until you dig down into them.*

Returning to what she had said at the close of the programme, Barbara Helm contended that it would take a formidable super computer to solve all the problems that migrating birds have to solve simultaneously. Picking up on that, Tim Guilford tried to imagine a passenger aircraft that turned its wheels into fuel while it was in the air and then back into wheels when it needed them to land, and did away with different parts of its superstructure to make the journey more efficient while in the air. That is what migratory birds are capable of doing. They digest their internal organs so they do not have to carry as much weight, he said. 'It's a staggering business.'

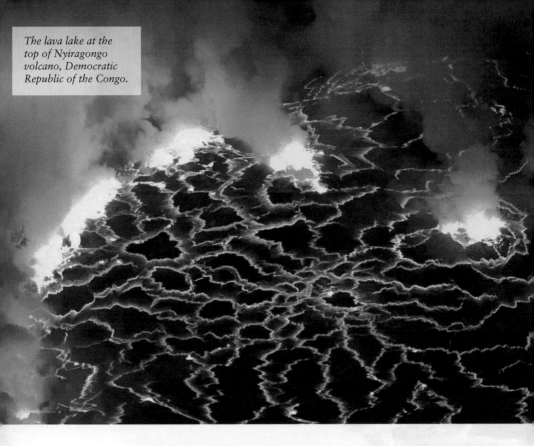

THE PALAEOCENE–EOCENE THERMAL MAXIMUM

About 50 million years ago, the earth's climate changed faster than at any time in our geological record, reaching temperatures much higher than they are today. That event is known as the Palaeocene–Eocene Thermal Maximum, the result, it's thought, of vast volumes of carbon dioxide being released into the atmosphere over a few hundred years, along with methane, another greenhouse gas. The Arctic and Antarctic became subtropical, with crocodiles where there's now ice. Some life forms went extinct, others adjusted in the warmer acidic oceans before the earth cooled 100,000 years later.

꘏꘏꘏

With Melvyn to discuss the Palaeocene–Eocene Thermal Maximum were: Dame Jane Francis, director of the British Antarctic Survey and professor of palaeoclimatology; Mark Maslin, professor of palaeoclimatology at University College London; and Tracy Aze, lecturer in marine micropalaeontology at the University of Leeds.

In geological terms, Jane Francis told us, where ages are measured in millions of years, this episode was a spike of warmer temperatures in a period when the normal temperatures were already warmer than today. This spike can be narrowed down to about 20,000 years, when there was more carbon in the atmosphere and, overall, the world's temperature increased by about 5°C, although the significance of that, as we were to hear, was greater than that number might suggest. Most of the dinosaurs had died out on the land surface around 10 million years before and, after that, life on earth was starting to recover. There is a lot of information available in the rock records about this period, as the relevant rocks are relatively young, while older rocks from this period are more compressed and it becomes harder in those to date a short period.

JANE FRANCIS: *We have a whole list of causes of the warming. Where did all the carbon come from? Did it come from volcanoes? Did it come from burning peat that was around, melting permafrost or methane that was trapped on the sea floor that was released? There's been a lot of work trying to understand why it happened and then what happened afterwards.*

The interest in this period started in the late 1980s with drilling near Antarctica, where scientists were looking at the sediments and the rock record. They noticed something very exciting, which was a sudden change in the sediment cores they extracted.

JANE FRANCIS: *They saw that some of these small shells, marine organisms that lived in the oceans, particularly on the bottom of the sea floor, suddenly disappeared from their cores, as they were working through. These things called forams, foraminifera, went extinct. Geologists are really excited when things go extinct because they want to know why.*

They also found a really dramatic change in the chemical signature in these rocks at this particular point.

Keen to place these prehistoric events in the right time period, Melvyn asked Mark Maslin for more context. We heard that geologists split the whole of the 4.5 billion years of the earth's existence into periods, to help identify and understand when massive changes in the earth have occurred, both environmental and biological. The end of the non-avian dinosaurs marked the start of an eon – the Cenozoic, the life period – and of the Palaeocene. That lasted for 10 million years with little change in the environment, before the very warm spike, which marked the boundary with the next period, the Eocene. This warm spike between these eons, the Palaeocene–Eocene Thermal Maximum or PETM, was abrupt.

The PETM was crucial for mammals, which had been expanding and changing since the end of the dinosaurs 10 million years before, and new species evolved. Melvyn suggested that the mammals used to be crushed by dinosaurs and started to peep out of their holes again after the dinosaurs were crushed.

MARK MASLIN: *Yesss, in some ways. Mammals evolved originally 225 million years ago and were oppressed by the dinosaurs for about 120 million years ...*

MELVYN BRAGG: *Slaves to the dinosaurs.*

MARK MASLIN: *Well, not quite. I mean there is a wonderful fossil from China of what can only be described as a killer badger and it has, in its stomach, baby dinosaurs and eggs, so we did actually occasionally get one back on the dinosaurs.*

During the PETM, there appeared animals like even-toed ungulates, which include camels, cattle, goats, giraffes and even whales, porpoises and dolphins. Significantly for us, this is also when primates first appeared and social monkeys evolved. This, then, was when human evolution started off. Monkeys became social, primates evolved from them and we evolved from these in east Africa later on. A lot of people have speculated about why monkeys became social, but one factor may have been that the warmer temperatures, with forests at the poles, meant there was suddenly a massive expansion of the environments that suited mammals.

MARK MASLIN: *You have warmth, subtropical temperatures up to Antarctica and the Arctic, you suddenly expand the range. Then you get groups of mammals moving into new environments that have no other competition, and therefore changes and different things have been tried out. And working as a tribe, as a group, as a social group seemed to be very, very successful, and that suddenly took over.*

If someone had been around then to look down on the planet from the sky and take a photograph, as Tracy Aze explained, the world would not have looked all that different from the way it does today. There would have been a recognisable Africa and North and South America. Some things, though, would have been quite different and these were significant to global temperatures.

TRACY AZE: *We don't have a Himalayan mountain chain because India is yet to crash into that tectonic plate that causes the Himalayan mountain chain. We also have South America still attached to the Antarctic continent. And the Arctic basin was much more restricted than we see in the modern day. There was a gap between North America and South America, so the Panama isthmus was open and that allowed for exchange between the Atlantic Ocean and the Pacific Ocean.*

As Antarctica was still joined to South America, there was no circumpolar current as there is today, a current that seems to aid the thermal isolation of Antarctica, keeping it cool by stopping the warmer waters from reaching it. The difference in the Arctic basin was significant, as this restricted the phenomenon we see today where the cold salty water in the high latitudes, north and south, moves down to the sea floor and drives ocean circulation. Until the PETM, the deep-water currents were probably only being generated in the Southern Ocean and this would have affected circulation. This is important as the oceans are regulators of heat distribution.

TRACY AZE: *One of the things we think happened in the Palaeocene–Eocene Thermal Maximum is this background state, where we think we were generating deep waters in the Southern Ocean, suddenly flipped and we started generating deep waters in the North Atlantic, which was a change in the state of ocean circulation and would have happened very rapidly. That would have had an impact on how we spread and distribute heat.*

Turning to the evidence of temperatures really rising, allowing crocodiles and rainforests at the poles, Jane Francis said there are many places across the world where we can find support for this. There is a really good sequence of plants in Wyoming, in the Bighorn Basin, with layer upon layer of fossil plants that originated before the PETM, during the PETM and then afterwards. Before the temperature rise, this Basin had plants like the Everglades, and then they became more like those of Mexico. The changes in the leaf shape edges and size also showed evidence of the warming.

MELVYN BRAGG: *Why the edges of leaf … ?*

TRACY AZE: *If you have a more jagged edge on a plant leaf, that is associated with cooler temperatures than leaves that have smooth edges, and we know that from modern [times]. When we look at the past and see assemblages of plants dominated by jagged leaf edges, we know that temperatures would have been cooler than assemblages dominated by smooth edges. And the size of the leaves can tell us about precipitation. When we see big leaves we know that there were higher levels of precipitation at that time as well.*

In some cores that have been drilled from sections of the ocean floor originating around the PETM, there is a very dramatic change in the colour of the rocks, from whitish grey to reddy brown. These grey rocks have a lot of lime in them, a lot of carbonate, and then, with the PETM, the rocks changed and the carbonate disappears. To find absolute evidence of the temperature, we can look at the carbon and oxygen isotopes in these cores extracted from the seabed.

JANE FRANCIS: *These are chemical signatures that are trapped in the shells of the small animals, the forams that were formed at that time. And we can use them to work out what the carbon was like in the ocean and what the temperature was like in the ocean. So that is direct evidence of what the ocean temperatures were at that time.*

The shells tell us which species existed at that time. Scientists have drilled over 400,000km of deep-sea sediments in over 1,400 different sites all over the globe since the 1960s. What those scientists drilling in the 1980s noticed, particularly Ellen Thomas, the micropalaeontologist and palaeoceanographer, was a clear extinction that occurred both at the surface and in the deep ocean, and then new species appeared. Mark Maslin pointed to another discovery in the shells, which is that we can see the different chemicals inside them. Sometimes the shells contain magnesium where calcium should be, and the amount of magnesium that goes into them is related to the water temperature, which can then be calculated.

MELVYN BRAGG: *We were talking about this warming spike. What was it? What sort of temperature is outside Broadcasting House now and what was it then?*

MARK MASLIN: *Global temperatures, on average now, are about 15–16°C for the whole planet. You are looking at the Palaeocene probably being somewhere more like 17–18°C. On top of that, we add another 5°C on ocean temperatures and global temperatures, so you're looking at an average temperature for the planet of about 22°C, which is 7°C warmer than the average today.*

MELVYN BRAGG: *It doesn't seem massive; it's more like a football score than a rugby score, isn't it? Can you convince us, Jane?*

JANE FRANCIS : *Let's go to the Arctic, [where] we've got ice at the poles now and we've got polar bears and seals. But if we go and look at the rocks that are 50–55 million years old, in the Arctic we can see crocodiles, we can see lemurs, we can see hippo-like animals, we can see Florida Everglade-type conditions.*

All of the environments, the trees and plants, that had lived much nearer the equator where it was warm, were suddenly able to spread to the high latitudes. We can use the fossils to track this migration into much warmer latitudes and the movement is quite distinct at this time.

Melvyn wanted to drill down into the evidence of what caused the sudden spike. There was, we heard, a massive injection of carbon into the atmosphere, thousands of gigatonnes (a gigatonne is 1,000,000,000 metric tonnes).

MARK MASLIN: *To put that into context, the amount of carbon that our huge industrial complex in the world puts into the atmosphere every year is about 4 gigatonnes. We're talking about 2,000 to 7,000 gigatonnes of carbon that were injected in [the PETM in] a very short period of time.*

One of the early ideas for the source of the carbon was coal, as there are seams from that period, and it was thought that this may have been burning freely. Another idea was that there may have been permafrost in the regions towards the poles, which melted as the temperatures increased, releasing trapped carbon. Jane Francis also suggested there may have been volcanic eruptions at that time, as we know that, in certain parts of the globe, there were plate tectonic activities, especially in the Atlantic region, which may have put more carbon in the atmosphere. One of the big ideas is that the warming released methane, which was trapped on the sea floor, frozen as nodules, and is thirty times more potent than carbon dioxide in terms of its greenhouse potential.

JANE FRANCIS: *A lot of it is stored, it comes from rotting animals and plants on the land. A lot of it gets stored in the oceans, it's frozen as nodules on the sea floor today. And if you have a little bit of warming or you have an event that disturbs the sea floor, these frozen*

*nodules are then released into the water and they melt and
the methane is released. At the moment, the jury's out on whether
there's one single cause, and I think that we are probably looking
at a mixture of all of those ideas.*

As more information comes to light, that jury has to reassess its
views. Until ten years ago, Mark Maslin suggested, the consensus
would have been that methane was definitely the cause of the
temperature spike. Now it is more likely to be one cause of several.
The methane hydrates on the seabed arise when bacteria break
down the organic matter for food, but because, without oxygen,
they cannot oxidise the matter fully, methane is produced. The
methane bubbles up to the surface of the sediment only to be chilled
by the ocean, so water freezes around it, enclosing it in icy cages or
clathrates. If you raise one of these clathrates onto a ship's deck, you
can light it and a blue flame appears from the ice as it melts. In the
Palaeocene, over several million years, huge reservoirs of organic
matter had rotted down and created these stores of methane. It is
thought that the warming at the end of the Palaeocene may have
just tipped the temperature of the seabed over and suddenly all this
methane erupted, creating what are sometimes called 'burps of death'.

MARK MASLIN: *The reason we call it burps of death is because,
if you do it slowly, what happens is the methane goes into the
water column and dissolves in the ocean. We know that, strangely
enough, from* Deepwater Horizon, *the BP disaster, [where] methane
was released but it just disappeared into the ocean. You have to
do this explosively, you have to really release all of it, and [then] it
gets through the water column and bursts out into the atmosphere.
That allows you to get thousands of gigatonnes of carbon into the
atmosphere and get this incredible piece of warming.*

The consequence of the warming was colossal, Melvyn observed,
even though the numbers involved were not spectacular. The impact
was worldwide, too, Jane Francis added, while other events in the
geological past were regional or in one half of the earth and not
the other. Moreover, while all were affected, there were some areas
affected even more than others.

TRACY AZE: *If you look at some of the local changes in the tropics,
for example, [with] some of the work we did in Tanzania, we were
looking at sea surface temperatures getting towards 40°C, which is
probably about as hot as your bath.*

Mark Maslin argued that the PETM helps us understand current
climate change, as the PETM suddenly became an event where nature
was injecting huge amounts of carbon, just as we have been injecting
huge amounts of carbon into the atmosphere over the past 100
years. One of the first things that interested researchers in the PETM
was that it appears as though, left to nature, it took about 100,000
years for all that extra carbon to be taken out. We have already put
about 1,000 gigatonnes of carbon into our atmosphere since the
industrialisation and we are looking at putting in another 1,000
gigatonnes by the end of this century. The PETM is so interesting

Leaf fossils from the Palaeocene–
Eocene Thermal Maximum.

when looking at climate change, he said, as the scale of carbon emissions that we could put in by the end of the century is at the bottom end of the PETM.

Mark Maslin: *We're actually doing our own natural experiment at the moment, which we can look back at [in] 55 million years and go, 'Well, what does that tell us?' The first thing it tells us is, if we don't actually take out CO_2 physically, the natural system will take 100,000 years.*

The cooling at the end of the PETM followed the reduction in the levels of carbon in the atmosphere. On short timescales, the carbon dioxide was absorbed into the oceans, which became more acidic, Tracy Aze said. Over hundreds of thousands of years, the carbon dioxide in a warm atmosphere would have increased the weathering rate of rocks, and then the weathered rocks would be flushed into the ocean via rain and rivers. Once there, organisms would have made their shells from carbon and that would have ended as sediment, locked on the sea floor.

Other periods of warmer temperatures were to follow the PETM, towards the end of the Eocene, but these built up slowly over millions of years, rather than in the sudden, dramatic way that had such an effect on evolution. Then, at the end of the Eocene, about 34 million years ago, there were the first signs of major ice caps on earth. We are now in a very cold period of time in earth history, with ice at both poles and a lot of increased sea level potential locked up in that ice, even if it seems relatively warm after the ice ages. Jane Francis thought that we are not going to get back into a glacial age for a very long time, as the carbon dioxide levels are high now and it is going to take a while for the earth to work out what to do with all this carbon in the atmosphere.

MARK MASLIN: *If ever.*

In the studio afterwards, Melvyn wondered how the modern age can be compared with the PETM when we are in a cold phase now, with ice caps. Tracy Aze suggested that the PETM is not a direct analogue to the modern age. The increase in carbon in the atmosphere now has happened over years measured in hundreds, while the PETM was over thousands. While it is not directly analogous, it is one of the only things we *can* learn from, because this kind of event has not happened that many times in the past.

There was evidence in 2016 of methane hydrates releasing methane from the bed of the North Atlantic, but Jane Francis understood that this was being trapped by seawater at present, even though that may change if ocean temperatures increase.

JANE FRANCIS : *There are so many cycles in the earth system and they're like cogs in a wheel, and one interacts with the other, and so trying to understand a very complicated cogged wheel system is what we're trying to do.*

MARK MASLIN: *About ten years ago, people were very worried about the clathrates in the bottom of the ocean. We now think that, in the next couple of hundred years, they will actually remain quite stable. But this has shifted the focus on to all of the methane hydrates in the Arctic underneath the tundra, because the tundra is melting, and all the permafrost. We're really worried about that methane. And we have no way of really estimating how much methane is stored there.*

PHOTOSYNTHESIS

Three and a half billion years ago, this planet was a hostile and barren place. The atmosphere was toxic and contained no oxygen, and life on earth was restricted to a variety of unsophisticated single-celled organisms that lived in the sea. But then a new type of organism emerged, one with an amazing new capability: it could harvest energy from sunlight and use it to fuel its own activities. This phenomenon is known as photosynthesis and is almost certainly the most important chemical process on earth. Plants and some other organisms depend on it for their energy, and almost all life is ultimately reliant on it for its survival. It is responsible for the food we eat and the air we breathe and, without it, the earth would still be sterile rather than as it is, teeming with life.

--◆--

With Melvyn to discuss photosynthesis were: Sandy Knapp, botanist at the Natural History Museum; Nick Lane, honorary professor of evolutionary biochemistry at the Department of Genetics, Evolution and Environment, University College London; and John F. Allen, honorary professor at University College London.

Photosynthesis, Sandy Knapp told us, is a very simple, elegant chemical reaction that involves an organism taking water and carbon dioxide and, with the help of light, turning those into glucose and oxygen. Without photosynthesis, that blue and green ball that we see from space would look like Mars. When organisms were able to make their own food by creating something from light, that, in turn, allowed other organisms to feed on them. Plants are autotrophs, organisms that make their own food, and (subject to the caveats raised by John Allen after the programme) anything that does photosynthesis is an autotroph.

SANDY KNAPP: *We are completely hopeless, we're heterotrophs, we depend on other organisms for our food. So, without these photosynthetic organisms, we would have nothing to eat and nothing to breathe and so all of life really depends upon autotrophs.*

The essential ingredients are water, carbon dioxide and light, but photosynthesis needs a few other things as well.

SANDY KNAPP: *Plants need nitrogen and phosphorous to make the enzymes that drive the reactions of photosynthesis and they also need an element, magnesium, which sits like a spider at the centre of the chlorophyll molecule, which is one of the light-harvesting pigments in leaves.*

Melvyn suggested that photosynthesis was like an engine room, and had nods back from all three guests. Nick Lane then took us to the structures within the plant that make photosynthesis possible. This happens in structures inside the cell called the chloroplasts, which were once bacteria in their own right and are now known as cyanobacteria. They became captured by more complex cells, probably 1–1.5 billion years ago, and they continued doing what they did before.

NICK LANE: *They were simply engulfed by a larger cell and put to work, not quite as slaves, but they did what they always did, they continued to photosynthesise, they continued to take electrons from water, put them on to carbon dioxide and make sugars that way. And so the host cell, which had captured them, gained those benefits of getting a free lunch, you might say.*

Within the engine room of the cell, as Melvyn termed it, there is a series of membranes, with enormous complexes of proteins. Taking that analogy further, Nick Lane invited us to shrink ourselves down to the size of a small molecule, at which point those engines would seem like a huge industrial complex sitting there in the membranes. What they do, as Nick Lane mentioned, is extract electrons from water and pass them down a kind of a chain and eventually push them on to carbon dioxide to make the sugars. That may be simple at a chemical level, but not at a biochemical one.

NICK LANE: *It's not easy to get electrons out of water in the first place. The largest storm, crashing water against a sea cliff, is not going to break water down into its component parts. But light can do that.*

Water is useful as it is everywhere. There are other materials that could be used, such as hydrogen sulphide gas or dissolved iron, but they are far less common.

The chemical processes in photosynthesis are known as the light and the dark reactions.

NICK LANE: *At its simplest, the light reaction is driven by the absorption of photons of light and it's simply dragging, stripping electrons from water. The waste of this is oxygen, which is just a waste product of photosynthesis, it's just let go, it accumulates in the atmosphere.*

Then there is the dark reaction that takes those electrons and forces them on to carbon dioxide, which does not require light at all, hence the name.

Picking up on Nick Lane's comments about oxygen, John Allen observed that oxygen was not just a waste product but a toxic waste product. Before photosynthesis, the whole biosphere was working fine without free molecular oxygen.

JOHN ALLEN: *This was dangerous stuff to have around, it's chemically highly reactive; 2.4 billion years ago, this trick was discovered, by accident, of taking electrons from water, producing this by-product. This was a big shock to the system. There's never been an equivalent environmental catastrophe for life that existed before that time.*

This process of taking electrons from water had such benefits overall that the organisms on this planet had to learn to live with this poison gas. There are still environments today, such as in the rocks, the lithosphere, that oxygen does not permeate and there is still anoxic life there without oxygen, a relic of this former time.

Chlorophyll, John Allen explained, is a word taken from Greek and simply means 'green leaf'. Its structure, as mentioned above, is like a spider's web with a magnesium atom at the middle and then four carbon atoms, linked in series with a fifth, nitrogen, and then folded around to make a circle or pentagon. There are four of these in the basic head group of chlorophyll and these are also arranged in a series, then folded into a circle with the nitrogen atoms pointing inwards towards the magnesium atom in the centre. There is, additionally, a hydrocarbon tail attached to one of the rings, which gives chlorophyll the property of being completely insoluble in water. The work it does is special and essential, but it is not magical.

JOHN ALLEN: *In the history of biology, people have always wanted to be focusing down on what's the smallest thing that we can say is alive and people got very excited about chlorophyll. It seemed to be a very special molecule, sustaining life on earth. But it's just a chemical; in fact, it's been synthesised by synthetic organic chemists in Harvard University in the '60s or '70s from scratch.*

There are two sorts of chlorophyll, both doing essentially the same thing. In the 1960s, Robin Hill and Fay Bendall, noting that there is a chain of electron carriers, added that there are two points in that chain of electron carriers where the electrons would not go unless they were given a push by some energy input, which is provided by light energy acting on chlorophyll. The special chlorophyll that loses its electron to start the chain is just one of 300 chlorophyll molecules, approximately. All the others take the absorbed excitation energy and pass it among each other until it arrives at this special one, and that sets the whole process going and sustains life on earth.

There is more than one type of photosynthesis. Most plants, Sandy Knapp said, are called C3 photosynthesisers as the first thing that happens to the carbon dioxide when split up is it turns into a three-carbon molecule. There is also a set of flowering plants that are called C4 plants, where the carbon dioxide is broken up into a four-carbon molecule and then the photosynthesis happens in two different types of cell. The carbon is stored in bundle sheath cells around the veins. These C4 plants are much more efficient at photosynthesis at high temperatures so, often, the plants that grow in deserts are C4 photosynthesisers.

SANDY KNAPP: *Corn, maize, for example, is a C4 plant, and this has been studied the most in the grasses. These C4 plants are highly photosynthetically efficient. One of the great holy grails in agriculture is to take a C3 plant, like rice or wheat, and turn it into a C4 plant, which would increase its efficiency and thereby perhaps increase its yield and its ability to grow in different parts of the world.*

There is a third kind, crassulacean acid metabolism or CAM, so named as it was first discovered in a sedum in a rock plant in the family Crassulaceae. In CAM plants, the stomates, the little holes that can open and close and through which CO_2 enters, keep closed during the day and open at night, when it is not so hot. They can store up all the components for photosynthesis and do it later, which is useful if you live in a desert. Cacti are CAM plants.

Melvyn returned to Nick Lane for what happens in the cells, and we heard how the flow of electrons is used to drive protons, the positive nuclei of hydrogen atoms, across a membrane. From this, there is a proton gradient across the membrane.

MELVYN BRAGG: *Gradient, like, you mean, slope?*

NICK LANE: *Well, yes. Essentially, on one side of the membrane, you have a large number of protons; on the other side, you have relatively few. It's essentially like a hydroelectric power scheme with a reservoir on one side and a turbine in the membrane itself. The turbine is an enzyme called the ATP synthase enzyme and that is powered by the flow of protons from the reservoir back to the side where it's downhill, in effect, and that produces ATP.*

ATP, he said, is generally called the energy currency of life and is used by all living cells. We could think of it like a coin in a slot machine where all proteins, if they are to do any work at all, must change their conformation, and to do that requires splitting an ATP. The current of electrons that is flowing from water to CO_2 is driving all of this.

In addition, all those electrons end up on carbon dioxide, converting it into a sugar, and those sugars are then converted into the rest of the organic molecules that the plants need to live, that we need to eat.

Besides photosynthesis in the plants, there is respiration. John Allen, for present purposes taking the definition of photosynthesis as release of oxygen and uptake of carbon dioxide, explained that aerobic respiration, which is the respiration that plants do and we do, is the uptake of oxygen, putting electrons on to it to make water, which is the reverse of taking electrons from water to liberate oxygen. However, he added, at the kind of level that Nick Lane had been describing, the power station was a good analogy.

JOHN ALLEN: *The way in which that is done is universal in biology, and photosynthesis and respiration are two ways of applying that same fundamental mechanism – electron transport, moving protons across a membrane to make a gradient, which is stored energy and used to make ATP. In that sense, they're the same process, except that the chlorophyll in the photosynthetic reaction centre gives the electron that initial push that it needs; in respiration, the electrons just sort of flow where they want to go.*

Nick Lane agreed that the source of electrons was really the major difference between photosynthesis and respiration. In respiration, we need an easy source of electrons – in our case, food – that will react spontaneously with oxygen. The enzymes in the mitochondria allow that to happen.

NICK LANE: *What's happening in photosynthesis is that light is providing that essential input of energy, which starts electrons flowing from far more difficult places, [from] water, in this case. Water really does not want to lose its electrons, but the input of light through chlorophyll extracts electrons from it, and sets them flowing in exactly the same way that they flow from food to oxygen in us. It's exactly the same process; the source of electrons differs.*

There are limiting factors for photosynthesis. Sandy Knapp mentioned the need for water, carbon dioxide and light, and also nitrogen and phosphorous, which are part of the reason we fertilise crops, to increase photosynthetic efficiency and thereby the yield. Temperature is a very important limiting factor for photosynthesis as well, as it does not happen efficiently at very high or low temperatures. Plants regulate the degree to which they photosynthesise, depending on environmental conditions.

SANDY KNAPP: *One of the things that's really interesting about plants is that people often think of plants as just sitting there. Plants behave – it's just on a very different scale to our human behaviour. And so, if there's not enough water, or if there's too much light, the stomates will close and thereby no carbon dioxide is taken in and photosynthesis goes down.*

As for why chlorophyll is green, it appeared there was no simple answer. Sandy Knapp said that it is not green – we see it that way because green is the only wavelength that is not absorbed. Nothing really has colour, we just perceive it that way because of the wavelength of light reflected off it. That prompted John Allen to offer his perspective.

JOHN ALLEN: *Why is chlorophyll green? Because it absorbs blue light and red light and doesn't absorb light in the middle of the visual spectrum that is green. That's true. But Melvyn's question could be rephrased: 'Why aren't plants black?' If they were black, they would be absorbing all visible light.*

MELVYN BRAGG: *We could start again.*

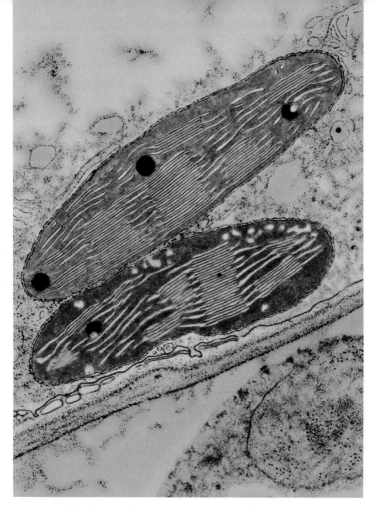

Colour transmission
electron micrograph of
two chloroplasts in the
leaf of a pea plant.

JOHN ALLEN: *No, why are they green? Why are they not making
use of green light? They should really – if they were interested in
getting the most energy, they would use the whole of the visible
spectrum and would be black, and they're not.*

While he did not have an answer to that question, Nick Lane
noted that plants use red light mostly, which is not energetically
particularly strong. Blue light has far more energy in it than red light
does. Chlorophyll does absorb blue light as well, but it does not use
that wavelength, for reasons that are not clear.

NICK LANE: *It may simply be the destructiveness of UV and blue
light; it can damage our own retinas as well. I think it's ended up with
red partly because that's the wavelength that chlorophyll absorbs and
partly because selection has adapted the wavelengths that chlorophyll
absorbs to being the gentlest on the plant itself. It's less likely to do
damage if you're absorbing light at that wavelength.*

The need for red light is such that many plants in the rainforest, nearer the ground and so shielded from the sun by the canopy, have a red layer on the underside of their leaves.

SANDY KNAPP: *It's actually very striking in deep rainforest plants. And David W. Lee published a really nice paper where they showed that what happens in this anthocyanin layer is that it reflects light back into the chloroplast so that they get more of the little light that's coming through. Anthocyanins are pigments that we see as red, so they're absorbing everything except the red.*

There is quite a lot of controversy over when photosynthesis evolved, according to Nick Lane. The first forms, 3.5 billion years ago, did not use water as the electron donor but chemicals like hydrogen sulphide and iron. Where iron was being used as the electron donor, this left behind rusty iron.

NICK ALLEN: *[This] precipitates out of the oceans and forms banded iron formations that are the major sources of iron ore we are using today. So some of the big mineral deposits derive from photosynthesis and are evidence that photosynthesis was happening at that time.*

Oxygenic photosynthesis, he added, the splitting of water and release of toxic waste oxygen, probably arose around 2.5–3 billion years ago. We know for sure it happened by 2.4 billion years ago because there was a tremendous catastrophe, a snowball earth, at that time.

NICK LANE: *There have been several episodes of these snowball earths across earth history. Probably what happened was, as oxygen was being released, it oxidised the methane being produced by other bacteria, and methane is a greenhouse gas … as it stripped out of the atmosphere, the temperatures plummet. The other thing we see around that time is the oxidation of rocks and so on, on the continent. We see what are called red beds, basically rusty iron everywhere.*

Until ten or twenty years ago, it was thought that, after the great oxidation event, when oxygen levels started picking up in the atmosphere, everything changed. In fact, it did not. It was stuck in a rut for another billion years or so.

MELVYN BRAGG: *The billion boring years.*

NICK LANE: *The boring billion, it's called, yes. So nothing really happened. Actually, complex cells arose in that time, the acquisition of chloroplasts and so on happened in that time. But there's very little in the fossil record. Then, at the end of this boring billion, we go into another global upheaval of more snowball earths, and right on the back of that is the Cambrian explosion and the appearance of animals, really for the first time, in the fossil record.*

While there are debates about what was happening at the Cambrian explosion, which was around half a billion years ago, it appears fairly certain that oxygen was produced at that time by plants and terrestrial algae rather than just cyanobacteria, and that gave the animals the energy they needed.

Photosynthesis itself, Sandy Knapp said, drives life on earth, it drives ecosystems and it probably drives the composition of ecosystems as well – namely why organisms are in a particular place and the relationship between them.

SANDY KNAPP: *So many heterotrophs depend upon autotrophs, which are these photosynthesising organisms, for their daily lives and their food, and then other heterotrophs depend upon those. We eat beef, which is a heterotroph, which is eating grass, so we actually are eating sunlight via this complicated chain.*

MELVYN BRAGG: *It's a bit 'Ilkla Moor Baht 'at', really?*

SANDY KNAPP: *Yes, basically. It's a tangled web, as Darwin said.*

The programme closed with a reference back to the discovery of photosynthesis, which John Allen placed at 1772 when Joseph Priestley published an investigation of different kinds of air. He quoted this from Priestley's paper:

I flatter myself that I have accidentally hit upon a method of restoring air which has been injured by the burning of candles and that I have discovered at least one of the restoratives that nature employs for this purpose. It is vegetation. One might have imagined that, since common air is necessary to vegetable as well as animal life, both plants and animals had affected it in the same manner and I own that I had that expectation when I first put a sprig of mint into a glass jar standing inverted in a vessel of water, but when it had continued growing there for some months I found that the air would neither extinguish a candle nor was it at all inconvenient to a mouse, which I put into it.

That, John Allen said, was the discovery of oxygen and the discovery of photosynthesis in one experiment.

In the studio afterwards, John Allen picked up on the comment that all photosynthetic organisms are autotrophic, they build themselves up. He argued that this was not true.

JOHN ALLEN: *Just tell me if this gets boring.*

MELVYN BRAGG: *We've been bored for a billion years … what's a few minutes?*

There are two things you can ask about any living creature, he said. Firstly, where does it get its energy? Photosynthetic organisms are phototrophs but they don't have to be autotrophs because they can get the energy and still eat food. Secondly, where does it get its stuff that it makes itself from? If it apparently gets it from nowhere, from the air, it is then an autotroph. If it gets it from other living things, it is a heterotroph, meaning other feeding. And yet …

JOHN ALLEN: *There are photoheterotrophs that get their energy from light but they still eat food, they need other organic compounds to assimilate. The obverse of that is there are also chemoautotrophs, which are organisms that are not interested in light, they live deep in rocks ...*

SANDY KNAPP: *Those are the vents ...*

JOHN ALLEN: *The vents, they're chemoautotrophs that get their energy from chemical reactions, but they fix CO_2 and make carbohydrate.*

SANDY KNAPP: *That's what always amazes me, that life on earth is absolutely incredible, the number of different ways in which organisms make their living, grow, survive and reproduce ...*

MELVYN BRAGG: *When I walk through London, I feel the same, every time I look in a shop. Dr Johnson said that – the way people make a living.*

SANDY KNAPP: *Nothing ever changes.*
Finally, Nick Lane recalled one of the points he had meant to get across, which was, while plants produce oxygen and animals consume oxygen, that is a complete balance. In the boring billion, nothing changed.

NICK LANE: *It's only ... if we die and we're buried and we are not then broken back down into CO_2 and oxygen again and water again, if we're just buried intact as a fossil fuel, in effect, then the oxygen that would have oxidised us was left over in the air, and so the dynamic over evolutionary time is nothing to do with how much photosynthesis there is, it's to do with how much carbon is buried, so it's a geological process rather than really a biological process.*

MELVYN BRAGG: *Do you think it would help the world if we all got buried?*

NICK LANE: *Yes. Except we'd end up with lots of oxygen in the atmosphere and everything would burn.*

GAUSS

Carl Friedrich Gauss, by those who know about these matters, is considered the greatest mathematician of his time and, arguably, of all time. He was born in 1777 in Brunswick, Germany, to parents too poor to pay for his education. But his brilliance brought him a royal patron and sponsor and, as a teenager, he solved problems that had baffled everyone since the ancient Greeks. By the time he died, in 1855, he'd been called the prince of mathematicians for advances in number theory, for predicting where to find asteroids, for thinking beyond Euclid's geometry and, on the way, for inventing the first telegraph. Later, his importance to the mathematical foundations of the theory of relativity was overwhelming, as Einstein acknowledged.

⊢⊶⊣

With Melvyn to discuss Gauss were: Marcus du Sautoy, professor of mathematics and Simonyi professor for the public understanding of science at the University of Oxford; Colva Roney-Dougal, reader in pure mathematics at the University of St Andrews; and Nick Evans, professor of theoretical physics at the University of Southampton.

Occasionally on *In Our Time*, Melvyn asks what is known of the famous subject's childhood and the answer comes back, 'Nothing.' In the case of Gauss, there were rather more fragments than usual. Colva Roney-Dougal told how his parents referred to his date of birth as eight days before Ascension, from which he later worked out the actual day (30 April 1777). His father could read and write and do arithmetic, though, and one of the first stories told about Gauss's early brilliance came from when he was with his father. Some of these stories have more weight than others.

COLVA RONEY-DOUGAL: *When he was aged three, he was sat in the corner of a room, while his father was handing out the weekly wages to the employees at the brick factory where he worked, and the father was having to work out how many hours each person had done and overtime, and Gauss suddenly pipes up, 'Papa, the calculation is wrong.'*

MELVYN BRAGG: *Do you believe that?*

COLVA RONEY-DOUGAL: *Maybe ...*

MELVYN BRAGG: *Well, let's move on then ...*
Gauss had taught himself to read and write by that time, we heard, so this story was plausible. Then, according to a story that Gauss loved to tell, when he was at school, around the age of six, his teacher asked the children to add up the numbers from 1 to 100 on their slates. Gauss immediately walked up with the right answer on his slate: 5,050. He worked it out by spotting that 1 plus 100, the first number and the last number, is 101. Carrying on in that way, pairing up each number at the beginning with the corresponding number from the end, he noticed the sum is always 101. Gauss reasoned that there were fifty pairs and so the sum of all of the numbers from 1 up to 100 is 50 times 101, which is 5,050.

The consequence of that, as Melvyn put it to Colva Roney-Dougal, was that the teacher thought this was a very, very clever boy and, when Gauss was about eleven, he took him to the Duke of Brunswick, the local duke, and said, 'Will you please look after his education because nobody else will?' Gauss, according to another story, explained to the duke how to tell that the square root of 2 is not a fraction. The duke, she said, was very impressed and agreed to sponsor his education, putting him through university and his doctorate. He studied intensely.

MARCUS DU SAUTOY: *On his fourteenth birthday, he got given a book of logarithm tables for his birthday present, the kind of thing we mathematicians like to get for our birthdays. And this book of logarithm tables began to obsess the young Gauss.*
Log tables, as older listeners would have remembered, were used before calculators to change complicated multiplication into addition. Gauss noticed the table of prime numbers at the end, the numbers that are only divisible by themselves and 1, 'the atoms of mathematics', as Marcus du Sautoy put it.

MARCUS DU SAUTOY: *The staggering thing is that Gauss managed to find a connection between the primes at the back of this book and the logarithms at the front of the book. And I think this really illustrates the brilliance of Gauss's mind. I think somebody [who] is a great thinker is somebody who changes the question.*

Until then, we heard, people had been trying to find a formula for the primes, to generate them, but Gauss could not find one so asked instead how many primes there were. He was interested in finding out if there was a way to predict the probability that a number would be prime as the numbers climbed higher and higher. He spotted that the logarithms would tell him the chance that a number would be prime and help him to count how many primes there were as he climbed higher and higher. This was his conjecture, it was right, although not yet published, and it was not proved until the end of the nineteenth century.

MARCUS DU SAUTOY: *This is staggering, this he discovered when he was fifteen. A fifteen-year-old boy had completely changed our perspective on the prime numbers and it's this perspective we use today. This was a completely new insight about the most fundamental numbers on the mathematical books. And Gauss wrote, 'You have no idea how much poetry is in a table of logarithms.'*

He enjoyed data, we heard, and he was quite an experimental mathematician. He liked just messing around with numbers and trying to see the patterns there.

For Nick Evans, a key part of Gauss's genius was just that he was obsessed, and could not really think about anything else. When he was a young child, he used a turnip to make a candle so he could study maths at night. There is the 10,000-hours hypothesis, which is that anyone can become really good at something if they spend five years of their life dedicated to it. Gauss had done that by the age of ten, and he had a potent mixture of intelligence and dedication.

NICK EVANS: *You can actually go and ask Gauss himself, because people did, and he said, 'No, I don't think I'm that much smarter than everybody else.' What he said was, 'Those who do great mathematics spend vast and deep and constant energy and attention on it.' And that's what he did all through his life.*

He was recognised as a genius from before his teens. At university, he was such a prodigious person that he would suck the mathematical knowledge out of his teachers quite quickly. He left, living on his own for a while to dedicate everything to maths. He was engrossed.

NICK EVANS: *There's a story, which is a little bit mean, from the end of his life when his second wife was dying from tuberculosis, when, allegedly, the maid came down and he was studying his mathematics and [she] said, 'Your wife's dying, you need to come.' And his response was, 'Can't she wait?'*

While still in his teens, Gauss took on problems that had baffled the ancient Greeks and everyone since. One, Colva Roney-Dougal told us, was about regular polygons, and the Greeks had been fascinated with the question of which of these shapes could be constructed using a straight edge and a pair of compasses only. The Greeks knew how to make an equilateral triangle, a square, a pentagon, how to make a regular fifteen-sided shape and how to double the sides of any one they could already make, but they couldn't make one with seven sides or nine sides or eleven sides or thirteen sides, and people had been trying since Euclid.

COLVA RONEY-DOUGAL: *Young Gauss comes along – this is while he's at university, he's eighteen at the time – and he finds a construction of a seventeen-sided shape. Now this is 2,500 years after people started thinking about the question and then this sprightly young eighteen-year-old just comes up with it. There's a notice in the local paper explaining that he's worked out how to do it, with a side note from one of his schoolteachers saying, 'By the way, he's only eighteen.'*

While the log table and primes idea were still in his private papers at that point, this discovery about polygons was published and started to make his reputation. Then, in 1801, Gauss showed something even stronger. He worked out exactly which shapes we can and cannot make and gave a complete justification for the ones we cannot make. Among the primes, we can do only 3, 5, 17 (which was the new one), 257 is the next one and then 65,537 is the one after that. 'And, as far as we know,' Colva Roney-Dougal concluded, 'at the moment, that's it.'

1801 was the year in which Gauss had a work published, *Disquisitiones Arithmeticae*, which collected together all his great thoughts about number theory. Marcus du Sautoy said that this was a subject that he studies now as a research mathematician, so he credits Gauss with forming his discipline. He invented something that, we were told, could be seen as a sort of clock calculator, where if we say it is 9 o'clock now and we are going to meet someone in four hours' time, we actually say we are going to meet somebody at 1 o'clock, we don't keep on adding the number. Gauss realised that, with this kind of calculator, you could use a clock with seven hours on, for example, rather than twelve, which would be a very powerful way to explore properties of solving equations and is now called modular arithmetic.

MARCUS DU SAUTOY: *Gauss pulled all of these discoveries about numbers together in this book and he was really hoping to impress the French Academy, because France was really where mathematics was being done at this time. And the French Academy was really dismissive of this book. It was quite a cryptic book, because Gauss didn't like to explain where he got his ideas from and so people called this book 'a book of seven seals' because you couldn't understand where rabbits were being pulled out of hats. And Gauss always used to say, 'Well, yes, but an architect doesn't leave up the scaffolding when he has built a building.'*

Gauss felt he was justified in this, but it caused him problems. He hated criticism and only published when he was sure he was right, and that meant he did not get the recognition he wanted. One of the last entries in his diaries is Marcus du Sautoy's favourite because

Gauss showed he understood how to solve an equation called an elliptic curve, the first example of something called the Riemann hypothesis for finite fields, which was discovered and proved at the beginning of the twentieth century. 'For me, it is absolutely staggering that he's beginning a journey that culminates in one of the great theorems that is proved in the twentieth century.' That, too, went unpublished in his lifetime.

MARCUS DU SAUTOY: *I think his conservatism actually held back mathematics by fifty years probably, that if he'd been more open, there would have been a massive explosion. The things he did were amazing but what he knew was even greater.*

COLVA RONEY-DOUGAL: *He's got some things other people would be rushing to publish because they're fascinating in their own right, but he feels [that if] he can't yet tell the whole story the way it ought to be told, then he won't publish. He's on record as saying, 'The first proof you find is not the proof you should publish, you should wait until you've found the right proof, the best proof, the one that shows why this is as it is.'*

He did, though, get recognition for his astronomy. As Nick Evans explained, telescopes had really improved since around 1800 and people were starting to find bits of rock in the solar system, smaller than planets, of which one was Ceres, around 1,000km across and in the asteroid belt. Astronomers observed it just before it disappeared behind the sun, so did not have a chance to plot its orbit and thereby predict where it would emerge. They thought it was lost. Gauss, though, matched the little data available to a range of ellipses, developing something called the least squares fitting method, which is now used across science to explain how to draw the best line through a bunch of data points. He then predicted where it would reappear and, a few months later, he was proved right. That brought him new fame.

NICK EVANS: *That [problem] made him think about not just the perfect case, but actually [about] experimentalists and the fact that they have errors. If you get 100 people to measure the length of a race, they will get slightly different times. And he came up with something called the Gaussian distribution, which is telling you the probability that you'll be a little bit out in the time, or the probability that someone will be a long way out in the time. And that is, to this day, our understanding of errors and how they occur in experiments across all of science.*

Gauss had, meanwhile, struck up correspondence with a French mathematician called Monsieur Le Blanc and this led to what Colva Roney-Dougal said was one of her favourite stories about Gauss. There was a young French mathematician called Sophie Germain, a woman living at a time when the establishment assumed it was not possible to be a woman in science, and she had become fascinated by mathematics while shut up for her protection during the French Revolution. She had read of the death of Archimedes at the hand of a

Roman soldier and been impressed that maths could be so fascinating to Archimedes that he did not realise he was in danger and was killed while studying geometries.

COLVA RONEY-DOUGAL: *Now Napoleon invaded Brunswick, and Sophie Germain was very worried that the fate of Archimedes might befall Gauss. She got in touch with a general in the invading army and told him to send someone to make sure that Gauss was safe. The person duly arrives at Gauss's house and says that a woman in Paris has come to check that he's okay and Gauss says, 'Well, I don't know any woman in Paris.'*

And then it turned out that his correspondent M. Le Blanc was Sophie Germain. Gauss sent her a letter, talking about her superior genius and amazing abilities at maths and saying that the customs and prejudices of the day made it so much harder for a woman to do maths than a man, and that he was overwhelmed by her abilities. When, about thirty years after that, Sophie Germain was dead, Gauss was asked to nominate someone for an honorary degree, he said he was incredibly sad that he could not nominate Sophie Germain because she would have been the best person imaginable to receive a degree. That was more than thirty-five years before the first woman was awarded a PhD in mathematics in Europe.

While Gauss survived Napoleon's invasion, his sponsor was not so lucky. He died in battle while leading Prussian forces at Auerstedt, aged seventy-one. That meant Gauss had to find a new way of making a living. As Marcus du Sautoy put it, Gauss thought there was no way he was going to get a teaching job at university because all he would do was teach boring low-level maths to undergraduates. He took up the role of head of the Göttingen Observatory.

MARCUS DU SAUTOY: *I blame Ceres a bit for dragging this wonderful mathematician away to doing things like physics and stuff like this, because he'd spent a lot of time doing astronomy and he called these things clods of earth: 'I've got to spend my time tracking clods of earth.' Later on, he got asked to do a survey of Hanover (I mean what a waste of time for this genius, but this was what he had to do in this position). But he used this to make yet another extraordinary discovery about geometry.*

It was out on this survey of Hanover that Gauss began to think the universe might be curved in some way. Gauss had been thinking about the geometry of Euclid and the parallel postulate, which says that, if we take any line and a point off that line, then there's only one unique line through that point, which is parallel to the first line. Gauss started to ponder whether there were other geometries with no parallel lines, or perhaps many, and came up with an idea of new geometries, what we now call non-Euclidian geometries.

MARCUS DU SAUTOY: *In Euclid's geometry, if I draw a triangle, the angles add up, as we all learn at school, to 180. But let me draw a triangle on the surface of the earth. I'm going to take a point at the North Pole, two points on the equator – the straight lines here are now lines of longitude, curved lines, and, if I measure the angles in here, I've got two 90-degree angles at the equator, they already add up to 180, and then I've got an angle at the top. So Gauss had discovered new geometries with different properties from Euclid and he wondered whether maybe the universe is like that.*

Einstein also believed there was a curved geometry in the universe and it was many years later, when we measured light from stars, that we understood that the geometry Gauss discovered was the one that models the way the universe works. Marcus du Sautoy added that this was another idea he did not publish ('silly fellow') and, when Nikolai Lobachevsky and János Bolyai announced these new geometries, Gauss said of Bolyai that to praise him would be to praise himself as he had already discovered them twenty years before, something that the diaries showed. Also from his surveys of Hanover came ideas about curvature, and an easy practical consequence of those, Colva Roney-Dougal told us, was that we cannot make flat maps of the whole globe.

Around 1830, as Nick Evans put it, 'This great theoretical physicist managed to pull himself away from pure mathematics.' Magnetism had been interesting since about 1820 when Hans Christian Ørsted had shown that a current-carrying wire generates a magnetic field. Gauss and his friend Wilhelm Eduard Weber built a famous magnetism lab that stripped out all the iron, which could be magnetised, and replaced it with copper, an idea that was copied in labs across Europe. He looked at the theory of electricity, which is very like the theory of magnetism, and he went back over the mathematical structure and devised something that is now called Gauss's Law of Electricity.

NICK EVANS: *Think of an electric charge as being like a hedgehog, with lots of spikes coming out of it. Where the spikes are near the charge at the centre, by the hedgehog, they're close together and the electric forces are strong. Then, as you go away, the spikes spread out in space, and that reflects the fact that the forces become weaker as you go away from a charge.*

The reason this is useful, Nick Evans explained, is that we can now think about taking lots of hedgehogs and sticking them to a wall, as charges on a wall, and now those spines can only escape in one direction, like the bristles on the end of a brush, straight out, parallel to each other, and so the density stays the same, which means that the electric forces do not fall away in that example. It became a way to think about electric problems and, almost immediately, to see the answers, at least in some cases.

Gauss also, almost as a game, invented the first telegraph with Weber, though again he did not pursue this. They strung a wire from Gauss's observatory to Weber's lab and found a way to send pulses of electricity down it and then detect these at the other end. They developed their own version of Morse code, sending messages such as 'one of the research assistants is coming over to your lab'.

Wilhelm Eduard Weber.

NICK EVANS: *Of course, once they'd done it they thought it was for other people to take it on. It didn't really progress from there. Apparently the wire got hit by lightning eventually and that was the end of it. But they'd understood everything that was needed to do it.*

MELVYN BRAGG: *Colva, you wanted to come in.*

COLVA RONEY-DOUGAL: *They did briefly have grand plans that you could send messages around Germany using the train lines, the rails that the trains would run on. And, sadly, I think that Gauss was not the best at communicating with business people, so that never quite came to light.*

One of the consequences of Gauss's work was that the centre of mathematical activity in Europe shifted from France to Germany. In France, Marcus du Sautoy said, the approach was utilitarian and intended to serve the state, which had a rather dismissive attitude to maths for its own sake. Coincidentally, Wilhelm von Humboldt was defining the education system in Germany and made sure that pure knowledge should be valued there. Gauss made tiny Göttingen the hub of mathematics and it remained that way until Hitler kicked out all the Jewish mathematicians.

Gauss's legacy was extraordinary.

NICK EVANS: *He's had a huge impact on all bits of science. His work on electricity and magnetism eventually led to the discovery of Maxwell's equations and radio, which I think we all agree is very important. But all of modern-day electronics and the lighting in your houses goes back to those equations. His work on error analysis is basically what defines sciences these days, the careful study of data and its application to theories. And then his work on non-Euclidian geometry, which did feed in through his students, led eventually to General Relativity, Einstein's theory of gravity. And, at the moment, we're seeing black holes colliding with gravitational wave detectors, all of which goes back to that work.*

COLVA RONEY-DOUGAL: *He founded my own discipline, namely group theory, with his study of modular arithmetic. He founded modern number theory, he founded the study of complex numbers. He made the shape of twentieth-century mathematics what it is now.*

In the studio afterwards, there was some talk of whether quadratic reciprocity should have been mentioned. As an example, Colva Roney-Dougal explained that 2 is not a square if we consider it in the ordinary whole numbers, but, if we consider it on the seven clock, then 3^2 is 9 and 9 becomes the same as 2 and suddenly 3 squares to 2 and so suddenly now 2 is a square ... And then there was the matter of pension schemes.

NICK EVANS: *At the end of his life, his university's widow scheme was going bust and he came in and did a probabilistic analysis of how likely people were to die and therefore how you should run the fund, which basically underlies the way people run pension schemes to this day.*

MELVYN BRAGG: *And he was this indigent professor who made a fortune on the stock market.*

COLVA RONEY-DOUGAL: *The students at Göttingen used to call him 'the newspaper eater' because he would come in every morning and work his way through all the newspapers, seeing what stocks were up and down, and invested accordingly.*

Finally, was he really the greatest mathematician, as we had suggested at the beginning? Yes, said Colva Roney-Dougal, who was prepared to consider Archimedes and Newton also, and yes, said Marcus du Sautoy, who was not and, as for Einstein, whom Nick Evans suggested, well, we heard he could not have done *anything* without Gauss.

ADA LOVELACE

Deep in the bowels of the Pentagon is a network of computers.
They control the US military, the most powerful army on the planet
and they are, in turn, controlled by a programming language called
Ada. It is named after Ada Lovelace, the (allegedly hard-drinking)
nineteenth-century mathematician and daughter of Lord Byron. She
became the Countess of Lovelace. In her work with Charles Babbage
on steam-driven calculating machines, Ada understood, perhaps
before anyone else, what a computer might truly be. Ada Lovelace
has been called many things – the 'first computer programmer',
a 'prophet of the computer age' – but, most poetically perhaps,
by Babbage himself, an 'enchantress of numbers'.

With Melvyn to discuss Ada Lovelace and her work were: Doron Swade, computer historian, and former assistant director and head of collections at the Science Museum; John Fuegi, visiting professor in biography at Kingston University; and Patricia Fara, fellow of Clare College, Cambridge.

There are three principal players in the story of Ada Lovelace – namely, her mother, herself and Charles Babbage – and to understand the significance of Ada Lovelace it helps to understand the role of the other two. Ada Lovelace was born in 1815 to two exceptional parents, Lord Byron and the aristocrat Anne Isabella Milbanke, also known as Annabella. Her parents were only married briefly, Patricia Fara told us, and Ada was only a few weeks old when Byron disappeared and Annabella Milbanke quickly took custody of her. Byron never saw his daughter after that, dying while abroad, athough, in one of his poems, he mentioned her blue eyes.

PATRICIA FARA: *Annabella Milbanke was a very, very courageous woman. She was also a very intelligent woman and she was very interested in mathematics herself. And she was determined to prevent her daughter following in the same footpaths as Byron had done.*

Annabella Milbanke was energetic and phenomenally interested in education and improvements. She had travelled to Switzerland to study the methods of education propounded by Johann Heinrich Pestalozzi and had established a series of schools and supported the establishment of a university in London. She was also part of the anti-slavery campaign and, at the National Portrait Gallery in London, she can be seen in a group portrait of the campaigners, right there with Wilberforce. She hired a succession of tutors to teach her daughter mathematics and other subjects, working her very hard, and there are messages from Ada Lovelace to her mother along the lines of, 'I'm sorry I didn't work hard enough yesterday and I'm really, really going to try hard to do my best tomorrow.' Ada Lovelace suffered intense headaches when she was quite a little girl and was paralysed for about three years before she was able to start walking and horse-riding again.

It was unusual for a woman to be so well educated in mathematics at this time, but not unique. Annabella Milbanke had a good education and so did several other women, so it could be an option open to those who had interest and aptitude and, above all, parents who were willing to invest in teaching.

PATRICIA FARA: *There were women who became very, very able in mathematics. There's the French woman, Émilie du Châtelet. Also, the woman who became Ada Lovelace's mentor, Mary Somerville, who was a very, very proficient mathematician. There were a few isolated women around who could learn mathematics, but there had to be a special combination of circumstances, and money was definitely one of the things you needed, as well as ability.*

Thanks to her mother's social circle, as Ada Lovelace grew older, she was able to correspond with some very prestigious friends of the family and she had private tuition, quite often by correspondence, with some very distinguished people, such as the mathematicians William Frend and Augustus De Morgan.

Intellectually speaking, the most significant relationship in Ada Lovelace's life would be with the mathematician Charles Babbage. He, as Doron Swade told us, was a colourful, controversial figure best known for inventing computers, and for then failing to build them. His ideas and his prototypes are what inspired Ada Lovelace.

An important development came in 1821 when Babbage and his friend John Herschel (1792–1871), the astronomer, were checking astronomical tables. In this period, the system for doing this was to hand the same set of calculations to two people, who were called 'computers', so that they could work out the answers, and then someone would check that their answers matched. If there were no discrepancies, then those compiling the tables could have confidence in their accuracy. While they were working on these astronomical tables, Babbage became increasingly agitated as the number of discrepancies was very high.

DORON SWADE: *And he clasps his hand to his head and he says, 'I wish to God these calculations had been executed by steam' – steam being a metaphor for not only the infallibility of machinery, but for the model of industrial production. And he devoted most of the rest of his life to the development of automatic calculating.*

These calculators were to be vast mechanical machines, the size of steam engines, and Babbage was a pioneer of computing with these methods. His first love was mathematics and he had published about a dozen papers by the time he was thirty. He was also, as Melvyn pointed out, a polymath and a Lucasian professor of mathematics at Cambridge, a post that had been held by Newton. He was prone to letting off his own steam, too, with extraordinary public outbursts, and he was touchy and proud to the point of self-destruction, on matters of principle, as if being right entitled him to be rude.

DORON SWADE: *His diatribes [were] of incontinent savagery against the scientific establishment, particularly the Royal Society. He impugns the personal probity of Sir Humphry Davy, people who lent him great support in his pursuit of government resources to build his engines. He alienated almost everyone whose support he needed.*

Babbage, we heard, was not only a gentleman of science and massively principled, he was hugely charming and a raconteur. His Saturday soirées were where you could find the intellectual glitterati of London. Ada Lovelace was seventeen when she attended one of these momentous soirées at which Babbage inspired her. John Fuegi explained that, at these sorts of gatherings, Babbage would demonstrate his ideas and, at one of them, he displayed a calculating machine called the difference engine, which still exists and is on show at the Science Museum in London. Annabella Milbanke and Ada Lovelace were struck by what they saw.

JOHN FUEGI: *Lady Byron referred to it as a thinking machine and she started to make sketches of it. And Ada – and I think this is amazing in terms of a seventeen-year-old – she sent around the next week to Babbage and said, 'Well, I'd like to look at the blueprints of this machine.' Now how many are going to do this?*

At this point, Charles Babbage was starting to develop his machines and Ada Lovelace's mind was starting to race, although the two of them would not collaborate immediately. Initially, this prototype for what he called the difference engine was exciting for Babbage, and he received government funding to make it. Soon, though, he became fascinated by the next stage of evolution, a machine of another order, which he called the analytical engine, and then, John Fuegi said, he did not really want to build what he had been given the money for. Doron Swade categorised the now less fascinating difference engine as what we would call a calculator, crunching numbers, performing repeated addition, evaluating and tabulating complex mathematical functions called polynomials.

DORON SWADE: *The huge leap from the difference engine to the analytical engine is the leap from something specific that has a fixed set of functions to something that is general purpose. The point about the analytical engine is it is a general-purpose computational engine and embodies, completely startlingly, almost every single significant logical feature of the modern digital computer.*

Although it so far existed only as an idea, the analytical engine was meant to be programmable, and it would automatically execute multiplication, division, subtraction and addition. Babbage, we heard, was led from mechanising arithmetic with his prototype differential engine to the level of a fully fledged digital computation, and that was the significance of the analytical engine.

Meanwhile, since the soirée, both Annabella Milbanke and Ada Lovelace became very seriously interested in what could be done with machines. They went on a tour of the Midlands to see other machines and find out what they could do.

JOHN FUEGI: *One of the machines that intrigues them is the Jacquard loom; the Jacquard loom constitutes part of the DNA of this project. Here was this person off in France who would program a loom to be able to do these enormously complex pictures. And I think it was something upwards of 30,000 cards that were used to do a portrait.*

MELVYN BRAGG: *I'm going to nail this. He's talking about cards, which he put in the loom, and so it replaced the handmade and closely woven flowers on this cloth and made it much more quickly and in much bigger quantities.*

JOHN FUEGI: *Yes, exactly. What is of particular interest in terms of computer history is that it's essentially an on or off switch, the loom: it either raises or does not raise the thread so that something is going to go through. And it is that central notion that is going to be of tremendous importance then, for the subsequent development within the analytical engine.*

Although the sight of the difference engine had an immediate impact on her, Ada Lovelace was busy on a range of other things for the next ten years. She was educating herself further, she married and had three children and, as Patricia Fara said, she was corresponding

*A model of the analytical engine
designed by Charles Babbage.*

with contacts such as William Frend, Augustus De Morgan, Mary Somerville and Charles Babbage himself, all of them helping her learn mathematics. It seems that she was not very good at routine algebraic manipulation of figures and equations, or understanding geometry.

PATRICIA FARA: *On the other hand, her great skill did lie in having a sort of visionary view of what mathematics could achieve, and I think that's why she did become so involved in describing the analytical engine, because she understood the concepts and really appreciated the possibilities, the potential, in this machine.*

A set of notes on the analytical engine were to define the reputation of Ada Lovelace and are a significant part of her reputation today, and John Fuegi explained how these emerged. Charles Babbage was getting infuriated in England, so went to speak abroad, reasoning that, if the Italians or Alexander von Humboldt became interested in the analytical engine, then the British government would get behind it. He delivered his presentation about his ideas in Turin and, while the more prominent Italian mathematicians declined the opportunity to write up what they thought of this, significantly there was one person who did take it up. This was Luigi Federico Menabrea, who was obscure at the time but, in the future, would be prime minister of Italy, and he published his report of the analytical engine in a Swiss journal, in French. This was the very point at which Babbage went to Peel, the British prime minister, to ask for funding for his analytical machine, only to be unsuccessful.

JOHN FUEGI: *Lovelace feels that Babbage's work is so important that there should be something done, and one shouldn't just leave it at that, with the government having made a horrible mistake. So she does the translation. Ada says, 'Okay, let's go for it and we'll publish it in English so that people can really see it.'*

Ada Lovelace was working with Charles Wheatstone, who was caught up in the idea of this project and had also been working on another calculating machine. Lovelace believed that Menabrea had made a lot of mistakes in his report so she went back to Babbage's original notes, which were three or four times as long as Menabrea's article. To Doron Swade, the significance of Babbage's notes was, primarily, that they were the most comprehensive and insightful account of the thinking of that time about computers. There was then a flurry of exchanges between Babbage and Lovelace in the months before the publication of these notes.

DORON SWADE: *The question is: is there something there that isn't Babbage's? Did she see something Babbage did not see? The answer, unquestionably, is yes, and, for all the other reasons that Lovelace has been lionised, the one that is defensible and does hold water is the notion of her as a 'prophet of the computer age'.*

He added that Lovelace saw that these machines were not bound exclusively by numbers, making the essential transition to a number representing something other than quantity. For Babbage, these machines were still about calculation, although he had some inkling that these machines could be used for algebra.

DORON SWADE: *We have Ada, who's not just suggesting this, but she is thumping the table and saying, 'This is the fundamental significance of the analytical engine.' And it's perfectly clear. And Babbage pays her a tribute, he says: 'I wish I'd given this further attention to see the great potential of these things. Having read your notes, I now see that I might have done so.'*

Ada Lovelace saw the essential distinction between calculation and computation. In such an analytical engine, numbers could represent something other than quantity, such as notes of music or letters of the alphabet. Ada Lovelace is the one who essentially made the transition from arithmetic to symbolic manipulation, as Doron Swade put it, a machine that can manipulate symbols according to rules, and that is the essential beginning of the concept of a computer.

PATRICIA FARA: *And she also has that marvellously poetic phrase that the machine will weave algebraic patterns like a Jacquard loom weaves flowers. And, I mean, that's such a perfect description.*

Patricia Fara agreed that what Lovelace did in the notes was very important. She also thought, though, that it was essential to recognise that Lovelace's visionary ideas were not actually put into practice.

PATRICIA FARA: *Looking back 100–150 years later, we can see that she conceptually grasped the difference between a calculator and what we now call a computer. In a sense, she and Babbage didn't* *really have any influence on the course of computing for the next 100 years. So, although it was a marvellous dream, I'm not sure it was a hugely influential one. And, if you're American, you tell a whole different story of the history of computing that goes through Herman Hollerith and the census at the end of the nineteenth century, and it's not necessarily traced back to Babbage.*

Doron Swade was in vigorous agreement with Patricia Fara about the tenuous connection between Babbage and modern computing, although there is a continuity in the legend and, after Babbage, nobody doubted one could build an engine. He also wanted to clarify the point about Lovelace often being credited as the first computer programmer. She published the first thing we would now recognise as a program.

DORON SWADE: *It's absolutely understandable that she should be so perceived because the first series of steps of instructions – we would now call it an algorithm – the first step of instructions was published under her name, or at least under her initials. The thing is that the work was Babbage's. The concept of a program was based on Babbage's work before Lovelace had any major involvement in the analytical engine.*

While there is dispute over the extent to which Lovelace influenced Babbage, John Fuegi has checked through the mountains of correspondence records. Her tone is directive, he found, stopping Babbage from including in the notes a diatribe against the government, which she thought would backfire, telling him not to mess with her language, chastising him for losing papers she sent him. There were five postal deliveries a day in London at that time, and they were exchanging messages continually.

JOHN FUEGI: *There can be no serious doubt whatsoever as to who is saying, 'We need to move to a new stage of things, you've done wonderful work and I'm deeply appreciative of it, but there are several things that need to happen, we need to stress the difference ... '*

MELVYN BRAGG: *And this is Ada in the driving seat?*

JOHN FUEGI: *This is Ada in the driving seat absolutely emphatically. 'We've got to move beyond difference engine discussion to analytical engine discussion. We've then got to move on, once we get this published, we've got to then line up the financing and we've got to build a prototype and we've got to do an advertising campaign.' Other people in this circle are Brunel and Wheatstone, who are used to raising capital on a large scale to carry things out. So she says, 'You've alienated the government, now we need to use other means.'*

There are stories that Ada Lovelace went on to be a hard drinker and a gambler but, from what he has seen in the records, John Fuegi found that she led really quite a dull life in comparison with many other figures of the day. Her husband, though, did have financial problems. He was the owner of 220 estates that stretched south from Hampton Court to the sea, but, by the end of his life, he was borrowing from Annabella Milbanke. Ada Lovelace was gambling, but she was not doing this as much as her husband, who was later described by his descendant, the Earl of Lytton, as being of a somewhat extravagant nature. Ada Lovelace went to the races but that is what other people did, too, and the idea that she was a heavy drinker may have its roots in another, sadder aspect of her life.

JOHN FUEGI: *What I think is a far more serious thing, and would be seriously compared with Coleridge, is the kind of medicine that you were given, because she dies very young and she has a very painful condition, probably cancer of the uterus but we don't know for sure. But what she was given were clearly opiates and this was standard, this was what you did at the time.*

In her last years, he emphasised, she was in rather a desperate condition, but the medications she was given were prescribed. Patricia Fara pointed to the school of historical thought that, for all the difficulties of retrospective diagnosis, she might also have had some sort of psychological illness. Then, between the drugs and the drink and possible mental illness, some of her behaviour could be extremely erratic.

PATRICIA FARA: *When you read what other people said about her, I think it's important to bear that in mind, because another interpretation of some of the encomia that have been made of her is that these are her friends trying to placate her, keep her on the straight and narrow, and to be flattering, even if they're not really quite sincere.*

Given that Doron Swade had made a case for Lovelace seeing further than Babbage, and that it was difficult to trace their direct influence on modern computing, Melvyn wanted to nail down their real impact. He was aware that Alan Turing had read Lovelace's notes, for one thing. Doron Swade said that there was no direct connection between Babbage and modern computing and, although Babbage is called the father of computing, that genealogical metaphor is actually incorrect. The details of his designs were not really studied until the 1970s. Until then, Lovelace's notes were the most that people had, other than encyclopaedia articles by Babbage primarily on the difference engine. There are conduits between their age and the modern computing age, but we should ask what people might have known of Babbage and Lovelace and by what route.

DORON SWADE: *We're talking about the Lovelace notes, top of the list, then we're talking about encyclopaedia articles. So, if we're talking about Babbage's designs being the DNA of modern digital computer design: absolutely not possible. But the small coterie of people that were continuously involved in automatic computation knew of Babbage, the legend persisted. Turing knew of Lovelace's notes, Lovelace's statements that the analytic engine has no pretensions to originate anything.*

The principles of modern computing, he said, were essentially reinvented by the pioneers of electronic computers in the late 1930s, early 1940s. For those years, John Fuegi suggested, there is no evidence that the first machines were moving beyond the difference machine in the way Lovelace's notes moved beyond. They were still continuing with calculation, as though they had gone back to the difference engine rather than the analytical engine. After that it is hard to define historically when computers moved from calculating, say, the simple trajectories of artillery shells and mathematics to general-purpose computing.

Turing, Doron Swade added, was the first person to define a computer in general ways that said, 'This is a machine that can manipulate symbols that represent things other than numbers.' In response to John Fuegi, he found that the continuity was where the work of Babbage and Lovelace re-emerged in modern times through Turing, one of the pioneers, who made explicit reference to Lovelace's notes.

Finally, Melvyn mentioned that, while Babbage never built his engine, Doron Swade did. It has 8,000 moving parts and weighs a number of tonnes. Like the original, it is not binary, but decimal, and those bases provide a very significant difference between Babbage's work and modern computers, to Patricia Fara's mind. It does, though, according to Doron Swade, work impeccably.

DARK MATTER

Something in our universe is missing, or rather, almost everything, most of the matter in existence. Scientists first noticed this in the 1930s, observing that galaxies were moving much faster than expected and, at such speed, should have dispersed or evaporated. They theorised that there must be something, as yet unknown, keeping the galaxies in place. A Swiss astronomer, Fritz Zwicky, called this 'missing mass' at first, and later 'dark matter', which is how we know it now. Before we went on air, at least one of our guests in this programme claimed that, once we do know what dark matter is, we will have solved one of the greatest mysteries in science, linking the Big Bang with the creation of galaxies, planets, earth and everything on it, including us.

⊰─●─⊱

With Melvyn to discuss dark matter were: Carolin Crawford, public astronomer at the Institute of Astronomy, University of Cambridge, and fellow of Emmanuel College, Cambridge; Anne Green, professor of physics at the University of Nottingham; and Carlos Frenk, Ogden professor of fundamental physics and director of the Institute for Computational Cosmology at the University of Durham.

The Sombrero Galaxy contains a vast black hole at its centre.

Carolin Crawford took us back to the 1930s and to the astronomer Fritz Zwicky, who was studying clusters of galaxies, which are swarms of galaxies, hundreds of thousands, all contained within a region a few tens of millions of light-years across, all bound together. Zwicky realised that he could use the motion of the galaxies to assess the mass of the cluster.

CAROLIN CRAWFORD: *He discovered that they're moving too fast, they're moving at speeds of the order of 1,000km per second. The whole system should have just dispersed out into space, unless you've got more mass there, more gravity there, than you would otherwise have guessed. And that mass, that gravity's anchoring everything, to keep it as one bound entity.*

That is the point at which Zwicky identified this idea of a missing mass, the extra gravity within the system that cannot be seen by an ordinary telescope. Zwicky, at first, called it 'missing mass', and it was later termed 'dark matter' as it does not interact with light in any way – it does not block it, reflect it or absorb it. Yet there this matter is, around five times the amount of ordinary matter but not visible to astronomers, to be inferred rather than seen directly, and extremely important.

CAROLIN CRAWFORD: *It is absolutely fundamental to everything in the universe. Dark matter is what anchors all structures together. Without dark matter, we couldn't have created galaxies and clusters of galaxies. We wouldn't have the current universe we see if we didn't have dark matter that initiated that process right at the beginning of the universe.*

There is something called the galaxy rotation curve, which has a role in this story. As Carlos Frenk explained it, a galaxy like our Milky Way is essentially a disc of stars rotating around the centre of the galaxy. A rotation curve describes how fast the stars are moving around the centre, at different distances from the centre. According to Newton's theory of gravity, we would expect the stars closest to the centre to be going around faster than the stars further out, just like in the solar system, but that is not what scientists noticed.

CARLOS FRENK: *To their horror, in the 1970s, they found that actually the stars were moving more or less at the same speed, a few hundred kilometres per second, regardless of where they were. And that was immediately recognised as a very serious problem, because essentially the stars in the outer parts of the galaxy were just going too fast.*

If all the material that produces the gravity was in the stars and visible, those far-flung stars should have been flung far from the galaxy. That they had *not* been ejected provided clear evidence, albeit not accepted by everyone, for the existence of dark matter in galaxies like the Milky Way. There were other computer simulations about the Milky Way in the 1970s by two Princeton physicists, Jerry Ostriker and Jim Peebles, which, at first, led to the discs of galaxies crumpling up into a kind of bar, but prompted the idea that, in order to make galaxies stable, one required this dark matter.

CARLOS FRENK: *The simulations were nothing compared to what we can do today, but they did manage ingeniously to assume there was some unseen 'halo', a clump of dark matter, and then a beautiful stable galaxy was spotted.*

MELVYN BRAGG: *Why did they call it a 'halo'?*

CARLOS FRENK: *It is a clump. I guess clump is not such an elegant word as halo. I think the idea is that most of it is outside the galaxy, but I always think that all astronomers have saintly tendencies and this is expressed sometimes in our language.*

The missing mass is described as dark, but optical light that we can see with our eyes is only a small part of the electromagnetic spectrum, and detectors that are sensitive to different wavelengths reveal very different things in galaxy clusters. Anne Green referred to the X-ray telescopes used by astronomers in the 1970s, which revealed that galaxy clusters contained a large amount of hot gas emitting X-rays, and gravity was trying to pull this gas in and the pressure was trying to stop it collapsing. Looking at this balance between pressure and gravity, it was possible to weigh the X-ray-emitting gas and compare that to the mass of the cluster as a whole.

ANNE GREEN: *What they found was there's actually a lot more [mass in the] hot gas in the cluster than [in the] galaxies, about a factor of ten roughly, but still that's not all of the missing mass – there's still five or six times as much stuff in the galaxy cluster on the whole as there is this hot gas. That added more information about what the dark matter had to be. It wasn't this gas, it was something else.*

Melvyn declared himself baffled by how it was possible to weigh all these things that his guests were referring to. Carlos Frenk explained that it is mass that, when put on a scale, registers as weight and, as we learn from Newton and Galileo, mass and weight are one and the same thing. Weighing something means measuring how much gravitating mass the object contains, so, if Melvyn had a mass of 80kg, that would be his weight as well as his mass.

Looking for more inferences of dark matter, Carolin Crawford turned to elliptical galaxies. Carlos Frenk had already referred to the way a flat spiral galaxy was rotating, and the way the rotation of the stars can indicate there is this extra dark matter. Most galaxies in the universe are ball-shaped elliptical galaxies, swarms of stars responding to the gravity of the galaxy, and again they are responding to much more gravity than can be detected from all the light and the stars of the galaxy. Elliptical galaxies are much more massive than spiral galaxies, with much more dark matter and, as with the clusters, there is a big halo of X-ray-emitting gas.

CAROLIN CRAWFORD: *This X-ray gas is at temperatures of millions of degrees Celsius – it's a plasma of fast-moving charged particles and these again should have just dispersed. They've got so much energy they should just scatter into space, unless you've got*

*more gravity there to anchor them to this galaxy. [This is] evidence
that this dark matter is endemic to all galaxies in the universe,
whether they be spiral or whether they be elliptical.*

This led to discussing the cosmic microwave background and the
corroboration that this offers for dark matter. Carlos Frenk told how
this background radiation is the heat left over from the Big Bang,
emitted when the universe was only 350,000 years old, the equivalent
of one day in a human life. As the universe expanded, the radiation
cooled and, by the time it had been discovered by two engineers,
Arno Penzias and Robert Wilson in 1964, it had cooled to 2.7°C
above absolute zero and appeared in the form of microwaves. At the
turn of the century, a NASA satellite mapped the temperature of this
microwave background radiation, the heat from the Big Bang, and
found that the temperature was not uniform but patchy, and, from
these patterns of hot and cold spots, we can read what the universe
must have had in order to produce such a pattern. From that, we
learn that the universe had not only ordinary matter, like
the matter of atoms of which we are made, but some form of
elementary particle, different from ordinary atoms, and that was
the dark matter.

CARLOS FRENK: *One way to think about it [is] if you're given a
present in a box that's wrapped and you don't know what's in it,
what do we all do? We shake it, right? And from the vibrations in
the box we try to infer what's inside it. Well, this is very similar. This
microwave background are sorts of vibrations and, by looking at the
vibrations, we can infer what the universe contains.*

MELVYN BRAGG: *That's terrific, isn't it? I mean I'm just in wonder
at all this sort of stuff. That's why we do the programme.*

Up until 350,000 years into its existence, the universe was a very
hot, dense place and everything was broken down into nuclei, which
are positively charged, and electrons, which are separate and, if an
atom tried to form, a very energetic photon, a particle of light, would
come along and kick the electron out of the atom again. Anne Green
described that as a thick gloopy mess of particles that were scattering
off each other all the time. However, at that point, in line with
conservation of energy, as the expanding universe had cooled down
enough, the energy dropped and atoms could form.

There is more evidence of dark matter from gravitational lensing,
an idea that follows from Einstein's theories of gravity, where his
theory of general relativity tells us that mass bends space and, when
light travels through space, its path becomes bent. By looking at how
the path of light is distorted, we can map out how space is bent,
and therefore how the matter is distributed. Sometimes, Anne Green
added, we have a big galaxy cluster and then a long way behind it is
a galaxy, the light of which gets bent around the galaxy cluster rather
than travelling in a straight line. The cluster acts like a lens, creating
multiple images of the galaxy distorted into arcs, from which we can
map out how much space has been bent and therefore how the matter
is distributed.

ANNE GREEN: *What you see are peaks where we know the galaxies are in the matter distribution, but surrounding the galaxies is a big additional lump of dark matter and this is the dark matter halo that Carlos has been telling us about already. So it's telling us where the dark matter is, spread out, extended around the galaxies.*

If, as it appears, there is dark matter, then one of the fundamental questions that remains is what might it be made from. The first place to start could be ordinary matter that just happened not to be luminous, perhaps a gas cloud, or black dwarfs that never became large enough to shine like stars. These are made of ordinary matter that, Carolin Crawford told us, is called baryonic matter as it is made of atoms, which are made of neutrons, protons and electrons, which, in turn, are known as baryons. There are problems with such an interpretation, as it is hard to get observations to sustain it. For example, if there is ordinary matter that is not at absolute zero, then it will give off some kind of radiation.

CAROLIN CRAWFORD: *If it's a planet, it could give off infrared radiation, a gas cloud maybe would absorb light. And you have the problem now that, with today's detectors, if there was enough of this ordinary matter, in the quantities we need to account for the dark matter, we would have detected the glow from it.*

With ordinary matter put aside, the trail leads towards non-baryonic matter. Carlos Frenk said that what clinches the fact, that the dark matter can't be ordinary matter, is the microwave background radiation mentioned earlier, as that unambiguously tells us how much ordinary baryonic matter there is in the universe, and it tells us how much total mass there is, and the two do not add up. The bulk of the mass has to be something different from baryonic dark matter.

Some of our listeners may have known that Carlos Frenk creates computer models of the universe. Melvyn certainly did, observing that he had 'a hell of a reputation'.

CARLOS FRENK: *I work on this day to day, and coming here allows me to step back and realise how amazing it is, what we actually do with these computers, because what we do essentially is to recreate the entire evolution of our universe. And it sounds grandiose, but it is. We now know that when the universe was very young, and I really mean very, very, very young ...*

MELVYN BRAGG: *What's young in your terms? I'm very suspicious of you lot with figures.*

CARLOS FRENK: *A decimal point and then imagine thirty-four zeros and one, that fraction of a second ...*

When the universe was very young, he went on, referring back to the microwave evidence, it was seeded with tiny little irregularities or quantum fluctuations. Carlos Frenk feeds these initial conditions, represented mathematically, into a computer. He then makes an assumption about what the dark matter consists of. Finally, he instructs the computer how to solve the equations of physics,

Swiss astronomer Fritz Zwicky inferred the existence of unseen matter. He initially referred to it as 'missing mass' and later as dark matter.

Einstein's relativity and so on, and lets the program work for months in a row. What astonishes him is that, when he makes the right assumptions about the dark matter, the models come out just like the universe in which we live.

CARLOS FRENK: *I like to challenge my battle-hardened astronomy colleagues by showing them images of galaxies that came out of a computer from this process, from these quantum fluctuations to the present, alongside images of real galaxies, and I challenge them to tell me which is which and, more often than not, they fail.*

As for particles that make up dark matter, there is apparently a range of possibilities with a huge spread of different masses and properties. Anne Green put forward the weakly interacting massive particles, or WIMPs for short, a term she said the astronomers had devised. This term was chosen as a corrective to the ordinary matter mentioned earlier, such as failed stars, which were known as massive astrophysical compact halo objects, or MACHOs. The WIMPs' weak interactions with each other could explain why they have not been seen to date.

ANNE GREEN: *They're very heavy, they weigh [from] maybe a few times a proton up to 1,000 times and they're a good dark matter candidate for two reasons. They'd be automatically produced a tiny fraction of a second after the Big Bang, in the right amount to be the dark matter. [And] they turn up in particle physics models that have been proposed for other reasons.*

Carlos Frenk thought the chances are that these are very strange particles because they're their own antiparticles, but so diffused that the particles of matter and antiparticles of dark matter never collide, except in very extreme situations such as in the centre of the Milky Way when they produce radiation. Following results from NASA's Fermi satellite, which was sent up to look for gamma radiation, there are claims that the centre of the Milky Way is glowing in gamma rays and that this is a signal of dark matter there.

Another candidate for dark matter, before the hypothetical WIMPs, was the neutrino and, as Carolin Crawford said, at least we know the neutrino exists and fills the universe. It does not have a charge, so does not interact with radiation. If each of these tiny particles had a certain amount of mass and there were so many of them, that could account for the dark matter. The problem with this is that experiments have shown that the upper limits to their mass are too small for neutrinos to account for the dark matter.

Carlos Frenk had tested neutrinos as candidates for dark matter with his computer models in the 1980s, when this possibility was termed 'hot dark matter', and the universe that came out of a computer did not look anything at all like the universe in which we live. That, he said, was a big disappointment for him.

CARLOS FRENK: *I was young then and cocky and I thought, 'Right, we've now ruled out hot dark matter, let's go for the next target,' which was cold dark matter. Let's rule that one out. That's the way you make science, you rule things out in order to eventually be left with the correct assumption. So I set out in the 1980s to rule cold dark matter out and now, thirty-five years later, I'm still trying to do it.*

Cold dark matter is a very different kind of particle and, he said, it is exactly the sort of particle that he needs to put into computer simulations to produce these faithful representations of our universe. It essentially explains everything we see on large scales; it explains something we call the cosmic web, which is the way in which galaxies are distributed in the universe, along filaments. The dark matter could still be warm, and it is very difficult to tell cold from warm, but he is continuing to try.

CARLOS FRENK: *To me, the discovery of the dark matter would be an advance to human knowledge on the same level as the discovery of Darwinian evolution.*

P vs NP

*The problem of P versus NP is so difficult to solve that there is
a $1 million prize on offer from the Clay Mathematical Institute
for the first person to come up with a solution. At its heart is the
question: are there problems for which the answers can be checked
by computers but not found in a reasonable time or can all answers
be found easily as well as checked if only we knew how? It has
intrigued mathematicians and computer scientists since Alan Turing
in the 1930s found that some programs, given a problem, could run
indefinitely without finding the answer. That is as true of today's
super computers as it was in his day. Resting on P versus NP is the
safety of online banking and all online transactions that are currently
secure. If access can be found as easily as checked, computers could
crack passwords in moments, and the chance to solve thousands of
practical problems would also be in sight.*

⊱─◆─⊰

With Melvyn to discuss (but not perhaps *solve*) the problem of
P versus NP were: Colva Roney-Dougal, reader in pure mathematics
at the University of St Andrews; Timothy Gowers, Royal Society
research professor in mathematics at the University of Cambridge;
and Leslie Ann Goldberg, professor of computer science and fellow
of St Edmund Hall, Oxford.

*The Pilot ACE was one of the
first computers built in the United
Kingdom in the early 1950s.*

Colva Roney-Dougal began by taking us back to the work of Alan Turing (1912–54), who was trying to solve some problems in the foundations of mathematics. He started thinking about how he could define whether or not it was possible to solve a problem, and this led him, at the age of twenty-two, to invent our modern notion of a computer. He defined an abstract machine, that we now call a Turing machine, and said it should be able to read input, it should be able to write output and it should be able to decide what to do, based only on what state it was in then and what symbol it was looking at. This was an imaginary machine, but he soon realised something important.

COLVA RONEY-DOUGAL: *One such machine can pretend to be any other machine, you can just give it the description of the other machine and it can simulate that machine. So that meant that we've only ever needed one mathematical model of a computer ever since.*

Algorithms were to be part of the studio discussion, and Colva Roney-Dougal described these as a collection of steps for solving a problem. An advantage of calling these an algorithm rather than just a sequence of instructions is the idea that, within an algorithm, you might want to loop. For example, a good recipe is an algorithm, if it is well written and gives clear, unambiguous instructions, such as 'dice the onions, fry them for ten minutes over medium heat'. That said, normally in a cooking recipe, if it turns out that you have burnt the onions, you might need to go back to the beginning and start again.

COLVA RONEY-DOUGAL: *Whereas with a computer algorithm, I might be wanting to do something like find a number in a sorted list of numbers and the instruction might be: 'Look at the middle number, is it bigger or smaller than the one you want? If it's bigger than the one you want, look at the middle of the next step down.' It's repeating there, 'Keep looking in the middle and going bigger or smaller depending on the answer.' You don't necessarily, immediately, know how many steps it's going to take.*

That established, it was for Tim Gowers to explain what lay behind the letters P and NP. P stands for polynomial and NP for non-deterministic polynomial, for reasons he said he would spare us for the sake of simplicity and brevity. When people started to build actual computers rather than Turing's imaginary ones, they realised that something was not as expected. At first, they looked at whether there was an algorithm for solving a problem, and then they slightly changed focus to see if there was an algorithm or systematic procedure that could solve a problem in a reasonable amount of time.

TIM GOWERS: *It turns out that there are quite a lot of problems for which it's very easy to write down an algorithm. The only drawback with the algorithm is that, if you program your computer to run the algorithm, it would take a trillion years or something like that.*

And, if you have got something as slow as that, then you might as well just not have an algorithm. Roughly speaking, he said, 'P stands for the class of problems for which there is a practical algorithm, an algorithm that can run in a reasonable time.' This is not exactly the technical definition, but it is the main point, so we can think of P as standing for practical instead of exponential and impractical. An example of a polynomial time algorithm is long multiplication. If you take two numbers of 100 digits, then, to multiply those two numbers together, the number of steps will be about a 100^2, roughly speaking, because each digit of one number has to be multiplied by each digit of the other number. That will be a polynomial time algorithm. An exponential one would be something where, as the input increases in size, the time it takes doubles and very rapidly will just blow up out of control. Exponential time algorithms will be ones that will take billions of years. Checking an answer to see if it is right is a slightly different thing, and that is where NP comes into all this.

TIM GOWERS: *There are certain problems that are search problems, where you're trying to find something, and you can think of it as a sort of a needle in a mathematical haystack. And sometimes it's easy to check an answer if someone tells you, 'I think this is the answer,' and then you can go away and do a simple calculation and verify that it really is the answer. If that's the case, we say that the problem's an NP. P are things that are easy to do, full stop, and NP are things that are easy to check as long as somebody gives you a massive hint.*

With the complex problems, so far unresolved and of interest, though, it appears it is slightly fantastical to talk of someone giving you a massive hint that could be checked and then found to be correct. That person is unlikely to be in a position to give that hint. Broadly speaking, exponential means hopelessly impractical.

In practice, there are workarounds for some of these exponential problems. As Leslie Goldberg explained, the obvious algorithm is exponential for most of the problems that she looks at, with exponentially many possibilities, but, for some problems, there is a clever way to narrow them down and find the right one. For example, there is one called the matching problem. If you want to find people who are compatible and put them together in a team so that everyone is with someone and no one is left out, then if you simply look at how many pairings there are, the problem would be exponential, as 100 people allow for more possibilities than there are atoms in the universe.

LESLIE GOLDBERG: *An exponential 'dumb' algorithm might just consider every possibility and say: 'Oh, is this possibility good – are all the people that were paired compatible? No? Let's try the next one. No, let's try the next one.' That's ridiculous. But this is actually an easy problem because we do know a polynomial time algorithm and we've even known it since the 1960s due to Jack Edmonds. So that's an easy problem.*

She commented that it would take more than the whole programme to explain *how* that polynomial time algorithm does something else and manages to find a good pairing, but she told us that it does not just look at every possibility but rather cleverly constructs the best one.

Alan Turing introduced the standard computer model in computability theory in 1936.

The next step in this discussion was to look at factorisation, which Colva Roney-Dougal described as relying on 'a lovely fact about whole numbers that's been known at least since the Greeks if not before', namely that there are prime numbers, which are numbers that can only be divided by one and themselves. It transpires that any whole number can be divided up into primes and that, if those primes are to come out in an increasing order, then there is only one way to do it. For example, twelve goes to '2 x 2 x 3'. That is easy enough for small numbers, but, for large numbers, perhaps those with 200 digits, it is very, very hard. This factorisation of primes has a property that, while it is so hard to find the answer, it is easy to check it by multiplying the primes, and that is important.

COLVA RONEY-DOUGAL: *All modern cryptography is essentially based on the fact that, if I multiply together two very big primes, that's easy to do. If I just give you the answer, you can find the two very big primes easily.*

This factorisation of primes, Tim Gowers said, was a very good example of an NP problem where it is easy to check but very, very hard to solve. After this, and helping us move towards an understanding, he said there was then something that does not apply to this factorisation problem, but which he described as 'a bit of a miracle', the NP-complete problem, which Leslie Goldberg was about to explain.

TIM GOWERS: *There are a lot of NP problems that turn out to be of equivalent difficulty in the following sense: that, if you've got a good method for solving one of them, then, by a completely non-obvious process, you can convert it into a good way of solving one of the other problems.*

MELVYN BRAGG: *Leslie Goldberg, give us the travelling salesman problem.*

This is the problem where there is one travelling salesman who has to visit several cities that are some distance apart, and the salesman has to work out the shortest route by which to visit each city only once, and then come back to the start.

LESLIE GOLDBERG: *That is an NP-complete problem or, more formally, the decision version of it is, but, anyway, it's as hard as everything in NP. So the amazing thing is, if you could solve that problem, you could solve factoring and you could also solve every other problem in NP, and there are thousands of them. DNA sequencing is one of the applications of that. I talk about cities but you could say a city is a DNA fragment.*

Prompted by Melvyn to say more about why this problem is so very difficult, Leslie Goldberg emphasised that there are exponentially many possibilities, so a 'dumb' algorithm certainly would not work. Besides, not only do we not have a 'clever' algorithm, we do not even know if one exists. Perhaps seeing a look on Melvyn's face that he was unconvinced, Tim Gowers suggested that he could think of it not as five cities but as 200, and then it might be more obviously hard.

Many of these problems may appear dissimilar, but they can have similar solutions. Colva Roney-Dougal offered that of the seating plan for a large wedding.

MELVYN BRAGG: *What's large?*

COLVA RONEY-DOUGAL: *Let's say 150 guests sitting down to dinner, and you've got a big long table to sit them all down, and you know that quite a few of your guests absolutely loathe each other; they must not be sat next to each other.*

MELVYN BRAGG: *So this is a typical wedding.*

This one turns out to be another one of these problems that is hard to solve but easy to check. If the plan is right, the couple can look around the room and see whether anyone is sitting next to anyone they hate. But to do that from scratch with 100 people, let alone 150, would offer more permutations than there are electrons in the solar system. This is essentially the same as the travelling salesman problem, which is NP-complete, and, if someone can find a way of solving the one, then that can be applied to the other. Tim Gowers added that mathematicians strip away the details of practical problems, such as seating plans and sales trips, and turn them into abstract mathematical problems. These two problems, mathematically, are ones of networks, with nodes and links between the nodes, where the nodes could be cities or wedding guests and the links could be roads or antipathies.

TIM GOWERS: *Once we've turned it into an abstract problem, we can then take it a little bit outside the realm of the practical, we can make these networks get larger and larger. And actually, when we* *study abstractly, we think we've got a network with N nodes, where we think of N as just some very large number and we're interested in how the difficulty of solving the abstract problem scales with N. Once you've slightly left the real world behind, I think it then becomes more plausible that these problems should be very hard.*

There are fine lines between problems that can be solved and those that become unsolvable. Leslie Goldberg referred to the pairing exercise she mentioned earlier. Forming twos is relatively easy, but, when that moves to forming threes, it becomes exponentially problematic. Tim Gowers added that what we have is a very precisely defined class of problems, called the NP problems, and, inside those, there is another very precisely defined sub-class of problems, the NP-complete problems. There is a well-understood method of reducing any NP problem to any given NP-complete problem, so, if we can solve the NP-complete problem, then we can solve the NP problem.

TIM GOWERS: *If one could prove that P does equal NP, that would be saying that things that are easy to check are actually easy to find, [that] would be enormous because you'd suddenly be able to solve a vast number of problems that, at present, we think you can't solve.*

By and large, it seems that people do not think that it is going to be the case that P equals NP, but there is still a tantalising possibility that somebody could just come up with an algorithm for the travelling salesman problem that would revolutionise the way we find algorithms in general. Tantalising it may be, but that is out of reach for now. Leslie Goldberg would not say that mathematicians have hit a brick wall as there is progress, even if that is slow. The problem has been known about since 1971, when people probably thought it would be solved in a year or two.

LESLIE GOLDBERG: *However, if we look at the history of mathematics, some problems take a lot longer to solve. For example, if you look at Fermat's Theorem, the famous thing about the margin, that was 1637. When was it solved by Andrew Wiles? 1994.*

Sometimes in mathematics, problems stay around for a very long time but that doesn't mean they cannot be solved; there is always the chance that they might be solved.

Melvyn was keen to know what the practical implications would be if it transpired that P is equal to NP – namely everything that can be checked can also be found. Colva Roney-Dougal was hedging her bets on this, saying it depended on how P and NP were found to be equal, but we might imagine a new fast algorithm that would solve all of these problems. She offered one bad consequence and then a good one.

COLVA RONEY-DOUGAL: *The one bad thing – we've already mentioned this: all internet security breaks instantly ...*

MELVYN BRAGG: *Why?*

COLVA RONEY-DOUGAL: ... *because we can now factorise numbers that are products of two very big primes and that's the basis for all of our current cryptography, so we would need a different way of exchanging information secretly. The good thing is that almost every single thing you buy becomes cheaper, because some of the problems that are in NP that are difficult to deal with at the moment are scheduling tasks in factories, transporting goods between factories.*

Tim Gowers said he thought it was incredibly unlikely that P would equal NP. Besides, the problem of finding proof, which is what mathematicians do for a living, is in NP. So, if P turned out to equal NP with the qualifications Colva Roney-Dougal mentioned, then mathematicians would be out of a job, because computers could very, very easily do all the work that mathematicians at the moment sweat away doing in their offices. As she put it, if P were equal to NP, you could claim all the Clay Mathematics Prizes because you would be able to run the code and generate short proofs for all of the remaining ones. One famous computer scientist, Donald Knuth, has said that he thinks it is so unlikely that P is equal to NP that, to the first person who shows this, he will award the prize of one live turkey in addition to the $1 million. Conversely, if we were to find conclusively that P is not equal to NP, Leslie Goldberg said that would be a good first step in our understanding of the difficulty of problems. The uncertainty may be solved, and the prize claimed, by showing that P is not equal to NP, rather than showing that they are the same.

In the studio immediately afterwards, Melvyn asked what else was on his guests' minds. Colva Roney-Dougal wanted to clarify that the word 'algorithm' came from the mathematician al-Khwarizmi, as he was doing equation solving and was giving step-by-step instructions for solving those sets of equations. Louise Goldberg mentioned that there is a whole field of study about how difficult NP-complete problems are to solve not fully but approximately. Melvyn checked that there was no sense in which mathematicians were going to give up trying to solve the P vs NP problem, and was reassured that the search would continue.

TIM GOWERS: *Some of the experts say, 'Well, I can't afford to spend too much of my time on this problem because it's such a hard problem and I don't want to end up with no publications whatsoever.' Most theoretical computer scientists ration the time they spend on the problem and spend some of their time working on slightly less ambitious ...*

MELVYN BRAGG: *I'd have thought so, like [how] I finish a novel instead of sitting trying to write the greatest novel ever written and never writing anything.*

TIM GOWERS: *It's a little bit like that.*

MELVYN BRAGG: *Ah, here's Simon. I think a double brandy and tea!*

A worker cold-shock tests copper vessels used in producing liquid oxygen.

ABSOLUTE ZERO

The coldest natural temperature ever known on earth was recorded
in July 1983 at a Soviet research base in the Antarctic. At quarter to
three in the morning, the thermometer registered -89.2°C. Beyond
our atmosphere, it can be dramatically colder even than this.
Astronomers believe that interstellar space has a temperature of
around -270°C. But the coldest temperatures yet known, colder even
than space, have been created artificially in the laboratory. Scientists
have been creeping ever closer to the lowest possible temperature,
known as absolute zero. The idea that temperature had a lower limit
was first suggested in the seventeenth century. The race for ever-
colder temperatures began 200 years later and has resulted in some
of the strangest, most important and useful discoveries of modern
science. But, although physicists can get within a billionth of a degree
of absolute zero, they will never quite get there.

With Melvyn to discuss absolute zero were: Simon Schaffer, professor of the history of science at the University of Cambridge; Stephen Blundell, professor of physics and fellow of Mansfield College, Oxford; and Nicola Wilkin, professor in the school of physics and astronomy and director of education at the College of Engineering and Physical Sciences, University of Birmingham.

Since we were looking at temperature, Melvyn started by asking Simon Schaffer what the early ideas were about this and what 'temperature' was. The Greeks lived in a culture in which all energy sources were either human, mechanical or thermal and understanding heat and temperature was fundamental to their cosmology. For Aristotle, for example, temperature, in the sense of possessing heat, was an essential quality of all bodies and, in his natural philosophy, he had proposed the possibility of what came to be called, in Latin, the *primum frigidum*, the fundamental cold.

SIMON SCHAFFER: *It was even supposed by many scholastics, followers of Aristotle, that cold was, as it were, a substance equivalent to heat. When substances became colder it was because they were absorbing cold and when they became hotter it was because they were absorbing heat.*

This idea was challenged in the seventeenth century with the development of new technologies such as the thermoscope with a sealed bulb full of air, plunged into water, where the height of the water would measure, in some sense, the temperature of the bodies surrounding the bulb. Experimenters such as Robert Boyle were satisfied that there was no such thing as the *primum frigidum*, that there was no fundamentally cold substance. Boyle thought, following Francis Bacon, that cold was a deprivation of motion and heat was a form of motion. That made possible the idea of an absolute limit to cold.

This was explored further by a Frenchman, Guillaume Amontons (1663–1705), who was an entrepreneur who wanted to drive a pump by the expansive force of air using what he called a 'fire engine'. He worked out ways of measuring what he, following Boyle, thought of as the spring of the air and designed a fairly accurate thermometer with which he could work out that, as temperatures drop, the springiness, what we might think of as the pressure of the air, also drops.

SIMON SCHAFFER: *And he projected the idea that there must be a point at which the air loses all its spring and that would be the limit of temperature, the absolute zero, in that sense, of temperature. He didn't pursue the speculation but, after this work, that idea of an absolute limit became thinkable.*

The next advancement came when Michael Faraday (1791–1867) began to explore lower temperatures at the Royal Institution in the 1830s. Stephen Blundell told us that Faraday started to do some experiments that followed on from one of the great achievements of his mentor Humphry Davy, which was to show that chlorine was an element. Faraday experimented with crystals of what was called chlorine hydrate at the time, basically ice with chlorine dissolved inside it.

STEPHEN BLUNDELL: *He put chlorine hydrate in a sealed glass tube and heated it up. Now the problem was that's quite a dangerous thing to do because the chlorine is released and goes to very high pressure and the glass tubes frequently exploded. So, after many of these experiments, Faraday found himself with glass all over his face and had to pick them out of his eyes, the shards.*

Faraday wanted to raise the pressure inside the glass tubes by heating them up. By putting chlorine under very high pressure, he made a little oily liquid on the inside of the glass, which was liquid chlorine. If the pressure of a liquid increases, the boiling temperature increases. Chlorine would normally go from liquid to gas at about -30°C but, by going to high pressure, Faraday could raise that point up to the temperature of the Royal Institution in February and, when he reduced the pressure, he had some very very cold liquid chlorine in his laboratory. He went on to do the same with hydrogen sulphide, nitrogen dioxide and sulphur dioxide.

William Thomson (1824–1907), later Lord Kelvin, was a theoretical physicist rather than an experimenter as Faraday was. He was very much concerned by the issue of thermometry because one of the problems was that any material that might be used to make a thermometer, such as mercury or alcohol, allows measurement by the expansion of that liquid, but that assumes the expansion gives a well-defined temperature, something that was not known. Messrs Fahrenheit and Celsius offered a particular scale for the expansion of liquid in a tube.

STEPHEN BLUNDELL: *Celsius, for example, set zero degrees at the boiling point of water and 100 at the freezing point, later inverted to give the more familiar Celsius scale. But essentially what they were looking for was fixed points on a scale but they were always reduced to thinking about how some material property behaves, whether it's mercury or alcohol or water or gas. And Kelvin wants to take us away from thinking about a material substance: 'Is there an absolute definition of temperature?'*

When Kelvin did look for a definition, the net result of his work was to see that absolute zero, the absolute zero of Amontons, -273°C, which we now call zero Kelvin, was the right zero of the scale.

Melvyn wanted more clarity on what was actually meant by temperature. Nicola Wilkin asked him to think of two cups of coffee that can be measured to see if they are equally hot or cold.

NICOLA WILKIN: *[The thermometer] is a bit like a speedometer, it's looking at the average speed of the atoms in your cup of coffee. So your cup of coffee looks like it's completely still but, inside it, all the atoms are moving around, they're bouncing off each other, they're bouncing off the walls, they're vibrating, they're rotating and that average speed is what's giving you the temperature.*

As the coffee cools, it looks much the same but the atoms have slowed down very slightly and that is what is picked up on the temperature scale. At the end of the nineteenth century, Nicola Wilkin said, before quantum mechanics, it was thought that everything was just slowing down with no other source of energy in there, which, at absolute zero, would mean that everything was pinned down, the electrons as well as the atoms. If that were the case, it could be conjectured that electrical resistance would become infinite at absolute zero as nothing would be able to move.

Among scientists in the nineteenth century, there was, as Melvyn put it, almost a race to the South Pole to be the first person to the lowest temperature. This, as Simon Schaffer pointed out, was a time when what were seen as the heroic triumphs of European imperial geography were on everybody's minds. James Dewar (1842–1923) was one of the British protagonists at the Royal Institution and his rival, William Ramsay, was nearby at University College, London.

SIMON SCHAFFER: *Dewar and Ramsay loathed each other. This was, in a certain sense, tragic for the development of London physics, London chemistry, the science of cold in London. What these two men had, if they'd been put together, was an absolutely unrivalled combination of experimental technique, theoretical understanding and high-powered engineering equipment.*

Dewar saw the move towards absolute zero as his destiny and, by assembling in the basement of the Royal Institution an almost unrivalled group of lab technicians and equipment, he was able to liquefy hydrogen before the end of the century, which was an extraordinary achievement. While Faraday had liquefied one range of gases, there had been another range of gases, including oxygen and hydrogen, which he had called the permanent gases as he thought they could not be liquefied. Meanwhile, Ramsay and his team were producing a range of hitherto unknown gases called the noble gases, argon, neon and ultimately helium, which also seemed to challenge liquefaction and offer the possibility of moving towards absolute zero. The rivalry was exacerbated by the lack of access to raw materials, as Ramsay had control over most of the helium in Britain, which happened to be in Bath, which made it difficult for his rival to work with it and make it liquid. As a side note: Dewar did, though, invent the vacuum flask.

Picking up from here, Stephen Blundell observed that one of the reasons that helium had not yet been liquefied was that it had only recently been discovered, and, even then, the discovery was in the solar spectra before it was found on earth. It is also essentially part of alpha particles from radioactivity, and the earth's radioactive compounds give rise to helium all the time, which means it is found in traces in some minerals.

STEPHEN BLUNDELL: *It was so special because, once liquid nitrogen, liquid hydrogen, liquid oxygen had all been made, it was discovered that, when you put helium gas in contact with those liquids, it wouldn't itself liquefy. Which means that helium had to liquefy closer to absolute zero than anything else. So it was going to be the gas that gave you the closest approach to absolute zero.*

Helium was therefore the final part in the race for the Pole. There was also another scientist of interest, Kamerlingh Onnes (1853–1926) at the University of Leiden, who had many highly trained technicians and, at that time, the most equipped and the best organised laboratory in the world. Onnes, Nicola Wilkin said, investigated what might happen to other materials if they were subjected to the same low temperatures. He chose mercury and cooled it down, anticipating that the electrical resistance would reach a constant and nothing would flow. Instead, to his surprise, he found that there was no electrical resistance.

NICOLA WILKIN: *He managed to set up, within a ring of mercury, a current flowing. And he let it stay there. In fact, he let it stay there for a year. So he set this current flowing without any batteries, left it there undisturbed for a year, [and the] current was still flowing. Because there was no resistance, he had this persistent current and hence it became a superconductor.*

This was a completely new phenomenon. Onnes could see extraordinary technological possibilities for this, such as building the huge magnets we have today.

Taking this further, Stephen Blundell turned to the quantum mechanics that began in the twentieth century, which showed that electrons would go around an atom for ever, with no need for a battery. The superconductivity spotted in the ring of mercury was similar to what happened to an atom, where a current of electricity would go round a loop of wire for ever.

STEPHEN BLUNDELL: *It was a scientist called Fritz London, working in Oxford in the 1930s, who made the connection that superconductivity was essentially like a giant atom, a phenomenon that would normally only be operative in the microscopic world of atoms, electrons going around and around for ever. [It was] now seen in a macroscopic way, seen in large objects.*

Noticing that quantum mechanics was manifest in this way was a crucial observation. It turned out that these kinds of phenomena were disrupted by the thermal vibrations that we heard about earlier, the jiggling around at high temperatures, so they became low temperature phenomena.

These enquiries were driven by curiosity, Simon Schaffer said, but the scientists were also helping to develop machines such as fridges, which went on to become so essential to civilisation.

SIMON SCHAFFER: *There were two key techniques that Dewar and Kamerlingh Onnes principally drew on. On the one hand, the Joule–Kelvin effect – when a gas escapes from a containment at very high pressure through a nozzle or syphon into an area of very low pressure, you get an enormous, dramatic and very sudden cooling.*

Engineers such as one of Simon Schaffer's heroes, William Hampson (1854–1926), turned that process into an automatic air-liquefying machine, leading to the establishment of the British Oxygen Company. The second process that Dewar and Onnes drew on was called the cascade technique, which was to liquefy a gas and then use that liquid to liquefy a second gas and so on, so that

Scottish chemist and physicist James Dewar was the first to liquefy hydrogen.

there is a kind of regenerative feedback loop in which the ambient temperature of the gas and then liquid can be driven down fast and very efficiently.

SIMON SCHAFFER: *Combine the two, the Joule–Kelvin effect and the cascade effect, as Dewar, to a certain extent, did and Kamerlingh Onnes did amazingly, brilliantly, and you can reach the temperatures of liquid helium and below, that's to say 4K.*

When studying physics, Nicola Wilkin cautioned, just as you think you have understood it and you are going to prove what is going on, nature throws something in your way. For scientists at the turn of the twentieth century, that was quantum mechanics. One of the first points that arose from that, relating to absolute zero, was what became called the Heisenberg uncertainty principle. That tells us that we are precluded from knowing precisely where a particle is and how fast it is going.

NICOLA WILKIN: *You can immediately see that there's a problem with the physics describing absolute zero earlier, where we were going to have particles nailed down and absolutely no speed associated with them, because quantum mechanics says we can't do that. There has to be some sort of energy still left at absolute zero.*

As Melvyn was interested in the idea of superfluids, Nicola Wilkin went on to a discovery published in 1938 that came out of investigations of helium. Liquefied, helium had no viscosity so, if you could imagine wading through it, you would feel no resistance to your strides. That is a very strange liquid.

NICOLA WILKIN: *If you put it, for instance, in a beaker, it can climb the edges of that beaker. I did a back-of-the-envelope calculation: it's something like (depending upon how accurately you do this) about 30km it could keep climbing up.*

MELVYN BRAGG: *Okay, that's a sort of a weird feeling here, a strange feeling went through the studio then. That's the world, isn't it?*

The race to absolute zero, it turned out, was not one that can ever be won, in some sense. Stephen Blundell explained that any cooling process imaginable will essentially reduce the temperature by a certain fraction. That can be done in a series of stages, perhaps reducing the gap to absolute zero by half and then again by a quarter, one eighth, one sixteenth, but the gap to zero can never be closed in a finite number of steps. The limit is there but it can never be reached.

STEPHEN BLUNDELL: *In practice, it's even worse than that because, when you get down to very, very low temperatures, you find that, if you're trying to cool something, there will always be some environment that is warmer and that will leak heat in. So the closer you get, you then start finding the thing slightly warms up a bit, and so it's like travelling on an escalator that's going against you, you can never get to the top.*

With advanced cooling techniques, scientists have been able to get to a millionth of one Kelvin, that is a millionth of a degree above absolute zero. Recent techniques have been evolved to cool small collections of gas atoms in a trap to even lower temperatures, around a billionth of a Kelvin.

There is a silver lining to this sensitivity that allows these cold gases to reach such low temperatures but not quite absolute zero. Normally, that sensitivity to the environment is not something positive in an experiment.

NICOLA WILKIN: *In fact, these gases, because they are so sensitive, are now becoming sensors. One thing that they're sensitive to, for instance, is variation in gravity. People are investigating using it for searching for oil, underground water supplies, archaeology.*

STEPHEN BLUNDELL: *Really one of the most exciting areas of research is to try to get superconductivity, which is a purely low temperature phenomenon. We have to cool down all the magnetic resonance imaging magnets to get them to work. How can you get that to work at room temperature?*

Just as the programme closed, Melvyn asked about recent research in Germany that suggested that a temperature below absolute zero had been created. 'Is it below -273 or not? I mean the producer is crossing his arms saying I've got to get off the air. Is it below … ?' It is lower, we were told, but had not gone through T = zero to get there, and that would have to be something for another day.

LYSENKOISM

In 1928, as America headed towards the Wall Street Crash, Joseph Stalin revealed his masterplan: nature is to be conquered by science, Russia is to be made supremely modern at any cost, and the world is to be transformed by communist example. Into the heart of this vision stepped Trofim Lysenko, a self-taught geneticist who promised to turn Russian wasteland into a grain-laden Garden of Eden. Today Lysenko is a by-word for scientific fraud but, in Stalin's Russia, his ideas became law. They reveal a world of science distorted by ideology, where ideas were literally a matter of life and death. To disagree with Lysenko risked the Gulag and he damaged, perhaps irrevocably, the Soviet Union's capacity to fight and win the Cold War.

⊰━●━⊱

With Melvyn to discuss Trofim Lysenko were: Robert Service, emeritus professor of Russian history at the University of Oxford and Hoover senior fellow; Catherine Merridale, senior research fellow at the Institute of Historical Research and fellow of the British Academy; and Steve Jones, senior research fellow in genetics at University College London.

Crop threshing in the Soviet Union in the 1930s.

In order to understand why Lysenko appeared to be the right man at the right time for Stalin, Melvyn asked Robert Service to explain the context of the first five-year plan in 1928. We heard that it was a stupendous ambition to modernise agriculture, banking, finance, industry, the military, foreign trade, transport, communications, and it was a contrast to everything that was happening elsewhere in the world, because there was just about to be the Wall Street Crash and a crisis in capitalism. Since the Bolsheviks had come to power in 1917, there had been a dictatorship run in the interests of the working class, taking hold of everything and mobilising the people in the interests of the revolutionary cause.

ROBERT SERVICE: *For several years, it met all sorts of obstacles, it had a civil war, it then had to make compromises with its peasantry, and then came the great breakthrough, in 1928, when the first five-year plan was announced and this great transformation started to be attempted comprehensively.*

The regime under Lenin had been much tighter than anything that had existed in Russia before the revolution, and it was about to get tighter or, as Robert Service put it, 'absolutely cataclysmically worse'. This very, very authoritarian one-party state planned the biggest undertaking ever by a world power.

ROBERT SERVICE: *It was absolutely staggering at the time to people who were living in foreign states. And many people who were not communists in Europe and North America were positively impressed because this was a state, the USSR, that was offering something totally different from what all the other advanced economies were offering to the rest of the world.*

Lysenko's contribution was to be to agriculture, the occupation of most of the population. The peasantry were using old-fashioned methods of cultivation based on household units that were now to be combined into large farms, essentially owned by collective farm chairmen who would control the methods of production, deal with the state and trade with the produce. Steve Jones then identified some of the flaws in this. Firstly, large numbers of the better-off peasants, the kulaks, were shot, which removed many people with expertise and an overview. Secondly, Soviet agriculture followed a centralised, scientific model, and the science of Lysenko was 'complete nonsense'. In the USA, too, small farms were being merged to make large farms and there was an increasing role for science, but the main difference in the USA was that their model of science was correct and was being used to increase the yields. Soviet agricultural scientists had their views suppressed and some suffered the same fate as the kulaks.

The central problem with Lysenko and Soviet agriculture was that it was a 'lethal mixture of science and ideology', something that Steve Jones said has happened in his field of genetics and still can, to a degree.

STEVE JONES: *The difficulty was that the model the Soviets had was partly a scientific model. You could observe certain things – that if you gave a cold shock, for example, to maize then they would burst into flower, and that's true. But added on to that was the belief that somehow there was what they called the 'law of necessary progress', that biology had an end in view, that things were bound to get better.*

That fitted with the Soviet view, he said, that one generation of suffering would possibly generate a new kind of human being, for the better. This was in some ways a mirror image of the 1920s view in the west, which was that human nature was set, a flawed approach that was soon exposed. The Soviets echoed Lamarck (1744–1829), the French naturalist.

STEVE JONES: *Lamarck was the 'inheritance of acquired characters' [which] meant, famously, that giraffes would stretch up to get the leaves at the top and then their offspring would have longer necks as a result. And that was believed for a long time.*

Stalin lionised Lysenko. He was, Catherine Merridale told us, the son of peasants and always dressed as a peasant rather than as the agricultural scientists often did, in their high collars and starched shirts. He was Ukrainian and trained briefly in Kiev, but did not have much formal education. He first came to prominence in Azerbaijan in 1927.

CATHERINE MERRIDALE: *His first great breakthrough, which he was very good at publicising, was to get peas to grow in the winter in the Caucasus, and he said that he could actually produce a desert that was green through the winter so that the camels would have something to eat.*

Lyskenko's next major step was to go into the science of vernalisation that Steve Jones had mentioned, the idea that, if grains were chilled before they were sown, then crops such as winter wheat could grow within one season, avoiding the freezing winter that could kill them off. Lysenko did his first experiment by getting his father to bury forty-eight sacks of pre-soaked grain in a snowdrift and, without waiting for the results, he declared in spring that the experiment had been a success. This was another of Lysenko's traits, Catherine Merridale said: he was very good at producing results before finishing experiments, and declaring them a success. He was brilliant at self-publicity and even better at it once he had been adopted by people who wanted to promote him for political reasons. He was also intolerant of criticism.

CATHERINE MERRIDALE: *Anybody who said, 'Comrade Lysenko, this isn't right,' they might very well find themselves being attacked verbally by him and then attacked in other ways by the state later on, when he became more powerful. He was very intolerant. He was also very good at getting the establishment to adopt him. And he was always moving on to the next thing before the previous thing had been shown to be a total failure.*

He failed with winter wheat but did not admit it, then went on to spring wheat and tried making the grain warm and wet to shorten the growing time once cold and wet had not worked, though warm and wet only led to rotting grain, so he moved on to potatoes and then to maize, announcing his 'success' as he went.

The Soviet Union was one of the world leaders in plant biology in the 1920s, and yet the agricultural scientists encouraged Lysenko. Perhaps, Catherine Merridale suggested, some were socialists and believed it was important to encourage the coming generation. Some were intrigued. Some were frightened to speak out against him as that would make them look bad. For the health of agricultural science, that tolerance and accommodation of Lysenko's culture was a mistake. In the eyes of Stalin, though, Lysenko was just what he was looking for.

CATHERINE MERRIDALE: *He was called a barefoot scientist. He was credited, in fact, with restoring the confidence of a lot of peasants because collectivisation was such a blow and there was such demoralisation and famine in the countryside. Here's a man who actually works with peasants in their villages.*

Lysenko said there was no need for expensive laboratories, and that he did his science in five pots in the corner of his greenhouse. He could also move more quickly than classical scientists who wanted perhaps ten years to develop a new strain of wheat, promising Stalin he could achieve this in two or three years, thanks to vernalisation and cutting down on multiple experiments.

As Robert Service emphasised, professional people were being arrested in the early 1930s when there was a deep suspicion in Stalin's USSR of anybody who had a toehold in the old pre-revolutionary society.

ROBERT SERVICE: *Eventually, in 1937, in the Great Terror, they're named as groups that are to be eliminated and either thrown into the Gulag camps or shot ...*

MELVYN BRAGG: *We're talking about hundreds of thousands, even millions.*

ROBERT SERVICE: *We're talking millions of people. And the Gulag is kept topped up with new victims as the slave labourers die off. And that's going on right through to the death of Stalin in 1953. So it's a period of enormous utopian feeling and aspiration, combined with enormous, huge, intense trepidation.*

Lysenko was the right fit for Stalin, who was a great believer in the effectiveness of science. Not only science, Robert Service said, but *Soviet* science and modernity, which would be superior to American modernity. He picked out young men from the peasantry and the working class, and they were usually men rather than women, who might enhance the possibility of transforming society rapidly.

ROBERT SERVICE: *The thing for Stalin was not to proceed by gradualist science but to set the goals in advance and then cajole, encourage and intimidate people into finding ways to meet the goals.*

MELVYN BRAGG: *And, if they couldn't find them, to fake them?*

*Trofim Lysenko measuring the growth of
wheat on one of the kolkhoz (collective
farm) fields near Odessa, Ukraine.*

ROBERT SERVICE: *And, if they couldn't find them, you arrested
them and that induced scientists like Lysenko to say that they could
do things that they really couldn't do. The thing about Lysenko that
was different from the other scientists was that he came to Stalin with
apparent solutions.*

Lysenko was not the only one suggesting quick fixes for significant
problems. Catherine Merridale mentioned the idea of breeding
rabbits as a solution to meat shortages in the first five-year plan. All
factories and offices, even the secret police, were given a number of
breeding pairs of rabbits and a target for the number of rabbits that
they were supposed to produce at the end of the period, along with
the amount of fur and meat. There was some merit in the idea, with
rabbits being such fast breeders, but there was nothing green for them
to eat in the winter, so they starved and it was a failure on the quiet.
Later in his reign as king of Soviet biology, Lysenko came to Stalin
to offer to change the climate of Siberia by planting trees in clumps
where the best tree in the clump would survive.

CATHERINE MERRIDALE: *Peasants were supposed to put hundreds
and thousands and millions of bunches of acorns into the Siberian
soil, which they did in 1948. And, by 1952, the great Siberian forest
was supposed to have happened. Shostakovich actually wrote some
music,* The Song of the Forests, *to celebrate the future Stalin forest.
And of course, by 1952, 4 per cent of the trees were still alive, so it
came to nothing.*

All the time that Soviet agricultural science was supporting the ideas of Lysenko, it was falling behind with the understanding of genetics, which might have led to better crops. There was a reluctance to study chromosomes and this apparently was partly due to the fact that they could be seen through a microscope. Their physical structure, Steve Jones said, suggested that they were not changeable and this ran counter to the point of Lysenkoism, which was that there was a vague nexus of goodness and badness that could be altered so that the bad would become good.

STEVE JONES: *They hated the notion that things could not be changed by the environment. And, at the time, they seemed to be entirely wrong, the Soviets, and later the Russians. However, nowadays I have to say some of that view is beginning to have some truth emerge. I'm not saying Lysenko was right but he wasn't entirely wrong, which is pretty embarrassing for us geneticists.*

According to the genetics of Gregor Mendel, the appearance of the peas he studied was controlled by something hidden inside the DNA and, whatever farmers did to the peas, growing them in good or bad soil, that made no difference to the genes. There have been some findings in Sweden in the past decade, Steve Jones noted, that suggested otherwise, where grandfathers who had experienced famine had grandsons and granddaughters who are better at dealing with food shortages than the intervening generation. Somehow the DNA has been marked by this environmental experience, which sounds Lysenkoist. In case it appeared that Steve Jones was supporting Lysenko here, he emphasised that Lysenko was wrong and a fraud.

It seems that Stalin had a particular weakness when it came to agriculture. By and large, Robert Service said, he took the correct decisions about such matters as what the best tanks were, what the best military aeroplanes were, whether the Kalashnikov rifle was any good. He read popular science textbooks and even forced his children to read them, but that did not lead to the right outcome.

ROBERT SERVICE: *In science, he got things wrong. And yet, when that type of thing happened in military technology, the scientists were shot, but they weren't shot in agriculture. And I think this indicates that much as he took agriculture seriously, he didn't take it as seriously as he took waging war.*

In 1940, Lysenko was made director of the Soviet Academy of Science Institute of Genetics, and that made him unassailable. He opposed Vavilov, a very serious geneticist, described by Catherine Merridale as the great plant biologist of the 1920s. He was a collector of plants and did something Stalin did not like, which was to travel abroad and contact foreign scientists. He looked at plants in their natural environments and tried to find ways in which they could be made adaptable to inhospitable conditions.

CATHERINE MERRIDALE: *He and Lysenko clashed on a series of occasions and, finally, he was arrested in 1940. He was sentenced to death in 1942 and he starved to death in a prison in the middle of the war in Saratov in 1943. It was a great tragedy. And all his supporters also disappeared; some committed suicide. And it's at that point that several hundred thousand scientists lose their jobs for ever. Genetics became almost impossible to carry out in the Soviet Union until the early '50s.*

MELVYN BRAGG: *It does seem extraordinary. Agriculture's lumbering away, a total failure, they're now in the late '40s, having to take grain from America, and nobody's saying, 'Have you got this wrong?' Or, if they do, they're sent to prison.*

STEVE JONES: *It's the power of terror. It's ironic that the plant hybridisation institute in Russia now is called the Vavilov Institute, so he's actually back and absolutely in favour. When I was learning genetics, there were a number of Soviet émigrés who'd been through that and fled to the States and to Britain and they still were terrified to talk about it, it was an appalling business.*

In Steve Jones's view, the further irony is that, while people talk of the arms race as the main contest between America and the Soviets, or oil, it was actually agriculture. The Soviets had to import grain from the USA. The Americans could do that because Donald F. Jones and E. M. East had discovered that, if you crossed lines of maize together, there was a fantastic improvement in yield and, suddenly, the United States was the breadbasket of the world. What made Lysenko's rise all the more shocking to Catherine Merridale was that, in 1948, three years after the Great Patriotic War, Russia and America were allies and Russian scientists had access to American science. They could see the results of this and of selective weed killers, but turned away from it, preferring instead the mistaken methods from before the war. It was not a time to step out of line.

In case it appeared that every scientist outside the Soviet Union was querying Lysenko, Steve Jones stressed that he did have support. Ideology was not behind this, although a lot of scientists had sympathy for left-wing ideas. He said that J. B. S. Haldane, a famous geneticist and a towering genius in science, went along with Lysenko until 1956 and almost wished that Lysenko was right. And the industrial programme behind the Urals was very successful, which may have coloured perceptions of agriculture. The fundamental problem was that the agricultural scientists did not accept the truth of what they found. Sometimes, findings mean that you have to reconsider everything you believed, and that did not happen.

STEVE JONES: *We may not like it but we have to swallow it. And that was the problem, they didn't like it so they didn't swallow it. And that really was the difference between Soviet biology and western biology.*

Lysenko was being presented as the great new leader of a new kind of agrobiology, with which the Soviet Union was to transform itself and the world. People in the west had seen the ruination of their economy in the 1930s with the Great Depression and, as Robert Service said, they willed themselves into thinking that this way of planning everything from the centre was a better way of running things than the rather messy, chaotic contours of capitalism. Stalin was very pleased with a speech Lysenko gave in 1948, denouncing Mendel and Darwin. Even Khrushchev was well disposed towards him.

CATHERINE MERRIDALE: *When Khrushchev was party secretary in the Ukraine, he'd adopted one of Lysenko's earlier schemes for chicken breeding. And so he was ...*

MELVYN BRAGG: *What was that?*

CATHERINE MERRIDALE: *Don't ask ... it was what he fed them on. And the problem with Khrushchev is that he was already one of the previous regime. So to announce that the emperor has no clothes would actually be to leave himself naked, too.*

Lysenko did persuade Khrushchev that he could still be the great head of science, even while there was clearly something interesting going on in the west with genetics and, by then, Watson and Crick had won the Nobel Prize in 1962 'for their discoveries concerning the molecular structure of nucleic acids and its significance for information transfer in living material'. It was very hard to let Lysenko go. Quietly, meanwhile, in Novosibirsk, 1,750 miles east of Moscow, scientists were taking a growing interest in genetics. In his lifetime, Catherine Merridale said, he was not made the figure of vilification that others were in the Soviet period. At the end of his career, he was left to work at a little farm on the Lenin Hills outside Moscow, which was eventually shut down, but he was not attacked as he had attacked others.

PAULI'S EXCLUSION PRINCIPLE

In 1925, Wolfgang Pauli made a decisive contribution to atomic theory through his discovery of a new and fundamental law of nature, the exclusion principle or, as it became known, the Pauli principle. It asserts that no two electrons in an atom can be at the same time in the same state or configuration. It was groundbreaking as it explained a huge range of phenomena, from the chemical behaviour of the elements to why matter is stable, and, for this, he won the Nobel Prize in Physics in 1945. Pauli also correctly predicted the existence of the neutrino and astonished and intrigued his peers. He was called the 'conscience of physics', yet he was fascinated by mysticism, alchemy and dreams, which he explored with the psychoanalyst Carl Jung.

‡—•—‡

With Melvyn to discuss Pauli and his exclusion principle were: Frank Close, fellow emeritus at Exeter College, Oxford; Michela Massimi, professor of philosophy of science at the University of Edinburgh; and Graham Farmelo, fellow of Churchill College, Cambridge.

By 1900, the year Pauli was born, scientists knew that matter was made of elements and that the elements were all made of atoms. Starting at that point, Frank Close proceeded to introduce us as simply as possible to ideas of some complexity. It was also known at that time that scientists could order the atoms of the different elements by mass, where hydrogen was the lightest, then helium, and, finally, the heaviest naturally occurring element, uranium. While each element had some unique properties, there were some common features that kept recurring. For example, some elements are inert, such as neon, argon and helium, while others are very active.

FRANK CLOSE: *And they noticed that, when you looked at this ordering, the inert elements appeared regularly and either side of them would be an element that was very active, like sodium or chlorine, for example. And this periodic recurrence of common properties became known as the periodic table.*

This was an observable, empirical rule that worked but nobody knew why. Another thing about elements that was surprising was that, if the atoms were heated up, they would emit light but not the whole rainbow. Passing the light through a kind of spectrograph, they would make a bar code of individual colours, which became known as spectra. Again, nobody knew why atoms were doing this.

Just before Pauli's birth, scientists learned that atoms had some inner structure. The electron was discovered, which was negatively charged, and the atoms were soon shown to consist of these electrons orbiting a central nucleus with positive charge. The problem with that was that it was impossible, according to Newton's laws of physics, as electrons whirling around a nucleus, held together by the electrical force, should spiral into the nucleus in a fraction of a second. There would be no atoms, and that was a great paradox that had to be solved, Frank Close said.

Niels Bohr (1885–1962) had an insight into what was really going on with atoms. He deduced that the electrons were restricted to what he called 'orbits' and were not free to travel anywhere. Using maths, he said that, with the rotary motion, as they whirl around, the angular momentum has to be a multiple of an integer, a whole number times some fundamental quantity, which became the quantum.

FRANK CLOSE: *Electrons can't go anywhere – they have to have one of these magic values. And this gives rise to an analogy that it was like having a ladder with rungs on: if you hold the ladder vertically, you can be on a high rung with high energy or a low rung with low energy but you can't be between rungs. So the electrons had to be on a rung somewhere. And they could jump from a high rung to a low rung.*

If, metaphorically, the electrons did jump from a high rung to a low rung, then the energy that they lost was emitted as light of a characteristic colour. These ideas emerged around 1913, when Pauli was a schoolboy.

Pauli came from an affluent family of Czech-Austrian origin, Michela Massimi told us, and his father went to a school in Prague with a son of the great physicist and philosopher Ernst Mach (1838–1916).

Mach was the author of *The Science of Mechanics* in which he famously criticised Newton's ideas of space and time and he was hugely influential, with Einstein regarding Mach as a precursor of relativity theory. He was also a philosopher who influenced the Vienna Circle of logical empiricists with his well-known anti-metaphysical attitude. Pauli's father had converted to Catholicism, married Bertha Camilla Schütz, a prominent Austrian woman who had written on the French Revolution. When Pauli was born, Mach was invited to become his godfather. The story goes, that many years later, Pauli said, jokingly, that, because Mach was such a great influence on him, he was baptised not so much Catholic but anti-metaphysical, a line of reasoning that remained for the rest of his career.

When he was eighteen, Pauli went to Munich to study with the leading spectroscopist of the time (someone who studies the interaction between matter and electromagnetic radiation), Arnold Sommerfeld (1868–1951).

MICHELA MASSIMI: *Arnold Sommerfeld was so impressed by the mathematical ability of the young Pauli that, when Albert Einstein declined the invitation to write an encyclopaedia article on relativity theory, he asked his student, his eighteen-year-old Pauli, whether he wanted to write the article. And so here we have a young university student producing an incredible encyclopaedia article on relativity theory.*

The result was published in 1921 and was welcomed as an outstanding achievement by some of the great mathematicians of the time. Beyond writing a simple survey of the theory, Pauli pointed out problems in relativity theory, such as the problem of the structure of matter, to which he himself was to turn. He spent a period in Copenhagen with Niels Bohr, and, in 1928, he got his first full professorship at the Swiss Federal Institute of Technology in Zurich, or ETH, although the story is that this was only after that position had been declined by his rival, Werner Heisenberg.

There was another quantum nettle to grasp when understanding Pauli's contributions.

MELVYN BRAGG: *Can you tell us about Pauli's idea of two-valuedness in (I was reading that carefully) two-valuedness in electronics?*

GRAHAM FARMELO: *This was perhaps his greatest contribution. We wind the clock back to about 1924. He's in Hamburg, he's a night owl, visiting the red-light district, having loveless sex in the evening, showing up very late in the mornings, thinking very deeply about these spectra that Frank was talking about …*

MELVYN BRAGG: *All human life is here.*

The spectra questions were those mentioned above, where atoms were making jumps from rung to rung, and the experimenters were trying to make sense of the discrete frequencies of light. This was a big problem.

GRAHAM FARMELO: *The thing that Pauli did so brilliantly was concentrate on one particular set of problems, and that was what's called the alkali element, lithium, sodium, potassium and so on. Now the reason these were special was that those particular elements, people had worked out, consist of shells, which you can imagine very crudely as a kind of sphere, like a soccer ball of electrons with one electron around the outside, which you call a valence electron.*

Graham Farmelo told us that, if the atoms, mentioned above, were subjected to a magnetic field, that could alter the frequency of the spectral lines and that was puzzling to scientists. Pauli said that he could account for those spectral lines if the electron did not just have 'three quantum numbers that specified the state of the electron'. But, if that outer electron, the valence electron, had what he called a two-valuedness, that accounted for the spectral lines and also for the number of electrons that were in that shell.

MELVYN BRAGG: *So what is this two-valuedness?*

GRAHAM FARMELO: *Well, he didn't know.*

MELVYN BRAGG: *I love it when you say things like that.*

People asked Pauli what he meant, and he was very cautious in his replies. Graham Farmelo continued, 'He wrote it in his very, very clear way that it was due to a particular non-classically describable two-valuedness of the valence electron.' He was saying that there was something doubled about that but he was not prepared to say what it was. We moved on, much like Pauli's peers, in hope of clarification later.

Melvyn asked Frank Close to explain the exclusion principle, the idea for which Pauli is best remembered. He started by saying that this related to electrons, one of the fundamental constituents of all atoms, in that, if there is an electron already in an atom in a place, you cannot put another electron in there, it is excluded. As an example, if Frank Close were to rap the table, his hand would not pass through the table because the electrons in the outer rim of his knuckle were trying to occupy a state that was already being occupied by an electron in the wood of the table, so it was excluded. This requirement that electrons have to go in special places, as occupied states are already excluded, gives rise to structure and to the different chemical natures of the atoms. Returning to the ladder analogy, we can start on the bottom rung with hydrogen, which has a single electron, and the rungs higher up grow wider to accommodate more electrons. The bottom rung, the simplest one, can only be occupied by two, which Frank Close said related to the two-valuedness that Graham Farmelo was mentioning.

FRANK CLOSE: *One electron, that's hydrogen; two electrons, that's helium, and you fill that rung, and helium is chemically inert because the rung is full. Now, if you want to go to the next element, lithium, you have to go to the next rung. Lithium is very active. The next rung's got a different shape, it turns out you can fill that, and they're eventually filled when you've got up to about ten altogether. And there, I think, you're now at neon, if I'm keeping track of things, which again is inert. Every time a rung was filled, you got chemical inertness. Add one or remove one, you get chemical activity.*

The filling of the rungs was because of Pauli's exclusion principle, that you cannot put an electron on a rung that is already full, you cannot put one in a state that is already occupied. This principle, he added, forces the electrons to go into different places in the jigsaw and build up structures. From this, you get atoms and chemistry, you get solids, you get crystals. The significance is vast.

Michela Massimi told how the news of Pauli's idea spread very quickly. He called it a rule that could account for a series of anomalies when looking at spectra and problems with the periodic table. As far as she knew, the first person to call it a principle was Paul Dirac (1902–84) in 1926.

MICHELA MASSIMI: *Pauli announced it in a letter to Alfred Landé who was a prominent experimental physicist at Tubingen at the end of 1924. The news spread. A month later, Niels Bohr sent a letter from Copenhagen to Pauli saying, 'We're all very excited for the very many beautiful things you have discovered, and I don't have to hide any criticism because you, yourself, Pauli, have described the whole thing as sheer madness.'*

People really were scratching their heads about the exclusion rule and what it meant, we heard. But Pauli's insight was visionary. People who came after him introduced the term of electro-spin. A young PhD student from Columbia called Ralph Kronig said that maybe we can interpret the two-valuedness by thinking of the electron as a spinning top that can be spun clockwise or anti-clockwise, and that gives you the two values, plus one half and minus one half. Pauli, we heard, dismissed that idea as witty nonsense but, soon afterwards, two Dutch-American physicists, George Uhlenbeck and Samuel Goudsmit, published a paper introducing the idea of the electro-spin.

Graham Farmelo picked up on Michela Massimi's mention of Kronig who, he said, could have had a Nobel Prize-winning discovery, but Pauli broke him with his criticism. With his personality as it was, he could take ideas and crush them in people's arms. One of his ex-wives later said he used to walk around their apartment polishing his barbs to make them as funny and poisonous as possible.

GRAHAM FARMELO: *There's another physicist called Paul Ehrenfest, who walked up to Pauli. Allegedly, their first words were, he said to Pauli, 'I like your physics better than I like you.' And Pauli said, 'Well, for me, it's the other way around.'*

In that case, though, Pauli and Ehrenfest became firm friends. Pauli also, to the surprise of some, became close to Carl Jung, the great psychoanalyst. For someone so rigorous and logical, Pauli was very interested in the paranormal. In 1927, soon after his mother had killed herself, his father married a woman Pauli's age and Pauli had his ill-fated marriage with a cabaret dancer, toured America and, drunk, broke his arm. His father steered him towards Jung. And then, Graham Farmelo said, they formed an improbable friendship. Pauli

Albert Einstein with
Wolfgang Pauli.

had become interested in psychology, partly from his closeness to Niels Bohr, who had very wide interests, and he agreed to have his dreams analysed, probably by one of Jung's students.

MELVYN BRAGG: *Frank, are these two things irreconcilable or is it just the way a man lives his life?*

FRANK CLOSE: *I'm just making this up as I go along, but Jung, with his idea of the collective unconscious, the feeling that there is something going on beyond that that we are immediately aware of, is not radically different from Pauli, who is here at the birth of quantum mechanics and, fifty, sixty years later, we still use quantum mechanics without being quite comfortable as to what's going on.*

Pauli's second *pièce de résistance*, as Graham Farmelo described it, was his idea that predicted the neutrino. The nuclei of atoms can, in some cases, decay randomly and this is what we call radioactive decay, and there are different types. In one particular type of decay, a very high-energy electron comes out of the atomic nucleus unpredictably. From measurements, it appeared that the total energy before the process was not the same as it was afterwards. Some energy appeared to go missing. Niels Bohr thought that this may mean that energy conservation, which was a really sacred principle, might even be wrong. What was more, the electron came out with a range of energies, not one, which was odd. Pauli took his time and thought all this through, and came up with a third particle to go with the proton and electron.

GRAHAM FARMELO: *He wrote to a conference of physicists suggesting, very tentatively, that what was going on was that, in addition to the electron charging out of the nucleus, there was a particle that we don't see. Now this particle, he deduced, very cleverly, from looking at the data, would have no electrical charge. It would have the same spin as the electron and very, very little mass. So he suggested this particle – it was later called the neutrino.*

He and many others at the time thought this particle would be undetectable. (Speaking after the programme, Graham Farmelo told how Pauli learned of the discovery of the neutrino while he was at CERN and read it out to a seminar, which must have been a wonderful moment. Frank Close added that Pauli handed over a case of champagne, which he had promised to do years before, on its discovery.)

For all the importance of his ideas, it took twenty years for Pauli to be awarded a Nobel Prize and, in 1934, it was not as though he was edged out by a rival. In that year, no prize was awarded for physics as it was thought there was no one good enough. The view of the committee apparently was that 'Pauli's receptivity exceeds his originality'. He won it, though, in 1945 for his exclusion principle.

MICHELA MASSIMI: *The great legacy of Pauli is his visionary ability of realising the limits of classical physics in dealing with quantum entities. He was one of the few people at the time really working, still, within the old quantum theory that realised the limits of applying classical models to describing quantum entities. [He] remains one of the unfairly overlooked figures of quantum mechanics.*

GRAHAM FARMELO: *I think Pauli [was], unquestionably, a great physicist. He did say later on, towards the end of his life, that he thought of himself, as a young man, as a revolutionary but, later on, he realised that he was a classicist rather than a revolutionary.*

In the studio afterwards, Melvyn wanted to know more about Pauli's fixation with the number 137 to the point that, on his deathbed, he was reportedly excited to learn that he was in a room with number 137 on the door. Graham Farmelo told him that this is a number related to the strength of the electromagnetic forces, a pure number that appears, and many people were fixated by it. Melvyn asked for clarification.

GRAHAM FARMELO: *In quantum electrodynamics, there is a scale that has to be set somewhere, and this scale is encoded in a number that happens to have the value empirically of almost 137 – so near to it that people thought it was precisely 137 and that this somehow was significant. And, even today, people say that, if you're trying to guess a theoretical physicist's PIN, try 137.*

This prompted Graham Farmelo to tell a joke about Pauli, God and 137, which would be ruined if transcribed here, but can be heard at the end of the podcast. Michela Massimi recalled an odd book that Pauli and Jung wrote together, before, finally, Frank Close, confessing he had never fully understood Pauli's fascination with the psychic phenomena, remembered one of Pauli's comments.

FRANK CLOSE: *He's made a prediction that perhaps we ought to enshrine in the* In Our Time *archive. He said that, in his view, the science of future reality will neither by psychic nor physical, but somehow both, and somehow neither.*

PHILOSOPHY

Philosophy has always daunted me. The homespun philosophy of 'Doc' in John Steinbeck was a joy, the ruminations of Montaigne are immediately understandable, some Greeks could tell it comprehensively – indeed, Socrates, thought by some to be the originator (through the writing of his admirer, Plato), made it his life's work to break through obfuscations and reveal the light of logic clearly. Zeno's paradoxes are brilliant brainteasers. Nietzsche, in parts, is a heady romp to a teenage autodidact. Confucius can be as accessible as a ten times table and the great tradition of Arab philosophers in the Middle Ages speak directly to the reader – and all of these have been included in the philosophy programmes.

So, when in a magazine interview with an English philosopher, I said, 'I know damn-all about philosophy,' a remark that condemned me out of my own mouth, what did I mean? Largely, contemporary philosophy, reaching back three centuries to Descartes' 'cogito ergo sum' (I think therefore I am), gaining traction in the Enlightenment and becoming a specialism that is now, to outsiders like myself, as daunting as physics. Yet its practitioners whom we have had on the programme have been generous in trying to reach across the divide that has undoubtedly developed between philosophy and other thinking and given us a hand. But, to my loss, I find that they are burrowed so deeply in what has become an esoteric pursuit (to many of the rest of us), as mysterious as medieval alchemy and carrying out not dissimilar processes of turning dross into gold.

I'm sure it all comes down to teaching. If you take up philosophy at or just before university and are well taught, the odds are you will be for ever after blessed with a set of intellectual tools of outstanding pleasure and utility. Even so, I'd guess that rather like, say, Sanskrit scholars, you will be aware that your expertise is not everywhere available and communicable. The Vienna School, so dazzlingly represented in this country by A. J. Ayer, became something of an imperial movement in thought but, I'd guess, only a few of its more memorable catchphrases were ever in general circulation. The work of Bertrand Russell could be said to have bridged the gap like no other. His *History of Western Philosophy* still reads like a meat-and-potatoes thriller. But his mathematical philosophy is caviar for the general.

Philosophers themselves have not been kind about philosophers. Cicero wrote, 'There is no statement so absurd that no philosopher will make it.' He led the way.

And then there were the more general thinkers, from Voltaire – with what he unashamedly called his *Lettres Philosophiques* (which would not pass muster as philosophy today) – to John Gray (his work and various other essays of ideas are equally accessible today and can claim the word 'philosophy'). Though I doubt this would be allowed into the masonry of today's hard-core professional philosophers who can make your eyes water.

And yet, however intractable they seem, we/I have an appetite for 'real' philosophers. Like mathematicians and physicists, they are cleverer than the rest of us and, if they need their own language, so be it. One day in the future, we will catch up and all will be revealed.

For me, there have been golden moments, as when I was discovering string theory in the company of scholars to whom it was as easy as pi, and, yes, I understood it! On that Thursday morning, I was a string theorist for a full twenty minutes. There have been similar epiphanies in discovering modern philosophy.

I am here talking about philosophers who are leagues away from the thoughtful essayists and intellectual observers of our life and times. The word 'philosophy' in the tradition of Voltaire can be applied to the latter, I think. What is often impenetrable is the philosophy so closely taught in universities today, which, sadly, has cut it off from the commonwealth of general knowledge. Temporarily, I hope.

KANT'S CATEGORICAL IMPERATIVE

Immanuel Kant (1724–1804) was one of the great thinkers of the Enlightenment, an age in which reason was the dominant force in philosophy as it was in science. Rather than relying on emotions or faith, Kant argued that the best way to distinguish right from wrong was to be rational. He argued that when someone was doing the right thing, that person was doing what was the universal law for everybody. This idea has been influential on moral philosophy ever since and is known as the 'categorical imperative'. Taking this further, Kant argued that simply existing as a human being was valuable in itself, so that every human owed moral responsibilities to other humans and was owed responsibilities in return, a fundamental aspect of modern human rights.

With Melvyn to discuss Kant's categorical imperative were: Alison Hills, professor of philosophy at St John's College, Oxford; David Oderberg, professor of philosophy at the University of Reading; and John Callanan, senior lecturer in philosophy at King's College London.

In his childhood in Königsberg in East Prussia, now Russian Kaliningrad, Kant's family had fairly modest but reasonably comfortable means; his father was a harness maker, and Kant was devoted to his mother.

DAVID ODERBERG: *He had an education in a Pietist school, the Collegium Fridericianum, which emphasised evangelicalism, fundamentalism, rigorous morality, personal Christianity and so on. He rebelled against that; he found it quite stifling to his independence of mind.*

Kant went on to study at the University of Königsberg where he was to spend the rest of his life, starting off lecturing on science, mathematics, geography, geology, everything under the sun, but philosophy was his main interest and he became a philosopher, studying the branch of philosophy called ethics, or moral philosophy.

DAVID ODERBERG: *[Moral philosophers] are concerned with concepts of right and wrong in the moral sense not just as in 'What's the right wallpaper for my bedroom?' but morally right. 'What are the right actions that we should carry out? How should we act towards other people? How should we act towards ourselves? How should we develop our character? What is the concept of moral obligation? What are the grounds of right and wrong?'*

Kant was taught in a rationalist tradition at Königsberg, one in which philosophers were extremely optimistic about what human reason could tell us, where we could think for ourselves and could come up with knowledge of God, of our own souls, of our freedom and of what is morally right and wrong. He was also influenced by two philosophers who were much more sceptical about the powers of human reason.

ALISON HILLS: *Hume had ideas about theoretical reason, about these ideas about knowledge of God, thinking that human reason is much more limited than the rationalist philosophers thought. We just cannot prove the existence of God, and much of what we think of as our knowledge of the world is actually instinct, or habit. We don't know what the future will be like, there are lots of things that we just don't know.*

Hume thought that human reason was not a powerful thing at all. Reason is pushed about by our desires. It can tell us how to get what we want, but it cannot tell us what we ought to do, and Kant talked of Hume 'waking him up from his dogmatic slumber'. He also said that Rousseau was a huge influence on him, in his moral philosophy, in his ideas about equality of humans, and in reason being something that can be destructive or problematic.

ALISON HILLS: *Rousseau talks about how I can be happy with my life, and then I compare myself to other people and think, 'It is fantastic that I am on the radio, I am so excited. But Melvyn's on the radio every week. Actually, it is not so great after all!' These sort of reasonings, giving me these comparisons ... I turn out to be less happy than if I hadn't had reason at all. And Kant says happiness cannot be the basis of our morality.*

Kant's huge, monumental work of theoretical philosophy was *The Critique of Pure Reason* and, in that, he asked how we can have knowledge of the world, and among the pages of that really enormous, important, influential book are ideas that were really important later for moral philosophy.

ALISON HILLS: *Kant thinks that there are limits to what we can know about the existence of God, we cannot prove that God exists. He attacks all these arguments that the rational philosophers have put forward, people like Descartes, trying to prove the existence of God, we can't know that. So we can't base ethics in knowledge of God, that won't work. Another very important limit is on human freedom; we cannot know that we are free; we also can't know that we are not free; we also can't know that God doesn't exist.*

These are questions we cannot answer, with reason, and that is where Kant thought practical philosophy could come in.

In 1785, Kant wrote *The Groundwork of the Metaphysics of Morals*, the focus of this programme. In this, he was trying to extend the Newtonian analysis into philosophy, to extend the use of reason to the questions of morality.

JOHN CALLANAN: *The central questions are: what is moral value? Is there such a thing, and what is it? How would we define it? Once we have defined it, is it possible that we might even realise it in our day-to-day actions? His core idea that begins* The Groundwork *is that you have to look to the subject, and to the subject's will, as the source of moral value. The subject being the individual.*

Kant's question is: what is moral goodness? Moral goodness, he said, has this character of being unconditional. An umbrella is good for keeping dry, if that is what you want, but we think that there is a different category of goodness, such as actions like refraining from torture, which is not just good in this or that circumstance but good in every circumstance for every person, always. He calls these 'unconditional goods'.

JOHN CALLANAN: *If there is morality, it is something unconditional and he wants to know: what is that? His answer is the only thing that can be a source of unconditional value is a good will, that is the individual subject's own capacity to form their intentions and plans, to perform actions.*

Will is your capacity to form intentions to perform an action and commit to them. They are your plans. They are the reasoning that you have engaged upon in forming those plans. Where that takes Kant is the idea that there is an inward turn.

*Kant was influenced by the
work of Isaac Newton.*

JOHN CALLANAN: *We are not looking for moral value now, out
in the consequences of our actions. We are not looking for moral
value in a divine lawgiver or something like that, or in conventional
values. We are looking for moral value inwardly, which is akin to
the Lutheran background. We are looking for that very personal,
authentic, moral, sincere activity.*

The question then is: if we are now turning towards the subject's
reasoning processes as the source of moral value, how do we get
to objectivity? It is for that reason that Kant wanted to appeal to
the categorical imperative as a way in which a subject can realise
objective truths. It is not enough to have a plan to do the right thing,
you have got to do the right thing for the right reasons.

JOHN CALLANAN: *He uses an example of a shopkeeper who doesn't rip off his customers, he keeps his prices the same for everybody, that's the right thing to do. But what has been the shopkeeper's motivation? His motivation is: if it got out that I was ripping people off, I would be ruined. So it is very prudential reasoning. However, another shopkeeper might keep his prices the same simply because it is the right thing to do, it is the fair policy.*

When looking at Kant, David Oderberg suggested, there is the exoteric and the esoteric, where the exoteric is really what John Callanan was talking about – doing things for the right reason.

DAVID ODERBERG: *The deeper motivation in Kant is this idea that morality has to be pure, it has to be purified of anything contingent, anything empirical, anything to do with personal happiness, personal desire, and even things that we normally regard as moral, such as love, sympathy, benevolence, desire for the welfare of others, things that we normally take as moral philosophers to be central to morality, are absolutely contaminating for him of morality.*

The only thing for Kant that is absolutely unconditionally good is a good will. That is not quite the same as intention; the good will is the subject as the personal legislator of morality.

MELVYN BRAGG: *So if the person thinks: if I do this, and everybody does this, we are okay.*

DAVID ODERBERG: *He gives examples. The first formulation of the categorical imperative: 'Act only on those maxims or principles that can be willed to be universal laws of nature for all rational beings.' I have to ask myself, as a moral legislator, can the principle that I am considering – should I lie, should I do this, should I do that, should I treat people this way or that way, shall I treat myself this way or that way? – can I will that to be a universal law?*

Kant gave examples of what he held to be categorically true, and they were chosen carefully because he thought they were examples of every type of duty, which is his word for the reason to act morally, Alison Hills said. There are duties to other people, and there are duties to yourself. Among those, there is the duty not to make a promise you do not intend to keep; Kant says that we should think what it would be like if everybody acted on that. There is a duty to help others, since another feature of us, he thought, is that we depend on other people.

ALISON HILLS: *There are things that I will for myself that I can't achieve unless other people help me. So I can't, at the same time, will that no one ever helps any one. Similarly, I have a duty not to will the maxim of never helping anyone. I have a duty (he calls it an imperfect duty) to help other people sometimes.*

Before Kant, John Callanan continued, there was the Golden Rule of 'do unto others as you would have them do unto you', and there are some similarities here, but Kant is quite emphatic that what he is proposing here is *not* the Golden Rule. The Golden Rule would encourage him only to act on the desires where he will be happy if someone else were to act on those desires towards him, but that was not really the type of moral psychology Kant thought appropriate.

JOHN CALLANAN: *What if someone has, for example, masochistic desires, he doesn't mind receiving pain every so often. Does the Golden Rule then sanction that they can inflict pain on others now and again? Or perhaps someone would reason: it is okay for me never to help someone, so long as I never receive any help. That satisfies the Golden Rule as we have just understood it. But Kant thinks it is just obvious that, if someone is in need, drowning in front of you, it is no excuse to say: 'Well, I wouldn't accept any help if I were drowning, so therefore I don't have to offer you any help.'*

We have some basic moral responsibilities, obligations to others, which are issued by reason itself. What if everybody did this? If you believe in reason at all, then you can see that you can use it for moral reasoning also.

Where, Melvyn asked, was God in all this? For Kant, David Oderberg said, it was not clear. Biographers disagree over whether he was an atheist, an agnostic or a sincere theist, which goes to show how difficult it is to know exactly what Kant did think about God. From his statements in *The Groundwork* and other writings, we understand him to say we must believe in God.

DAVID ODERBERG: *Why must we believe in God? Well,* The Critique of Pure Reason *is that we can't prove the existence of God through theoretical means, those proofs are folly. But we don't want to give up on God, as it were. So where do we find a foundation for belief in God? We find it in morality, in duty, this wonderful duty that he rhapsodises about in* The Critique of Practical Reason, *particularly: 'The starry heavens above me and the moral law within me.'*

How is it possible that this moral law has been given to us from somewhere? It is possible, Kant thought, as we are free, we are able to legislate for ourselves and we are immortal as well. Not that he could theoretically prove it, but we must hope for it and we must postulate the existence of God. Is God the supreme lawgiver? Kant never said.

DAVID ODERBERG: *He wants to extricate himself from the Enlightenment idea; you know, morality is not imposed on us by a divine lawgiver, but somehow God is the backing. Maybe one of the most helpful ways of looking at it – and it may be incorrect, it is just my take on it – I think he identifies God with the moral law.*

Alison Hills turned to the place of happiness in Kant's moral philosophy. There are lots of moral theories that say happiness is the important thing, and utilitarianism is the key one there. Kant did not think that happiness played that important a role, partly because he thought it was a very elusive goal for us.

ALISON HILLS: *We are never really sure exactly what will make us happy, so we can't base anything as important as duties on that. But he also says that we must do our duty even if it is not going to make us happy, or even anybody else happy. We must not lie, we must not torture people, even if that would make ourselves, or other people, happy.*

Kant did think that the highest good is virtue rewarded, with the good will and happiness combined. And he asked: do good people get rewarded in this life? No, they do not. We must hope that there is another life where we will be able to perfect our virtue because, Alison Hills suggested, Kant thought it would just be too depressing if it weren't true and it would undermine our motivation.

Melvyn queried this, as we had heard that Kant's idea was that we were doing something not because of some higher authority figure, but because of some inward authority figure that somehow had accreted to us.

JOHN CALLANAN: *Kant seems to have religious and anti-religious moments. The anti-religious moment seems to be the one that you just described. We look to ourselves for the source of moral authority and moral decision-making. There are other moments where thinking of ourselves as God's creatures, thinking perhaps that there might be some reward for us in an afterlife, has to find a place in his system.*

There was a deep ambivalence frequently in Kant's thinking, it was noted, and this was one example.

David Oderberg introduced what has been called the humanity formulation of the categorical imperative, which is the second formulation and has perhaps been more influential in its long-term legacy than the first formulation.

DAVID ODERBERG: *The second formulation: always act on those maxims such that you treat humanity never merely as a means, but always as an end, an end in itself. The idea there is we use people as means to ends all the time; when I go to the supermarket, I am using a checkout person as a means to get my bottle of milk, that's okay. But what Kant objects to is the idea of using other rational beings as pure means to our own ends. To put it in contemporary jargon: exploitative behaviour that treats people purely as objects for furtherance of one's own ends.*

We can see immediately the influence of that kind of idea and the notion of dignity. We are rational beings and that makes us an end in itself, to be respected absolutely. We can say that human rights, human dignity, the dignity of the person, a lot of that can be traced back to Kant.

Probably the most difficult question mentioned so far, Alison Hills suggested, was how free we are to act morally. It was absolutely crucial to Kant and he thought that, if we have a duty to do something, it must be possible for us to do that thing.

ALISON HILLS: *He is very concerned that we might be just a member of the causal order, like anything else, where one thing happens after another, and there aren't actually options open to us that we can freely choose between. Another really important strand is that one of the grounds of the value of the will is our capacity to act freely, to make choices for ourselves, but, as we mentioned before, he thought we couldn't prove that we are free.*

In the third part of *The Groundwork*, Kant tried to show that there is room to think of ourselves as free. He said there is a shift where you think of yourself as acting, and you see that, when you act and you are making a decision, you must think of yourself as having an option.

There is another formulation of the categorical imperative, the autonomy formulation, which John Callanan said was very influential, and it relates to that notion of freedom. We have to presume that we are free and we have a responsibility to decide for ourselves. This is about growing up and not outsourcing moral responsibility to some parental figure, to conventional morality or religious figures, but rather deciding for yourself what you think is the morally correct thing to do. Kant described that as acting autonomously.

JOHN CALLANAN: *It can't be that I perform moral actions because it is God's will, Kant says, that can't be my moral motivation. If it is, then the reason I am helping someone who is, say, drowning in front of me is because God would like it. There it seems like my motivation is just to win the approval of some divine parental figure, but that's distorting proper moral motivation. You should help someone in need because it is the right thing to do.*

To this, David Oderberg added his thoughts about how to place Kant in the history of philosophy, and this emphasis, this almost 'fetishisation' of duty. Moral philosophers believe in duties but there are also other things in morality, such as what is permissible, what is admirable, what is praiseworthy and so on; there is the building of character.

DAVID ODERBERG: *For Kant, it is duty, duty, duty above all else, only holy duty, that is the holy thing. It is Prussianism, it is Prussianism. I know that I am probably going to get my colleagues trying to kill me on this one, but that is Prussianism. It is so easy to say, 'Oh, well, of course duty, so therefore obedience to the moral law' – that is kind of a caricature. Unreasoned obedience to the moral law is absolutely crucial for Kant.*

Alison Hills found lots to disagree with there, asserting that obedience to the moral law is something that reason gives to itself; it cannot be unreasoned. Other works that Kant wrote were all about other aspects of character, including the importance of some kinds of love and some kinds of sentiment, and respect was hugely important. Those, David Oderberg suggested, were arguably dilutions of the official theory, as found in *The Groundwork*. John Callanan contended that Kant, when he talked about duty, was using his name for a very ordinary kind of moral psychology that he thought everyone did – it was the notion of reasoning and doing something simply because you thought it was the right thing to do.

Kant's influence was diverse and diffuse throughout the nineteenth century and beyond, David Oderberg said, affecting the Romantic philosophers in both positive and negative ways. In a positive way, there was the idea of the human being's own contribution to the construction of an interpretation of reality. In a negative way, some of the Romantic philosophers feuded with Kant over his destruction of any firm ground for faith. Alison Hills added that Kant is still a really dominant thinker in terms of being against that other strong tradition of utilitarianism or consequentialist thinking that says that what matters is the end result. John Callanan noted that Kant was interested in establishing a culture of reason, where we value reason as the way in which we engage in dialogue with each other; we do not think that our moral transactions are just about who has the stronger passion, who has the stronger desire. 'And I think, to a large degree, he has been successful.'

HANNAH ARENDT

Hannah Arendt was born in 1906 near Hanover in Germany, where her family rarely mentioned their Jewishness. She said she first encountered the word 'Jew' in the anti-Semitic remarks of children as she played in the streets. She escaped to America in 1941 and spent much of her time trying to understand why totalitarianism had dominated Europe so murderously in the twentieth century. To prevent its return, she argued, everyone should engage in political life as in an idealised ancient Greek city state. She also wanted to know what motivated so many to act so atrociously in the Second World War and it was at the trial of Eichmann, one of the main organisers of the Holocaust, that she described what she called the 'banality of evil'.

━┥━●━┝━

With Melvyn to discuss Hannah Arendt were: Lyndsey Stonebridge, professor of humanities and human rights at the University of Birmingham; Frisbee Sheffield, director of studies in philosophy and bye-fellow of Girton College, Cambridge; and Robert Eaglestone, professor of contemporary literature and thought at Royal Holloway, University of London.

Hannah Arendt excelled at school, studying ancient Greek from a young age, which, Frisbee Sheffield said, led to a lifelong interest in classics. She went on to the University of Marburg to study philosophy and theology, where she met the philosopher Martin Heidegger, before moving on to the University of Heidelberg for her doctoral dissertation on the concept of love in St Augustine, studying with another philosopher, Karl Jaspers.

MELVYN BRAGG: *Can we spool back to Heidegger? Because she had a big affair with Heidegger that marked her for the rest of her life. His wife was anti-Semitic; he then became a Nazi and an admirer of Hitler.*

FRISBEE SHEFFIELD: *I think that's why she moved to work under the direction of Karl Jaspers rather than staying at Marburg. And, yes, there was a rupture in their relationship, of course, when he joined the Nazi party and proclaimed support for their views when he was rector at the University of Freiburg. She struggled to come to terms with that.*

Arendt moved to Berlin and came face to face with the growing Nazi movement; she gathered information about anti-Semitism, and was detained for a time by the Gestapo.

She began with philosophy but was to work across politics as well. The events of the war were to politicise her, and she said she learned to think politically from her second husband, Henrich Blücher, who was a revolutionary socialist.

FRISBEE SHEFFIELD: *She resisted being called a 'political philosopher' because of what she saw as an inherent hostility towards politics in most philosophers. One might call her a political thinker, or theorist. But even there she is quite hard to pin down; she doesn't seem to fit into established categories of political thinking. She is not a liberal in any straightforward sense.*

If Blücher taught Arendt to think politically, she said it was Heidegger who had taught her how to think and how to think about things, or how to think in order to do things, and this was what drew her to him. Heidegger taught Arendt that thinking was a way of being a person.

LYNDSEY STONEBRIDGE: *It means that how you think is how you exist. You establish yourself in the world through thinking and through language. As soon as you think about being, you are using words. Arendt will always come back to the thing she borrows from Socrates, and from Heidegger, which is the two-in-one dialogue we always have in our heads.*

The conversation to be had within ourselves was so important to Arendt. She loved the speech at the beginning of Shakespeare's *Richard III*, the soliloquy where Richard is talking to himself and says, 'I am determined to prove a villain.' That was exactly Arendt's model for the thinking, moral self.

LYNDSEY STONEBRIDGE: *Richard, who is, of course, evil, talks himself into doing evil. The non-thinking self won't even have that conversation. She says that, if you are having a dialogue with* *yourself, your actions in the world must reckon with the fact that you are going to have to come home to that voice inside your head. Richard had that voice. It didn't mean that he wasn't evil, but he at least had that voice, 'to prove myself a villain'. Someone like Eichmann didn't have that voice, didn't have that conversation.*

Arendt escaped from the Nazis to Czechoslovakia and, after time in detention camp, was lucky enough to get a visa for America, where she learned English, her third language. She found the people in America socially conformist, which she disliked, but she liked the political structures and political freedom there, which she felt were lacking in Europe.

LYNDSEY STONEBRIDGE: *She was very conscious of her status as a refugee. Earlier in her work, she had written about the distinction between the Jew as pariah, as 'other', as the troublemaker, and the Jew as parvenu, the refugee who wants to assimilate, who doesn't want any trouble. It had become very clear to Arendt, and a lot of other people by the early twentieth century, that the assimilation option was not working, so, in her thinking and her being, she adopted the position of the pariah.*

Hannah Arendt's book *The Origins of Totalitarianism* (1951) brought her some fame. It had a lot of history in it, but was really about her philosophical enquiries into the core of totalitarianism. She found two essential things, one about ideology and the other about terror.

ROBERT EAGLESTONE: *She says that totalitarianism arises when people are disconnected from each other, when they are atomised, when social bonds aren't as strong as they had been. A movement, or a strong man, arises and offers a story, an ideology, which claims to explain everything, why people are unhappy, to its adherents. This story becomes more and more powerful; it means that you can't argue with people who have become Nazis or Stalinists.*

With that power, there becomes only one way to think and, bizarrely, the adherents cannot even experience their own experiences. Arendt had an example from the Stalinist trials of the 1930s, where a man was arrested and accused of being a factory saboteur.

ROBERT EAGLESTONE: *He says: 'Well, the party is always right. I don't think I was a saboteur, but the party is always right. And, if the party says I was a saboteur, I must be a saboteur.' It even takes other people's experience of their own lives. And she calls this the 'rule from within'.*

The terror aspect related to some thoughts that emerged out of Aristotle and Heidegger, the idea that there are two parts to what it is to be a human being. Part of that is the animal, and part is your social, political and legal life.

ROBERT EAGLESTONE: *What totalitarian terror does is split those two bits. Totalitarian regimes take away your name, your identity, your rights, your 'bios', Aristotle calls it, your socio-political world, and reduces you just to your body. Once you are made just to be a body, Arendt says, you are superfluous and, once human beings are made superfluous, you can kill them the way you might kill a flea.*

There are several factors that will allow totalitarianism to happen, Lyndsey Stonebridge added, namely ideology, anti-Semitism, racism, uncontrolled imperial expansion and the elites getting together with the mob. Any one of those things alone cannot cause totalitarianism, there has to be a perfect storm of the different elements working at the same time.

In Arendt's view, there had been a rupture in political thought after the Second World War and the established categories of political thinking needed to be fundamentally rethought. For her, the ancient Greek philosophers were part of that rethinking project.

FRISBEE SHEFFIELD: *Central to her reading of the Greek philosophers is a contrast between the active and the contemplative life. Aristotle and Socrates had a very positive conception, she thought, of the active life, that came to be degraded by Plato.*

Socrates, to Arendt, was the last great philosopher citizen. She thought Socratic conversation was about adjusting to the plural perspectives of other people in a communal space like the Agora, the marketplace where Socrates taught. She was interested, too, in some of Aristotle's thoughts – for instance, that man is, by nature, a political animal.

FRISBEE SHEFFIELD: *She held that what was important for Aristotle was that he thought we realise a distinct human freedom by acting together, talking together with others in a communal space. There was a particular historical moment, which was the trial and death of Socrates in 399 BC. She says that Plato's despair at the death of Socrates motivated an inward turn and a flight from the political realm.*

Arendt was also concerned by the growth of the social or, as she called it, the blob, in place of a political space where ideas were discussed. People became jobholders or functionaries, whereas what she wanted at the heart of any vibrant political community was the notion of consent and dissent.

LYNDSEY STONEBRIDGE: *There had to be a conversation, there has to be something new. When she is looking back to the Greeks, as Frisbee was saying, a lot of people say she was nostalgic for the Greek polis. I don't think that's quite right. What she was nostalgic for was the marketplace of ideas, the idea that something else might happen, that something might change.*

She borrowed the concept from Herodotus of 'isonomia', the principle of equal liberty that any vibrant community needs. There are moments of 'that's not fair' in life that provoke discussion and you need a vibrant political community that can produce change, without risk.

LYNDSEY STONEBRIDGE: *The other two things you need to keep that political community in place are a community that is okay with promising – because if you promise to do things, you make things* *less dangerous, you stabilise things; sometimes you have to break promises, but you have to have a good trust/promise community – and you need a culture of forgiveness, because things go wrong.*

Since 1945, Hannah Arendt had been thinking a lot about the question of evil. She was present at the Eichmann trial in Jerusalem, in 1961. He was a high-level desk-killer in the Holocaust who had been seized by the Israeli secret service in 1960.

ROBERT EAGLESTONE: *He spoke in clichés, he couldn't follow a train of thought, he couldn't understand other people's point of view, he was vulgar. And, she used to think, this man is the evil mass killer? How can this be? She was always opposed to giving the Nazis satanic greatness; the Nazis loved that with their SS uniforms and death-head scarves. These are just people, men, how can they be evil? And she thinks about this phrase, the 'banality of evil'.*

We might think of that phrase as describing the normalisation of evil, the means by which something as evil as mass murder could be turned into something that happens every day.

ROBERT EAGLESTONE: *She talks about (this is the crucial thing) Eichmann's thoughtlessness. It is not carelessness, it's his inability to think, and she says he is hedged around by these linguistic clichés, by his refusal to question, by his lack of sense of the past. And that makes him thoughtless.*

MELVYN BRAGG: *Is that back to what Lyndsey was saying, about him not being Richard III?*

ROBERT EAGLESTONE: *That's right, it is like a living example of exactly that, Eichmann is unable to talk to himself about what he is doing.*

One of the things to be clear about, Frisbee Sheffield continued, especially in light of the vitriolic criticism Arendt received from her use of that phrase, is that she made a very sharp and robust distinction between the doer and the deed. There was nothing banal about the deeds; they were monstrous and wicked.

FRISBEE SHEFFIELD: *Some of her reviewers said that she was claiming that the Holocaust was banal. You have to have a serious amount of ill will to read it [that way]. She neither says nor implies that. Also, she did mean something quite specific by 'banality' – she didn't mean commonplace. She meant specifically that it wasn't rooted in some evil motivation, some satanic greatness. It was an absence.*

Besides, one of the reasons that evil was allowed to thrive, albeit in that banal form, in Arendt's view, was the bureaucratisation of modern life. This is when we become alienated from a way to relate to one another and we start relating to each other through systems.

LYNDSEY STONEBRIDGE: *One of the first things she did when she was a refugee in the States was to write two very good essays on*

Adolf Hitler at a Nazi rally in 1933, the same year that Hannah Arendt escaped Nazi Germany.

Franz Kafka, and it is that world that Kafka could already see. When people have been reduced to jobholders, to identities, to names, [that] allows you to function without having that two-in-one conversation. She is saying that there is a context for radical thoughtlessness, and that context is everything to do with how we organise our social life together.

Arendt said this phenomenon was like a fungus, Melvyn recalled, a growth; you look like you are a bureaucrat sitting at your desk, but there is a fungus inside you that has taken over your brain.

LYNDSEY STONEBRIDGE: *And it spreads. Rebecca West talked about a 'yeasty darkness' in that period. Yeast and fungus don't have roots. This isn't deep evil. This isn't Richard III. This is evil without roots, it is on the surface, it is sticky, it gets everywhere. You can't get rid of it.*

Hannah Arendt's *The Human Condition* (1958) followed *The Origins of Totalitarianism* and, in that, she took on the task of rethinking our established categories of political thought. One of the central strands of that work was an attempt to clarify the active life that was dethroned, for her, by Plato.

FRISBEE SHEFFIELD: *She tries to analyse the three fundamental activities of the active life and to think about how they've been conceived differently in different periods. Those three fundamental activities in* The Human Condition *are labour, work and action. She assesses each of those activities in terms of the contribution they make to human self-realisation and freedom, and how they are able to meet certain conditions of our human life.*

She talks, in the chapter on action, about natality. Heidegger said that philosophy begins in our awareness that we are going to die, and that makes us think about ourselves. Arendt took that idea but turned it the other way around. She, Robert Eaglestone said, held that philosophy began at our birth, both our first birth and when we are born into society and take our role in the marketplace.

There was a sense, Melvyn suggested, that, now and then, Arendt put her foot in it and was careless of the consequences. Robert Eaglestone mentioned a famous case about integration, an article or essay 'Reflections on Little Rock', where she was on the wrong side of history, while saying her tactlessness and mistakes came from deep engagement in her thought and in civic society.

LYNDSEY STONEBRIDGE: *When she wrote* Eichmann in Jerusalem, *she wrote it in the ironic mode. This did not go down very well with the Jewish community. This is the first time some survivors got to speak of their trauma, and it was an extraordinary and emotional outpouring of grief, in Susan Sontag's words. To miss this and to be ironic was seen as deeply wounding.*

Arendt also thought that the testimonial culture of the trial was getting in the way of inventing a new law that could cope with crimes against humanity and, if we were distracted from that, those crimes were going to keep on happening.

Despite the darkness of her themes, Arendt in *The Human Condition* was optimistic that change could happen.

FRISBEE SHEFFIELD: *She thought of calling the book* Amor Mundi, *love of the world. That brings out this sense that she was re-throning the political space, in contrast to the rejection of it that she saw in the Platonic and Christian tradition. It is the principle of natality here, that is the principle of optimism in the work, and she describes that with a quote from Augustine, 'A beginning be made, Man was created.'*

Despite her optimism that change could happen, Arendt feared that totalitarianism might recur.

ROBERT EAGLESTONE: *Nazism had been defeated, Stalinism had gone, but all the conditions were continually moving around, continually about, and we should be constantly aware of the dangers of totalitarianism, particularly whenever human beings are made superfluous.*

FRISBEE SHEFFIELD: *And a stateless person.*

LYNDSEY STONEBRIDGE: *She said that elements of totalitarianism linger in the political culture: the idea of organised lying – she was very concerned about the Pentagon papers and Watergate. You can't just think that totalitarianism is this big dark cloud that descends on other histories and other places. Potential elements of it are always there.*

STOICISM

The philosophy of Stoicism was founded by Zeno of Citium in the
fourth century BC and flourished in Greece and then in Rome. Its
ideals of inner solitude, forbearance in adversity and the acceptance
of fate won many brilliant adherents and it became the dominant
philosophy across the whole of the ancient world. The ex-slave
Epictetus said, 'Man is troubled not by events, but by the meaning
he gives them.' Seneca, the politician philosopher, declared, 'Life
without the courage for death is slavery.' The stoic thoughts of
Marcus Aurelius, the philosopher emperor, provided a rallying point
for empire builders into the modern age. But what was Stoicism?
How did its ideas of inner retreat come to influence the most
powerful and public men of the classical era and does it still have a
legacy for us today?

With Melvyn to discuss the philosophy of Stoicism were: David Sedley, former Laurence professor of ancient philosophy at the University of Cambridge; the philosopher and historian Jonathan Rée; and Angie Hobbs, professor of the public understanding of philosophy at the University of Sheffield.

Stoicism took its name from the colonnade, or stoa, in Athens where Zeno of Citium and his followers discussed their ideas. Stoicism, Angie Hobbs explained, had a coherent system based on the integrated three pillars of logic, physics and ethics. Stoics argued for a materialistic and deterministic cosmos that was composed, at the conceptual level, of passive matter interpenetrated by active, divine reason. At the observable level, this passive matter took the form of earth and water, and the divine reason took the form of a mixture of fire and air known as *pneuma*.

ANGIE HOBBS: *The key point is that this divine reason organises everything for the best, this is the best of all possible worlds. As an organic entity, the cosmos has a set lifespan and, at the end of each cosmic cycle, all the matter is transmuted into pure, creative, rational fire, out of which the next perfect and absolutely identical cosmos is formed. It has to be identical, because it was perfect to begin with.*

Human reason is a spark of the divine fiery reason, Stoics would say, and so we are part of a greater whole. Our happiness lies in acknowledging that fact and accepting that whatever happens to us, even if at the time it seems to be terrible, is actually part of a greater providential plan. To understand this divine plan, we need to understand human reason, *logos*.

Zeno was setting up the stoa in about 300 BC after Alexander the Great and Philip of Macedon had, effectively, destroyed the Greek city state, the polis, as an independent political unit. It was a time when people were feeling far more powerless than their grandparents had.

ANGIE HOBBS: *This has two particular effects: on the one hand, people are starting to look inwards, and are thinking, 'Well, I can't control my immediate political environment, I can search for my inner peace of mind, I can practise philosophy as a therapy of the soul to give me stability and tranquillity.' On the other hand, perhaps partly as a result of the barriers of the Greek world breaking down under the Macedonian Empire, we have people thinking of themselves as part of a greater unit than the old polis, and starting to think of the way that human beings connect up.*

There were other schools of philosophy in the Greek world at this time, such as the Cynics and the Epicureans. Rather than being diametrically opposed, Jonathan Rée said, they were more like friendship networks, with Socrates the father of them all. Choosing between them was more like choosing between two high street coffee chains than choosing between rationalism and empiricism.

JONATHAN RÉE: *All of them promised to teach you how to lead a better life, how to lead the life of a philosopher, how to imitate Socrates, how to lead a life of virtue where virtue would lead you to happiness, where you would understand that being good and being happy were one and the same thing. This was true of Epicurus and the Epicureans, it was true of Diogenes and the Cynics. Despite their later reputations as diametrically opposed, they were all offering you the happy life of a philosopher.*

The Cynicism of Diogenes had nothing to do with the modern sense of the word cynicism. His Cynicism consisted of taking Platonism very seriously, so seriously that he absolutely despised the social world, he despised human convention, as reflected in later stories of his life.

JONATHAN RÉE: *He lived in a tub, he walked around naked, he masturbated in public to prove that he didn't care what anybody thought. His pupil Crates, a rich man who carried on the tradition, gave away all his money and said that it was wonderful because he got in exchange a quart of lupins and the ability to say, 'I care for nobody.' That was the great prize.*

Crates became Zeno's mentor when Zeno, aged thirty or so, arrived in Athens after a shipwreck and asked if there was anybody in Athens who carried on the tradition of Socrates. He was introduced to Crates, who was walking past.

JONATHAN RÉE: *Here's how Crates teaches him: he tells him he has got to carry a pot of lentil soup around, something servile. Zeno is not happy about this; he tries to hide it under his cloak. Crates smashes the pot so that he has this brown stuff dribbling, like diarrhoea, down his legs, and Crates insists, 'You must not feel ashamed of this.' This is philosophy teaching through humiliation.*

Zeno never became as extravagantly exhibitionist about his contempt for the world as Crates. Stoicism, Jonathan Rée would say, was Cynicism for the shy.

Socrates had made it top of his agenda to ask how we should live, David Sedley continued, but he had also raised some very difficult issues about what goods we should be pursuing in our lives. Socrates pointed out that wisdom is an unconditional good, and you cannot go wrong so long as you know what you are doing. All the other things that people value in their lives are neither good nor bad.

DAVID SEDLEY: *Everybody wants to be rich, everybody wants influence and reputation; but actually wealth is no more good than bad, because if you use it for good purposes it is good, but if you use it to commit genocide, for example, it is a greater bad. So, too, for all of these other supposed goods. The legacy of Socrates, to Zeno among others, is the question: in that case, should we be pursuing these things at all?*

Zeno was too conventional to go for the opt-out solution that the Cynics went for. His great breakthrough was to see there was a way in which you could adopt the same Socratic value system but, nevertheless, lead a very conventional life. The reason he gave was that, although it is true that things like wealth are not intrinsically good, nature has created us to pursue these things. It is our instinct from birth to pursue certain things and to avoid other things; and, as we grow up and become rational, we find increasingly that we are simply, by nature, pursuing rational goals.

DAVID SEDLEY: *The goal of life, according to Zeno, is actually to make your life totally in conformity with nature, and that doesn't mean back to nature, it means a rational cosmic nature that has an overall plan of which you are just a tiny part. As you learn to conform your activities to nature's rational plan, you discover that the things that, as a matter of course, are natural to pursue, such as good health, may have to be varied.*

In the end, if you succeed, you will understand what nature wants for you and you will go along with it willingly. Chrysippus, who was the most important of Zeno's followers, remarked that, if he knew that he was fated to be ill, he would want to be ill.

DAVID SEDLEY: *One remark that Zeno and Chrysippus both made about this is you should think of yourself as like a dog tied to the back of the cart. You are going to have to follow anyway, you have got no choice, but either you can be dragged or you can go willingly. The aim of Stoicism is to find out where the cart is going and to follow willingly.*

The inheritors of Plato's Academy said that, in this materialistic, deterministic universe, the Stoics had taken away human responsibility and made people lazy. Why call the doctor if you are fated to be ill? To that, the Stoics would say that they are fated to get better ... but only if they call the doctor first.

ANGIE HOBBS: *In terms of human responsibility, they say, it is also up to you how you respond to fate, how you react to it. Are you the willing dog, or are you the reluctant dog? They likened fate to somebody pushing a cylinder down a hill and they said, yes, it is that push of fate that gets the cylinder rolling, but it is the fact that it is that cylindrical shape that keeps it rolling down the hill. Our characters are absolutely crucial, and things are up to us.*

Stoicism was an extremely prestigious philosophy in Athens by the middle of the second century BC, but other philosophies were competing with it. From this position, thanks to what became known as the Embassy of the Three Philosophers, it went on to become very influential in Rome.

DAVID SEDLEY: *The year 155 BC was the year in which philosophy arrived in Rome; the Athenians had been fined a huge sum of 500 talents for pillaging the city of Oropos. Because Greece was under Roman control at this time, if they wanted to appeal against the fine, they had to appeal to the Roman senate. They took the most extraordinary decision: they decided they would send the three heads of the three major philosophical schools as their ambassadors to Rome.*

That delegation included Diogenes of Babylon, who was then head of the Stoic school, along with the head of the Academy and the head of the Peripatetic school. When they arrived in Rome, these philosophers turned out to have the status of superstars (and they did get the fine reduced to 100 talents). They gathered crowds around them and gave demonstrations of their philosophical virtuosity and all of them made an impression.

DAVID SEDLEY: *The Romans were particularly impressed by Diogenes the Stoic, who was said to speak with great common sense and sobriety. I think the Roman love affair with Stoicism really did begin at that point.*

The Greek delegation was not received without opposition, and the older Cato was absolutely revolted by these Greek philosophers who were coming, as he thought, to corrupt the youth of Rome. Despite that, by the time of the civil war, 49–46 BC, the great figures Scipio, Pompey, Brutus and Cato the younger had a certain respect for this idea of philosophy. Cato even took his own life in a manner that was seen as consistent with Stoicism.

JONATHAN RÉE: *The story that was told, again and again, was that, after he had been defeated, he had retreated to Tunisia and spent a night reading Plato's* Phaedo *over and over. He had Plato's* Phaedo *in one hand and he had his sword in the other and, the next morning, he disembowelled himself.*

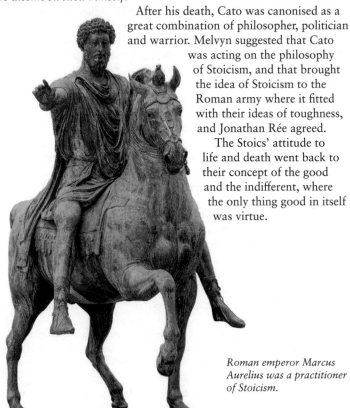

After his death, Cato was canonised as a great combination of philosopher, politician and warrior. Melvyn suggested that Cato was acting on the philosophy of Stoicism, and that brought the idea of Stoicism to the Roman army where it fitted with their ideas of toughness, and Jonathan Rée agreed.

The Stoics' attitude to life and death went back to their concept of the good and the indifferent, where the only thing good in itself was virtue.

Roman emperor Marcus Aurelius was a practitioner of Stoicism.

ANGIE HOBBS: *Other things, such as life and death, in themselves are indifferent, although usually, under normal circumstances, [life is] to be preferred. They make this rather strange distinction between the good and the naturally preferred. However, there can be exceptional circumstances when life is not actually to be naturally preferred, if you are being forced to do something that's against your will, which would sully your inner purity and moral integrity and freedom.*

Cato had felt it was going to sully his integrity to accept the pardon of his arch-enemy Caesar, so killed himself in line with his philosophy.

We tend to think of the Roman Stoics as obsessed with suicide, David Sedley said, but what they saw was what they called a rational departure from life. The point was that your happiness depended not on how you felt or behaved on any given day, but on the shape of your whole life.

DAVID SEDLEY: *No single feature of your life was more important than the way you ended it. Not only how you ended it but also choosing the time at which to end it. In the case of Socrates, that had required simply deciding to obey the law when he had the opportunity to escape from prison and escape the death penalty.*

Seneca, the playwright and Stoic philosopher, was employed by Nero's mother when Nero was twelve as his tutor in rhetoric. He did exercise a strong influence on Nero and, when Nero became emperor at the age of seventeen, Seneca was kept on as his adviser. Stoics had always thought that being an adviser to a monarch was one of the ideal positions for a philosopher. Seneca was quite clear that the Republic could not be resuscitated, and that enlightened monarchy was the right way forwards, so initially it was not problematic for him to help Nero. Besides, the first five years of Nero's reign, David Sedley said, were regarded by historians as one of the best periods of Roman rule.

DAVID SEDLEY: *It was only after five years into Nero's reign, when he murdered his mother and went onto a whole string of other atrocities, that he really went off the rails. That was the point at which one might have wondered why Seneca didn't get out. In fact, he did make a number of attempts to get out of the imperial service, but that was not easy because to resign would be taken as a sign of disloyalty.*

Seneca published great treatises on mercy in which he was praising Nero, as if Nero really were a merciful emperor, as a devious way of getting him to become that merciful emperor. Seneca probably knew that Nero had already committed his first atrocity, which was the murder of his main rival for the principate. Picking up from that, Jonathan Rée called Seneca the greatest of the Stoics, because he recognised that, if you were in a state of sorrow, there was nothing you could do to control it; the point was not to trick yourself out of your misery, but to conquer the misery.

Melvyn mentioned Marcus Aurelius, who was emperor for about twenty years in the second century AD. He wrote things in his *Meditations* that were taken up in the nineteenth century in Britain, such as: 'It is possible to live out your whole life in perfect contentment even though the whole world deafens you with its roar and wild beasts tear apart your body like a lump of clay, for nothing can shake a steady mind of its peaceful repose.'

For all that, in Jonathan Rée's view, Marcus Aurelius was a tremendous step down intellectually.

JONATHAN RÉE: *I find Marcus Aurelius rather prim, simple-minded and Pollyanna-ish. There is one very good sentence in it, which is where he says, 'If anybody says to you "I will speak to you quite frankly," then you know that they are a hypocrite, because if they have to say that they are being frank, their frankness can't come to them naturally, so don't believe it.'*

MELVYN BRAGG: *Noted by all broadcasters from now on! 'To tell you the truth … ' serves the same purpose, doesn't it?*

Whatever the status of Marcus Aurelius as a philosopher, Melvyn suggested, Stoicism had come a long way from people strolling around in Athens in 300 BC under the Colonnade and discussing how the universe was made, and how matter came into existence, for it to end up with the ruler writing his *Meditations*. Stoicism had become hugely important in the Roman Empire and, *pace* Jonathan Rée, Angie Hobbs had a sneaking affection for Marcus Aurelius.

ANGIE HOBBS: *The intriguing thing about Stoicism is that it doesn't just appeal to those in power, it can appeal to those in the very lowest ranks of society as well, and another of the most famous Stoics writing in the Roman imperial period was the freed slave Epictetus, and this was going to be crucial because it is going to lead onto one of the reasons Stoicism is going to appeal to Christianity.*

The Stoics were defining virtue and happiness in such a way that it did not matter what your circumstances in life were, it was up to you and your reason to choose whether to accept to live in accordance with the divine plan. With that went the notion of Stoic cosmopolitanism, where all fellow humans were linked, which fitted in nicely with Roman imperial ambitions.

Stoic ideas were very widely read, and very widely known to the early Christian writers, David Sedley said, and those writers read a huge number of works that are now lost. St Augustine was absolutely steeped in Stoicism. Yet, soon after Marcus Aurelius, Stoicism was swallowed up into Platonism.

DAVID SEDLEY: *Platonism was a great theoretical edifice that could compete with Christianity, and did for many centuries, and what the Platonists found they could learn from Stoicism was practical ethics. The best writers in antiquity on practical ethics were writing as Stoics, especially if you include Cicero when he was writing in a Stoic voice.*

Stoicism was relaunched in Europe after the sixteenth century, Jonathan Rée added, when some people thought that Stoicism was exactly the same as Christianity, even if serious Christians themselves did not.

JONATHAN RÉE: *Milton, for example, is absolutely appalled by the fashion for Stoicism. He talks about 'Stoic pride'. The ideal of Stoicism is self-sufficiency, and Christianity (certainly the kind of Christianity that flourishes after the Reformation) says that there is no such thing as self-sufficiency, there is no such thing as salvation, except through Christ and through the gospels.*

There was something deeply pagan about Stoicism, so that, when people started having doubts about Protestant Christianity in the nineteenth century, characters like Matthew Arnold talked of Marcus Aurelius as a great friend to him in times of adversity. Stoicism, Angie Hobbs noted, has been called the 'religion of the nineteenth-century British public school'. When the Victorians thought the tide of divine providence had gone out, Stoicism left them with some kind of comfort; and, Jonathan Rée thought, all those ideas about empire and self-sacrifice, in the name of some greater good, came in to occupy the space vacated by Christianity.

COMMON SENSE PHILOSOPHY

In the first century BC, the Roman statesman Marcus Tullius Cicero claimed, 'There is no statement so absurd that no philosopher will make it.' Indeed, in the history of western thought, philosophers have rarely been credited with having much common sense. In the seventeenth century, Francis Bacon made the point rather poetically, writing, 'Philosophers make imaginary laws for imaginary commonwealths, and their discourses are as the stars, which give little light because they are so high.' Samuel Johnson picked up the theme with some pugnacity in 1751, declaring, 'The public would suffer less present inconvenience from the banishment of philosophers than from the extinction of any common trade.' But, as Samuel Johnson scribbled his knockdown in The Rambler *magazine*, the greatest philosophers in Britain were locked in dispute about the very thing he denied them – common sense. It was a dispute about the nature of knowledge and the individuality of man, from which we derive the idea of common sense today. But what is common sense philosophy? Who are its proponents? And how did it emerge from the ties of scepticism, empiricism and rational enquiry running through eighteenth-century Europe?

Roman politician and lawyer Marcus Tullius Cicero.

With Melvyn to discuss common sense philosophy were: A. C. Grayling, master of the New College of the Humanities, London, and professor of philosophy; Melissa Lane, class of 1943 professor at Princeton University; and Alexander Broadie, emeritus professor of logic and rhetoric at the University of Glasgow.

Before moving to the main subject of the programme, A. C. Grayling mentioned an earlier, different connotation of common sense that went back to Aristotle, which was that there must be something in the mind that makes common the data that comes in from all the senses, so we get that unified experience. This 'common sense in the mind' makes common cause between all the different sense organs. And that was quite a different sense of common sense to the one we are used to today.

A. C. GRAYLING: *What we mean today is: very fundamental, general, much-agreed views, beliefs, concepts about the world, which it would be absolute lunacy to deny or to reject. Common sense being, as it were, the touchstone of the ordinary person in the street.*

MELVYN BRAGG: *Can you give us some concrete examples, so we know how concrete we are being?*

A. C. GRAYLING: *Well, that there are physical objects, that we have spent most of our lives near the surface of the earth, that if you put your hand in a flame it will burn and so on.*

The seventeenth-century Catholic theologian François Fénelon is often quoted for the way he expressed exactly, in the course of one of his dispositions, what common sense beliefs were.

A. C. GRAYLING: *He said common sense notions are those that you cannot contradict or deny, or even, indeed, examine. They are just so basic to us that you can't call them into question and try to examine them. And, yet, they are premised in all our thinking and doing otherwise. He said that if somebody (and this might be a lunatic or a philosopher, that collection of two types of people) were to call them into question, 'all I could do is smile'.*

In the seventeenth century, some of the great debates of philosophy in antiquity were revived, especially on the idea and nature of knowledge and the grounds of certainty in knowledge. People were looking for an answer to the question: how is it that we can have beliefs about an external world that seem to work, or about moral realities, or the existence of a deity?

A. C. GRAYLING: *There were various attempts by well-known philosophers, it might be the empiricists Locke and Berkeley, and, later on, Hume, to talk about how we acquire knowledge of the world through sensory experience alone, as if our minds were, as Locke began by saying, 'blank slates on which experience writes'. And there were others who were saying we have got to know certain things at the moment of birth, because we wouldn't be able do any kind of thinking or experiencing at all.*

On innateness, the knowing from birth, Plato thought our immortal souls, when in their disembodied existence, were in immediate contact with all the great truths, and that, when we are embodied, we forget everything. The process of education was about being reminded, at least partially, of some of what we knew in our pre-birth existence.

Moving on to the Cambridge Platonists, Melissa Lane mentioned that there was a second great image in this debate, after the blank-slate idea from Locke.

MELISSA LANE: *The Cambridge Platonists countered that with the notion of reason as the candle of the Lord, the image that God has put a candle of understanding into our minds, and we can use that in order to know the world with certainty.*

They followed Plato's idea that the mind already had certain knowledge, but took that more in a Stoic sense in which it was not so much that we were always born with the knowledge, but that our minds had a disposition to form certain judgements and concepts. For example, the Cambridge philosopher Ralph Cudworth took up this idea that the mind could only know what was native and domestic to it, and that enabled us to know God, to know morality.

MELISSA LANE: *The main argument was to show the other side, the empiricist, materialist, sensationalist side, that their arguments were faulty. The [Cambridge Platonists'] arguments were to say, for example, how could you possibly ever form, just through sensations alone, how could you possibly form concepts like geometry, for example? You never encounter a perfect triangle in nature, so how would you be able to form the notion of a perfect triangle? That must be an innate idea.*

The moral ideas were also seen as being among these innate ideas, so that we were not just machines for processing data coming in from the senses, but we actually had reason in our minds given by God and that included moral notions. Very often, for innatists, the way that we can have a guarantee that our innate ideas are true is because they come from God. If one tried to dispense with that premise, it was harder to make that argument.

In 1690, Locke launched a blistering attack on certain innate-ideas theorists, including the Cambridge Platonists. He asked: if you say that there are these universal ideas that are innate, well, which ideas are they?

MELISSA LANE: *He went back to some of the ancient sceptical claims, saying that we look at the diversity of human kind, we look at the diversity of beliefs and senses, and we can't say that there are these universals. He also thought and argued that believing in innate ideas makes us lazy. It is a cover for just accepting certain kinds of prejudices and accepting what we are told on authority.*

Alexander Broadie turned to René Descartes, who wanted to found science upon an absolutely certain base for which he needed some propositions that nobody could deny. He found one that was affirming his own existence, and his philosophy developed from that. This was the 'cogito ergo sum' argument in which the crucial word was 'sum' – I exist. Descartes was starting in his own head.

ALEXANDER BROADIE: *His problem is that this doesn't seem a very suitable place for founding a basis for science, because the science he was talking about was all going on outside his head, it was about the real world. His big question, philosophically, was how to get outside his head. He managed this by constructing a series of arguments for the existence of a God who has all the perfections, including the moral perfections, and who is therefore not a deceiving God and therefore is a God who would not deceive Descartes into believing certain things when they are completely false.*

To reach this, Descartes started with beliefs that, roughly speaking, were common sense beliefs in the form outlined earlier. He realised that such propositions as these were doubtable, as we know very well that sometimes our sensory receptors serve us ill, as well as serving us well, just as our memory can serve us ill, as well as serving us well.

ALEXANDER BROADIE: *This means that those sources of information that tell us about the outside world now, and the outside world in the past, are not entirely reliable. He goes on doubting and doubting until he finds something that can no longer be doubted. Because to doubt the proposition in question, namely his own existence, and the fact that he is doubting, is, in effect, to affirm the proposition that he is trying to deny.*

MELVYN BRAGG: *So, when it comes to the doubt about his own existence, that's proof that he exists?*

ALEXANDER BROADIE: *The very fact that he is doubting his own existence proves that there is himself, a thinking thing. Because doubting is a form of thinking, so there is thinking going on and so there must be a thinker who is at it.*

Descartes got outside his head by noticing that there were, inside this head of his, a number of ideas. Among these was the idea of God and the question was, then, is it possible to argue, from the idea of God to the reality of God, the existence of God, not just an existence that depends upon an activity of Descartes' mind but a God who has to exist for Descartes' mind to exist?

In the case of Locke and Berkeley, who were empiricist philosophers, a different route had to be engineered from the experience inside the head to this external world.

A. C. GRAYLING: *Locke tried to do it by saying that there were certain properties of things, what he called their primary qualities, the qualities of objects that you can measure (their position, their dimension, how big they are, how many they are and so on), that give us direct access to objects outside our heads. So there is a bridge, in experience, to the external world.*

*Scottish philosopher, historian,
and economist David Hume.*

This left Hume with the very interesting problem that, if you are
really going to base everything on your experience, you are going
to have to trace every one of your ideas or concepts to (what he
called) an impression, either of sense or an internal impression, from
which these ideas and concepts originated. His successors and his
contemporaries, including Thomas Reid, thought that this landed him
in a universal scepticism.

Hume was, on the one hand, committed to the notion that this
is how all of our information had to come in. On the other hand,
Melissa Lane continued, he was very aware of the ancient sceptical

arguments, known as Pyrrhonism, that the senses do give us contradictory information all the time. The mind has to try to sort that out, and create a notion of an external world despite that.

Hume was based in Edinburgh, but there was a philosophy club in Aberdeen with a minister of the kirk there, Thomas Reid (mentioned earlier), and they discussed ideas, particularly Hume's ideas. Hume's ideas went down, in a sense, very well indeed in Aberdeen in the Wise Club, because Hume gave them something to argue over.

ALEXANDER BROADIE: *There is a famous letter from Reid to Hume in which he tells Hume to keep publishing, 'because otherwise I will run out of things to talk about'. We have the paradoxical situation that the Wise Club in Aberdeen was a fan club of Hume's while, at the same time, being totally opposed to his ideas. The reason that they were opposed to his ideas is that the Aberdonians were not sceptics, and they reckoned that Hume was very much a sceptic.*

It was not just that Hume could not find a proof of the external world, he was also locked into position by way of the ideas that he had adopted within his own system. In that case, if there was an external world, this had to be a world that was somehow constructed out of impressions and ideas.

ALEXANDER BROADIE: *The position that Hume adopts is that what we are pleased to think of as reality is, in fact, almost entirely a construction of our own imagination going to work on the impressions and the ideas that we have. And that means that, in effect, each of us is a creator of the world, we are all of us world-makers, so that the world, the external world, stands to us roughly in the way in which a novel stands to an author.*

On several occasions in his *Treatise of Human Nature*, Hume spoke of the external world as a fiction, and he meant fiction in the modern sense as something that we have made and that, Alexander Broadie explained, was clearly scepticism in a very tough sense.

A. C. Grayling raised the point that philosophers were interested in whether this was *indeed* what Hume was trying to say. It may be that Hume was sceptical about the possibility of Rationalist (with a capital R) philosophy – philosophy as an enterprise of reason – to provide us with arguments.

A. C. GRAYLING: *He also says in the* Treatise *that when he gets up from his study desk and goes off to play backgammon, which was his favourite occupation, he couldn't help but believe that there is an external world; and so what he was implying there was that our human nature actually equips us with convictions about these very, very basic things.*

It may then be that Hume was not at all a sceptic about the external world, but about the potentials of reason to prove it.

Reid was very important in this debate and he wrote an influential book in 1764, *An Inquiry into the Human Mind on the Principles of Common Sense*. Hume read a draft of this and then wrote in a letter that Reid was reviving innate ideas.

MELISSA LANE: *But that wasn't at all what Reid took himself to be doing, or not exactly that. Because Reid rejected this very notion of ideas that has been mentioned, the thought that the only thing that is real is the impression in our mind from the outside world. He wanted to restore a direct connection between ourselves and external reality, and he did that by these common sense principles.*

For Reid, the common sense principles were principles like, 'you exist and have a mind', 'this table is real', 'I exist' or 'I can have reason to trust my senses and testimony generally'. Reid picked up on Fénelon's thought to say that people who denied these really were either lunatics or what he called 'metaphysical lunatics'; they are mad philosophers. We could not ever reason or think without these premises; we had to accept that this was part of the constitution of our minds.

On the one hand, Alexander Broadie observed, there was Hume writing his philosophy, in the course of which he was declaring the external world, and therefore all his friends, to be a fiction, a product of his own mind, as mentioned earlier; and, on the other hand, he was leaving his writing and going out and playing backgammon and talking with his friends in the common sense world, in the real world.

ALEXANDER BROADIE: *As far as Reid is concerned, what this demonstrates is that there is something desperately wrong with Hume's philosophy, because it is not a philosophy that you can live. If you actually do think that your friends are products of your own imaginative activities and that's the end of the story, then you can't possibly treat them in the kind of way that nature forces you to treat them, namely as other centres of consciousness and centres of moral principle.*

It was an essential part of the philosophical insight of the common sense school that there should be a unity between the life that you lived in the real world and the philosophy that you theorised about.

There was a paradox there as, in a way, Hume and Reid could be brought together.

MELISSA LANE: *There is a wonderful nineteenth-century Edinburgh story that said that really what happened was that Reid was shouting out very loudly, 'We must believe in an external world,' but whispering, 'We have no reason for our beliefs.' And then Hume was saying very loudly, 'We have no reason for our beliefs,' but then whispering, 'But we must believe in an external world.' There is a sense in which, one can argue, are they in some ways saying the same thing?*

Having suggested ways in which Hume and Reid were very similar, there are also ways in which they are very different, on some points.

MELISSA LANE: *In this question of this relation to God and miracles, Hume had argued that we have no grounds on which to believe in ancient biblical reports of miracles because there is no* *reason for us to trust that testimony unless we have experience of its reliability. Reid countered that, saying testimony is just as basic a way of knowing about the world as our senses are, and we can't escape having a principle of believing in testimony.*

Immanuel Kant was influenced directly by what he had heard of Hume. He claimed to have been inspired by this idea that it was the way our human nature was constituted that gave us our most fundamental beliefs about the world and responses to them, and he turned it into a very powerful system of thought.

A. C. Grayling: *He did it on the basis of a crucial change. Whereas the empiricists before his time had asked: where do our ideas come from? Kant said: don't ask that question, ask instead what work do they do?*

The utilitarians, Melvyn suggested, would seem to have a lot to offer common sense philosophy, with Jeremy Bentham's *An Introduction to the Principles of Morals and Legislation* (1789). There, though, Melissa Lane saw a paradox.

Melissa Lane: *In one way, one might say that the utilitarians are looking for the one, big, great principle of common sense that they think no one can deny, which is that the rule of our actions should be to do that which increases the greatest happiness of the greatest number. But, on the other hand, they didn't think that that was something everybody actually did agree to, they thought that was something that people might disagree about.*

The other thing that happened was that one of Reid's successors, Sir William Hamilton, developed Reid's ideas in the nineteenth century, and John Stuart Mill, one of the great utilitarians, launched a blistering attack on him in a book. It was probably that attack that really put paid to common sense philosophy, at least in Britain.

The common sense ideas influenced G. E. Moore, a twentieth-century Cambridge philosopher, who made a very similar argument to the one that Reid was making.

Melissa Lane: *He said that, if we have the proposition that there is at present a living body, which is my body, it would just be lunacy to deny that. And he held up his hand and said, 'You can't deny that this is a hand.' That feeds into some of the ideas of the later Wittgenstein as well.*

Moore titled of one of his works *In Defence of Common Sense* and he was a direct inheritor of this tradition, A. C. Grayling added, and Wittgenstein in his last work, *On Certainty*, was also an inheritor, via Moore, of Reid's ideas.

A. C. Grayling: *But there is a famous case in which Moore, having used such examples as, 'I know that I have a hand here, and another hand there, and I know that I have been close to the surface of earth all my life,' and so on …*

Melvyn Bragg: *'Almost all my life,' he says.*

A. C. GRAYLING: *Yes, almost ... he was giving a lecture at an American university in a great hall, the walls of which were hung with curtains, and he said, 'I know with absolute certainty that there are windows behind these curtains.' And, in fact, there weren't.*

CONFUCIUS

In the fifth century BC, a wise man called Kung Fu Tzu said, 'Study
the past if you would divine the future.' This powerful maxim
helped form the body of ideas that, more than Buddhism, more than
Taoism, more even than communism, has defined what it is to be
Chinese. It is a philosophy that we call Confucianism – Confucius
is the Latinisation of Kung Fu Tzu – and, as well as asserting the
importance of learning from the past, it embodies a respect for
hierarchy, ritual and self-cultivation through learning. Confucius said,
'Learning without thought is labour lost; thought without learning is
perilous.' But who was Confucius and how did his ideas manage to
become the bedrock for a civilisation?

With Melvyn, to go over 2,000 years of Chinese past in the hope of divining the future of Confucianism, were: Frances Wood, retired curator of the Chinese collections at the British Library; Tim Barrett, emeritus professor of east Asian history at the School of Oriental and African Studies, University of London; and Tao Tao Liu, emeritus tutorial fellow in oriental studies at Wadham College, Oxford.

Confucius was a kind of itinerant teacher, Tao Tao Liu began, from a class of people who were coming to the fore, the Shi, which is variously translated as the 'scribes' or the 'knights', people who were not inheriting a great deal from their family but belonged to the noble houses.

TAO TAO LIU: *They were well educated, and they went around trying to find a job of their own, and they propounded their own ideas. He wasn't the only one at that time; in fact, there were quite a lot of other people propounding their own ideas.*

Much of the material about him was written down not by Confucius but by his disciples. There are references in Daoist texts to him going around with those disciples; some of the other schools tended to laugh at him, saying he was not going to get anywhere.

TAO TAO LIU: *[His system] put a great deal of emphasis on human interaction, and a human society. He said that he was a reformist, not really an innovator. He said that people are the most important, and you should think about how you treat people with love, or humanity. The word Ren, as it has been called, is the sense of caring, if you try to translate it that way.*

Frances Wood underlined this statement of Confucius, that he was not the great innovator, even if we sometimes think of him that way. He was expressing views that were commonly held at the time.

FRANCES WOOD: *It is simply because his disciples wrote down what he said that we have this body of literature, which gives us the idea that this is something very important. He has stressed the importance of family, family relations, relations with people within society and so on, but he was just saying what pretty well everybody knew. He was reacting to what he saw as the breakdown of an ideal system. This ideal system lay in the past.*

Rather than ideas of reciprocity, and people being nice to each other, Frances Wood highlighted the concern Confucius had about statesmanship. He believed things should be right: *let the ruler be a ruler, let the subject be a subject.* There was a right way to behave, and that went all the way down through society.

MELVYN BRAGG: *Let the ruler be the ruler, the minister be the minister, the father be the father, the son be the son and then the states are stable. All male, by the way.*

FRANCES WOOD: *We can come to women. Whether you can rescue your sister-in-law from drowning if it involves touching her hand was a big argument. The idea was that it was actually so improper for a* *man to touch a woman's hand, if he was not married to her, that it would be better to leave her to drown.*

There was an almost Christlike idea of Confucius from Tao Tao Liu, Melvyn summarised, and a very strict hierarchical idea from Frances Wood, and there was also the part of Confucianism to do with government, which made him attractive to bureaucracies. Confucius believed that the key to good government was education, which put him in a minority when sheer efficiency was increasingly valued, especially as the Zhou dynasty was breaking up and its former vassals were beginning to compete to take its place.

TIM BARRETT: *These rising powers put a premium on efficiency, especially military efficiency. To talk about rituals, to talk about kindness in human relationships, this all seemed very remote. However, Confucius look[ed] backwards towards the institutions, towards the texts concerning better times in the past. He was laying the foundations of an educational curriculum, which conveyed a cultural heritage.*

In the short term, possibly to his contemporaries, certainly for a few centuries thereafter, Confucius's approach looked plain silly. However, once China was unified and there were no more enemies to fight, it became important to find a way to keep the empire together. The solution took some time to emerge, but held good for a couple of millennia thereafter.

TIM BARRETT: *[This] was the idea of having an elite who were all brought up on the same sort of education, familiar with all the same texts and so forth, held together because of their cultural knowledge, and who, through their cultural knowledge, gained the kind of prestige that, at least in settled times, allowed them to dominate local society.*

There were said to be 100 competing schools in the time of Confucius, yet his ideas survived to be taken up by the first Han emperor in about 200 BC. Survival was thanks to that large body of work of the disciples, recording what he said, something that did not happen to other philosophers who vanished without leaving much of a system.

FRANCES WOOD: *[They are] always in the form of these little 'the master said this' or 'in response to questions from so and so, he said this, that and the other'. He spoke about all sorts of things, some things have already been mentioned; he also said odd things like 'a gentleman should never wear scarlet at home'. Lots of anecdotes about him were repeated; it was said that he couldn't sleep if his mat was not straight.*

This body of material about him and his gnomic sayings were to form the basis for the examination system that created the bureaucracy in China.

The bureaucracy itself came from the heritage of those who were striving for efficiency. The theory of bureaucratic management, Tim Barrett said, was not in itself Confucian but, 'After the experience of autocracy under the terrible first emperor of China (the man with all those terracotta warriors), they were looking for something that

would make that kind of totalitarian bureaucracy more bearable.'
To have people in the bureaucracy who had been examined for
their knowledge of the Chinese heritage, rather than their ruthless
efficiency, was a way of achieving that goal.

Later, in AD 600–900, Buddhism was in the ascendant in China.
The Tang dynasty marked a period of unification after lengthy civil
wars. People may have been disappointed that they had an imperial
government that did not, at that stage, seem to work, and they were
looking for solutions at a more personal level, and that looked as if it
could be Buddhism.

TIM BARRETT: *What it offered, above all, was an answer to
questions as to what happens after death, a personal salvation, a
chance of remedying the situation. Even if you end up killed in a
battle, there is a chance of a further incarnation. In particular, the
number of people who died in the fighting who were not cared for as
ancestors within the Confucian setting, the wandering ghosts – who
would take care of them? Buddhism offered that possibility.*

The Buddhism that arose in China, especially Tang China, was
very different from the original, rather ascetic preachings of the
historic Buddha. The Chinese transformed Buddhism enormously so
that it would fit in with the Confucian family setting.

FRANCES WOOD: *For example, Buddhism should be a monastic
religion. That means it takes you away from your family, and you
have got the problem that you must stay within your family because
you need to look after your elderly parents, and you also need to keep
feeding the ancestral spirits back for three generations.*

In a Confucian family, obligations to your ancestors meant you
should be at home, offering sacrifices, offering food to them, incense
and prayers, informing them what was going on in the household,
and you could not do that if you were away in a monastery.

*Silk painting depicting
Confucius lecturing students.*

FRANCES WOOD: *This is putting it very simplistically, but you get the development of Zen, which is sudden enlightenment, which is through self-cultivation; you don't have to go into a monastery, but you can become a Buddhist and you can achieve enlightenment through your own cultivation.*

There was some reaction against the foreignness of the new ideas, Tao Tao Liu suggested, and the Chinese retrenched a bit. There was a form of neo-Confucianism, starting from about the tenth century up to the twelfth, culminating in a great thinker, the 'Thomas Aquinas of Confucianism', who was Zhu Xi and who lived in the twelfth century.

TAO TAO LIU: *He had a rather different interpretation. He made Confucius less of a state institution, and made it much more the idea that everybody can participate. He tried to get from the much more politicised ideas of Confucianism to the idea that, within each person and within each household, you could have a sense of what is right, and everybody knowing their places and so on.*

The continuity between Confucius and Zhu Xi was possible because of the literary culture in China, where so much was written down. Back in the Han dynasty when Confucianism was first being adopted by the state, before they had invented woodblock printing, they had the Confucian texts carved in stone.

FRANCES WOOD: *Then you would take rubbings from that with paper, so that people could have copies of it. They always had this great thing about the correct text and, whatever the fate of the cult at any time, you have got this continuous re-examination of the texts, and re-examination of one's heritage, one's past.*

Melvyn mentioned *The Book of Songs*, which he understood was a key Confucian text even though a lot of the songs in it were bawdy. Confucius himself never actually denied people's appetites, Tao Tao Liu said, and that included sex and food and general shelter. *The Book of Songs* really contained folk songs, as well as hymns and poetry, and described the whole of life.

TAO TAO LIU: *He thought that this really took poetry, and the arts, as an expression of things that are perhaps too deep emotionally to be expressed easily in verbal form. He loved music as well. I don't think one should get an idea that Confucius was somehow a purely dull old stick. There is one record of him actually getting so enraptured by some music that he didn't eat or sleep for three days.*

While Confucianism was embedded in China and had been for millennia, the arrival of the industrial west in the nineteenth century had a disruptive effect. It broke up the entire Confucian world. China regarded itself as bestowing civilisation on its neighbours, like Korea, Japan and Vietnam, and, when these countries fell under colonial influence or went their own ways, there was a blow to Confucian self-esteem. It was unclear whether Confucianism would be able to create a society that was fit to survive in the modern world.

TIM BARRETT: *Once again we see some of the slogans that had dominated China, in the terrible period after the life of Confucius as it moved towards unification by brute force. Originally, perhaps in Japan, but then in China, too, as these countries perceive themselves as under threat in an immensely competitive situation, [we see] the slogans 'we must enrich the country, strengthen the army'. These became, once again, dominant.*

It was an awful new world, he added, but one that had echoes in east Asia of times long distant.

In the twentieth century, Mao attacked Confucianism and, in the Cultural Revolution, attempted to eliminate the past and Confucianism along with it. There were some successes but, on the whole, the plan did not really work.

TAO TAO LIU: *In many ways, Mao himself was a bit of a Confucianist; he was a great believer in hierarchy, you knew your place, and, as far as he was concerned, he was at the top of the tree and everybody else was somewhere on different rungs well below it. He also actually went against the Confucian spirit of being fairly catholic in the ability to take on various aspects; he just decided that everything had to be one politically correct voice.*

One of the areas in which Mao seems to have been trapped in a Confucian way of thinking was when he tried to transform China through his own personal efforts.

TIM BARRETT: *One of the distinctive aspects of Confucianism was this belief that great people can transform cultures. Confucius looked back to earlier sage kings and, in his turn, was looked back to as a sage himself. Although Mao's idea of what China should be like may have been more than coloured by Marxism, the effort single-handedly to transform China, and the effects of failure on him personally in making him more and more autocratic, bear an uncanny echo of earlier problems in trying to act as a sage and single-handedly transform a whole society.*

Tao Tao Liu noted that Confucianism was still observed in places like Taiwan, Singapore and Malaysia, where there is a sense of upholding the old traditions and the old Chinese-ness. It may spread back to China as a mark of being Chinese and, considering the strength of the family and responsibility of the family, there are ways in which Confucianism has never vanished from Chinese life.

FRANCES WOOD: *Even in things like the family having to pay for the bullet if one of its members is shot as a criminal. Things like slander – you can't slander for three generations back – that's got all sorts of resonances that are very Confucian. It hasn't been used in any sort of self-strengthening yet, but they have started re-doing the rituals at Confucius's birth place. They play music that is 3,000 years old and dance to strange rituals. There will be another coming of Confucianism.*

NIETZSCHE'S ON THE GENEALOGY OF MORALITY

What price have human animals paid to become civilised? That's one of the questions posed by the German philosopher Friedrich Nietzsche in On the Genealogy of Morality: A Polemic, *which he published in 1887 towards the end of his working life. In three essays, he argued that: having a guilty conscience was the price of living in society with other humans; Christian morality, with its consideration for others, grew as an act of revenge by the weak against their masters, the 'blond beasts of prey', as he calls them; and the price for that revolt is endless self-loathing. These and other ideas were picked up by later thinkers, perhaps most significantly by Sigmund Freud, who further explored the tensions between civilisation and the individual set out in Nietzsche's essays.*

With Melvyn to discuss Nietzsche's *Genealogy of Morality* were: Stephen Mulhall, professor of philosophy and a fellow and tutor at New College, Oxford; Fiona Hughes, senior lecturer in philosophy at the University of Essex; and Keith Ansell-Pearson, professor of philosophy at the University of Warwick.

Nietzsche was born in 1844 in Saxony, a province of Prussia, and his father and grandfather were both Lutheran ministers with connections to the royal court and the government.

STEPHEN MULHALL: *His father died when he was five, as did his only brother, and that meant that the family suffered various kinds of financial difficulties. Nevertheless, they put him on the standard track, educationally, to go to university and that meant he went to a very reputable boarding school at which he acquired a great facility with languages.*

That led Nietzsche to an interest in philology, a study of language, which he pursued at university, first at Bonn and then at Leipzig, initially with theology, although he soon dropped that. At the age of twenty-four, which was incredibly young, he was offered a chair in classical philology at the University of Basel. He was regarded as an extremely promising philologist until, in 1872, he published his first major work, *The Birth of Tragedy*.

STEPHEN MULHALL: *That received a generally very lukewarm reception, but one very eminent scholar wrote a ferocious critique of it. And, at that point, the possibility of going onwards and upwards as a philologist was pretty much closed to him. Although he spent a lot of time in Basel and did a regular amount of teaching, his health got a great deal worse and he became increasingly disenchanted with academic philology; he took the chance to retire in 1879.*

Nietzsche became an independent scholar, travelling around Europe on a small pension, with bouts of ill health that were to worsen drastically in later life.

As a young child, he had been very comfortable with his Lutheran upbringing and seemed to have been very dutiful and obedient.

KEITH ANSELL-PEARSON: *His schoolfriends and family called him the 'little pastor', such was his earnestness; but things began to change quite dramatically when he went to Pforta, the boarding school. That's between the ages of fourteen and twenty and, in the middle of that period, when he is seventeen (so it is 1861), he has a religious crisis, a crisis of faith.*

Nietzsche was moving from a fundamentally religious orientation, based on belief and imagination, to a critical orientation, where the emphasis was put on reason and evidence. In the first year at Bonn, he wrote to his sister, Elizabeth, 'If you want peace of mind and happiness, then believe; if you want to be a disciple of truth, then you should search.'

KEITH ANSELL-PEARSON: *The Lutheran religion leaves its mark on Nietzsche's subsequent thinking. In one of his mature texts,* The Gay Science, *from 1882, he says: what does your conscience say?*

And he answers: you should become the one that you are. And that's a sort of Lutheran idea, that what's really important, having an individual conscience, having an individual relationship to God and the Bible.

For him, the conscience that was at stake was not so much a moral conscience as what he called an intellectual conscience. He thought mankind had the duty to marvel at the fundamentally enigmatic character of existence and to keep questioning existence.

Nietzsche produced *On the Genealogy of Morality* in 1887 in the later stages of his career. After the congenial texts of his middle period, this later work was aggressive and polemical. He was concerned that Europe was about to enter a period of decadence and nihilism and that all the illusions people suffered from, as modern human beings, needed exposing and attacking.

The overall project of *On the Genealogy of Morality*, Fiona Hughes explained, was to evaluate morality, its value and worth. There are three essays within the work and, in the first, Nietzsche focuses on putting forward a contrast between noble morality and slave morality. The nobles are the masters of society, who he also called the 'blond beasts' initially, and they are the instinctive, powerful individuals who determine their own fates, and they have values rather than morals.

FIONA HUGHES: *Their morality is that of creating their own values, on the basis of their own interests. For them, values come from themselves, they are self-regarding values. They are not really very interested in those who are not powerful. They want to have power over those other powerless people, but they are basically interested in controlling their own fates and, in order to do that, controlling those around them so that they don't get in their way.*

It is possible to argue that this description does not necessarily capture the identity of a particular social class, it may be more to do with a mentality.

The slave morality is a morality, or believes itself to be a morality, and it is a reaction against the noble values, with a belief that it is good to restrain the self, which is presented as particularly developed within Judaeo-Christianity.

FIONA HUGHES: *There is a negative strength in that redefining of what is good, and the introduction of what, from the slave morality's perspective, is now called evil, rather than bad. The evil, from the slave morality's perspective, is strength, is powerfulness, is exactly what the nobles would have thought of as good. There has been a reversal of what counts as good and, in that respect, the slaves have a strength; but the problem about it, in Nietzsche's view, is that supposed strength is directed in a negative way not only against the nobles, but against themselves.*

Stephen Mulhall, following on from this, said it was no accident that what slave morality defined as evil was what the master morality defined as good, and vice versa. You just have to look at it from the perspective of the slaves, the weak and feeble.

STEPHEN MULHALL: *They are in a master morality world, they are disdained by the masters, they just get kicked into the gutter, while the masters go about their business. If they are going to improve their situation, they don't have the direct, physical, natural endowment to do it directly. What they want to do is create an environment in which forms of behaviour that are to the advantage of the weak and the feeble are praised, celebrated, affirmed as the good way of living. All the forms of behaviour that are to the disadvantage of the weak, they get redefined as evil.*

Since Nietzsche thought that master morality was not just historically prior but, in a certain sense, a more fundamental expression of what human life is, what vitality is, then that meant slave morality was a negative phenomenon.

STEPHEN MULHALL: *It is basically expressing a kind of hatred of life. You have a paradoxical situation where, on the one hand, the slaves are manifesting strength by imposing themselves on the world, redefining it in terms that are to their own advantage. On the other hand, they do it by presenting a code in which, as it were, life is denied and a certain kind of negative force is imposed.*

The slaves had been in a weak position but, in Nietzsche's view, within the space of a few decades of that redefinition, the whole

Sigmund Freud further explored the tensions between civilisation and the individual set out in Nietzsche's essays.

world was turned upside down and it was suddenly great for the weak and feeble. That change centred around the role of the priest because, according to Nietzsche's account, the priests were a branch of the aristocracy, a kind of noble, but without the direct physical force to back them up. They still wanted to have power, so they used intelligence, they sought indirect ways of winning the battle against the other branch of the nobles.

STEPHEN MULHALL: *The way they do that is by recruiting the slaves to bring about this revolution. They put themselves at the head of the revolution, that gives them power, but, in order to achieve that revolution, they need the masses behind them, and sheer volume of numbers is going to allow them to win the battle, but only under the leadership of the priest. A certain sort of internal fracturing of the nobles led to a complete inversion of the value system that they were originally living under.*

What drove the slave revolt was an attitude or sentiment of *ressentiment*, a word that Nietzsche had encountered in a text of 1875 by a German thinker, Eugen Dühring, called *The Value of Life*. It meant something different from resentment or revenge, pure and simple, where a direct hitting-back at the source of hurt might prove cathartic.

KEITH ANSELL-PEARSON: *Ressentiment is different, it is the lingering sentiment of a poisonous revenge. You are impotent, you are powerless, you are not in a position to actually carry out your resentment, so it poisons your system and you compensate yourselves with an imaginary revenge.*

Nietzsche saw himself as a psychologist as well as a historian. What he really wanted, Fiona Hughes thought, was to identify certain ideal types rather than any particular period. He looked back to Greek history, he talked about the Celts and the Vikings, and he also suggested that the Romans were the noble type.

FIONA HUGHES: *It is absolutely clear, if anything can be absolutely clear in Nietzsche, that he thinks that the noble type is healthy, whereas the slave type is unhealthy, is sick. But the relationship between these two groups has a certain amount of ambivalence in it, because the slaves are the interesting human beings. It is once we become resentful, in the precise sense of* ressentiment *that Keith was talking about, that we begin to turn our attention back into ourselves.*

The blond beasts were not really self-reflective; the advantage of the slaves was that they were intelligent, reflective beings and Nietzsche had a sympathy with that, even though he was also critical of it.

These ideas had to do, partly, with the construction of the very idea of an inner life as something distinct from one's external public life. If you think about someone like Achilles, Stephen Mulhall suggested, you do not imagine him having a rich and complex interior life. It is part of Nietzsche's story that a confluence of entry into society and the restructuring of that society, by the values of slave morality, introduced a much sharper distinction between the inner and the outer in our lives.

STEPHEN MULHALL: *Christianity places a great value on that idea of self-examination and, in a certain way, it encourages you to believe that there is this rich, interior life for you to explore and perhaps partly to construct as you explore it. You are being told that seeking the truth about yourself is part of being a good person, the only way in which you can establish the right relationship to God. That's built into a context in which you are creating an occasion for punishing yourself, and for feeling guilty.*

There could be a system of punishment in which the only thing that mattered was whether or not you *did* something bad. With Christianity, following Nietzsche, you have to think not just about the actions you perform, but whether you have bad intentions. After all, Christ said that, if you contemplate adultery in your heart, you have committed the sin of adultery. That was a radical extension of the domain of guilt and punishment.

In the first instance, Nietzsche thought that we use guilt in order to try to make people morally better, but he considered that this approach was a mistake. Punishment actually makes people harder, more resistant, more alienated, rather than making them morally better. He gave the example of prisons, saying that prisons were not full of people with very finely tuned moral consciences; punishment tended to tame people, rather than to reform them.

FIONA HUGHES: *At a deeper level, he thinks that the ascetic priests use guilt in order to try to manage our horror in the face of suffering. Human beings, according to Nietzsche, find it intolerable that not only do we suffer, but that our suffering is meaningless. To introduce the idea of guilt gives us a handle on this, in that [someone] can think: 'Well, at least it is explicable that I am suffering, it may not make it feel better, but at least I can understand why I am suffering. I am suffering because I am guilty, because I am sinful.'*

Nietzsche's rejoinder was that suffering is just not explicable in that way, and that all that guilt helps us do is deal with the fear of suffering, not with the suffering itself.

Melvyn was keen to clarify whether the notional slave revolt could be associated with a particular period – for example, the development of Christianity where 'they walk in the doors in 100 BC and walk out the door in AD 100 and it is a different world, because of what's happened'. His guests thought it tended to be more general.

KEITH ANSELL-PEARSON: *That kind of history repeats itself, throughout history. He sees the French Revolution as the modern equivalent of another slave revolt of morality. He says, 'Yes, the slaves have won, the slaves have been successful, the weak have inherited the earth.' The French Revolution for him is a great symbol of that.*

On the one hand, Stephen Mulhall added, Nietzsche was tempted at various points to say that certain historically datable events were fundamental in the inception of this revolution. On the other hand, Nietzsche thought, partly because of the point that Keith Ansell-Pearson had made about the poisonous nature of *ressentiment*, that the slaves never felt as if they had won.

Nietzsche introduced the notion of the ascetic ideal primarily in the third of the three essays that make up *The Genealogy*. It was his label for the various ways in which slave morality, in its Judaeo-Christian religious form, mutated and evolved and permeated the culture of western Europe.

STEPHEN MULHALL: *It is perfectly possible for slave morality to be real and effective in the world without any theological trappings attached to it at all. Merely denying that God exists, while remaining committed to a value system that privileges altruism, compassion for the weak and so on, as good and evil as all the forms of behaviour that the masters naturally manifest, that would be a further form of slave morality, another form of asceticism.*

Slave morality has its non-religious forms, Nietzsche argued, and it also has forms in which a certain sense of what matters in the world, and what does not, is manifest in parts of culture that are not obviously moral. He talked extensively about art, science and philosophy. And he tried to identify, in each of those three cases, where it was that an ascetic, life-denying attitude to the world could be seen, even though none of those artists, scientists or philosophers would recognise themselves as having evaluative commitments.

To Keith Ansell-Pearson, Nietzsche himself displayed, as a philosopher, certain ascetic practices and was implicating himself in what he analysed.

KEITH ANSELL-PEARSON: *He has a certain investment in truth, he wants to find out the truth about our history, the truth about Christianity; and yet he realises that, if it becomes an unconditional value, then it is ultimately ascetic and life-denying. Why should truth be the unconditional value of life?*

In science, with its attention to seeking facts, and in the scholar's objectivity, there are ascetic traits, life-denying traits, and Nietzsche was really worried about these developments and what they meant for intellectual activity. Science and even atheism are not the enemies of the ascetic ideal, they are fully implicated in it. That is why Nietzsche thought that truth was not the sole important value in philosophy; he was quite radical in this respect, since we tend to associate the philosopher with the investment in truth and the concern for truth. He wanted a knowledge placed in the service of some new future life, Keith Ansell-Pearson continued, and that is why he wanted to carry out this genealogy, to revitalise history.

The issue here, for Stephen Mulhall, was not so much that seeking truth in itself is always ascetic. The question was where you find yourself locating the truth, and how much self-sacrifice you are willing to impose on yourself in order to achieve it. Much modern science, on Nietzsche's controversial account of the matter, locates the underlying nature of reality in realms that transcend the one that is open to our everyday senses.

STEPHEN MULHALL: *Modern science tells us you shouldn't believe what the senses tell you because they are misleading. We think things are coloured? Turns out they aren't. We think they have tastes? Well, they don't really have tastes, they just have these primary qualities. Then, as science develops, it locates the truth about things in a more and more distant realm. It is taking it away from what Nietzsche thinks of as the immediate, empirical world of becoming.*

Philosophy itself, for Nietzsche, was an ascetic discipline that involved turning away from the senses and cultivating a much more spiritual approach to things.

FIONA HUGHES: *At the same time, there is a possibility within philosophy, as Keith was saying, for a more vitalistic approach. Philosophy, in fact, becomes a very productive place to look for the new nobles, the nobles who are the successors of those blond beasts, but who now have a much more complex internal life and who are able to be much more playful, to laugh, to dance, to sing.*

Ultimately, Nietzsche's analysis is quite optimistic, particularly when compared to Sigmund Freud and his book *Civilisation and Its Discontents*, published in 1930. Although Freud did not refer to Nietzsche in that, the analysis that he offered was uncannily close to some of the things that Nietzsche had highlighted in *The Genealogy*.

KEITH ANSELL-PEARSON: *Freud posits an irredeemable conflict between, on the one hand, the demands of instinct and, on the other hand, the restrictions of civilisation, and he locates guilt as the fundamental problem of civilisation. What Nietzsche and Freud share is the idea that civilisation is built on the taming of our aggressive instincts, through their repression and sublimation. But, where Freud is a pessimist about the future of civilisation, Nietzsche is more optimistic.*

Freud thought that we have to make a pessimistic choice between civilisation or instinctual happiness; we cannot have both. Nietzsche thought there was at least a possibility of a form of moral self-determination that would be free of this self-lacerating guilt and self-inflicted cruelty. It is what he signalled at the start of the second essay as the 'super moral, sovereign individual'.

Nietzsche had a short life, Melvyn observed, and, not long after *The Genealogy*, he spent his last eleven years in sanatoria. He had a massive nervous breakdown and did not do any more writing. He was looked after by his anti-Semitic sister, who also took control of his papers, and his reputation took a long time to recover from the harm she caused. Now, Stephen Mulhall said, Nietzsche is having a lot of influence and is regarded as a genuine, intelligible interlocutor, particularly in moral philosophy, not just in the Franco-German traditions of philosophy but also in the Anglophone traditions, and, broadly, that is because of his naturalist inclinations. He was someone who wanted to explain things, without reference to the supernatural.

AL-BIRUNI

If you were to point a reasonably powerful telescope at the surface of the moon, at latitude 17.9 degrees, longitude 92.5 degrees, you would find yourself looking at the Al-Biruni crater. This lunar feature is named in honour of a tenth-century Muslim scholar, who was not only one of the greatest figures of medieval natural philosophy, but is also claimed as one of the most outstanding scholars of all time. Born in central Asia, Al-Biruni was an astonishing polymath, a master of mathematics, astronomy and medicine. He was fluent in five languages and he was as great a scholar of philosophy as he was a scientist. Perhaps Al-Biruni's most remarkable book is The India, *a comprehensive account of Hindu philosophy, religion and science. It is the first work about India by a Muslim scholar, and is so compelling a portrait of one culture, seen from the perspective of another, that it has been described as the first work of anthropology.*

With Melvyn to discuss Al-Biruni, and his groundbreaking work, were: Amira K. Bennison, professor in the history and culture of the Maghrib, University of Cambridge; Hugh Kennedy, professor of Arabic in the School of Oriental and African Studies, University of London; and James Montgomery, professor of classical Arabic at the University of Cambridge.

In Arabic, Hugh Kennedy began, Al-Biruni's full name is Abū Rayḥān Muḥammad ibn Aḥmad Al-Bīrūnī, and the Biruni part, by which he is always known, reflects the fact that he was apparently born in the suburb (or *birun*) of the city of Kath in Khwarezm. This region is in the delta of the Oxus river, which flows from the Pamir mountains down into the deserts of what is now Uzbekistan. The area was very fertile and densely populated, but, at the same time, also very isolated. His birth, around 973, was in the period after the universal caliphate had collapsed and the Muslim world in the tenth century was in a state of political disintegration that had not spread to the culture.

HUGH KENNEDY: *One of the features of the medieval Muslim world is that it retained a cultural unity and identity and, instead of having one centre in Baghdad, there were numerous different places where intellectuals worked. Among the many dynasties that followed the Abbasids, it was something of a statement, a legitimising device, to have intellectuals at your court.*

While we know relatively little about Al-Biruni's early education, he must have studied what are sometimes described as the religious sciences, becoming skilled in areas such as jurisprudence, law and the exegesis of the Qur'an.

AMIRA K. BENNISON: *He also studied what were often called the Greek sciences or the sciences of the ancients. He became very proficient in mathematics, astronomy, also astrology, which was closely associated with astronomy in those days. He was able to engage with all kinds of different scholars in the region in which he was living.*

He was a contemporary of people like Avicenna, and they all had access to the Greek sciences. In most of the region's cities, there were libraries full of Greek works that had been translated into Arabic, including the works of Aristotle. Muslims were using paper and that meant that volumes of works were much more readily available than they would have been with parchment, or other materials. There was relatively less of Plato, although some things, particularly Neoplatonism, had been translated.

AMIRA K. BENNISON: *The important thing is to remember that, at this point, there doesn't seem to be any disparagement of non-Islamic, or non-Arab science. It is fully integrated among these intellectual circles.*

Al-Biruni became part of the court of Ma'mun, one of the Khwarezm shahs, and his position is sometimes described as that of *nadim*, a boon companion, someone who did not necessarily have a formal position but who was an adviser and was probably also used as an ambassador to undertake missions for Ma'mun.

There was almost nothing that Al-Biruni saw around him that did not attract his interest, Hugh Kennedy commented, and his first book was an attempt to sum up how different cultures calculated their years. He wrote some 140 books, not all of them very long, but *The India* has 600 pages in the English translation and is a serious work.

It was in around AD 1000 that Al-Biruni came into contact with Avicenna, the foremost philosopher of his time and a recognised expert on the interpretation of Aristotle. What they would have had in common was the broad-based education, mentioned earlier, although they may have diverged in their teens when aspiring students could specialise.

JAMES MONTGOMERY: *Avicenna had developed his interest in philosophy through reading every bit of Aristotle that he could get by the age of sixteen or seventeen. They shared very much the same educational background, but they differed enormously in how they viewed natural philosophy. For Avicenna, Aristotle had begun to ask the right questions and provide most of the right answers. Al-Biruni took a slightly more quizzical stance towards the ancient Greek tradition when it came to accounting for natural phenomena.*

For example, the natural philosophy of the day said that, when an object was cooled, it would shrink. Al-Biruni asked Avicenna why it was, then, that when there is water in a glass jar and that freezes, the glass jar breaks. Avicenna did not provide a very convincing answer to this simple question. Al-Biruni posed a series of other questions, including the following one that appears insightful (although there is some contention over the interpretation).

JAMES MONTGOMERY: *Aristotle in* On the Heavens *says that planets must move in a complete circle because otherwise a vacuum would be created. Now Al-Biruni asks Avicenna: why is it that, when objects move around an axis in such a way that they either form an oval or a lentil shape, they don't seem to have any problem in completing the circuit?*

Al-Biruni seemed to be talking about the elliptical movement of the planets, something that Kepler took up in the seventeenth century in his *Laws of Planetary Motion*, and he appeared to reckon that the whole notion of circular movement of the heavens was something that Aristotle had invented.

JAMES MONTGOMERY: *Avicenna says, 'Well, we must remember what Themistius says. Themistius says that we should always interpret the philosopher Aristotle in the best possible way.' Avicenna effectively admits that Al-Biruni is right, but then deflects the argument by a quibble and says, 'Of course, things that move inside the celestial sphere are different from the celestial sphere itself, which is tantamount to perfection.' And that really is not a proper answer, in my opinion. Al-Biruni had Avicenna on the run.*

When he was twenty-seven, in the year 1000, Al-Biruni dedicated a work of which the title roughly translates as *The Extant Remains of By-Gone Eras*, and he worked on this book for the rest of his life. It was an exercise in the charting and the mapping of time and he asked how all the world religions, prior to Islam, calculated their religious feasts. He started off with the Persians. Those before Zoroaster were thought to be Buddhists, so he discussed them, and those after Zoroaster were obviously Zoroastrians. Then he moved onto the Sogdians, who were in what is roughly Tajikistan and Uzbekistan now, and then his own people, the Khwarezmians, then the Jews, the Christians and the late antique pagans, and then he moved onto the Muslims themselves. He was trying to work out how accurately time could be charted.

JAMES MONTGOMERY: *That's one of his big obsessions. He, after all, was occupied through numerous courts as an astronomer, and one of the jobs of the astronomer was determining the times of prayer. He has this deep-rooted fascination with time, and one of the things that he says is that counting is fundamental to man's existence.*

Al-Biruni had been enjoying the patronage of Ma'mun in Khwarezm, but that was about to be interrupted. Mahmud of Ghazna was a Turk by origin, from central Asia, and his father had been employed as a professional soldier by a local Persian dynasty, the Samanids. When his father died, Mahmud took over the warlordship and was determined to establish himself as a major political figure in what is now Afghanistan and the edge of India.

HUGH KENNEDY: *One of the things that he wanted to do was establish a proper court, a distinguished court that people would look up to. He needed a number of court intellectuals to make this a proper palace set-up, and Biruni, in Khwarezm, was an obvious target for his recruitment. He conquered Khwarezm and, effectively, kidnapped Biruni and took him back to his court and (this is about 1017). Biruni spent the rest of his life as a court intellectual with Mahmud of Ghazna.*

It was here he started *The India*, and it is remarkable that he wrote it at all because, for most Muslims, Hinduism was dismissed simply as polytheism and idol worship.

HUGH KENNEDY: *Biruni is the one Muslim intellectual of his time, or, indeed, of the pre-modern period, who tries to get behind that and see that Hinduism is, in fact, a complex religion with many different philosophical and intellectual sides to it.*

The India does not made it explicitly clear where Al-Biruni gained his knowledge of Hindu ideas and culture. His biographies talk very little about the period when he was at Mahmud's court, from around 1017 until Mahmud's death in 1030.

AMIRA K. BENNISON: *Mahmud was already engaged on the conquest of India. By India, we don't really mean the whole of the subcontinent. Mahmud's conquests and raids were primarily in the Indus Valley region, what is now Pakistan, rather than what is now India. He did make some raids into the Gangetic plain area, but relatively few. He was already engaged in India, going on annual campaigns, before Al-Biruni arrived at the court in Ghazna, by whatever means he arrived there.*

There are almost no references to Al-Biruni going to India. The text of *The India* has a list of places with very little description of the kind you might ordinarily find in geographical works, so it is difficult to see him as an eyewitness. His information may have come from Mahmud's conquests and the capture of individuals.

AMIRA K. BENNISON: *When Mahmud went into the Punjab, the Indus Valley region, he captured large numbers of people who were also brought back to Ghazna, just as Al-Biruni himself had been brought from Khwarezm. You can imagine in Ghazna, this kind of frontier border town, where Mahmud is trying to build up a court, he was actually collecting elites from all the regions he raided or conquered and bringing them together.*

Al-Biruni would thus have had a great deal of contact with many people of Indian origin. Mahmud of Ghazna had Indians within his army, as the Ghaznavid army was very ethnically mixed, with Turkish warriors as the elite commanding group, but with Arabs from Khorasan, Afghans and Daylamite soldiers from the Caspian Sea. He also captured intellectuals, craftsmen and scholars and brought them back to his city.

The India goes through the various areas of Hindu knowledge, and it is essentially about Hinduism. He says nothing about Buddhism, which was almost extinct there. The inspiration to write it was unlikely to have come from Mahmud of Ghazna, whose objective was raiding the major Hindu shrines for their gold and silver. There is no indication that Mahmud had any interest in Hindu culture whatsoever.

HUGH KENNEDY: *Biruni took a lot of interest in the measurement of time, how they measure their festivals, rituals of purity among the Hindus, how you become a brahmin, what brahmins were and so on. It is described as a work of anthropology, but it is only in a certain sense that; it is about the religious and intellectual life of the Hindus.*

If you wanted to find out what sort of houses the Indians lived in, what they ate, what they wore, then there is nothing of that in *The India*. But, if you want to find out their thought systems, then the work is very eloquent.

Al-Biruni was particularly interested in how Hinduism compared with Greek ideas of science and wisdom.

HUGH KENNEDY: *He is discussing the mathematical aptitude, but he is saying about Hinduism that it is much more than just simple idol worship with tons of Gods. There is a system to it, it has philosophical background. And that's what distinguishes him from the other people.*

There is an Aristotelian aspect to the structure of the work. Al-Biruni described in the introduction to *The India*, using what James Montgomery called 'very disingenuous terms', that he had tried to apply a geometrical method in analysing the thoughts and beliefs of the Indians. What he meant by that was that you do not talk about something unless you have first defined all of the functions and the meaning of the words, and the terms on which you are going to use them.

The arrival of an Indian embassy before Mahmud of Ghazna.

وانیال ایشان مینت یاوردند وخاص وعام در فوایدان عنایم متساوی شدند

ت غنا واسفا رسید ونا جیه ناردین درعرصۀ اسلام افرود این غزود حا دمقامات وناریخ غزوات سلطان معین الدوله ثبتا قاد

JAMES MONTGOMERY: *He begins with the Hindu vision of existence, he begins with God, he moves onto philosophy, ontology, how the soul is liberated from the body, talks about heaven and hell, and so on. He does this roughly over the first seventeen chapters, but he also mentions the religious literature of the Hindus in order to prepare you for the next stage of his argument.*

He then turned to how the Indians described their own universe, a cosmography. He began with mathematical geography and, from there, he moved onto astronomy. The bulk of the book was again concerned with how Indians calculated time, a chronography. He began with the measurements for night and day and went on through every conceivable permutation that the Indians had. If other people were doing this kind of work, theirs has not survived, so we can be fairly confident this interest was something unique to Al-Biruni.

MELVYN BRAGG: *It is still itching away in the back of my mind, I am awfully sorry, to take up Amira's more or less definite declaration that he didn't go there [to India]. Where do you stand on that?*

JAMES MONTGOMERY: *I agree with Amira. There is one reference to a trip to India, it is in a later work. Al-Biruni had devised his own method for measuring the radius of the earth, through observing the*

height of a mountain, and he goes to Mount Nandana in the Punjabi mountain range of Salt, and that's the only time, that I am aware of, that he actually mentions being in India.

Besides, in *The India*, he does allude to restricted freedom, saying at the introduction, 'I haven't been able to move freely,' which James Montgomery took as a reference to the fact that, for thirteen years, he was, effectively, a hostage of Mahmud.

Al-Biruni was a good Muslim and, for him, Islam was a perfect religion. He was in no sense an atheist or freethinker, but he did recognise that other religions shared certain core values even if, on the face of it, they were very different.

HUGH KENNEDY: *He also includes in that Greek philosophy and Plato and so on as having a valid religious point of view. And this is very important not just intellectually but also socially, because the view of most of the people at the court of Mahmud was that Hindus were not people of the book, they didn't have a fundamentally worked-out religious faith and they were essentially expendable.*

When Al-Biruni explained that Hinduism was a valid religion (as was Christianity), he was making a pitch for the rights of the Hindu subjects of Mahmud of Ghazna, with implications that went beyond just the intellectual.

Even if Mahmud thought Hindus were expendable, he still was bringing the Hindu elite back to Ghazna, so obviously he was not killing everyone.

AMIRA K. BENNISON: *Al-Biruni is special, he does stand out by his intellectual curiosity, but I think that one would want to counterbalance that also by saying that, obviously, for some time, within the earlier Abbasid court in Baghdad, there had also been appreciation of Sanskritic knowledge. Where he is unique is taking it so much further and writing such a lengthy book about the belief systems and chronology and cosmology of the Indians.*

Al-Biruni, in his view of how human civilisation developed, was of the opinion that the ancient Greeks and the ancient Indians shared the same set of ideas. He actually said that the doctrine of transmigration, which the Hindus believed in, was borrowed by them from Pythagoras.

JAMES MONTGOMERY: *The further back he goes in time, he becomes a religious syncretist: the Greeks and the Indians share the same effective set of beliefs. This is an exercise in historical archaeology for him. Islam, of course, is at the top, but the Greeks have formed a very important stream in Islam, and Al-Biruni is pondering why the Indians haven't progressed according to this pattern.*

With the death of Mahmud in 1030, it seems that Al-Biruni felt a lot freer, although he chose to remain in Ghazna under Mahmud's successor, his son Ma'sud. He dedicated his next work to Ma'sud, which suggests that the relationship between the two was more like his earlier relationship with Ma'mun in Khwarezm.

AMIRA K. BENNISON: *And, of course, he chooses to spend the rest of his life in Ghazna, so he seems to have become reconciled to being there and to becoming a much more prominent court intellectual rather than the figure in the background that he is with Mahmud.*

He wrote a book of instruction for his patron, the *Canon of Mas'ud*, a re-writing of the *Almagest* of Ptolemy, which had been the most important work of astronomy in the classical period both in late Greek antiquity and Islamic culture.

JAMES MONTGOMERY: *Al-Biruni sets out to provide the new ruler with a comprehensive guide to the structure of the universe, the movement of the planets, together with a number of his own observations. Some historians of mathematics, for example, have seen, in one or two of Al-Biruni's calculations, anticipations of functional relationships.*

He certainly anticipated later discoveries, yet his immediate legacy in the Muslim world was very small, Hugh Kennedy suggested, with no direct connection to what came after. There is only one significant manuscript of *The India*, so his reputation survived by a narrow thread.

HUGH KENNEDY: *It appears again in the Ottoman period and was taken up by nineteenth-century European intellectuals and, in the twentieth century, by Muslims, particularly in Iran, because he is considered to be an Iranian. But nobody seems to have read his book very much, nobody took the research any further. It is a bit of a shooting star.*

With what we know now, it is clear that Al-Biruni had a very brilliant and very flexible mind. He was very inquisitive, and his interest in the natural world was enormous.

AMIRA K. BENNISON: *He did write about minerals, he wrote a book on pharmacy and, in that, he lists all the different herbs and plants you can use and gave their names in five different languages, which is a remarkable achievement. In total, about twenty different dialects and languages are employed in the work. He was a hugely intelligent man.*

COGITO ERGO SUM

There are few sentences in the history of philosophy that have become as famous as their authors. 'The unexamined life is not worth living,' said Socrates, reputedly, in the fifth century BC. 'Man is born free,' wrote Rousseau, two millennia later, 'but everywhere he is in chains.' Pithier still is Nietzsche's statement, 'God is dead.' But perhaps the best-known saying in the history of philosophy is one usually quoted in Latin, cogito ergo sum *– 'I think therefore I am.' This statement first appeared in 1637 in a work by the French philosopher René Descartes. Despite its simplicity, it is the starting point for an entire system of thought; today, Descartes' 'cogito' argument is commonly regarded as one of the foundations of modern philosophy. What does this apparently unassuming sentence mean, and why does it still provoke criticism and comment, almost 400 years after it was written?*

With Melvyn to discuss Descartes and his statement 'cogito ergo sum' were: Susan James, professor of philosophy at Birkbeck, University of London; John Cottingham, professor emeritus of philosophy at the University of Reading, professor of philosophy of religion at the University of Roehampton and honorary fellow of St John's College, Oxford; and Stephen Mulhall, professor of philosophy at the University of Oxford.

Descartes first used this short phrase in passing, in the work that he published in 1637 called *The Discourse on the Method of Rightly Conducting One's Reason and of Seeking the Truth in the Sciences*, to which Melvyn referred above, and which Descartes wrote in French.

SUSAN JAMES: *There he wrote, 'Je pense, donc je suis.' That was translated into Latin as 'cogito ergo sum' – I think therefore I am. This is the origin of this phrase, and there Descartes presents it as what he calls the first principle of philosophy, the first metaphysical principle of philosophy.*

It was not until 1641, in *The Meditations*, that he began to spell out the argument he was summarising there, which the programme explored.

Descartes was born in Tours, France, in 1596 and he went to the Jesuit College of La Flèche, which provided a very sound and solid education with Latin and Greek and rhetoric, mathematics and philosophy.

SUSAN JAMES: *After he had finished school, he went to study law at the University of Poitiers briefly because, in spite of his father's wish that he should become a lawyer, he went off to be a soldier. In Holland, where he joined an army, he came into contact with a famous mathematician, Beeckman, and began to produce really original and creative work in geometry and algebra.*

This was the beginning of Descartes' intellectual project, a fascination with the clear method that he was to develop for solving mathematical problems, and that became a more ambitious explanatory system for the whole of nature.

In his education, he would have imbibed the dominant system, scholasticism, which had been going strong for several centuries. This was based on the principles of Aristotle, elaborated so as to be consistent with the Bible and with Christian doctrine.

JOHN COTTINGHAM: *One of the most important [features] was that each subject was, in a sense, separate, it had its own methods and standards of precision, as Aristotle himself originally said. It was also qualitative – that's to say, things were explained, things behaved the way they did because of certain real qualities they possessed. For example, things fell to the ground because of the quality of gravitas or heaviness.*

Although this was the system in which Descartes was educated, he thought that this approach was not really valuable as an explanation of natural phenomena.

JOHN COTTINGHAM: *Instead, you ought to look for quantitative explanations, that things behaved the way they did because of their size and shape and motion. The scholastic system was largely purposive; things were explained as moving towards a goal, or purpose. Again, Descartes reacted against this, and thought instead that we should search for mechanical explanations.*

This was an inspiring time for Descartes, with so many developments in the understanding of the natural world. While Descartes was still at school, Galileo's discoveries of the moons of Jupiter had been published. These were the first clear experimental confirmations that earth was not the centre of the universe, and confirmed the Copernican view from a few decades before Descartes was born.

Descartes also drew inspiration not from others, but from three powerful dreams he had in November 1619, when he was twenty-three and travelling as a gentleman soldier in southern Germany.

JOHN COTTINGHAM: *[He] spent the whole day shut up in a stove-heated room, and he had three very vivid dreams. The first one involved a hurricane, which pushed him around and frightened him severely. He took refuge in a chapel and met someone who presented him with a fruit, which he thought was a melon from a foreign country. The second dream was very quick, it involved a thunder clap and sparks. In the third dream, there was a series of books. There was a Latin poem that begins with the line, 'What path in life shall I follow?' Then a motto of Pythagoras appeared; then, finally, an unfinished encyclopaedia, which he took to represent all the sciences connected together.*

One of the things that Descartes drew from these dreams was the idea of the essential unity, or continuity, of human knowledge. In certain contexts, he famously used the image of the tree of human knowledge with metaphysics, first philosophy, as the roots, then physics as the trunk and all the other sciences as the branches.

STEPHEN MULHALL: *On the one hand, he seems to think that there is a fundamental unity in the whole system of human knowledge, and so it must be possible in principle to articulate those various bodies of knowledge as forming part of a fundamental unity. And yet there is a certain kind of hierarchy built into that image. Physics gets a certain kind of priority in relation to the other natural sciences and, in turn, metaphysics, first philosophy, has a certain priority over physics.*

Descartes was committing himself to that project, to explore a certain kind of unity of human knowledge, and perhaps this is what he interpreted from the image of the encyclopaedia in the third dream.

There was another aspect of this context that was fundamental to his sense of how to go about developing that project. If first philosophy, or metaphysics, was the root of the whole enterprise, then one needed some way of establishing genuinely reliable knowledge to feed into that.

STEPHEN MULHALL: *The reliability of that knowledge can then be transmitted through the rest of the edifice, if you like. The method that Descartes uses is that of scepticism, a kind of methodical doubt.*

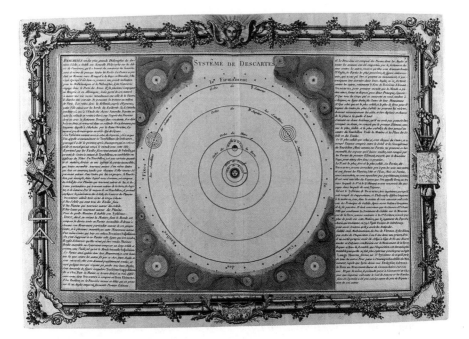

The centre of this plate depicts
Descartes' system of the universe.

This was not just a radical break with Aristotelian ways of understanding nature, it was one that revealed that the vision of the world, which is delivered to us naturally through the senses, is fundamentally unreliable.

In 1637, Descartes had produced *The Discourse on the Method*, mentioned earlier, a conception of method that he cleaved to throughout his intellectual career. There were four aspects to these, and the second, third and fourth had to do with principles: that one should break down the areas that one tries to study into the simplest possible parts; that one should build from the simple to the complex; and that one should try to make sure that the chain of reasoning, from the simple to the complex, is as comprehensive as possible.

STEPHEN MULHALL: *The first principle is the one that turns out to be much more fruitful, and radical, than it might look. According to the first rule of this method, Descartes says that one should only rely upon that which one clearly and distinctly perceives to be true, and that turns out to be the core of the method that gets much more systematically articulated in* The Meditations.

The 'cogito' argument, Susan James continued, was something that Descartes adapted from Augustine and, in its simplest form, it is the idea that, when you are thinking something, when you are doubting something, you know that you are doubting it. It was later, in the context of *The Meditations*, that he explained what use he was going to make of this claim.

JOHN COTTINGHAM: *To find something stable and secure, you have to demolish the whole lot and start again right from the foundations, that's what he says in the opening of the first meditation. There are six meditations, perhaps modelled on the spiritual exercises of the Jesuits who brought him up. And it starts with these waves of doubt, you push doubt to the limit to see if anything survives. He starts by doubting the senses, our basic source of knowledge, the five senses.*

Descartes mentioned the stick in water that looks bent but is actually straight, or the sun and the moon, which look roughly the same size to people on earth even though the sun is enormously bigger. Then, he said, here he was, sitting by the fire in his winter dressing gown, surely that was so certain that he could not be wrong? He reasoned no, that was not certain, because sometimes he had vivid dreams and thought that something like this was going on, only to wake and find he had been asleep in bed.

JOHN COTTINGHAM: *Then he broadens the doubt to think: maybe the whole of life might be a dream, maybe the whole external world, all the images are just beamed into my mind by a malicious demon, bent on deceiving me. Then he comes out of that into certainty because he reasons: even if I am being deceived, even if I am doubting, I must still be here in some sense to do the doubting. So I, at least, must exist. So, as he phrases it in* The Meditations: *'sum, existo' – I am, I exist.*

The 'cogito' argument was meant to serve the purpose of finding something that was not doubtful, but this was, Susan James suggested, a very small Archimedean point with which to move the world. What Descartes could be sure of was only that, as he was having a thought, he knew he was having it.

SUSAN JAMES: *As I am remembering that I was walking down the street, I know that I am having this thought of remembering myself walking down the street. Of course, I don't know whether it is true that I was walking down the street. As long as I am thinking some thought or other, then I know that I exist. But it seems that, at this stage, all I know about myself, at the most, is that I'm this succession of momentary thoughts.*

In Stephen Mulhall's view, there is a certain kind of performative aspect to the argument (if it is an argument) that is being presented. The force of the conclusion is only going to have an impact on us in so far as we are actually engaged in the process of reflection that delivers that conclusion. This connects with a bigger issue, which is that 'cogito ergo sum' would have looked like a very peculiar kind of argument at the time Descartes put it forward.

STEPHEN MULHALL: *The canonical example that philosophers always offer of argument structure involves Socrates: 'All men are mortal, Socrates is a man; therefore Socrates is mortal.' You only get to the conclusion because you have two premises from which the conclusion follows. When someone tells you 'cogito ergo sum', you* *naturally start looking for what the premises might be and, usually, at least in the form of a syllogistic argument, one premise isn't enough.*

To his objectors, Susan James explained, Descartes would reply that this was not really the way he wanted one to take the argument. The order of discovery is that you perceive with a simple intuition of the mind, 'I am, I exist,' and that is how you get started. In fact, John Cottingham added, Descartes said in his introduction that he did not want to have anything to do with those who were unprepared to follow him along this path and meditate for themselves.

Descartes had to get out of this tiny flickering candle of subjective certainty to a whole system of knowledge, and this was where God came in.

JOHN COTTINGHAM: *Once he is aware of himself as existing, he is immediately aware of his imperfection of himself as finite. There are many things he doesn't know, there are many things he can't do. And yet he has a sense of something infinitely greater than himself. He has the idea of this infinite being, and this idea, he reasons, couldn't have been created by him, from his own resources, and therefore must have been put in his mind by God, as he puts it, 'like the mark of the craftsman stamped on his work'.*

Once God was in the picture, Descartes had something good and benevolent, and he could then reason that his mind was a reliable instrument and he could get going and build his new system of science.

Once Descartes had this distinct idea of the mind as something that existed, he could begin to explore it. One of the ideas he found was that of physical bodies.

SUSAN JAMES: *He says, 'What I do know about a body, for sure, is that, in order to be a body, it must have certain essential properties,' which Descartes calls 'extension' or 'extendedness'. Roughly speaking, it must have shape and size. He has got two clear and distinct ideas, one of his mind as something fundamentally thinking, the other of his body as fundamentally extended.*

From this, he argued he was in a position to see that the mind and body are distinct and that there is nothing in his idea of a mind that depends on his idea of a body, and there is nothing in his idea of a body that depends on the existence of a mind.

SUSAN JAMES: *Now he has done something quite dramatic really, which is that he has generated a quantifiable conception of body that can be the basis of physical science, and a quite separate idea of a mind, which is just something that thinks. This is against a background of an Aristotelian notion of a mind or soul, which has all sorts of capacities other than thinking.*

In *The Meditations*, this sense of a fundamental essential distinctness between mind and body came out of the application of the method of sceptical doubt. There is also a way in which this sense of mind and body fitted into a broader cultural context, particularly in theology.

STEPHEN MULHALL: *What it suggests is that, if the mind is essentially immaterial, a belief in the immortality of the soul is entirely consistent with the basic principles of first philosophy. Matter is the kind of thing that decays and decomposes, because it is extended, it is divisible. Something that is essentially non-material is indivisible, so what you get is a conception of the mind that is entirely constant with the conception of the soul as being of the essence of the human individual.*

There was concern among other philosophers about what became known as the Cartesian circle, which went back to the question of the function of God in the system, as presented in *The Meditations*. There, God gave a reason to treat not just our senses but also our reason as generally reliable.

STEPHEN MULHALL: *The worry, that is encompassed in the idea of there being something circular here, is on what basis do we believe in God's existence, if not the fact that we clearly and distinctly perceive the truth of the arguments that Descartes offers for that belief? But it is God who is supposed to underwrite the validity of that general criterion for truthfulness.*

Another way of putting this, John Cottingham added, was an earlier formulation in Descartes' *Rules for the Direction of the Mind*, which was 'sum ergo deus est' – I am therefore God exists. It looked as though the whole thing was a vicious circle.

Hobbes was one of the people whom Descartes invited to write objections to *The Meditations* and Descartes replied to them. Hobbes was a materialist and picked Descartes up on the 'cogito' argument in particular, and raised the question of what this 'I' was that was doing the thinking, which Descartes said was the mind.

SUSAN JAMES: *Hobbes says, 'You say it is mind, but how can you be sure that's all it is, maybe it is also a body.' Hobbes seems to think that it must be a body, because only bodies can be the subjects that are capable of having thoughts predicated of them. Descartes points out, quite reasonably, that Hobbes is begging the question there. But there is a problem, which is what exactly this 'cogito' argument establishes about who this 'I' is.*

As the centuries rolled on, John Cottingham said, there was a lot of emphasis on subjectivity; the movement we know as existentialism laid a lot of stress on the individual awareness of the subject, and the idea that the subject had to construct reality from him or herself. That was Descartes' starting point so, in a sense, the existentialists were inheriting that point of the individual existing self and starting philosophy from there.

JOHN COTTINGHAM: *The difference is that, when you get on to Nietzsche and Sartre, you have got Descartes but without God. You have got the whole thing depending on just the individual thinker, meditating and wondering what's going on. Whereas with Descartes, you have got this radical subjective reflection, but against the background of a firm traditional belief in the infinite source of* *his being, God. The moderns are very different, although they see Descartes as their ancestor.*

In fairness to Descartes, he added, as the programme came to a close, Melvyn and his guests had been discussing very transparent thoughts or conscious acts, like 'cogito ergo sum'. That was not all that mattered to Descartes. In his later work, he acknowledged that there was much besides, notably passions and emotions, love, hate, fear and so on, which were much more complicated and for which there was no such immediate, transparent awareness of all the implications of what was going on inside.

SUSAN JAMES: *The 'cogito' continues to be at the root of contemporary work on the nature of self-consciousness, and Descartes has recently become much more a figure studied for his work on the passions and these more obscure relationships between mind and body.*

SIMONE DE BEAUVOIR

*'One is not born, but rather becomes a woman.' So wrote Simone de
Beauvoir in her best-known and most influential work,* The Second
Sex, *her exploration of what it means to be a woman in a world
defined by men. Published in 1949, it was an immediate success with
the thousands of women who bought it, if much less so with some
of the male critics. Beauvoir was born in France, in 1908, to a high
bourgeois family, though her father lost his fortune when she was
a girl. Some commentators say that was her good fortune as, with
no dowry, she pursued her education to get work. In a key exam to
allow her to teach philosophy, she came second only to Jean-Paul
Sartre, who was re-taking it. They became lovers and, for the rest of
their lives together, intellectual sparring partners. Sartre concentrated
on existentialist philosophy, Beauvoir explored that and existential
ethics, plus she wrote novels, of which the most successful was* The
Mandarins, *and, increasingly in the decades leading up to her death
in 1986, wrote about the situation of women in the world.*

With Melvyn to discuss Simone de Beauvoir were: Christina Howells, professor of French and fellow of Wadham College, Oxford; Margaret Atack, professor of French at the University of Leeds; and Ursula Tidd, professor of modern French literature and thought at the University of Manchester.

Simone de Beauvoir had a bourgeois background, Christina Howells began, in a conventional family, with a younger sister of whom she was extremely fond, Poupette, while her mother was apparently a religious woman. Beauvoir was sent to a Catholic school and, while she was there, she discovered that she was an atheist. She excelled at school and studied literature and mathematics in particular, moving into philosophy when she went to the Sorbonne and, in Paris, somehow followed classes at the École Normale, which was for men only. Students at the École Normale were prepared for the *agrégation*, the very competitive exam after which the entrants could be allowed to teach in a school or, if they pursued it further, a university.

CHRISTINA HOWELLS: *She didn't go to the two or three years of preparation for getting into the École Normale, she wasn't allowed to go there officially. And she had a really stupendous academic record. She came second to Sartre when she took the* agrégation.

MELVYN BRAGG: *This is in the whole country?*

CHRISTINA HOWELLS: *That's right. She was twenty-one, he was twenty-four, and he had sat it before.*

Melvyn observed that Sartre was fascinated by Beauvoir, this young, brilliant woman, and she was slightly in awe of him, and they got cracking, then and there.

CHRISTINA HOWELLS: *It seems that he was fascinated by her. He was a very ugly man and she was lovely, so it is not surprising, and they were both so intelligent. I know she always claimed that Sartre was superior, but I think that was very modest of her, bizarrely modest given what she has done later.*

MELVYN BRAGG: *But she made (retrospectively, I think, but still) the statement: 'I knew that my life would be bound to his life, for the rest of my life.'*

CHRISTINA HOWELLS: *Yes, she did; it is hard to know, isn't it? Because we probably all feel a bit like that.*

It was an open relationship, Margaret Atack continued, and they never set up home together, which was very unconventional for its time and for her background. He was as dazzled by her intellect as he was by her looks and it was a meeting of minds.

MARGARET ATACK: *A very loving and affectionate and intimate relationship. She certainly wasn't interested in becoming a creator of philosophical systems in the way that he was. She was always within philosophy but she said, 'I don't have to invent a philosophical system to feel myself Sartre's equal, or independent.'*

Melvyn pictured these two people of supreme intelligence meeting each other, sitting in Les Deux Magots or Café Flore along the Boulevard Saint-Germain, talking philosophy all the time, along with gossip about their entourage.

MARGARET ATACK: *She was working within the importance of his apprehension of being in the world, of the existentialist framework, of freedom of choice, of commitment, and all their works were jointly (almost) edited. She used to send him her manuscripts; he used to send her his. Her elaboration of the nature of self and other, interaction with other people, they were both very involved in that.*

Beauvoir saw herself primarily as a writer and began her novels when France was occupied, first *She Came to Stay* and then *The Blood of Others*. *She Came to Stay* (1943) was Beauvoir's first published novel and, Ursula Tidd said, it is a novel that explores one of the grand themes of Beauvoir's intellectual life, the whole theme of the 'other', looking at what happens when we realise that there are other people in the world, and how we respond to other people in the world.

URSULA TIDD: *One of Beauvoir's philosophical concepts is the notion of the existential situation. Other people are part of our existential situation. Beauvoir, in this novel, is exploring what it is to begin to take into account the presence of the other, and she explores it through a triadic relationship, loosely based on the relationship that she was having with Olga Kosakiewicz, a triadic relationship they had in the 1930s.*

One can read that as a novel of personal relationships, but it is really about the terror of the other. *The Blood of Others* (1945) was very much a product of Beauvoir's wartime experience and she was again exploring the presence of the other, but in the context of situated action. One of the main characters is Jean Blomart, a resistance leader, and much of the action takes place in the context of the Second World War.

URSULA TIDD: *One of the main decisions that opens the novel is Jean Blomart trying to decide whether or not to sanction actions of sabotage against the Nazis in occupied Paris. It is a novel about the ethics of responsibility and the ethics of action. The epigraph to the novel is taken from Dostoevsky's* Brothers Karamazov *and it sums the novel up: 'Each of us is responsible to everyone, and for everything.' Which is, of course, a terribly tall order.*

Beauvoir brought out *The Ethics of Ambiguity* just two years after that novel. Ambiguity was a very strange word in this context, Christina Howells thought. It was more about the ethics of complexity or the ethics of existentialism. The problem for an existentialist, trying to compose an ethics, is that, for existentialism, there are no pre-given values.

*Simone de Beauvoir
with Jean-Paul Sartre*

CHRISTINA HOWELLS: *You make yourself, but you also make
your ethics. In common sense, we might think that we know,
roughly, what's good and what's bad: we mustn't steal, we mustn't
hit people, we mustn't kill people. If you are a more rigorous
philosopher, say a Kantian philosopher, then there are also categorical
imperatives, things that definitely are always wrong, such as lying
or killing. For the existentialist, it is situational: what are the
consequences of this behaviour?*

The means could contaminate the ends. For example, what should
someone in the resistance do in a wartime situation where killing one
of the occupiers could lead to fatal reprisals?

Existentialism is about choosing, Ursula Tidd continued, where you are free to make your choices, but that choice is constrained by the consequences, which are the kind of person you become, and the kind of world that you create through your behaviour.

MARGARET ATACK: *The choices are eloquent of your values. You are always on this treadmill, you can never stop. The ambiguity is also that, yes, you go for action, but you can never go with a quiet conscience. You can never think, 'Well, that's it, I have ticked it, and I have done it,' because you can never have clean hands.*

In *The Second Sex* (1949), Beauvoir's best-known book, one of the big ideas is that gender is constructed, by which Beauvoir meant something specific.

MARGARET ATACK: *[With] existentialism, we have no human nature, we are free, we are totally not determined. There is a philosophical rejection from the outset that there might be an* éternel féminin, *as the French call it (you know, 'just like a woman'). We do not have gendered natures in the sense we don't have any kind of nature.*

There are the givens of one's situation, but what matters is what you do with the cards that life has dealt you.

URSULA TIDD: *Beauvoir is encouraging women in* The Second Sex *to throw themselves into the world and to seize their lives and to make their essence. When she is talking about becoming a woman and not being born a woman, her point really is an anti-naturalist one: that there is no inherent nature that decrees that men are like this and women are like that.*

Patriarchal ideology has certain (what Beauvoir would call) *myths* about women; there are also myths about men, but here Beauvoir was interested in writing about women. For example, there is the myth that motherhood is a natural situation that all women are destined to fulfil.

URSULA TIDD: *Beauvoir argues controversially that there is no maternal instinct, and that the experience of real mothers is terribly variable. In the same way, one could argue that the experience of paternity is terribly variable as well. In the second volume, which is subtitled* Lived Experience, *Beauvoir is at pains to show the micro-politics of gender relations and the ways in which girls and women learn very quickly, both at conscious and at unconscious levels, how to become women who conform to patriarchal ideology.*

Women become the second sex, relative to the masculine, yet women do have choices, and it is up to women to seize those choices. Women respond to that situation in various ways, Beauvoir argued, and sometimes women are complicit with patriarchal ideology.

The Second Sex had a mixed reception. It was very popular, but, at the same time, was seen as rather rude.

CHRISTINA HOWELLS: *Mauriac was very indignant and said that he didn't wish to know about the workings of the author's vagina,* *which caused quite a scandalous reaction. Beauvoir is quite explicit about bodily functions. She talks about menstruation, for example, and abortion. She says that women smell and women get constipated, all to do with menstruation. At the time, it was really rather revolutionary to be talking about it at all.*

Beauvoir also talked about women without really talking about femininity, which some feminists found difficult to deal with.

Before the war, it is unlikely that Beauvoir would have said she was a feminist. She, like Sartre, was not very interested in politics and they were much more interested in themselves.

MARGARET ATACK: *After the transition they went through in the war, she became much more interested in the rootedness of experience, and the rootedness of women's experience, and the disparagement and the oppression and the inequality and the systematic denigration of the female in this gender relationship between the sexes. That's hugely feminist. I find her works are never hostile to women, but that's not widely shared in some circles.*

Around the time of the May 1968 protests, young Marxist feminists such as Christine Delphy approached Beauvoir as they wanted her support in the second wave of feminist activity in France. Beauvoir was very humble towards them, for an intellectual.

URSULA TIDD: *She could have played the grande dame, but she didn't do that. She lent her support in a very discreet way, she financed political campaigns, she lent her support for the campaign for legalising abortion in France, which was passed in 1975. That was very much appreciated by young feminists, who needed that kind of support to get some of these campaigns off the ground.*

After *The Second Sex*, Beauvoir wrote *The Mandarins* (1954), which won the Prix Goncourt. There was a perfect storm around this novel, which gave it more momentum, as she was already notorious after *The Second Sex*. Existentialism had been flavour of the month, and Beauvoir and Sartre were intellectual celebrities. The novel took on the relationship between France and America, Margaret Atack said, with the increasing domination of America, and the relationship between the intellectual left and the Soviet Union. It had a group of intellectuals who were writers, who were grappling with the ambiguities of being committed, politically, in a world where it no longer seemed so black and white to them as it had been in the resistance. Readers liked to spot the people in Beauvoir's circle, behind the story, something she reportedly hated.

Christina Howells teaches it to students as a *roman à clef*, as readers can clearly see who is who in *The Mandarins*.

CHRISTINA HOWELLS: *There is Camus in it, there is Beauvoir in it, Sartre in it. Camus was very upset by it because the character Henri drives his wife insane in the book and, of course, Camus' first wife sadly did go to a mental asylum. Henri is very promiscuous in the book; that's also true of Camus.*

With Beauvoir, Ursula Tidd added, her own life was also the stuff of literature, so, in a sense, she lived to write and she wrote to live, and everything was witnessed in her writing.

URSULA TIDD: *[The Mandarins] is also about the politics of truth telling in the immediate Cold War period in France. One of the central ethical dilemmas in that novel is whether to expose the existence of the Soviet gulags to the French left, and that particular question is something that the character Henri Perron, who is this editor of [an] independent left-wing journal, has to agonise over.*

MELVYN BRAGG: *What's his agony? Letting down the communist side by telling the truth?*

URSULA TIDD: *Exactly, exactly.*
It was also letting down the workers, Margaret Atack said, as the communists were the biggest party in the elections after the Second World War.

Beauvoir went on to write her autobiography, which is perhaps no easier to categorise than her other works. The novels are philosophical, Christina Howells suggested, while the philosophy involves a lot of examples and the autobiography itself is a literary work, not simply a recounting.

Since Beauvoir's death, letters have been discovered between her and Sartre that have shown a more complex side to their characters. In the public discourse that was hostile to her, Beauvoir was very much treated as the little woman next to Sartre, until the letters appeared.

MARGARET ATACK: *Then one realises everything she had said about them exchanging views was perfectly true. They write to each other at great length about their relationships with other people, about the nights they pass with them. It is very intimate, and it is very detailed. And here was a level of shock – suddenly they became a centre of a web of intrigue.*

Sartre and Beauvoir shared young adult women between each other, it transpired, and readers were shocked by the way they wrote about the intimate details. Ursula Tidd thought Beauvoir recognised, at the end of her life, that they had made some serious mistakes in the relationships that they had had with the women they drew to them.

In the studio afterwards, Christina Howells observed that, while *The Second Sex* was written over fifty years ago, it is still an eye-opener. Some of the topics in there are things that we still do not talk about. And Beauvoir's argument was apparently persuasive; in late interviews, she actually made Sartre say that the feminist struggle was more important than the working-class struggle (although whether he really thought it was another matter).

ZENO'S PARADOXES

*The ancient Greek thinker Zeno of Elea flourished in the fifth century BC.
His great innovation in philosophy was the paradox, a tool to highlight
the unexpected consequences of common sense ideas, to question
assumptions and to provoke new theories. For example, according
to Zeno's paradoxes, motion is not possible. An arrow in flight does
not move. The fastest runner in Homer, Achilles, could never catch up
with the tortoise in a race, if he gave it a head start. Philosophers from
Aristotle to Bertrand Russell have tried to refute his ideas, or explain
them, with varying success. Innovations in mathematics with Newton
and Leibniz went some way to demonstrate flaws in Zeno's arguments,
but the questions he raised 2,500 years ago about time and space are as
relevant as ever and they have re-emerged in quantum physics.*

⊱─◆─⊰

With Melvyn to discuss the paradoxes of Zeno were: Marcus du
Sautoy, professor of mathematics and Simonyi professor for the public
understanding of science at the University of Oxford; Barbara M.
Sattler, senior lecturer in philosophy at the University of St Andrews;
and James Warren, professor of ancient philosophy at the University
of Cambridge and fellow of Corpus Christi College, Cambridge.

*In the arrow paradox, Zeno claims
that, if someone shoots an arrow, it
never moves but is always at rest.*

Zeno lived in the middle of the fifth century BC and came from Elea, a town on the west coast of southern Italy and, James Warren said, we know that he travelled a lot in Greece and wrote maybe just one work, which included these paradoxes, of which we know about seven or eight, some to do with motion, some to do with plurality.

JAMES WARREN: *One of the most important people in Zeno's intellectual life was from the same city, a character called Parmenides. Parmenides wrote a very peculiar poem in hexameter verse, in the style of Homer, and he attempted to set out to prove that there was only one thing, and that it was changeless and motionless and perfect. Whatever else you think there is, if it is not this one thing, it isn't actually there.*

Plato wrote a dialogue in which the two of them came to Athens, and Zeno was cast as a defender of Parmenides. That is one way to think of these paradoxes – as Zeno's attempt to undercut possible objections to Parmenides' curious thesis. They travelled to the great festivals, such as the Panathenaia, and they would have given demonstrations and public recitations and met people there.

JAMES WARREN: *Parmenides is reacting to a tradition of cosmological thinking, of people attempting to explain the world and how the world worked and functioned, often in terms of identifying some basic principle, or element, out of which the world was constructed, from water, or air, or something else.*

Those people were relying on there being a plurality of things and on there being things that changed and were in motion in order to account for the way the world worked. Parmenides set out to show how that view was grossly mistaken.

Turning to paradoxes, which Zeno would use, Barbara Sattler explained that the word comes from the Greek, being something that is against (*para*) common expectations or beliefs (*doxa*).

BARBARA SATTLER: *In a philosophical context, by paradox we normally understand that we derive a problematic conclusion from sound premises. It seems we have good starting points and we do right reasoning, and yet we get to a conclusion that is untenable. Why is it untenable? Either because it is inconsistent in itself or it contradicts other beliefs, opinions, that we hold.*

One paradox that is quite famous is that of the bald man. We would all agree that, if somebody has no hair, that person is bald. If the person has one hair, we would still call the person bald; two hairs, probably still bald; three hairs, the same, and so on.

BARBARA SATTLER: *One hair doesn't seem to make a difference, but yet, if this person has 10,000 hairs, it seems this person is not bald any longer. So where does that stop? Is it from 100 hairs onwards we say, 'This person is not bald,' but at ninety-nine hairs, 'This person is still bald'? That doesn't seem to be right.*

MELVYN BRAGG: *Why not?*

BARBARA SATTLER: *Because it seems baldness is not a concept or notion where we can give a clear quantitative determination.*

We all agree on certain ideas of baldness and we all have a problem with saying when a person stops being bald. What that shows is that there seem to be some notions that can be called 'vague'. Another example might be: how many grains do you have to take away from a heap of grain before it is no longer a heap? Paradoxes such as these are very fruitful for philosophy.

BARBARA SATTLER: *In philosophy, a lot of what we do is actually done conceptually, so our theories are not falsified or verified by the world outside. Paradoxes are very important because they tell us something has gone wrong. You have to go back to your concept and look again.*

In Greece, in Zeno's time, mathematicians were exploring abstract ideas and to these, too, paradoxes would apply. The Egyptians and the Babylonians had been trying to describe the world with the new language of mathematics, but their approach was often geometric and functional.

MARCUS DU SAUTOY: *They are measuring areas of land, volumes of pyramids and things like that. But then, in the 100 years before Zeno, we have the Pythagoreans beginning to appear on the scene and they are trying to prove things. They are trying to prove that it is not just a calculation they want to do, they want to produce a proof that something will always work.*

Perhaps the idea of analytic thought came from Greeks wanting to do politics, trying to prove that laws would work and would always apply. The idea of paradox was starting to appear at this time in mathematics, perhaps a little after Zeno, as a tool that was a proof, a *reductio ad absurdum*.

MARCUS DU SAUTOY: *Make a hypothesis, for example, that the square root of 2 can be written as a fraction. Then you follow that through, and you end up with a ridiculous conclusion that odd numbers equal even numbers, and then you realise that that's absurd, it is a kind of paradox. But the paradox is very useful, because you can then work backwards and say, 'Okay, something along the way was wrong.'*

The Pythagoreans discovered that the square root of 2 could be approximated by fractions, more and more; but this idea of teasing out a logical argument, arriving at something absurd, was a very powerful tool for complex problems, such as the one the Greeks had with infinity.

MARCUS DU SAUTOY: *Infinity doesn't seem to exist, I can't see anything infinite. They have this idea of actual infinity and potential infinity. There is a potential for infinity. For example, Euclid proves that the primes have the potential to go on for ever, but there is a claim that this isn't an actual infinity, you can't actually have infinitely many primes, they have the potential to go on for ever.*

By using paradoxes, the mathematicians could reveal that their ideas of infinity might be wrong, something that was explored later in this programme.

Another thing to bear in mind, James Warren suggested, was that these paradoxes were playful, a way of Zeno embarrassing an interlocutor just as Socrates embarrassed people. He could take someone and say, 'Well, you think things move, don't you?' 'Yes, of course I think things move.' 'Well, you would agree, wouldn't you, that, in order to get from A to B, you must get halfway from A to B?' 'Well, yes, of course.' 'Well, surely you would then agree that, to get from A to halfway to B, you would have to get halfway from A to halfway between A to B?' And so it would continue. This is a dichotomy paradox, the 'cutting in two' paradox.

JAMES WARREN: *What's problematic then is that you have got your person to agree that to cross any spatial extension entails an endless series of prior journeys; in order to do something, first I have to do something prior. If that's an endless series of prior requirements, the killer line will say, 'But you don't think you can complete an infinite series of tasks, can you?'*

There is obviously a sense in which the impossibility of completing an infinite number of tasks is true, in which case asking someone to cross a room would be asking for something impossible.

The mathematicians and philosophers were grappling with similar problems, if in different ways and with different outcomes. Aristotle thought there was a distinction between potential and actual infinity. Potentially you could think of your journey as including as many sub-journeys as you liked, but you do not actually have to do all of those in order to cross the room.

JAMES WARREN: *Aristotle is working from the assumption that, of course, Zeno must be wrong, because, of course, things do move, and there are many things. He is of the opinion that the absurdity of the conclusion licenses you to think there must be something wrong with the argument ... and he can just carry on writing his book on physics.*

Aristotle did not kill the argument over infinite prior steps with this. It continued, it emerged and it re-emerged.

Perhaps the best known of Zeno's paradoxes is Achilles and the tortoise, which Barbara Sattler noted was a variation of the dichotomy paradox. In this, Achilles, the fastest runner in the ancient world, had a race with a tortoise and gave the tortoise a head start. If we imagine they are racing on a 100m track and the tortoise is starting 10m ahead, Achilles first has to cover those 10m but, during the time that Achilles takes to cover the 10m, the tortoise has moved on. By the time Achilles has reached that point where the tortoise has been, the tortoise will have moved on again.

BARBARA SATTLER: *The distance between Achilles and the tortoise will get less and less but will never get to zero. It seems that Achilles, the fastest runner in the ancient world, will never be able to overtake this slow tortoise. That's the paradox. I don't think that Zeno wanted to show we will never experience somebody overtaking somebody else. What he is telling us is, 'Okay, you describe what is going on, and you will get into contradictions.'*

In this paradox is the challenge of the infinite, and particularly something called an infinite series, because we are having to add up infinitely many things and are trying to understand whether that is actually physically possible.

MARCUS DU SAUTOY: *Let's say he does the first step in half a minute; the second step he does in half the time, so a quarter of a minute; the third step in an eighth of a minute; the next step in a sixteenth of a minute. It looks like he is having to do infinitely many tasks, but we understand that he can do infinitely many tasks because it can take him a finite amount of time. This infinite series actually adds up, if you take infinitely many of them, to the answer 'one'.*

Mathematicians had to come up with some way of understanding the adding-up of infinitely many things and whether that had some sort of physical reality, and that advance did not really happen until the seventeenth and eighteenth centuries.

In the physical reality, we do not have a problem with these things, as we see the tortoise being overtaken, but, in mathematics, which we use in order to describe the physical reality, there seems to be a real problem with dealing with infinity.

BARBARA SATTLER: *We have, in the nineteenth century, a new way of dealing with actual infinity. Remember Aristotle had this distinction between potential and actual infinity, and there was always this idea – there can't be actual infinity, there can only be potential. Then, with Cantor and others, we had this idea: there can be an actual infinity that just needs a different way of dealing with it. That goes against our intuitions, by the way.*

Georg Cantor was examining the questions underlying these paradoxes over 2,000 years after they were raised.

There is another famous paradox, which is the arrow in flight. Parmenides argued, and Zeno put it forward, that, if someone shoots an arrow, it never moves but is always at rest. If you think of *any* point in the arrow's journey – an instant, a temporal point – at that point, the arrow is occupying a space, exactly arrow-shaped and arrow-sized.

JAMES WARREN: *It is not moving within that space, it is stationary at that instant. You can think of it as either too snugly held by space, or there is not enough time for it to do any moving, because we've specified that we are talking about a durationless point in time. You could pick any instant in the arrow's journey and it would always be the case that, at that instant, the arrow is stationary, so it seems to be true throughout the journey that the arrow is not moving.*

The challenge of this arrow, Marcus du Sautoy suggested, was that it was decelerating as it went forwards, so had a different speed at every particular time and, for it to be moving, it had to have a speed.

Bust of Zeno of Elea.

MARCUS DU SAUTOY: *If you just take an instant of time, the time interval is zero, the distance that's gone is zero, but speed is distance divided by time, so it doesn't have a speed then, does it? Zero distance divided by zero time.*

What Newton and Leibniz did was realise that actually this thing did have a speed, but the time interval that you are measuring gets smaller and smaller. Calculus was a way of making sense of this challenge that Zeno had set, as Newton and Leibniz had developed a mathematics to understand a world in flux.

JAMES WARREN: *I don't think Zeno would be impressed by that.*

MARCUS DU SAUTOY: *Really?*

JAMES WARREN: *I think that's mathematically clever, but philosophically not so smart, because you have cheated. You have assumed the arrow is moving, and then have described how it can be moving at a time, at an instant, on the assumption that it is crossing* *some distance. That's precisely what is at question. You can't help yourself to the conclusion that you are trying to get.*

In support of Marcus du Sautoy, Barbara Sattler said philosophers did later try to think of motion in that way, with Bertrand Russell and others developing the 'at-at theory of motion', where motion was nothing but being at a particular point at a particular time, and the difference between motion and rest was observed from the surroundings. Something in motion would be at a different point in space at the next moment of time and something at rest would still be at the same point.

There is a modern-day effect in quantum physics, Marcus du Sautoy observed, which says that motion does not happen. It is called the 'quantum Zeno effect', where an electron can be in two places at the same time but, when you observe one, it has to make up its mind where it is, so it is 'there'.

MARCUS DU SAUTOY: *This is called the quantum Zeno effect because, if I keep on looking at it, I can stop this thing evolving. I have actually brought a pot of uranium into the studio, which is the same effect. If I keep on observing this, I can actually stop it radiating, it never has the chance to move because of my observations.*

MELVYN BRAGG: *That's like magic, it is marvellous.*

MARCUS DU SAUTOY: *I know. Anyone who is a Doctor Who fan will know that this is the key to the Weeping Angels, which, provided you keep on looking at them, are these statues that don't move.*

The responses to Zeno's paradoxes have been fruitful; they sparked the natural philosophers, who followed him, to come up with solutions.

BARBARA SATTLER: *All natural philosophers after Zeno, in some way or other, had to find a way to deal with them if they wanted to do natural philosophy.*

The idea of a paradox is still very much used today to tease out and challenge our view of reality. The idea of 'infinitely many tasks' was the challenge at the heart of trying to overtake the tortoise, and there have been more recent challenges. Is our universe, as the ancient Pythagoreans thought, finite in its nature and without infinite decimals in its make-up?

MARCUS DU SAUTOY: *There are these new challenges called 'super tasks'. Can you switch on a light, on and off, and on and off, and halve the time between your switching the light on and off? And, if you do that in one minute, is the light on or off at the end of this?*

Is that experiment actually ever physically going to be possible and, if so, what is the end result when you add all of these actions up at the end of the minute – is the light on or off? Such paradoxes, with their roots in Zeno, are still very relevant today when teasing out the nature of reality and our intuitions about it.

CULTURE

＋＝＝●＝＝＋

We have looked at cultures from around the world. The unexpected consequence of the initial eclecticism is that, over the years, patterns have emerged, ambitions unsuspected in 1998 have been quietly established. For example, we decided to pay full and proper tribute to the great scholars and translators of the early Islamic Renaissance – in the west's Dark Ages and early Middle Ages. For centuries, their contribution had been ignored or, if recognised, described as a sort of donkey work, as translators heavy-lifting Greek culture into medieval Europe. They did that, too, but, more importantly, their own philosophers, scholars of medicine, and poets greatly enriched and, in some ways, enabled the growth of the western European Renaissance – not as translators but as exemplars.

Similarly, we went to ancient China (though not enough); to ancient India (again by no means enough); to South America (another field to be tilled more sedulously as time goes on). This is not to mine the exotic. It is to chime in with parallels to the western experience; higher civilisations occur at different times in different locations.

The listeners seem to enjoy it when we spread our wings and, because of the ubiquity of the podcast, we receive instant feedback from these programmes – from northern China to Mexico, Hawaii, North America, Australia, Mumbai … It is as though there are those in the world who want to see their own cultures shoulder to shoulder with others and also stay listening to savour the differences. Radio 4 is giving us a unique opportunity.

So where should we begin? Once again, Simon has had the enviable task of selecting a few from the many; ten from about 150. He includes the *Epic of Gilgamesh*, 4,000 years old, said to be the first great masterpiece of literature, from Mesopotamia in modern-day Iraq. Today we would call it Magical Realism and it would be worth a thesis to see if there is a line from Gilgamesh to Salman Rushdie.

Then, I think, he threw his hat in the air and went for ultimate variety. Frida Kahlo was born in Mexico City in 1907 and, over the decades, despite horrific disabling accidents and perhaps because of her involvement with the left-wing revolution in Mexico, her work grew, largely under the radar of the oligarch-dealers. Only recently has she been given the highest accolades. Her subject matter emphatically drew on herself as a Mexican, claiming both Mexico and herself as a source of art. And there is so much in Mexico's past for instance – the Museum of Anthropology in Mexico City is one of the museum wonders of the world. So, if we can wedge in, we can prise open a past that informs both modern Mexico and stands alongside pre-Christian civilisations from the other side of the Atlantic.

When you are given the liberty of a continuing series, you can try things that might not work because you can always pick up the stitch in the following weeks. For instance, we have discussed in detail several paintings on *In Our Time*. Turner's *The Fighting Temeraire Tugged to her Last Berth*, for instance. What most pleased me is that the art historians discussed it as though everyone at the listening end had a print in front of them.

What I most liked was that the contributors on Turner did not stint on detail, the direction of the wind, the relationship of the ship to the sun, what Turner had left out of 'reality' and what he had added for his composition.

We did a not dissimilar exercise recently with Beethoven. We/they talked about his music without, in forty-five minutes, hearing a single note – rather like Beethoven himself in his later years – but it was a demand on the listeners' imagination that they seemed to enjoy.

What brings rapture from the audience can also be a classic novel. *Emma* brought a surge of Austenites, *Middlemarch* possessed George Eliot enthusiasts, but the novel that, as it were, scorched the listenership was *Jane Eyre*.

I don't do Twitter. Nor do I read it. Save once a week when Simon passes on the tweets about the programme. The contributions generally begin at about 8.30 a.m., when I trail the subject inside the *Today* programme. On *Jane Eyre* day, tweeting began at 8.30 a.m. and went on throughout the morning.

And so we sweep along having a great time and hoping our enthusiasm engages the listeners. The Icelandic sagas, Rabindranath Tagore, *The Anatomy of Melancholy* (which shot up the Amazon sales list), and John Clare, the 'peasant poet', so patronised for so long, so terribly confined to what was then called a lunatic asylum – 'I am, yet what I am, none cares or knows ... ' – now emerged as one of our leading poets whom more readers wished to embrace.

FRIDA KAHLO

The painter Frida Kahlo was born near Mexico City in 1907. Though not widely known by the time she died in 1954, her reputation has grown dramatically in the past thirty years and she's now seen as one of the most important artists of the twentieth century. Her self-portraits are at the core of her work. She's often dressed in the traditional costume of native Mexican women and she emphasises her one continuous dark eyebrow and the faint shadow of a moustache. Many show her body damaged by polio and broken by the bus crash that almost killed her and left her with chronic pain for life. She became part of the cultural revolution that followed the violent Mexican Revolution. She sheltered Trotsky in her home when Stalin had exiled him from the Soviet Union, leading to one of many affairs.

–»•«–

With Melvyn to discuss Frida Kahlo were: Patience Schell, chair in Hispanic studies at the University of Aberdeen; Valerie Fraser, emeritus professor of Latin American art at the University of Essex; and Alan Knight, emeritus professor of the history of Latin America at the University of Oxford.

Patience Schell introduced the political background to Frida Kahlo's life, which was so important to her that, although she was born in 1907, she later claimed she was born in the year in which the Mexican Revolution started, 1910, so that she would then be a child of the revolution. This revolution had started with the overthrow of the dictator Porfirio Díaz and then continued among different factions for a decade, with the moderate reformists winning eventually.

PATIENCE SCHELL: *The decade following 1910 was one of mass movements of people, mass disruption. Mexico City, near where Kahlo grew up, although it wasn't itself a battlefield, was a prize for these different factions. Invading armies were coming and going, there were problems with disease, with shortages of food, so there was a lot of disruption in the first years of her life.*

When she was a teenager in the 1920s, Mexican civil society was trying to figure out what the revolution meant, how Mexico would be reformed, and Frida Kahlo wanted to be part of that reimagining.

Her family, Alan Knight told us, was an interesting mix of cultures. Her father was intellectual and austere, an immigrant from Germany with a Hungarian Jewish background, who had moved from jobs in retail to be a successful photographer, becoming almost the official photographer of the Porfirio Díaz regime. The fall of that regime hit him hard financially. Frida Kahlo was the favourite of his six daughters and she helped him in his darkroom from time to time, work that may have had an impact on her art.

ALAN KNIGHT: *Her mother was a Mexican woman, from the southern state of Wahaca, of part Indian parentage. Frida did have tenuous claims to have Indian ancestry as well. She had this family background, part European Jewish, rather intellectual, reading Schopenhauer, playing the piano. On the other hand, she had this much more traditional maternal Mexican background, also very Catholic.*

With her mother's influence, Frida Kahlo was brought up as a Catholic until her teenage years, and she went to communion and to confession. As a teenager, she went to a secular college with about 2,000 boys and only three dozen girls, and this is where she broke with the Church and became strongly anti-clerical.

ALAN KNIGHT: *She stopped going to church entirely, and clearly her whole lifestyle, her beliefs, her communism, were repudiations of the Church in almost all senses. But she used a lot of religious motifs; one particular would be the St Sebastian image of a saint being punctured by arrows and stab wounds, and she repeats that in a lot of her pictures, including of herself.*

There was a lot of poor health at home. Her father was chronically ill, with epileptic seizures, and Frida Kahlo's childhood illness with polio damaged her right leg and left her isolated in bed, recuperating, for a long time. Much worse was to come, though, as Valerie Fraser explained, after a terrible accident.

VALERIE FRASER: *She was travelling on the bus and a tram ran into it and it was the most horrific accident – a handrail of the bus went right through her abdomen. She broke her leg in twenty-two places, she broke her collarbone, she broke her spine, she broke her pelvis. It's astonishing that she survived it all.*

Again, Kahlo was confined to bed for a very long time at home, with plaster corsets supporting her back and her legs, and she later had to go through over thirty operations. She did initially recover and she could even dance in her twenties and early thirties, before becoming less mobile and spending more time in bed. Ironically, she had planned to take up medicine before her accident. She had always doodled and made drawings, and she loved medical illustrations in particular.

VALERIE FRASER: *She loved medical drawings, she loved the insides of bodies as well as the outsides of bodies. She has to abandon her medical studies, except that she doesn't, because she becomes her object of study, it's her body, she's now become the subject of her medical investigations, if you like. And a lot of her paintings are of the insides of bodies, as well as the outsides of bodies.*

Kahlo extended this into the natural world, often showing the veins of plants as well as how things were put together, and Valerie Fraser thought that came from her medicine. All the while she was recuperating in bed after the bus crash, her mother was helping her, providing her with a special easel that fitted on the bed, with a mirror above the bed so that Kahlo could look at herself and paint. That is where her interest in depicting herself began.

As she recovered, she met Diego Rivera, a pre-eminent muralist of the Mexican muralist period who was twenty years her senior, and, in 1929, she married him. He had made a name for himself by creating enormous murals of Mexican history, reimagining this through the prism of the revolution and affirming Mexican history and culture, using techniques he had learnt in Italy.

PATIENCE SCHELL: *He was a massive man. He had a big belly and he had bulging eyes and even he admitted that he looked a bit like a toad. By the time he and Frida got married, he had already had many affairs. He was a total womaniser throughout his life, and he had a habit of leaving the women who bore him children – he'd done that three times by the time he and Frida got married.*

Although he fashioned himself a revolutionary and carried a pistol, Rivera had spent that turbulent decade in Europe, mostly in Paris, making friends with (and then falling out with) Picasso. Shortly before he and Frida Kahlo married, he had spent a year or so in Russia as part of his commitment to communism.

On the face of it, to Melvyn at least, Kahlo and Rivera seemed an odd couple. As Alan Knight noted, Diego was a serial womaniser and Frida had numerous affairs with women and men, including one with Trotsky, so it was not a happy relationship in that sense. They had repeated separations, with one of them culminating in divorce, only for them later to remarry.

ALAN KNIGHT: *On the other hand, it does seem to have been very creative. They encouraged each other's work, they were each other's most fervent admirer and critic. Although, of course, their work is substantially different. Diego was up on the scaffolding doing these vast wallscapes in Mexico or the US; she was doing these very small, precise, more miniaturist pictures.*

While Rivera was somewhat infantile in his behaviour, Kahlo was vivacious, lively, bohemian and quite hard-headed, so she was more capable than he was at managing finances. Oddly, for a Trotskyist, Rivera had a lot of commissions to create murals in America for Ford and the Rockefellers, and, in these, he combined a Marxist message and a populist message for the people, along with his reverence for the Ford V8 engine. Diego Rivera was entranced by American modernity, something that Frida Kahlo did not like.

ALAN KNIGHT: *She continued to paint in the US, but she was in some ways an appendage of Diego while he was working, and he was a workaholic when he was doing the murals. She felt isolated and their relationship was on and off. She had a very serious miscarriage when in Detroit in 1932, and she yearned to go back to Mexico. In the end, they did, partly because he fell out with the Rockefellers. There was a huge spat, because he put Lenin in a picture without telling them.*

One of Frida Kahlo's most famous paintings dates from this time, *Self-Portrait on the Borderline Between Mexico and the United States*. Melvyn invited Valerie Fraser to describe it, and she set this image very much as a product of the time, when Kahlo was dislocated, with her miscarriage, when she was travelling to and from Mexico when her mother was dying. Kahlo depicted herself in 'a fancy frilly pink prom gown, with nice lacy gloves, but carrying a Mexican flag and a cigarette'.

VALERIE FRASER: *On the right-hand side, behind her, there are windowless, very tall tower blocks and strange anthropomorphic machinery heading towards her, and, in the clouds, in the steam, there are four chimneys that say 'Ford' written across them. On the other side, in contrast, there's a lot of crumbling Aztec ruins and bits of Aztec sculpture. Kahlo herself stands on a little plinth, plugged in on the US side to three machines, and on the other side to ridiculously fecund Mexican plant life.*

It is unclear, she said, whether Kahlo in the middle is generating the electricity that makes all these things work; it is weird. At this point, though, Kahlo's works had not yet been put on public display or made available for sale. She was so powerful and self-confident, it was almost as if it did not matter whether she was going to have exhibitions at this point; she was simply going to paint.

This self-confidence appears in the gaze with which Frida Kahlo stares out at the viewer. One of Valerie Fraser's favourite Kahlo paintings is *My Nurse and I*.

VALERIE FRASER: *There is a huge brown woman with an Olmec mask, holding in her arms a tiny little baby Frida, but with an adult body, and feeding from these gigantic breasts that are oozing milk.*

And there's this sense of X-ray; you're looking inside as well, so there're all the glands of the milk, bubbling out.

The rain in this painting, coming down behind, is milky, and the huge trees and leaves around the image are so full of life and fertility. And, as with *Self-Portrait on the Borderline Between Mexico and the United States*, Frida Kahlo herself is a part of the fullness of life; she is being fed by it and she is also feeding it.

Frida Kahlo was inspired by Mesoamerican culture and pre-Columbian art and ruins, and, Patience Schell said, many of the objects that she painted were in Kahlo and Rivera's personal collection. Kahlo dressed in the loose clothes of indigenous Mexicans that her mother wore, which concealed her injured leg and appealed to Diego. She was also very influenced by Catholic iconography and by popular art such as retablos, portraits of saints and particularly the Virgin Mary, showing their suffering, including ex-voto images, which were narrative paintings of the intercession of a saint or of Mary to save someone.

PATIENCE SCHELL: *They're very small, painted on tin, and had an inscription on the bottom that would describe what was happening. The Catholic iconography also comes through in terms of the doves, in terms of the thorns that she uses, obviously coming from Christ's crucifixion. And she also picked up on the popular press in Mexico in the late nineteenth century, which had lurid illustrations of crime and satire.*

One of these lurid illustrations inspired another work, which shows a woman who has been stabbed to death, called *Unos Cuantos Piquetitos*, or 'A Few Small Nips', inspired by a court case in which the accused defended himself by saying he did not really stab his victim so much as give her 'a few small nips', a phrase that incensed Frida Kahlo. Another translation of the Spanish phrase chosen by Kahlo for the title, offered by Alan Knight, would be 'A Few Little Pricks'. It is a small image, about 12 x 15 inches, and is in the style of an ex-voto, while also picking up on the gruesome woodcuts of murders that were popular in the nineteenth century. The other important aspect of this picture is that it reflects Frida Kahlo's personal turmoil at that time.

ALAN KNIGHT: *It was done in 1935. She'd returned to Mexico with Diego. Diego then began an affair with Frida's younger sister, Cristina. This was more serious and prolonged and the fact it was her sister, to whom she was close, obviously made it worse. She and Diego separated for a time, but didn't get divorced, and this picture is a cry from the heart about a woman being betrayed and stabbed. Interestingly, the woman lying there looks much more like Cristina than Frida, and the killer does look a bit like Diego.*

Frida Kahlo's continued choice of herself as subject was partly the consequence of her recurring need to be in bed while she recovered from injury and illness. She was also fascinated by herself, Valerie Fraser suggested, as a way of dealing with her own pain, with being confined, and yet presenting herself as a still-independent, powerful woman. Kahlo tended to emphasise aspects of her appearance, too, or exaggerate them.

Frida Kahlo with one of her paintings.

VALERIE FRASER: *She had very bold black eyebrows, which met in the middle. And she has very, very black hair and olive-coloured skin and she emphasises the olive-coloured skin to emphasise the Indian associations. Very often she adds a slightly dusky moustache, and she wasn't embarrassed about that – she would add the moustache, I think, and exaggerate it.*

MELVYN BRAGG: *Why did she make the eyebrows into one continuous eyebrow so it looks like a stealth bomber?*

VALERIE FRASER: *To make herself different, I think. She just didn't want to be like anybody else, she wanted to be really independent. And the wonderful hair, and then (I think it's after the divorce) she does this wonderful portrait where she cuts off all her hair and says, 'Oh, well, you only loved me for my hair,' and there's this hair everywhere, like snakes, all over the floor and over the furniture.*

Before their divorce in 1939, Kahlo had been to collect some guests from the dock at Tampico as Rivera had been unwell. These were Trotsky, his wife and his secretary, whom Rivera had asked the president of Mexico to admit so that they could have a place of refuge from Stalin. They had already left Russia for Turkey, France and Norway and, needing somewhere new, they were being allowed into Mexico on the condition that they did not interfere with domestic politics.

ALAN KNIGHT: *The Trotsky entourage stayed for two years, rent-free, in Frida's childhood home. And the couples became very close. We've heard already about the affair that Frida had with Trotsky, and there was a falling-out between the couples afterwards, not directly related to the affair. Some of it was about politics; some of it was that Diego was a bit of a pain. He gave Trotsky a little candy skull that had 'Stalin' written on it, things like that.*

Rivera and Kahlo did not have to deal with Trotsky and his entourage for long. There were two assassination attempts on Trotsky while in Mexico, and the third one there in August 1940, with an ice pick, was successful.

Slowly, as an artist, Frida Kahlo was starting to emerge from the shadow of Diego Rivera. People like Breton, Picasso and Kandinsky had seen some of her paintings and were saying she was someone to be reckoned with. What worked for her, when coming to wider attention, was a combination of her self-portraits and her persona. She had her first show in 1938 in the Julien Levy Gallery in New York where, Valerie Fraser said, 'She would dress in her Tijuana outfit and people would crowd around behind her in the streets and say, "Where's the circus?"' Kahlo was being advertised as the wife of Diego Rivera and was included as such in *Vogue* and *Vanity Fair* and she seemed happy to be used in this way. She began to be bought by galleries; the Louvre bought a painting, as did New York museums and big private collectors such as Edward G. Robinson, the film actor. She had a second solo show in Mexico in 1953, Patience Schell told us, but she was also starting to be featured in shows of Mexican art in the United States and Mexico, and it was then that she gained a name for herself in her own right in the last decade of her life, rather than being known mainly as Diego Rivera's wife.

Those last years of Kahlo's life were sad and tragic, Alan Knight indicated. Again, she was confined to her bed and tried to control her pain with drugs and alcohol. She had remarried Diego Rivera by then, and he was supportive in his fashion, continuing his affairs on the side. She was still painting, but her work was becoming less precise and her journal, with its doodles and lack of structure, suggests that she was becoming disconnected from the world. At the same time as she declined physically, Alan Knight added, she was becoming more and more respectful of Stalin as the great hope for humanity, and she was working on a portrait of him when she died.

Kahlo lived long enough to be relatively famous in her own time, and her house in Mexico became a museum soon after her death. It was still another twenty years before she became truly prominent.

PATIENCE SCHELL: *It was in the 1970s in the United States, the Chicano movement, which was part of the civil rights movement, recognising the unique identity of the Mexican-American population in the United States. And she was seen as an artist who spoke to that experience and also a feminist icon, and she became quite prominent as a feminist icon in Europe as well.*

ALAN KNIGHT: *She's almost like a Che Guevara icon that's instantly recognisable. And Diego's reputation has gone down, partly because those great big historical murals have come to seem very passé, whereas she represented something different, something surreal, something more personal and, above all, something feminist.*

In the studio afterwards, Melvyn's guests recalled the road trip that the Bretons, the Trotskys and the Riveras had all taken together around Mexico, an extraordinary combination of individuals, a story to be saved for another day. There was some debate about whether it was right to mention Rivera so much and to feature so much of Kahlo's life story, though it was soon agreed that those elements were so intertwined with her art that they were inseparable, and the paintings do not make as much sense without knowing about Kahlo's life. Valerie Fraser's one concern was that there was a whole generation of wonderful women artists at the same time as Kahlo whose profiles could also be raised, though it was noted that this, of course, was not Kahlo's fault. And there was a word of appreciation for Melvyn, whose cab had not turned up at all on that Tube strike day and who had jogged across Regent's Park to reach the studio five minutes before the live broadcast. He was still catching his breath as the live programme began.

JOHN CLARE

John Clare is seen now as one of the great poets of the nineteenth century and, according to one of my guests on this programme, the greatest labouring-class poet that England has ever produced. He was born in Helpston on the brink of the Fens near Peterborough in 1793 and knew the world around his cottage intimately. His work describes nature and country life in an extraordinary level of detail that few, if any, have equalled before or since. Clare also fires up against the threat to that countryside. For this, he achieved fame in his late twenties, though often with condescension from the London literary world, who made allowances for the man they called the 'Northamptonshire peasant poet'. The last twenty-four years of his life were spent in what was then called a lunatic asylum.

With Melvyn to discuss the life and works of John Clare in this 750th edition of *In Our Time* were: Sir Jonathan Bate, provost of Worcester College, Oxford; Mina Gorji, senior lecturer in the English faculty and fellow of Pembroke College, Cambridge; and Simon Kövesi, professor of English literature at Oxford Brookes University.

John Clare was born in 1793, just after the French Revolution, and was a contemporary of Lord Byron and John Keats. He was born deep in the countryside, Jonathan Bate told us, in a little village called Helpston, halfway between Peterborough and Stamford in what was then Northamptonshire but is now part of Cambridgeshire. This home was on the edge of the Great Fen, the eastern flatlands of England.

JONATHAN BATE: *His community was one that had really not changed for hundreds of years. His father was a casual agricultural labourer, he was brought up in a tiny cottage. But the way in which the agricultural system worked there was unchanged since the Middle Ages. It was the old open-field system where each peasant would have a little strip of land, and the commons were available where you could maybe graze a cow.*

This was very different from the kind of landscape that emerged later, as we were to hear.

Clare had a twin sister who died as an infant. Much of Clare's work is bound up with the sense of loss, and Jonathan Bate suggested that losing his baby twin may have influenced this. That work began with another incident in his later childhood.

JONATHAN BATE: *He was out working in the fields as a teenager and there was another boy who was reading a book. Clare had got some education at the little local school. The book was a volume of poems called* The Seasons *by James Thomson, very popular genteel poetry but a poetry of landscape. And Clare read it, loved it. He saved up his little bit of earnings and went along to the bookshop in Stamford and arrived before the shop was open but duly bought a copy of this book. And that really got him hooked on poetry.*

This interest in verse was supported by a great tradition of folk culture in the village, where Clare's father would love to sing ballads and folk songs in the pub and play the fiddle, and Clare learned the songs of gypsies living on land near Helpston.

John Clare spent much of his time outdoors. He was a great noticer of the natural world, Mina Gorji said, paying attention to minute changes such as how the hawthorn bud would unseal, or how the catkin became covered in downy white. He recorded these in his poetry, with the tiniest details that other poets before him had not mentioned.

MINA GORJI: *He also celebrated the local landscape, which was not a very glamorous place really, it was a sort of 'swampy desolate place', [as] his publisher described it, and he found beautiful things there to celebrate: the wild flowers; the weeds like the ragwort, which most farmers wouldn't like very much because it kills livestock; the fleabane. His poetry is full of the celebrations of these unsung things in the natural world.*

Whereas Thomson in *The Seasons* was talking about nature and the landscape from above, John Clare was very much inside nature, noticing it on his rambles, sharing his local world through his verse. Reading Clare's poems, there is a strong sense of him being in the place, as with the sound of snow underfoot, which he described as 'crumping', a word that readers could look up in the glossaries in his books if they could not glean it. He was not a dialect poet, where every other word might have to be looked up by the uninitiated, but he used words like 'crumping' sparingly and to great and powerful effect.

Mina Gorji: *A word like 'gulsh', which is the sound a tree makes when it falls on wet ground, or a word like 'prog', which is a dialect word for prodding, which he uses in a poem called 'The Mouse's Nest'. And when a word like that appears, like 'prog', we can sense that it means prod, but it also gives his readers a bit of a startle, in the way in which he was a bit startled when he saw this mouse scurrying out of the nest.*

Clare told how he used to write on scraps of paper and tuck them into a hole in the wall of his parents' cottage, only for his mother to find them and use them as firelighters. This can be construed as a negative comment on her, but Simon Kövesi stressed that, although Clare's mother was illiterate, she valued literacy and supported his education. His parents saved really hard for this and Clare started threshing, when he was a boy of nine or ten, to help pay for school, and, with all the extra labour, there was not much room for leisure or writing. There was support for Clare in the village, but also suspicion of his unusual habits.

Simon Kövesi: *He was born into a world of war, 1793. Britain's already at war with revolutionary France; it doesn't end really until the Napoleonic Wars finish in 1815, when Clare's in his twenty-second year. There is a suspicion of anyone walking around the countryside on their own, which is one of the reasons when he buys* The Seasons, *coming back from Stamford, he jumps over a wall into the Burghley Estate in order to secrete his reading. There was always a sense that he's got to be secret, and secrecy is a really important motif in Clare's life.*

After reading and being inspired by *The Seasons*, Clare was writing poetry in his teens and early twenties while earning his living by working in the fields or as a lime-burner. But then, Jonathan Bate said, his poetry was seen by a local publisher called Drury, who happened to have a cousin, John Taylor, who was a London publisher and who had a very good eye for new talent. He was the one who, arguably, had discovered John Keats.

Jonathan Bate: *Drury says to him, 'Look I've found this local poet, I think he's really good, let's join together and publish his work both provincially here in Stamford and down in London.' So, in 1820, Clare's first volume, called* Poems Descriptive of Rural Life and Scenery by John Clare, the Northamptonshire Peasant Poet, *is published in London. And Taylor brings him to London and does a brilliant marketing campaign.*

Robert Burns had been enormously successful a generation earlier in Scotland, so publishers in London were on the lookout for the 'English Burns'. Clare was a great success, even having his portrait painted in London. This success, though, unsettled him and made him very anxious.

MINA GORJI: *He worried that he'd be forgotten very quickly as he knew people like Burns had been forgotten. Even Wordsworth was neglected when Clare was writing in the early days. He worried that he'd be picked up and then tossed aside by the world of fame. Also, in those brief years of fame, he was treated like a cultural curiosity. He said he hates what he calls the peep show – the 'puppet show', he calls it – it makes him very uncomfortable.*

It could be that John Clare's anxiety over this insecurity contributed to the decline in his mental health since, as he feared, he was lifted up to great excitement and later dropped into neglect and obscurity, and that neglect coincided with the beginnings of his mental decline. The interest in him was not entirely negative, by any means. Although Clare was part of a puppet show, as he termed it, the people who came to see him in the fields at Helpston did so because they liked his poetry, and the local aristocrats supported him with small pensions. One of these was the Marquess of Exeter, one of the Cecil family, who owned Burghley House and the land around it, where Clare had hidden on the way back from Stamford on the day he had bought *The Seasons*.

MINA GORJI: *Clare had worked as a gardener there in Burghley House, and then the marquess invites him to visit and offers some support. Clare finds it mortifyingly embarrassing. The clatter of his hobnail boots on marble, he says he's so ashamed of the sound they utter on the marble. Still, he was being offered help, even though the shift of worlds made him uncomfortable.*

Even at the height of his celebrity in London, when he had been introduced to Charles Lamb and to Coleridge, John Clare kept coming back to his home in Helpston. There, Simon Kövesi said, he would receive letters from labouring-class poets, enclosing their poems and asking him how they could get into print, too. This would annoy Clare sometimes as, in those days, the recipient paid for the letter on delivery and he did not have much money. In Helpston, though, he was at home and there he was a great celebrant of ritual and habit and custom in village life.

SIMON KÖVESI: *In the open-field system before enclosure, before the sowing of seed, the whole village would go and collect stones from the fields. If you're a kid and you found a stone with a hole in it, you would try to string that to the back of the master's coat and, if you did that, then you would win a prize off all the other kids. There're these fantastic rituals, there was an enormous amount of tactile play with sticks, with pudges, little puddles, with stones. Clare says the moment enclosure comes, the sense of the village coming together in those big fields, those big jobs together, those customs disappear.*

There were fertility rituals around Helpston, and marriage rituals, and rituals around predicting who was going to marry whom, and going to a local spring and drinking the water to get healthy, and these were very much curtailed by the process of enclosure.

The land was inseparable from Clare. He had mapped out everywhere in his village in great detail, and everywhere for a day's walk around. He knew the names of lanes and gave names to the bushes, and described the birds' nests in great detail.

JONATHAN BATE: *He'll take the reader on a walk and then he'll spot a bird's nest and he'll look at the markings on the egg and say that it looks 'pen scribbled', like writing. That's the yellowhammer's nest. But then, also, this very, very strong sense of particular places. For instance, there was a bush called Langley Bush where the village always used to meet in a parliament that almost went back to the Middle Ages. And there's a lovely poem of his called 'Remembrances' where he just recites the names of bushes, lanes and trees, and these, he says, are all things that have gone because of this thing, the enclosure.*

With so many mentions of enclosure already in the discussion, Melvyn provided his own summary – 'in infinite wisdom, they decided this open land, which had been going for centuries and so on, and was common land for many people, should be privatised, and the privatisation consisted of fencing it off, barring ordinary people from it, diverting streams, cutting down woods, taking it over and trespassers were prosecuted'.

The Enclosure Act for Helpston had been passed in 1809, when Clare was sixteen, and the landscape was transformed over the next ten years. Consequently, he always associated the old open fields, the open moor, the common lands, with a childhood that had gone, and he saw enclosure as an offence not only to village customs but also to nature.

JONATHAN BATE: *All of a sudden, the villagers couldn't go to that little spring because it was on a piece of enclosed land with a 'no trespassing' sign. He says even the birds are prevented from going there and trees get cut down because of the enclosures. [There is a] wonderful poem of his called 'The Fallen Elm' where he looks at this elm tree, huge tree, that had been part of village life for generations, and suddenly a man owns it and decides he's going to cut it down for profit and that's the end of that tree, that's the end of a long history. It's a form of tyranny, he says. In the poem 'Remembrances', he says enclosure 'like a Bonaparte' came, and destroyed everything.*

Clare was a contemporary of Keats, they shared the same publisher, and some people compared or rather contrasted them. They both wrote poems inspired by nightingales, although Keats thought Clare, in his works, merely described the birds, and Clare thought Keats only described things as they appeared to his fancies, not as though he had seen them for himself. But Keats died before Clare's best poetry got going, Mina Gorji said, and one of his best poems is 'The Nightingale's Nest', which is so different from Keats's wonderful ode, so informal, where Clare gets down on his hands and knees and watches the bird while she sings.

MINA GORJI: *Not only does Clare's nightingale tremble in her ecstasy – her feathers stand on end (where Keats doesn't see the nightingale at all) – but also Clare, very importantly, takes us to her nest, and her nest is made of dead oaken leaves, he said, and velvet moss and scant and spare of scarce materials, down and hair. He's taking us into the centre of this nightingale's universe and the texture of this nest.*

John Clare also had a line, as Melvyn recalled, in which he says it 'made me marvel that so famed a bird should have no better dress than russet brown', which was very down to earth. More than that, Mina Gorji said, Clare knew full well that russet was associated with labourers and peasants, the colour of their home-spun cloth, which was a way of connecting this songbird with him and his poetry. Keats, meanwhile, was not so interested in the real nightingale; his nightingale is an immortal bird, a symbol of poetry, a symbol of music.

MINA GORJI: *What's special about Clare's is it's a real, trembling, actual bird and Clare's worried about how the bird is made anxious when he comes close. Clare, in many of his bird poems, is thinking about how the bird is feeling. It's panicking, it's scared. And Keats isn't thinking about the bird in that way at all.*

Clare's first couple of collections in 1820 and 1821 were very successful, especially the first one, which went through four editions in the first year. The reviewers, as Simon Kövesi told us, were surprised by someone from what they called an uneducated background, with very little formal education, sold by his editor and his publisher, John Taylor, in the introduction as being the poorest of the poor. There was a vogue then for not just regional and dialect verse but also poetry that included the poor, which may have begun with Wordsworth and his *Lyrical Ballads*, poems like 'Old Man Travelling' and 'We Are Seven'.

SIMON KÖVESI: *The life that Clare lives, for Taylor's readers, is shockingly poor and [Taylor] makes sure that you know that. The reviewers are surprised and amazed at his work and the quality of his work, but also there is always that, 'But if only he knew grammar a little bit better ... and maybe all these dialect terms, well, they're okay, but where's the organising principle?'*

This was one of the big tensions for Clare, Simon Kövesi thought, and also one of his great contributions to literary tradition, in that he did not always want to drive a poem's narrative, so there was not an organising principle telling a story. He did not want to have an overarching concept of how rural life or the natural world should be packaged.

The matter of Clare's mental health has been referred to throughout the conversation, and, in his lifetime, this was called lunacy. In 1837, he went into a private asylum in Epping. He came

out in 1841 and then he went into an asylum in Northampton where he stayed for the last twenty-four years of his life, although he was allowed to come and go during the day. There are some insights into his mental health in his letters and journals and from what people wrote to him.

JONATHAN BATE: *It looks as though he had what we would now call bipolar disorder. There would be periods of weeks where he would struggle to get out of bed in the morning. There would be other periods where he couldn't stop writing: he wrote over 3,500 poems, he was one of the most prolific of all English poets.*

There was also, Jonathan Bate added, something significant about Clare's poetry, which, as it got better, became less well known. There was a recession, poetry publishing got into trouble and Taylor went out of business. By the early 1830s, Clare had been struggling to publish his poetry and he was beginning to feel very cut-off, both from the world of fame and from his own community. His friends had provided Clare and his family with a cottage in another village, about 3 miles from Helpston, and it was at this point that he lost his sanity. Clare said that he had lost his own sense of who he was. This was the place from which he was sent to the asylum in Epping, 80 miles away, later setting off from there on a long walk home, which he wrote about in a three- or four-page piece of prose, 'Journey Out of Essex'.

JONATHAN BATE: *The lunatic asylums at the time were relatively liberal places – we're not talking about straitjackets and iron bars. He was allowed to walk in the woods and that's why he was able to escape to go back home. But, by this time, he is increasingly having delusions. In that first asylum, the private asylum, in the Epping Forest, he's written poems in the voice of Lord Byron and he's announced that he is Jack Randall, a famous prize-fighter, and there seems to be a real psychological disturbance there.*

For a poet who is regarded as eco-centric rather than egocentric, Simon Kövesi said, Clare did write a lot of poems that were considerations of the stormy self and the depressed self. He adopted the voices of poets like Byron and Burns to give himself a sense of identity that was confident with women and the literary marketplace, though sometimes their air is of utter despair. Still, physicians at both asylums regarded writing as a good thing for him to be doing. One of the most beautiful poems he wrote in the asylum, Mina Gorji thought, was 'Clock-O'-Clay', a Northamptonshire dialect word for ladybird.

MINA GORJI: *He imagines himself into the being of a ladybird, hiding in a cowslip pips – bell – cowslip bell, in a storm, and he imagines what it's like to be this little ladybird buffeted by the tempest in a storm. And, on the one hand, it is an expression of his own feelings, but, on the other hand, which other poet imagines what it's like to be a ladybird in that way, inside a cowslip bell? And it's a beautiful poem:*

267

In the cowslip pips I lie,
Hidden from the buzzing fly,
While green grass beneath me lies,
Pearled with dew like fishes' eyes.

That poem's expressing a sense of menace, as well as the cosy safety
of being inside the cowslip bell.

Effectively, Clare was isolated from his family in the asylums, with
a visit from one of his sons and no visit from his wife in the twenty-
four years he was living there. He was not entirely cut-off from
society, though, by any means.

JONATHAN BATE: *They let him go into Northampton, into*
the town, and he sits outside the church and he writes poems for
local young men to give to their girlfriends on St Valentine's Day
in return for some tobacco. He's got a little cottage industry
going there.

In many of the poems written at that time, there is a sense of being
cut-off from nature, family and places that Clare knew. Fortunately,
Jonathan Bate said, the enlightened asylum superintendent William
Knight wrote them down, and many of them were published after
Clare's death.

JONATHAN BATE: *And probably the greatest of them all is this*
poem 'I Am'. 'I am the self-consumer of my woes.' And it's an
extraordinary poem about loss:

Into the nothingness of scorn and noise,
Into the living sea of waking dreams,
Where there is neither sense of life or joys,
But the vast shipwreck of my life's esteems;
E'en the dearest – that I loved the best –
Are strange – nay, rather stranger than the rest.

[There is an] extraordinary sense of isolation there. And then, in the
final stanza, he longs to go back to childhood, to be lying with the
grass below, above the vaulted sky.

Clare dropped out of fashion partly as, with the death of Byron,
Romantic poetry petered out and there was a transitional period before
Tennyson and Victorian poetry came along. He was talked about a lot,
though, Simon Kövesi said, and, at one point, a rumour went about
that he had died and this was discussed in newspapers, which gave the
asylum superintendent a chance to raise a subscription to meet his fees.

SIMON KÖVESI: *Throughout the 1850s and '60s, big Victorian*
writers, like Samuel Smiles, Edwin Paxton Hood, Eliza Cook, write
really celebratory verse about Clare. A lot of people used Clare as
an example and a warning to working-class people: don't have
literary aspirations because you'll end up mad or drunk or dead.
They'll talk about Chatterton or Burns, and Clare becomes an
example of that.

Dickens did not think much of Clare, which affected Clare's reputation, but he started to be promoted by twentieth-century poets such as Ted Hughes, Tom Paulin and Seamus Heaney. Until recently, he was not even one of the big six Romantic poets – Blake, Wordsworth, Coleridge, Keats, Shelley and Byron – who are taught in schools.

JONATHAN BATE: *It really has only been in the past twenty or thirty years that – largely because of the work of poets who've admired his extraordinary eye for detail – it's only in that time that he's come to be regarded as one of the absolutely central great poets of the nineteenth century.*

In the studio afterwards, Simon Kövesi confessed that he was one of the few Clare fans who did not like 'I Am', as, he said, it imagines a world without women, which was the opposite of what Clare would have wanted. Jonathan Bate mentioned Mary Joyce, Clare's childhood sweetheart, whose father was a farmer who prevented their relationship, and it was towards Mary Joyce, his imaginary wife, Clare walked when he left the Epping asylum. Jonathan Bate also mentioned a letter a doctor had sent him after he wrote Clare's biography a few years ago, in which the doctor linked Clare's mental health to syphilis and the mercury given to treat it. There was mention of Clare's relationship with enclosure, which Simon Kövesi said was not clean. He worked on the enclosure gangs for about four years, building walls and fences, and in a limekiln, which produced lime for recovering soil for agriculture on the newly enclosed land. We want Clare to be this great environmental protest poet, he said, but his socioeconomic position was such that he did not really have a position to resist it economically.

EPIC OF GILGAMESH

'He who saw the deep' – that's a quotation, the first words of the
Epic of Gilgamesh, *said to be the first great masterpiece of literature,
a poem with roots more than 4,000 years old in Mesopotamia,
modern-day Iraq, and rediscovered in the nineteenth century. It tells
of Gilgamesh, the king of Uruk, who, with his best friend Enkidu,
fights a giant and kills the Bull of Heaven and, alone, travels across
the waters of death to meet the one man who survived the great
flood in the vain hope of learning from him how to live for ever.
In his adventure, Gilgamesh becomes a wiser man and a better king
and learns to accept his mortality. We have much, but not all, of the
ancient text from clay tablets gathered near Mosul and it is hoped
more discoveries will continue to fill the gaps.*

*Statue of a figure
often identified as
Gilgamesh from the
palace of King Sargon
II at Khorsabad in
northern Iraq.*

With Melvyn to discuss the *Epic of Gilgamesh* were: Andrew George, professor of Babylonian at SOAS, University of London; Frances Reynolds, Shillito fellow in Assyriology at the Oriental Institute, University of Oxford, and fellow of St Benet's Hall, Oxford; and Martin Worthington, senior lecturer in Assyriology at the University of Cambridge and fellow of St John's College, Cambridge.

Andrew George took us back to the origins of the poem, which was written down on clay tablets in cuneiform script in the very first centuries of the second millennium BC, nearly 4,000 years ago, although this was probably once a poem told by bards before it came to be written down. The clay tablets are very durable, and pieces of the poem have survived that were created over a very long period, from about the nineteenth century BC down to 100 BC. The poem was not static, but evolved and developed over that time. It may well be that there was one creative genius behind the first written version, drawing on existing material and folklore. The version of the poem of which we have the oldest fragments has a different mood from the poem that is much better preserved, from 1,000 years later, which has a distinctive voice.

ANDREW GEORGE: *The mood changes from a poem about the glory of an epic hero, the glory of the greatest hero and king of old, to one that is essentially a meditation upon the facts of life and, particularly, on death. This, it seems to me, is an intervention in the poem that is very considerable and changes it completely, and then I would think that this is also the work of an individual.*

The poem largely fell out of human knowledge for 2,000 years, the story forgotten and the tablets lost or undecipherable. Then clay tablets started to come to light in the 1850s in their tens of thousands and the first great discovery, in 1850, resulted in 20,000 clay tablets with cuneiform script on them being sent to the British Museum in London. In 1866, George Smith started to study these and, within ten years, he was able to give a fair translation of the preserved parts of the epic. Since George Smith, there have been more discoveries.

ANDREW GEORGE: *We are essentially pioneers in Assyriology, recovering the world's oldest literature. There's not just Gilgamesh, but many other compositions. This is a work that continues. I've been the latest person to have had the privilege in bringing together the texts about Gilgamesh but it's work that must continue. But our problem is that Assyriology is not very well financed and always vulnerable to cuts, so we're not sure if this field has a future – we desperately hope that it has.*

The story of the poem is amazing, Frances Reynolds said, starting with a poetic prologue and a hymn before the narrative gets going.

FRANCES REYNOLDS: *We have Gilgamesh as a king in Uruk who's abusing his power, it's a period of tyranny, the city can't function as it should. As a result, there's an outcry, he's preoccupying the people, particularly the young, in martial exercises, he's abusing his rights. And, in response, the mother goddess creates a wild man, Enkidu, from clay to be a match to Gilgamesh. And the idea is that this will therefore absorb his energies, his aggression.*

After being moulded from clay, Enkidu is brought up with the herds, eating grass, drinking at the waterhole with the gazelles. In order for Enkidu and Gilgamesh to meet, there is a bridging device, which is Shamhat, a prostitute from the temple of the city of Uruk, a high-status cultic prostitute who was living in the heart of the city and is sent out to trap Enkidu. He goes on to meet Gilgamesh and they fight.

MELVYN BRAGG: *Hold on, I mean, let's talk about the entrapment, it's worth talking about. He comes, she seduces him. It's very important that he is humanised through contact with a woman, which takes place unabashedly and unashamedly for seven days and seven nights.*

FRANCES REYNOLDS: *Absolutely.*

MELVYN BRAGG: *And, in the end, he is humanised. He's more of a human because of this particular sort of contact, particularly for so long.*

Enkidu cannot then live with the gazelles any more, Frances Reynolds said, and he has the intelligence and wisdom to connect with humans. Gilgamesh and Enkidu fight and the outcome is a draw; they become firm friends and set off to the Cedar Forest where they fight and kill the guardian, an ogre called Humbaba. This is an act of hubris, an offence to the gods. After that encounter, Gilgamesh and Enkidu carry on.

FRANCES REYNOLDS: *When Gilgamesh is washing after the battle, the goddess Ishtar sees him and desires him and proposes marriage. We have a wonderful inversion then of the classical proposal of marriage from a man to a woman, with the goddess proposing marriage to Gilgamesh. However, Ishtar is the goddess of sex and violence – a proposal from her is an extremely dangerous matter. Gilgamesh rejects her advances.*

MELVYN BRAGG: *Because her previous lovers have come to a very dire end, every one of them.*

FRANCES REYNOLDS: *Exactly. If one looks at her dating history, one is not encouraged to be the latest partner of Ishtar.*

Enkidu, in dreams, discovers he is going to die and these dreams come true, he does die, which causes great grief to Gilgamesh. In response, Gilgamesh sets off in the path of the sun to find a man who has survived a great flood, in the hope of discovering from him the secret of immortal life. Gilgamesh is given a test before being immortalised, which is to stay awake, but he falls asleep for seven days and the humiliation for this great king is that he cannot even conquer sleep, let alone death. Gilgamesh has also been given a plant of rejuvenation, but this is stolen while he is bathing. He then travels back to Uruk with the ferryman who had helped him cross the waters to reach the flood survivor.

FRANCES REYNOLDS: *When he reaches his city, he is able to reach a reconciliation that, while every mortal individual will die, the human race is eternal, and he can see the city as an expression of humanity and of future generations. It's the classic story of a journey that ends where it's begun, but with different perception.*

Since it was first translated, the story has been called a poem and, if we are able to call it that rather than prose, it is because we are lucky, Martin Worthington told us. In Babylonia, when they wrote works that we call poems, they would lay them out in poetic lines, with each line a complete clause or sentence, syntactically complete, which was not the case for unvarnished prose, and this good fortune allows us to make the distinction.

MARTIN WORTHINGTON: *Also, what we call Babylonian poems have verses that are normally constructed around three or four nuggets of meaning, meaning one principal word. And this makes them tremendously economical. If you take a verse of Babylonian poetry and translate it into English, you often find the number of words doubles.*

The Babylonian poems do not have rhyme in the way that we might expect, and they do not have a rhythm in the way many English poems do, but there is a great force in the words and a lot of verbal artistry, so we can comfortably call *Gilgamesh* a poem, even if the Babylonians themselves did not seem to have talked about poems in the way that the western tradition does. There is also repetition, a feature of Mesopotamian poetry in general.

MARTIN WORTHINGTON: *It already starts in Samaria and it carries through to Babylonian. And it can take many forms. You can have the repetition of an entire passage, so ten lines appear here and then they appear later. You can have repetition within a line or you could, for example, have a string of lines that start with the same word. And, at different times, different poets use all of these strategies.*

We can speculate as to why this repetition happens, he said, based on our own literary sympathies, but it is a striking feature of Mesopotamian literature.

The qualities of Gilgamesh the king are not static, they develop. He starts as king, a bad one, which was in line with political thought in Mesopotamia that, if a king were to exercise power properly and to everyone's advantage, that king must be counselled.

ANDREW GEORGE: *Our problem with Gilgamesh – this great giant hero living in Uruk, whose mother is a goddess – is that he's superhuman, he doesn't have a counsellor. And therefore the story has to bring a counsellor to him and that's one of Enkidu's jobs, to make him a counsellor. But, later on in the poem, we discover that the kingship of Gilgamesh is not really at issue any more, that he becomes just one of us, and the reason this poem resonates for us is because we can identify with his human struggle as a man.*

Gilgamesh and Enkidu complement one another in several ways, Frances Reynolds said. They match physically, with their supreme beauty, their stature and, in the sense of their abilities, their aggression, their energy. Gilgamesh, for the first time, finds a peer, somebody with whom he can travel, with whom he can have these adventures. When Shamhat and Enkidu are on their way back to Uruk, they pass shepherds who tell Enkidu he looks like Gilgamesh. The word 'love' is used between them, too.

FRANCES REYNOLDS: *This has been a matter of much debate, what the nature of the relationship actually was between Gilgamesh and Enkidu. And this obviously also reflects the responses to the poem of the readers of the time. But it seems clear that, as well as a very close friendship, there was also a sexual relationship between them.*

Within the text, there are other indications of how Enkidu and Gilgamesh relate to each other, Martin Worthington told us. For example, Gilgamesh prefigured Enkidu's arrival in dreams: first, where he saw a meteor; and, in the second dream, where he saw an axe. Meteors were an important source of iron at this time for tools and weapons. One way of looking at this would be to interpret the way that Enkidu had been created by the gods from a pinch of clay and then made human by Shamhat over seven nights.

MARTIN WORTHINGTON: *In the first dream, we have a meteor, i.e. a raw material that comes down from heaven, and, in the second dream, we have an axe, i.e. a humanised artefact made out of the raw material from the first dream. And so you can interpret these two dreams as a tacit prefiguration of Enkidu's transformation.*

Also, Enkidu is going to be Gilgamesh's axe because he is the friend at his side, he protects him. Once Enkidu is dead, suddenly Gilgamesh has an axe, a replacement for the lost Enkidu.

There was no timber in ancient Mesopotamia, it had to be brought in from the mountains, so the Cedar Forest, which Gilgamesh and Enkidu cut down with an axe, was a well-known idea in ancient Mesopotamia. The poet of Gilgamesh visualises it somewhat differently from they way one might expect for a forest in this region.

ANDREW GEORGE: *Only recently a new manuscript has come to light that plugs a gap in the story and describes the Cedar Forest to us. It's actually a jungle. It's a jungle filled with the shrieks of birds, the cacophony of insects, and monkeys yelling in the trees, all entertaining the guardian, Humbaba, who lives in the middle, like a king, surrounded by his musicians.*

Gilgamesh and Enkidu go to the forest to kill Humbaba and chop down his trees, but the poet brings ambivalence into this episode, which might be thought heroic and glorious until the heroes realise they are acting against the will of the gods.

ANDREW GEORGE: *Indeed, the new piece of tablet tells us, at the end, after Enkidu and Gilgamesh have chopped down the trees, that Enkidu looks back and he says, 'My friend, we've created this wasteland, what shall we tell the gods when we get back home?'*

In that, there is awareness that humankind lives in an environment and can destroy and damage that environment, and that is wrong, and to invade someone else's country and kill their king and pillage the resources is also morally wrong.

It is after this important episode in the Cedar Forest that Gilgamesh has the encounter with Ishtar, when he rudely rejects her offer of marriage and she takes her revenge. She calls down the Bull of Heaven from her father, who is the sky god, to kill Gilgamesh and destroy Uruk.

FRANCES REYNOLDS: *This is a ferocious animal, its breath withers vegetation and pits open up in the earth; it can destroy anything that's in its path. But Gilgamesh and Enkidu do prevail. And there's a very nice codicil to that where Ishtar's so angry she goes up on the ramparts of Uruk and is actually abusing the heroes. So Enkidu tears off the haunch of the bull, the hind leg, and throws it at Ishtar. And this is part of the aetiology for the constellation of Taurus and how it appears in the sky to have one leg missing.*

Tablet containing part of the Epic of Gilgamesh.

When Enkidu dies, Gilgamesh is overcome with grief. He is very reluctant even to bury him for a long time, Martin Worthington mentioned, 'until a worm drops from his nose'. He then worries about his own mortality, and sets off to find the man who became immortal, the flood hero Utnapishtim. On his way, Gilgamesh takes on some of the traits of Enkidu, roaming the wild, wearing lion skins, something that the god Shamash, the sun god, had foretold to Enkidu on his deathbed.

The story of Utnapishtim, the flood hero, is found elsewhere in Babylonian literature, but the poet of Gilgamesh has used it as a story within a story, Andrew George told us, for a very good reason. Gilgamesh asks Utnapishtim how he became immortal, and, in reply, he tells the story of how, a long time ago, the gods sent a great flood, but had first warned him to prepare a boat and bring into it the seed of all living things, and his family and kith and kin, to survive the deluge.

ANDREW GEORGE: *There's a very moving bit here where Utnapishtim describes how, when the rain ceased and things had gone quiet, he opened a hatch and looked out and he could see only water. And then he reflects on his position, on what has happened. He sees that all men have died and he says, 'I knelt me down and sat there weeping, and over the sides of my cheeks the tears did flow.' And when I read this with my students, many students say they're actually moved by the original Babylonian here, which is interesting in a poem that's 4,000 years old.*

The purpose of the flood story, it appears, is for Utnapishtim to tell Gilgamesh that he only became immortal because of a one-off event a long time ago, and the same was not going to happen to him. He does, though, tell Gilgamesh something about life and death.

ANDREW GEORGE: *He teaches Gilgamesh that life is something the gods have given to mankind but, as for each individual, they're like a mayfly on the river: they're there for a moment and then they die. But the human race, symbolised by the family, recreates itself cyclically, so that the human race is immortal but the individual is mortal, the individual must die.*

By way of compensation, Utnapishtim gives Gilgamesh a plant of rejuvenation, only for a snake to steal it and then shed his skin on the way.

This flood story, when it was first deciphered by George Smith in 1872, had an extremely high impact. There was an account of how Smith was so excited and amazed that he tore off his clothes and ran around the room at the British Museum. An ancient flood story, outside Genesis and without Noah, was extraordinary.

FRANCES REYNOLDS: *This became a matter of national discussion involving prime ministers, heads of state – it was internationally discussed. And, of course, for some people it was seen as a threat. The question was: was it something that somehow undermined the Bible, or, indeed, was it something that supported the Bible? Could it be seen as supporting the belief in the Bible as a literal text?*

The argument continued and still continues, we heard, and tends to be resolved by Assyriologists and Old Testament scholars, with each generally in favour of their own areas of study. Old Testament scholars may make a strong case, but we had Assyriologists in the studio.

ANDREW GEORGE: *The evidence of archaeology is clearly that these tablets, on which the flood story survives in Mesopotamia, date back 4,000 years from now. There's nothing that suggests that the story in Genesis, of Noah, dates back anything like that long. So, in terms of precedence, the Mesopotamian story, both as an independent story and probably also in Gilgamesh, is considerably older than the story in Genesis.*

There may have been a further element of futility in Gilgamesh's quest for immortality. While he was given the rejuvenation plant, it is not clear if listeners of the poem were ever to expect that this would turn out well for him.

MARTIN WORTHINGTON: *If you ask Gilgamesh, he'll probably tell you, 'Oh, I was so close, I had this plant, it would have given me youth or eternal life or something, and the damn snake bore it off and here I am without it.' But actually he had to go and get that plant down in the subterranean waters called the Apsu, which are the realm of the god Ea, who's the trickiest of Mesopotamian gods.*

Knowing the guardianship of the tricky god, it followed that Utnapishtim always knew that the gift of the plant would never work out.

Gilgamesh returns to Uruk and tells his companion, the ferryman, to go up on the wall and look at the city. We assume that Gilgamesh must have been transformed by his experiences, but that is not explicit.

ANDREW GEORGE: *When he gets home, everything stops. All the verbs are in what we call the stated form that describes inaction, as if, when he got to the end of his journey, which you might think is the end of a human life, he stops doing anything and he doesn't do any more. He's like Pierre Bezukhov in* War and Peace *– he suddenly finds contentment in actually observing life and not doing anything himself.*

That state may be taken as an ascension to wisdom, and there are many people who think the *Epic of Gilgamesh* has a spiritual side to it. There may also be gaps in the story that could be filled by discoveries, to make this interpretation clearer. While the spiritual side is part of the story's appeal, another allure is the intellectual adventure for those studying the originals, and another is the strength of the story itself.

MARTIN WORTHINGTON: *You talk to people who specialise in Dante and they say, 'Dante's so great because you can never get to the bottom of him, you can always re-read him.' Talk to people who study Thucydides and they say exactly the same. And I think we can say the same about Gilgamesh. You have got everything – you've got sex, you've got the gods, you've got loss, you've got getting old, you've got youthful adventure, you've got a monster. What isn't to like?*

In the studio afterwards, there was discussion of the uncertain timescale of the poem, which could have been anything from a few days to a millennium, so scarce are the clues. There was some doubt raised over the attractiveness of immortality as represented by the flood hero Utnapishtim, who appeared to be in a living hell. There was wonder at the interplay of the semi-divine Gilgamesh and the many different gods, and their attitude to humanity, particularly in the context of the flood. And there was discussion of the gods as forces of nature, where they act to address the humans who were disturbing the world with their behaviour and large numbers.

ANDREW GEORGE: *Embedded there is the idea of a view of ecology in which human beings do not, as in the Bible, have dominion over the earth, but they're actually part of a world that is very carefully balanced, and there are opportunities for them to endanger this balance by cutting down the Cedar Forest, by growing too fast in numbers, which, I think, is a very sophisticated notion and anticipates modern ideas about humans on the planet.*

THE PRELUDE

The winter of 1798 was a terrible one across Europe, allegedly the coldest of the century. In the small town of Goslar, in northern Germany, a bitterly cold young English poet wrote some of his finest short poems and, feeling dreadfully homesick, then wrote a few consolatory verses about his childhood. That was William Wordsworth and the poem he started writing was to be his masterpiece, The Prelude, *an epic retelling of Wordsworth's own life and a foundation stone of English Romanticism.*

━━◆◆◆━━

With Melvyn to discuss *The Prelude* were: Rosemary Ashton, emeritus Quain professor of English language and literature at University College London; Stephen Gill, emeritus professor of English literature at the University of Oxford and supernumerary fellow of Lincoln College, Oxford; and Emma Mason, professor of English and comparative literary studies at the University of Warwick.

Rosemary Ashton explained what Samuel Taylor Coleridge, William Wordsworth and Dorothy Wordsworth were doing in Goslar in 1798, the small town mentioned by Melvyn above. The two men had met the year before when they were both writing and, she said, they fell in love with each other's genius. *Lyrical Ballads* had just been published in Bristol when they set off for Germany. Coleridge wanted to study philosophy there, particularly Kant, to learn the German language and to get away from his wife and their two young children. William Wordsworth and his sister Dorothy were drawn to him like a magnet, though they also had more prosaic reasons for leaving England.

WORDSWORTH.

ROSEMARY ASHTON: *They went off to Germany together, Wordsworth and Dorothy, because they were hard up. Both Coleridge and Wordsworth had no income of any sort, they hadn't got a profession. They wanted to be poets. They wanted to be poets together, they wanted to live cheaply and they had heard that life in Germany was cheaper.*

For all this, it soon became clear that the Wordsworth hearts were not quite in it; they felt homesick and Wordsworth started writing poetry, remembering his childhood in the Lakes. This became the start of *The Prelude*. Melvyn noted how abandoned they both felt when Coleridge left them to study elsewhere, and that Wordsworth felt a longing to be back in a childhood that he and his sister had not spent together, which set Wordsworth off writing.

ROSEMARY ASHTON: *Wordsworth and Dorothy had been separated as children after the death of their mother, when Wordsworth was eight and Dorothy was a year or so younger. And they had come together more recently. And they just were desperate to stay in one another's company. And Dorothy was a perfect helpmate (until Wordsworth later married) for a poet.*

There were tensions between Coleridge and Wordsworth; they had different agendas. Coleridge wanted Wordsworth to write a philosophical poem, and yet he would not provide him with the notes Wordsworth wanted for this, and Wordsworth was still chasing him for these as late as 1804 when Coleridge was in Malta for his health.

Melvyn suggested that the poem at the end of *Lyrical Ballads*, 'Lines Written a Few Miles Above Tintern Abbey', could be said to be a prelude to *The Prelude*. Emma Mason thought of that work as a springboard or blueprint, one of the few poems that Wordsworth felt he really finished, and he felt so strongly about it that he argued with Coleridge over it when they were deciding what should be the final poem for *Lyrical Ballads*.

EMMA MASON: *Wordsworth wanted it to be 'Tintern Abbey' because that poem is so different from the other poems in that volume. The other poems tend to be about suffering individuals and, when the readers come to those poems in the* Lyrical Ballads, *they feel the suffering of those individuals, and then 'Tintern Abbey' gives a way to feel affection for them at the end, it produces a different kind of feeling.*

Even though Coleridge wanted Wordsworth to write a philosophical poem, Wordsworth said that one of the reasons he could not do this was that he was more invested in memory than in philosophy. He thought that individual memories were important springboards for poetry, partly as everybody could have them, and, in 'Tintern Abbey', he found a space to develop his self through memories and their emotional content. In *Lyrical Ballads*, Emma Mason said, he had found what he thought poetry should do, which was to foster one's feelings and make more subtle the sensibility of others.

EMMA MASON: *His poetic vocation comes very strongly from the fact that he thinks he's the figure to re-emotionalise a dead society in Britain. And he's reacting very much against strong ideas of rationality and reason that the Enlightenment has pushed on people, invested in industrialisation and capitalism, in ideas that are about an abstract idea of collective good, as opposed to a real individual idea of collective feeling.*

Melvyn asked Stephen Gill to provide a broad outline of *The Prelude*. He described it as an autobiographical poem, where the first part concerns Wordsworth's childhood in the Lake District, with its rich evocation of childhood joys and sports with friends. The poem follows chronologically from that youth in the Lake District to his time at the University of Cambridge, then to an amazing walking tour of Europe with Robert Jones, a friend, where they walked something like 2,000 miles to reach and cross the Alps. There is the life in London, and then his time in revolutionary France from 1791 to 1793. The poem concludes with Wordsworth back in England, meeting Coleridge and writing *Lyrical Ballads*. It marks the growth of the poet's mind, from birth to the age of twenty-eight. It also reflects Wordsworth's growth as he worked on the different versions of *The Prelude*. He started with two books in 1778–9, which many feel to be the most wonderful compressed high-quality poetry Wordsworth wrote, and he then extended it to thirteen books in 1805, writing many thousands of lines of concentrated blank verse.

STEPHEN GILL: *He lives with this poem for the rest of his life. There are no more bursts of composition of such intensity and length as there were in 1804–5. But we have to imagine Wordsworth growing old, forty years old, fifty years old, sixty years old. He's sixty-nine years old when he last revises this poem. And he's an old man and he's writing about himself in the French Revolution. He's going back to it and he's living with it.*

He was living with it but, significantly, he was not publishing it. He read his 1805 version to Coleridge and other friends and they praised it as a masterpiece, but Melvyn stressed that *The Prelude* was not published until after Wordsworth's death, when his wife arranged it. Emma Mason thought that there was never a point at which he had finished the poem; for a long time he was trying to write his philosophical poem and, until he finished, he could not complete the prelude to that poem. There was something that Wordsworth wanted to say about the nature of existence, that it was fractured and it was always in process and, if you fixed those details, you crushed life itself. Stephen Gill mentioned the declared position on this, which Wordsworth included in the preface to his philosophical poem *The Excursion* in 1814.

STEPHEN GILL: *He explains to everybody that there is another poem, an autobiographical poem, which is a prelude to this one, which is where the poem gets the title. Wordsworth never ever used the title 'The Prelude'. He says this autobiographical poem does exist, but, of course, I shan't publish it until the philosophical work is complete.*

Rosemary Ashton noted this, but said that there was something else. Wordsworth was writing to his patron, Sir George Beaumont, to say it was unprecedented that anyone should write at such length about himself, and he was aware that it was preparatory to another poem, which did not itself get written. What Wordsworth failed to grasp was that *The Prelude was* the philosophical poem they were anticipating. While he went on to write *The Excursion*, that Rosemary Ashton said she found that almost unreadable as he does not talk about himself but about a wanderer, with some of his childhood experiences but only at a distance.

Melvyn quoted a line from *The Prelude* where Wordsworth described himself being brought up by nature, 'fostered alike by beauty and by fear'. Wordsworth ran around the Lakes wherever he chose, climbing trees and cliffs, stealing birds' eggs, as he wrote in *The Prelude*. He also appears to relate nature to religion.

ROSEMARY ASHTON: *Early on, he's rather pantheistic, so that God is found in nature. And, to some extent, because he lost his mother at eight and his father at thirteen, there is a school of thought, with which I have some sympathy, that says that nature stood in as parents for him and he more or less says that himself, with 'fostered alike by beauty and by fear'.*

Many extracts of *The Prelude* show the power that nature came to bear over Wordsworth. One, recalled by Stephen Gill, describes the poet as a schoolboy, playing with his friends in front of an inn by the side of a lake, and as evening comes on, he describes the pleasure they have taken in the afternoon.

> The garden lay
> Upon a slope surmounted by the plain
> Of a small bowling-green; beneath us stood
> A grove, with gleams of water through the trees
> And over the tree-tops; nor did we want
> Refreshment, strawberries and mellow cream.
> And there, through half an afternoon we played
> On the smooth platform, and the shouts we sent
> Made all the mountains ring. But ere the fall
> Of night, when in our pinnace we returned
> Over the dusky lake, and to the beach
> Of some small island steered our course with one,
> The minstrel of our troop, and left him there,
> And rowed off gently, while he blew his flute
> Alone upon the rock,— O, then the calm
> And dead still water lay upon my mind
> Even with a weight of pleasure, and the sky,
> Never before so beautiful, sank down
> Into my heart, and held me like a dream!

What Stephen Gill particularly liked about this passage was the way Wordsworth gave a sense of the pleasure he took with his friends, the little boys shouting and making the mountains ring.

STEPHEN GILL: *Most of all, look at the language of this; it's all about your body being taken over by the outside world. The 'dead still water lay upon my mind'. The sky sinks down into my heart. And the pleasure of it all is a weight. One of Wordsworth's most-used words is joy. And one of the things that I value most in him is the emphasis he puts on trying to foster that in children.*

One of the many things that people pick out of *The Prelude* is the notion of 'spots of time' ('There are in our existence spots of time / That with distinct pre-eminence retain / A renovating virtue'), which Emma Mason said took us directly into Wordsworth's main interests, namely consciousness, the way in which we get to know ourselves, and affection, the way in which we learn to love others through knowing ourselves. 'Spots of time' is his phrase for memories that he can call on from the past and use to renovate or fructify himself.

EMMA MASON: *In the earlier editions, he uses the word 'fructify', to suggest that memories are fruitful for him. In the later editions, and in the very last edition, he uses the word 'renovate', to suggest that memories somehow restore him. He's not suggesting that we go back into our memories and sit there and indulge in them. Memories are only important to Wordsworth as they impact on your present moment.*

Melvyn suggested that present feeling can be underpinned by past feeling, even if the past feeling was opposite to the present feeling, so that pleasure today can be enhanced by looking back on a bleakness of a very similar situation long ago. As well as joy, Wordsworth's other concern was grief, and Emma Mason thought his whole poetic process was to think how to translate grief into joy through recalling memories in poetic form, not as massive adventures, but in everyday activities. Poetry gives us that rhythm of everyday life and teaches us how to feel. Rosemary Ashton noted the passage in the 'spots of time' section where Wordsworth talks about those moments in childhood 'by which our minds are nourished and invisibly repaired', where *nourished* suggests the mother and baby hinted at elsewhere and the invisibility of the repair makes it harder to grasp.

Melvyn quoted one of the most famous lines from *The Prelude*: 'Bliss was it in that dawn to be alive but to be young was very heaven.' This again, Rosemary Ashton said, was a reference to his feelings, as he remembered them, of when he was a young man immediately after the French Revolution when he hoped that revolutionary fervour would sweep through the whole of Europe, bringing freedom and equality and brotherhood of man. The line that Melvyn quoted comes after Wordsworth had already told readers of his disappointment when the Terror occurred, the guillotine was being used every second minute, the Jacobins and the Girondins fell out, and all the hopes for France and the rest of Europe, by analogy, had fallen flat. That is the point, she said, at which he went back to remember what it was like before, changing the chronology for dramatic emotional effect.

EMMA MASON: *For all that the poem is about nature, really nature didn't mean, in the eighteenth and nineteenth centuries, what we think it did. It doesn't mean non-urban, rural, National Trust-y places. It means a realm of intuitions and affections that is linked to the natural world, but he's not a pastoral poet, he's not someone that idealises the landscape.*

Relating to the world had to be a particular and a human experience, not an experience where people went abstractly into nature on their own, but something that was carried through their relationship with other people. Wordsworth was very keen on describing his encounters with other people, his interactions, usually outdoors, usually when walking somewhere.

ROSEMARY ASHTON: *The main thing is the effect that the meeting with other people had on him and on his mind, because this point is absolutely wonderful in connecting that direct love of external nature with a real attempt at psychologising himself. It's the first great psychological poem.*

In 1807, once Wordsworth had read his poem to Coleridge and his friends at George Beaumont's house, Coleridge almost immediately sat down and wrote a poem about listening to that poem and he performed the great compliment of writing it as a consciously Wordsworthian poem. He actually became quite rhapsodic, Rosemary Ashton said, talking about it as a prophetic lay, an Orphic song. The poem ends, 'Thy long-sustained song finally closed, / And they deep voice had ceased … I sate, my being blended in one thought / (Thought was it? Or aspiration? Or resolve?) / Absorbed, yet hanging still upon the sound— / And when I rose, I found myself in prayer,' where the 'hanging still upon the sound' was actually a Wordsworthian phrase, the physicality of the mental response to the poem.

Wordsworth's sister Dorothy and his wife Mary supported the writing of *The Prelude*, as did Coleridge, but there was another figure, namely his brother John Wordsworth, whom Emma Mason believed had an immense impact on Wordsworth as a model of affection and feeling. With the early deaths of their parents, the siblings had been spread among the homes of relatives all over the north of England. Wordsworth was addressing the impact of that. He was not saying that you had to have love as a young child, but that you had to learn how to repeat or get that feeling in your adult life, if you had not had it as a child.

Wordsworth referred to his brother John as a silent poet. Unlike Dorothy, John never wrote poetry, but the idea of being a silent poet suggested that, for Wordsworth, poetry was not about the reading or linguistic content, but the emotional content.

EMMA MASON: *Which is why it's so important that he reads it to Coleridge, because it's the feeling that the readers have at the end of the poem that is important to him, rather than the process of reading. And he says that very clearly in the preface to the* Lyrical Ballads, *where he says that feeling is what gives importance to actions and situations, not actions and situations to feeling itself.*

Samuel Taylor Coleridge.

People in Wordsworth's circle knew of *The Prelude*, from readings and from talking to him about it face to face at his home in the Lakes. According to Stephen Gill, though, it did not have great influence at that time. Wordsworth's impact upon writers such as George Eliot, Elizabeth Gaskell and Tennyson was huge, but there was already a lot of Wordsworth in circulation when he died. In 1850, Stephen Gill asked, did anybody really want to read another thirteen-book poem? Matthew Arnold was the most influential taste setter regarding Wordsworth in the later Victorian period.

STEPHEN GILL: *Arnold regards Wordsworth as a lyric poet and barely makes a mention of* The Prelude. *As late as the 1880s and '90s, publishers are still putting out collections of Wordsworth in which they don't include* The Prelude *(well, they can't, as a matter of fact, for copyright reasons, but we'll let that pass). They put in little notes at the front saying,* 'The Prelude *is not the equal of his other works.'*

Wordsworth had tinkered with the poem for so many years and, Rosemary Ashton argued, part of the consequence of that tinkering was a watering-down of the original freshness and the boldness. The idea that Wordsworth was a favoured son of nature went, and a few more references to Christian God crept in as he became more conventionally religious. It was still a great poem but it was a slightly duller poem. It was also a long time since the French Revolution, since the pre-railway age and, by the time the poem was published, the Victorians were interested in other things.

ROSEMARY ASHTON: *One of the criticisms that was made of the poem was that it was all about himself, it wasn't about humanity and other people, readers thought, and, by the Victorian period when you've got all the social problem novels of Gaskell and Dickens and so on, it somehow didn't seem to be a poem of the era in which it was published, and nor was it.*

Although the novel was overwhelmingly popular in the Victorian period, Wordsworth did hold an enormously important place for many poets who are read less often now, Emma Mason noted, particularly women poets gathering their sense of self for the first time, such as Dora Greenwell and Adelaide Anne Procter, who were extremely popular in their own day. Victorians found immense consolation in *The Prelude* as they did in Tennyson's 'In Memoriam', both providing an alternative space to the Church for allowing religious sensibilities to operate.

If, instead of the long delay, *The Prelude* had been published in 1807, Stephen Gill thought it could have been dynamite. Wordsworth did not hold back from revealing his political sensitivities from the 1790s.

STEPHEN GILL: *In book ten, I think it is, there's a passage where Wordsworth describes himself praying for French victories, kneeling in an English church and being the only person there not offering up prayers for our nation's victories. By the time he wrote those words, William Wordsworth was a member of the Grasmere militia and was a staunch patriot, but he wrote them, that's the point. And he did not delete them.*

With that, Melvyn concluded that there was nothing else for anybody to do but go and read *The Prelude* over the next month or two, 'with enormous pleasure and delight'.

RABINDRANATH TAGORE

It is claimed that Rabindranath Tagore was, at one time, one of the most famous poets in the world. Born in Calcutta in 1861, he became the first non-European to win the Nobel Prize for Literature. W. B. Yeats and Ezra Pound were great supporters. A commanding figure in the Indian renaissance of the nineteenth century, Tagore also played a major part in India's independence movement. The first prime minister of India, Nehru, said he had two gurus: Gandhi was one, the other was Tagore. He wrote novels and plays, he painted; he composed thousands of songs, and two of his many poems became the national anthems for India and Bangladesh.

With Melvyn to discuss Tagore were: Chandrika Kaul, senior lecturer in modern history at the University of St Andrews; John Stevens, research associate at the School of Oriental and African Studies, University of London; and Bashabi Fraser, professor of English literature and creative writing at Edinburgh Napier University.

There was a cultural movement in Tagore's part of India in the nineteenth century known as the Bengal renaissance, a movement in which he, his family and his ancestors played a large part. Chandrika Kaul explained that Ram Mohan Roy (1772–1833), an influential reformer, is the one traditionally credited with starting this. There was social and religious reform, a literary and scientific movement, as well as a political strand that became more prominent towards the end of the nineteenth century. In part, the social and religious reform came out of a British cultural project of understanding and gathering knowledge, which led to the establishment of schools and universities.

CHANDRIKA KAUL: *People like Ram Mohan Roy and others begin to assimilate western cultural, literary, philosophical traditions, the western Enlightenment traditions, as well as the teachings of Christ and Christianity, along with an approach to reviving and reforming Hindu religion and faith.*

There was a cultural dimension to this, with the revival of Bengali as a literary language, and there was an assertion of the Hindu faith as one of the great religions of the east.

There was a close connection between Tagore's family and the East India Company. His great-grandfather had made his fortune in the eighteenth century working for the company as a revenue collector, and his paternal grandfather had consolidated this fortune by investing in mining, indigo and sugar plantations, becoming an extremely wealthy entrepreneur in Anglo-Indian society in Calcutta (Kolkata) where he was referred to as a prince.

CHANDRIKA KAUL: *Calcutta was the capital of the East India Company, and also the British until 1912. He was at ease with Anglo-Indian society, he twice went to Britain, he dined with Queen Victoria, he was fêted by the Lord Mayor of London. He was an assimilated Indian who benefited from the commercial and economic opportunities thrown up by the East India Company. He is reputed to have formed the first British Anglo-Indian Company, Carr, Tagore and Co., in Calcutta.*

One of the driving forces behind the Bengali renaissance was the Brahmo Samaj, which Ram Mohan Roy had founded in the 1820s and, initially, functioned as a small place of worship.

JOHN STEVENS: *Debendranath Tagore, Rabindranath Tagore's father, took over the Brahmo Samaj in the 1840s and he really revitalised the movement and turned it into a very powerful force in Bengal in terms of the spread of education, in terms of reforms to do with improving the condition of women in Bengal and also in terms of promulgating a form of Hinduism that was reformist, that was universalist and that was monotheistic and rational.*

The group split into many factions over the century, but generally, John Stevens said, they trod a middle path between those in Bengal who wholeheartedly embraced the west and those who rigorously defended what they saw as the traditions of India and Bengal.

Rabindranath Tagore was the fourteenth child in a wealthy, energetic family, although he termed it a servocracy as, to him, the servants appeared to run the place rather than his parents. He grew up in a culturally stimulating environment, in a large house in north Calcutta, and, among his siblings, there were many great writers, artists and poets.

JOHN STEVENS: *The family were very well connected. But one does get the sense, from his writings about his early life, that there was also an element of loneliness to it. He was largely raised by servants. It doesn't seem that he was particularly close to his parents and he never got on very well at school.*

Initially, his verse was influenced by the devotional Vaishnava tradition of poetry, and, Bashabi Fraser told us, he went on to write *Bhanusimha Padabali* under a pseudonym. She described this work as being a bit like Macpherson's *Ossian*, as Tagore claimed he had discovered this work by a medieval poet who was using not Bengali but Brajabuli, a dialect between Hindi and Bengali. At first, it was accepted as genuine, although, after people praised it, he owned up that it was his. While still young, he travelled to London with his brother Satyendranath and started to study law, but did not progress much and returned home.

Tagore wrote several collections of poems in this period of his life after his return, and one of his famous ones is 'The Golden Boat', which Bashabi Fraser recited in Bengali before improvising a translation into English.

BASHABI FRASER: *Just the gist of it. 'There are clouds that are thundering, the rain is a heavy downpour. I sit alone on the bank of the river. I have a certain sense of hopelessness. I finished reaping the harvest of paddy, there's loads of it now beside me. The river is in full spate but, while we were harvesting, the rain came.' And, in this poem, somebody comes in another boat and he feels he has seen this person. Who is he? He asks him, 'Can you take my paddy?' And he does. He fills the boat and then he says, 'Can you take me?' He says, 'No, there is no room.' And the boat goes away, and he's alone.*

When Tagore came back from London, he was about nineteen or twenty, and that was when his father put him in charge of some of his vast estates. In Chandrika Kaul's view, some of the romantic rural idyll that is at the heart of Tagore's poetry, such as that just recited by Bashabi Fraser, was influenced by him being thrown from the security of his urban Calcutta existence to managing his father's estates in rural Bengal. This was when he met villagers, the common sharecroppers.

CHANDRIKA KAUL: *He spent most of his time travelling by the houseboat that the family owned, moving down the Padma River, visiting various households and householders. And this greatly influenced not just his attitude towards reconstruction and social reform, particularly among the peasantry, but also his poetry. His creative spirit was reborn in this new, invigorating, if isolated, environment where he was communing with nature.*

Melvyn, having read some of the poems for the programme, observed that Tagore had, indeed, gained an awful lot of material from his rural experiences, which were outside the world in which he had grown up. Chandrika Kaul noted this rural romanticism in the collection of poems *Gitanjali*, which, in their English version, were later to form the main basis for his Nobel Prize.

Rabindranath Tagore was relatively detached from politics for a while, but he became drawn in more tightly after the partition of Bengal in 1905. The British, John Stevens said, claimed that this division would make a very large province easier to administer. It was generally understood, though, that one of the British aims was to weaken the growing nationalism there. It was at this time that the seeds of a Muslim East Bengal and a Hindu West Bengal were sown. Very quickly a movement grew against the partition, the Swadeshi movement, which was an economic form of resistance favouring indigenous goods over British ones. Tagore was very much in favour of the boycott of British goods, although not the destruction of British factories. He wrote songs and poems in favour of Swadeshi, we heard, and led a big Swadeshi procession through Calcutta. He was open to British culture, but that did not mean he supported British rule.

JOHN STEVENS: *In the end, he did turn against the movement and this was because, in 1907, there were some very serious riots, communal riots, and part of the problem with Swadeshi was that Swadeshi goods, these indigenous goods, were more expensive than the British goods. And the largely Muslim peasantry often couldn't afford these Swadeshi goods, but were forced into buying them. This created tension; there were these very serious riots. Tagore was appalled by the violence.*

It was at this point that Tagore really moved away from the Swadeshi movement, we heard, and from organised politics in general.

It was in 1910 that Tagore published the poems in Bengali that were known as *Gitanjali*, or 'Song Offerings'. In 1912, he travelled to London with these, translated into English, to meet with his supporter W. B. Yeats and the artist William Rothenstein, although, of this new collection of 103 poems in English, only fifty-three were in the original Bengali *Gitanjali*.

BASHABI FRASER: *He had delayed his journey because he hadn't been well and he had retreated to his estate. Rothenstein had earlier expressed an interest in reading his writing in English when he came to England. There's a story that he had given them to his son Rathindranath, who had left them in Victoria station and some kind soul had found them. So it might have been lost altogether and it would have been a different story.*

Tagore was introduced to Yeats in June 1912 and, in July, Yeats read three of Tagore's poems to a gathering of seventy people, which

*Rabindranath Tagore
with Gandhi.*

seemed to change the game for him. The India Society went on to publish the book, and Thomas Sturge Moore, who was a fellow at the Royal Society, nominated Tagore for the Nobel Prize.

Tagore went on to win the Nobel Prize in 1913, the first non-westerner to be awarded that prize for literature. It was a great achievement but no one, Chandrika Kaul said, was more surprised than Tagore. He was on a reading tour and it was not until he reached India again in November that he heard about it. There were other contenders, such as Thomas Hardy, who were seen as the leading horses in the race. Perhaps his Swedish followers helped sway the decision away from the favourites, although there were several other works of Tagore in the Nobel library, so someone there may have read him in depth, and the award did not have to rest on *Gitanjali* alone.

CHANDRIKA KAUL: *You have to remember the context of Europe at this time, the lead-up to the First World War, the growing militarism, the war clouds on the horizon. What Tagore's poems, at one level, represented was this breath of fresh air, this hope of communion with nature, this romantic idyll of peace. And Tagore, with the long beard and piercing eyes, seemed to represent everything that the oriental sage of Kipling's time would have represented.*

In 1915, largely in recognition of his Nobel Prize, Tagore received a knighthood from George V. Four years later, he renounced it, after one of the defining events in twentieth-century Indian history. This was the notorious Amritsar Massacre of April 1919, which John Stevens described.

JOHN STEVENS: *There was a large group of protestors, they were protesting against the arrests of a number of congress leaders and against some very unpopular legislation, which had, effectively, made these arrests possible. They had gathered in Amritsar and Brigadier-General Dyer was there with his troops in the area. He became very worried by this protest, he saw it as evidence of a coming full insurrection in the area, which it wasn't – this was an unarmed protest …*

MELVYN BRAGG: *And men, women and children …*

JOHN STEVENS: *Dyer ordered his troops to open fire on the unarmed crowd. Which they did. Reports state that they carried on firing for as long as ten minutes. They were shooting people who were running away, it was really awful.*

The number of casualties, he said, was contested – perhaps 400 dead and 2,000 injured – but there were different figures. The British tried to suppress news of this massacre getting out, but it did get out. Dyer was severely criticised in Britain and forced to retire. Tagore got to hear of the massacre in May 1919 and his immediate response was to write to the viceroy to renounce his knighthood. That letter, John Stevens said, in which he renounced his knighthood, is now a very celebrated document of Indian resistance. Tagore was saying that he did not want to receive any special honours when his countrymen were being treated as insignificant.

Tagore used his Nobel Prize money to fund education. He had founded a school at Shantiniketan in 1901 and then his university in 1921, and the Rural Reconstruction Institute in Sriniketan in 1922. As a Nobel Prize winner, he was invited to lecture across the world and the funds from these lectures went back into his educational establishments. He supported interdisciplinary studies, with science alongside culture and arts, a liberal education bringing east and west together.

BASHABI FRASER: *He also felt that university shouldn't be separate from the surrounding areas and he worked very hard at Sriniketan through his rural reconstruction centre to replenish the villages around, which were Hindu, Muslim and Santhal, and to dispel the sense of apathy and to help them in self-awareness and self-reliance.*

Gandhi had already heard of Tagore while he was in South Africa and, on arriving in India, he sought him out. They became good friends, Chandrika Kaul said, admiring and respecting each other's views, although, in time, coming to disagreements over ideology and political practice. Gandhi wanted political freedom; Tagore was more interested in social reform.

CHANDRIKA KAUL: *For Tagore, social progress and social reconstruction took primacy over political independence. He felt that, if India didn't get her own house in order, then the grant of political independence in itself wouldn't solve the problems besetting the country. There was a difference in emphasis.*

When Gandhi launched the non-cooperation movement in 1920–22, Tagore was travelling around Europe trying to raise funds for Shantiniketan and advocating cooperation with western universities and intellectuals. He felt Gandhi was talking about non-cooperation not just with the British, but with everything modern and western. Tagore was opposed to Gandhi's emphasis on the burning of foreign cloth and on the boycott of schools, because he felt these actions were essentially nihilist.

CHANDRIKA KAUL: *[Tagore thought] you cannot ask the poor to burn the only clothes they have without supplying them with cheaper alternatives. Similarly, you cannot and you shouldn't ask students to leave universities and schools without giving them a viable alternative. Given his emphasis on education, he felt very strongly about this.*

Gandhi and Tagore both expressed their opinions in public, in print, so there was no escaping the disagreements. Tagore took particular exception to what he saw as Gandhi's aversion to science and progress. In the 1930s, there was an earthquake in Bihar, which Gandhi talked about as a divine visitation because of the sins of untouchability, and Tagore was furious.

In the sphere of Bengali literature, Tagore's influence was boundless. He was constantly quoted, people had his poems at home, they learned his songs by heart and he was translated into other Indian languages.

JOHN STEVENS: *Another thing about Tagore's output is there was so much of it and in so many different genres. He wrote novels and poems and plays, short stories, songs, dance dramas, you can go on and on. It came to the point where, really, if you were writing anything in Bengali, you were immediately compared, usually unfavourably, to Tagore.*

Tagore travelled widely, reportedly to thirty different countries across five continents. He was familiar with advances in technology and, as an example, Chandrika Kaul mentioned his attitude to the birth of broadcasting in India. Gandhi, we heard, shunned broadcasting, while Tagore embraced it to spread his political and social message and to read his own poetry, including one called *Akashvani* to celebrate the opening of the medium-wave transmitter in Calcutta. He firmly believed that shunning technology would isolate India and would not help it even when it gained independence.

His popularity as a poet dipped for a while, particularly with the groups of younger poets who felt they could not be heard in Bengal because of Tagore. There were several translations into English of his Bengali poems but these were not generally successful.

CHANDRIKA KAUL: *He reinvents himself now as a painter, as an artist, and his paintings are widely exhibited in Paris, in Berlin, in London, in Moscow, and receive very flattering praise. He's a polymath who doesn't quite go away, though the attention shifts, to some extent, from him as a poet.*

Tagore's popularity also took a dent as he was lecturing against nationalism at a time when it was on the rise, internationally and in India. He died before Indian independence and became disillusioned that India was not yet free and that the world was being dragged into war again, as it had been at the start of the century. It was not until the centenary of his birth, and then again at the 150th anniversary of it, that his reputation resurged.

In the studio afterwards, there was agreement that Tagore's critiques of sectarian nationalism were important, as was his universalist philosophy, the idea of unity in diversity that was later picked up by the Indian government. There was also mention of some of the incidents that tarnished his name in the west. While he was in America in 1917, there was a claim that he was a German agent.

BASHABI FRASER: *The British foreign secretary told the American government that he was dangerous and he was actually colluding with the Germans. He had been very popular in Germany earlier. And, also, there was this fear when he went to Japan in 1916 that he went there to solicit Japanese assistance.*

What was emphasised, though, by John Stevens was that Tagore absolutely believed that the way forwards for the world was for different cultures to interact with each other. He did not think that India should be transformed in the image of Britain, although he was very welcoming to British culture, and he never thought that India should isolate itself from other parts of the world. His very wide international travels were really about Tagore putting that philosophy into practice.

TRISTAN AND ISEULT

The story of Tristan and Iseult was one of the most popular of the
Middle Ages. From its roots in Celtic myths, it passed into written
form in Britain a century after the Norman conquest and almost
immediately spread throughout northern Europe. It tells of a Cornish
knight and an Irish queen, Tristan and Iseult, who accidentally
drink a love potion at the same time, on the same boat, travelling
to Cornwall, where she is to marry someone else. They have no
choice: they consummate their love at sea and, from that point, must
navigate the physical and moral dangers that follow. In one version,
he slays a dragon and she saves him from certain death. They are
a perfect match and their love is heroic, but could that excuse their
adultery in the minds of medieval listeners, particularly when the
Church was so clear they were wrong?

With Melvyn to discuss Tristan and Iseult were: Laura Ashe, associate professor of English at Worcester College, Oxford; Juliette Wood, associate lecturer in the School of Welsh at Cardiff University; and Mark Chinca, reader in medieval German literature at the University of Cambridge.

Before the story of Tristan and Iseult was written down in the forms that survive, there were other stories being told in the British Isles with related themes. Juliette Wood told us of the Irish story of Deirdre of the Sorrows, who was forced to marry an older king yet fell in love with someone else and put her lover under *geas*, a form of compulsion common in Irish folklore, which led to his death and then hers. There was also the story of Diarmuid and Gráinne, in which Gráinne, who was married to Fionn MacCoul, approached Diarmuid, again with *geas*, and they escaped constantly, until they were both killed. These were part of the wide body of folklore from which stories developed.

There is no historical evidence for Tristan and Iseult; they appear to be completely the products of fiction. All the same, from the seventeenth century, their story has been linked to geographical locations in Cornwall, and that has inspired archaeologists looking for historical evidence of the castle of King Mark, the intended husband of Iseult.

JULIETTE WOOD: *Tintagel, Castle Dore, places like that, have been excavated. The problem with the archaeological histories is that they have, in turn, created a lot of folklore, particularly in the 1930s when the first big excavations were done. People were actually looking for proof of Arthur and Tristan and Iseult and these stories, and, of course, when you look for proof, you find it.*

One of the first to write down the story was Thomas of Britain, about whom little is known, although Laura Ashe could tell us that he refers to his name, Thomas, twice in the text of his story, and the German poet who translated his work a few decades later described him as Thomas of Britain, which almost completes the scant detail. He was probably from Normandy, though working in England for aristocratic courts, and he was writing in French between the 1160s and 1180s, but that is about all that is known. As for the text of Thomas's Tristan and Iseult, that probably contained between 12,000 and 15,000 lines, of which only 3,500 survive in manuscript fragments and, up to a point, in translation into German by Gottfried, as well as, more faithfully, in a translation into Old Norse in its entirety.

LAURA ASHE: *It's worth bearing in mind that, as Juliette's been implying, there's no such thing really as a whole story of Tristan. I mean Thomas himself, when he's writing, it's one of the earliest extant texts we have, but he still says this story comes in many versions, many people have told this story, I've heard many different ways of telling it in many different plots and here's my version. And he says, 'My version is definitive.'*

Even from the perspective of someone in the twelfth century, Thomas sets the story in the distant past. At some point in pre-history,

Tristan's parents had an illicit affair that ended with his father's death in battle. His mother died of grief in childbirth, hence his name, from *triste*, or 'sorrow'. Tristan does not know his background, but he is brought up as a favourite at King Mark's court in Cornwall, where his connection to him as Tristan's uncle becomes known. Tristan defeats an Irish prince, Morholt, who came to demand tribute from Cornwall, leaving a chip of his sword in Morholt's skull, and he has various adventures in Ireland, winning the right to take Iseult from Ireland to Cornwall for King Mark, who had already heard from Tristan what an astonishing woman she is after he had met her on an earlier adventure. And then, Laura Ashe continued, the couple drank a love potion at sea by mistake; by the time they land, Iseult is no longer a virgin and her lady-in-waiting, Brangaine, takes her place in the marital bed on the first night. After that point, we have the substance of the story, which comes in three sections.

LAURA ASHE: *There are the long periods when they're at court conducting their affair clandestinely and Mark is riven with suspicion. People attempt to expose them and there's never quite proof and they're repeatedly challenged and then reinstated. Then there's a phase when Mark can't bear it any more and he banishes both of them. And they go into the forest and the final end game (and Thomas's version kicks in here): Iseult is back at court, now Tristan is banished alone and he meets another woman, a beautiful woman [also] called Iseult, and he decides, for a series of psychologically mad reasons, that he will marry this other Iseult. And now we have a love quadrangle. Finally, he's wounded by poison. Only Queen Iseult can save him, she is on her way to save him; his wife tells him that she is not coming and he dies of despair. And then Iseult comes and finds his body and she lies down and dies also in despair.*

· One measure of the popularity of this story is how quickly it spread. Mark Chinca noted the move from England to continental Europe and Scandinavia. Gottfried of Strassburg reworked Thomas into Middle High German, the literary form of German at the early thirteenth century, probably around 1210. There was also another translation of Thomas into German, made somewhere in the northwest of the continent in a literary language that is usually called Low Franconian, the forerunner of literary Dutch, and fragments of that survive. There is also the Old Norse version, as a saga.

MARK CHINCA: *That saga is very important because it enables us to reconstruct the whole of the plot of Thomas because it is, in fact, the only, I think, translation of Thomas surviving that actually completes the whole story. It survives mainly in manuscripts of the seventeenth and eighteenth centuries, but those manuscripts contain a prologue in which they say that the translation was made by a monk called Brother Robert in 1226 at the court of King Haakon, that's Haakon IV of Norway.*

There can always be doubts about authenticity, but the statement fits what we know about the court of King Haakon, notably that he was interested in promoting European literature in the early thirteenth century. There is also a version by Béroul, about whom we again know nothing, and this was in continental French, so not from England, and from the second half of the twelfth century, and it had a different approach to the story.

MARK CHINCA: *The most striking difference is that the love potion in Béroul is time-limited. In the Thomas tradition of the story, the potion causes those who drink it to love until they die, so it's absolute and unending love. In Béroul's version, we're told that the potion's effect wears off after three years; it works only for that period of time.*

Where Thomas appears more interested in creatively mining the story for general problems that he can put up for intellectual debate and discussion, Mark Chinca added, Béroul prefers the maximum of narrative suspense and excitement from the story. There is an episode in Béroul in which Mark has sentenced the lovers to death, with Iseult handed over to a colony of lepers and Tristan captive in a chapel high on a rock, from which he makes a death-defying leap onto the cliffs below, just in time to rescue Iseult and ride with her into exile in the forest, all told for narrative suspense.

The moral position in the raw material of the folk tales was fluid in that this would have been left for the teller to insert as he chose. Looking at the early versions, according to Juliette Wood, the stories are all about conflict between duty and love, the *duty* owed to an overlord, as with Diarmuid and Fionn, and the *love* of a woman, as with Diarmuid and Gráinne.

As well as the narrative suspense, there is something else that is unusual in Béroul; he includes a rather strange story.

JULIETTE WOOD: *King Mark has horses' ears, probably for comic purposes. I think understanding medieval humour is something that we have problems with. Now 'mark' in Cornish, Breton and Welsh means horse. So it's not surprising that you get that story. And you find that story quite well attested, particularly in Welsh. It suggests that Béroul has got closer to the localisation of the story in Cornwall.*

While there may have been no defined moral position in the folklore, the Church had a view that was hardening at the time these stories were being written down. Laura Ashe explained that the Church had dramatically attempted to have a greater role in marriage in the twelfth century, in which it was no longer just an alliance between noble families but a sacrament that relied on the absolute consent of both parties.

LAURA ASHE: *It's possible to argue – many people have – that the growth in the 'romance', the fiction of love, is a response to that, saying, 'If marriage has to be about consent, then we now need to understand what consent to that kind of bond would mean.'*

This sacramental approach runs straight into a problem with Tristan and Iseult, where the couple consents but the love is adulterous and directly against the bonds of marriage. On the face of it, Thomas's narrative of adultery runs counter to orthodox Christian teaching, and some critics have argued that he must simply be showing the lovers' sufferings as a just punishment for their sins. Alternatively, he is elevating love itself as an alternative religion, a cult, although Laura Ashe finds that tendency more in Gottfried. To her, Thomas's narrative shows something that is real, something that happens to people.

LAURA ASHE: *Thomas develops a moral sense, based not on the question 'Are they sinning or not?', but based on the question of the effect they have on others. He shows us, very painfully, the hurt they cause to others all around them, and that, I think, develops a much more interesting kind of moral ambiguity than the simple question 'Are they sinning by loving adulterously?'*

The moral ambiguity continues in Gottfried who, like Thomas, put phrases into the lovers' mouths that were often borrowed from the Church's own definitions of marriage. Mark Chinca gave examples of this. In the Thomas version, when Tristan agonises over whether to marry this second Iseult, he frames the problem to himself in terms of breaking his faith with the first Iseult, his fidelity, and, in canon law, the phrase used for adultery is that it breaks the bond of marital fidelity. In Tristan's mind, entering into a legitimate marriage could itself be an act of faithlessness and, implicitly, of adultery. Canon law often says the wedding ring symbolises the consent and the bond of the two hearts, the *marital* fidelity. In Gottfried, when the lovers are parting for the very last time, Iseult presents Tristan with a ring of *adulterous* fidelity.

MARK CHINCA: *She says, 'Take this ring so that you will remember me by it.' But she then says it is a seal or symbol of fidelity. Again, that exact formulation is borrowed from canon law. It's very striking that both of these authors, Thomas and Gottfried, allow the adulterers to talk about their own relationship as though they were legitimately married in the eyes of the Church, and that obviously magnifies the moral ambiguity and ambivalence of the story.*

With the popularity of the story came more retellings. The Welsh version, Juliette Wood told us, was very different. It dates from the sixteenth century or earlier and has Tristan and Iseult living in the forest, and nobody can attack Tristan because, if they do, his blood would cause their death, so no one can wound him. By this time in the Welsh tradition, Mark, Tristan and Arthur were all associated.

JULIETTE WOOD: *Arthur is brought in and he says, 'Well, look, one of you is going to live with her when there are leaves on the tree and one of you is going to live with her when there aren't leaves on the tree.' And Mark says, 'Well, I want winter because the nights are longer.' And it's Iseult who says, 'There are three trees that never lose their leaves therefore I'm going to stay with Tristan.' And off she goes. It has a happy ending. She picks the evergreens and it's interesting that it is Iseult who does this.*

Iseult is a very active heroine, like Deirdre and Diarmuid's Gráinne, and they are quite different from many of the other medieval heroines.

French fifteenth-century miniature depicting Iseult on horseback accompanied by knights.

Melvyn asked Laura Ashe to explain Thomas's handling of the psychological complexity of the four characters: Mark, the first Iseult, Tristan, and Iseult of the White Hands (the second Iseult). In Thomas, it begins with Tristan's debate with himself over whether to marry the second Iseult. He thinks the first Iseult has forgotten him, or she has not, but she is married and has pleasure with her husband, and perhaps, if he were married, he would know what she felt. He then says at least the first Iseult cannot blame him for exercising lust with someone else, because he would be married to that person and that would be allowed. He then realises that he only wants this second Iseult because she represents the first Iseult to him.

LAURA ASHE: *This comes to fruition horribly when, on the wedding night, he is getting undressed for bed and the ring that Iseult gave to him, which Mark mentioned, is pulled off his hand by the shirt that he pulls over his head, and he is stricken with the realisation that he has done something terrible. And now he has to betray both women because he's married another woman and betrayed Iseult, but also he cannot bear to sleep with this woman and so he betrays his wife by refusing to consummate the marriage.*

He never does consummate the marriage with Iseult of the White Hands. Thomas gives us a psychological exploration of how Tristan could have done this, then talks about what these four suffered in this terrible pattern.

LAURA ASHE: *Mark has the body of the woman he loves but will never have her heart, and he knows it. Iseult must submit to her husband in bed but does not want him and does not love him, and she cannot have or be with the man she does love. Tristan, meanwhile, cannot have the woman he loves and he lies in bed next to a woman he cannot bear to touch. And Iseult of the White Hands longs for her husband, loves her husband, and he cannot and will never touch her. And this description of this quadrille of hurt is, I think, just profound.*

This pattern gives a psychological insight to all of the characters. What is important in Thomas is not just that our hero and heroine have feelings, as is the case in other versions, but that there are other people whose feelings matter, and we see that.

LAURA ASHE: *There's an astonishing episode worth mentioning. Iseult of the White Hands is one day riding along with her brother when her horse steps in a puddle and water splashes up her thigh and she starts laughing uncontrollably and her brother, who's a bit paranoid, says, 'Tell me why you're laughing,' and she says, 'That water touched higher up my thigh than my husband has ever touched me.' And it is the most astonishing moment. So it's that psychological realism, which is incredible in Thomas.*

What happens in this quadrille of misery, Mark Chinca added, is that Thomas goes through each of the characters and explains why they have a claim to be miserable in love, which is quite a striking thing to do if he is telling a love story. But then the narrator in this story stops his narration and says he is lost for words.

MARK CHINCA: *He says, 'Now I don't know what I can say, which of the four of these has the greater suffering in love? I will hand the judgement over to lovers in the audience because I, myself, have no experience of it.'*

MELVYN BRAGG: *Him being a monk, I presume?*

MARK CHINCA: *We assume he is a cleric, so he probably doesn't if he's being a good cleric and an unmarried cleric and a celibate cleric.*

LAURA ASHE: *He's fairly knowledgeable, though.*

On the one hand, it seems he puts the audience above him in knowledge but, on the other hand, experience is a very double-edged sword in Thomas. Tristan's decision to marry Iseult of the White Hands is based precisely on this idea of wanting to try things out, of gaining experience, and that is disastrous.

Melvyn recalled that a key factor in the story was that, as Tristan was bringing Iseult over to Cornwall from Ireland to marry Mark, they are given the love potion together by Iseult's servant, and then that was it.

MELVYN BRAGG: *Why was a love potion introduced? Why didn't they just fall in love with each other like they do in movies?*

There are lots of different interpretations of this, Laura Ashe replied. In Béroul, it was very clear that it was just a potion that wore off and then the plot could go in different directions. In Thomas, you can reasonably claim it is just symbolic, a way of saying to readers, 'You may not doubt this love now.' That then has a bearing on the moral question, the question of whether they are free to act or bound into their love.

LAURA ASHE: *If we take it as symbolic, if we then ask ourselves the question, 'If our emotions are this strong, if this is a love that means that you would burn yourself in the world to be with this person, does that then justify actions you take for that love or does it not?' And, in the Middle Ages, there's a strong Christian line that says that the goal of life is to deny the self's longings in order to reach God. Now we are much more likely to have an ideal of self-fulfilment, to say, 'It is to be true to myself to fulfil who I am, to pursue love, to pursue my highest desires.'*

Thomas, she added, was ahead of both of those camps. He developed a genuine ethical exploration. Thomas showed that their emotions explained everything they did, but also that they could not justify anything that they did, and he showed us that through the pain of others. Laura Ashe summarised this: 'Can you justify what they do? Well, it's impossible to say; others are hurt by it. Should they not have done it? They could not do otherwise.'

The idea of not being able to act otherwise is found in other stories, even if it is not explored in such a way.

JULIETTE WOOD: *In the Diarmuid and Gráinne story, Diarmuid has a love spot and it's only …*

MELVYN BRAGG: *A love what?*

JULIETTE WOOD: *A love spot, something that makes all women fall in love with him. And this is only actually in the oral tales, which*

*we get from Scotland. And Gráinne, when she realises she's
married to this old man, puts everybody under a sleep spell and
[puts] Diarmuid under geas, which is a compulsion, almost like a
love potion. She says, 'You have to love me.' And Deirdre does
much the same.*

Melvyn wanted to know why the themes in Tristan and Iseult
appealed to medieval audiences as much as they appear to have done
when they seem so foreign to most of the experience that we find in
other literature at the time. Mark Chinca pointed to the changes in
marriage practices that had been affecting aristocratic families for a
century before this story of adultery at court was written down. Until
the Church had taken over, a couple married because the parents had
exchanged contracts. It was the way of producing legitimate heirs, the
way of passing down landed property.

MARK CHINCA: *With the Church's insistence on consent also
defining and constituting a marriage, there's a new element, which is
that you get married because you want to, the individuals concerned
have actually wished it. And, if you think about it, what you've got
in the adulterous relationship is this mixture of must and should
and want. The lovers must love because they're compelled, they
drank a potion; they should because they're so suited to each other;
and they actually want to, they make statements about how they
want to be together.*

The appeal of the story was thus that it offered a fictional
medium through which an aristocratic public could begin to think
about what it was that determined why two people were together for
life: because they must; because they should be; because they
want to be.

There is a famous Wagner version of the story, featuring the
liebestod, the love death. Anticipating this, Laura Ashe said that,
within the format of the story in the twelfth century, love could only
end in two ways – either someone died or it went wrong. Therefore,
as soon as a narrative of love appears, if an author wants to say that
someone's love is perfect, then, logically, we must see the characters
die. Marie de France, who was writing in England at about the same
time as Thomas, gives us a series of short romances, or lays, with
different structures of love, and she shows the idea that someone's
willingness to suffer is a measure of how noble his or her love is and
ultimately, when someone loves perfectly, love endures until death
and, implicitly, love brings with it death. Marie de France retold a
short version of the Tristan story in which she said their love was so
perfect that it brought them to death on the same day. In the Thomas
legend and in Gottfried, Laura Ashe added, we are told that, when
they drank the love potion, they drank their death; they drank love,
they drank death – both are the same.

Melvyn recalled how, in Wagner, this was taken up very seriously
in one of his greatest works, *Tristan und Isolde*, with the love death at
the end, 'the music waiting, waiting, waiting for it' and then resolving
itself in the love death. He asked if that was Wagner's addition or
something that had become an accepted part of the story by then.

MARK CHINCA: *I think that's Wagner, this notion of the* liebestod, *the love death that's the fulfilment and the culmination of love. Death is what actually ensures the perpetuation of your love because it means you won't ever wake up from the night of love. That's what the lovers sing in that duet in the second act of Wagner.*

JULIETTE WOOD: *In the early versions, when the two lovers die, they are buried on opposite sides of a river and plants grow out of their graves and unify. They're cut down and they grow again, and they're cut down and they're finally left. There's this folk motif of lovers united in death by the image of these twisting plants, which, of course, Marie takes up very much in her lay. Certainly Wagner's romanticism takes it to the highest levels, however one sees Wagner, but I think the implication is there beforehand.*

In Marie de France, Tristan and Iseult are the hazel and honeysuckle bound together for ever. Laura Ashe thought that Thomas did something very different from the *liebestod* as the couple do not die together.

LAURA ASHE: *Tristan dies and then Iseult comes and finds his body and lies down next to it and dies out of despair. It's not the same: he dies for his love, she dies for pity; they're separated by death. And I think this is because Thomas is not trying to write a symbolic* liebestod, *he's not trying to write something celebratory and glorious, he's trying to write something about real suffering.*

JULIETTE WOOD: *That says something about the power of these storytelling patterns, they can go on and they can spread and they can be reinterpreted, they can fall out of fashion and they can come back into fashion.*

In the studio afterwards, Melvyn's guests discussed some of the humour in the stories, such as the supposed disguise of Tristan when he passes himself off as 'Tantris' and no one but his dog recognises him. Another example was the idea of the older king being outsmarted by his young wife and her young lover, such as the time, in one version, when Tristan disguises himself as a monk and attends the ill Iseult to 'cure' her in private, and Mark thanks him profusely. That, Juliette Wood said, was pure Boccaccio.

Frontispiece to Emma.

EMMA

At the end of 1815, the great London publisher John Murray
brought out a novel by an anonymous writer identified as 'The
author of Pride and Prejudice etc. etc.' This writer we know to be
Jane Austen and the novel was Emma, described by some of the
speakers in this programme as her masterpiece and, by one, as the
greatest novel written in English. The plot revolves around Emma
Woodhouse, described by Austen as 'a heroine whom no one but
myself will much like'. Several of the other characters do very much
like her, though – particularly the conceited vicar Mr Elton (for a
while), the gentlemanly Mr Knightley and, in his way, the charming
Frank Churchill. Emma, meanwhile, tries to arrange marriages for
her female friends; she claims success for that of her governess and
wants even greater success for the lowly Harriet Smith. It all takes
place in a small Surrey village, a place in which Emma is virtually
immured. Her father wouldn't let her leave the place and she has little
inclination to displease him.

◦━◦━◦

With Melvyn to discuss *Emma* were: John Mullan, Lord Northcliffe professor of modern English literature at University College London; Janet Todd, professor emerita of literature at the University of Aberdeen and honorary fellow of Newnham College and Lucy Cavendish College, Cambridge; and Emma Clery, professor of English at the University of Southampton.

It was around the time that *Emma* was written and published, Emma Clery told us, that Jane Austen began to define her field as a novelist. She wrote in one letter, 'three or four families in a village is the very thing to work on', and, in another, that she specialised in scenes of domestic life in a country village. These were her roots and what she knew best. She had been born in December 1775 in the village of Steventon, 16 miles south of Basingstoke, and her parents had six boys and two girls. Her father was George Austen, a clergyman, who was very well educated, cultivated and hard-working.

EMMA CLERY: *He was also quite poor. He also, on the side, ran a boarding school for boys from his home and did a little bit of farming as well. Her mother, Cassandra, was also very intelligent; she had a dry sense of humour. She had aristocratic connections but was really willing to put her shoulder to the wheel as well.*

Jane Austen had drafts or first versions of *Sense and Sensibility*, *Pride and Prejudice* and *Northanger Abbey* by the 1790s, but did not have the connections to get these works published until, in 1810, with the help of her brother Henry, by then a banker in London, she succeeded with *Sense and Sensibility*.

Her parents, as Melvyn noted, supported their children in their literary interests and had a well-chosen library.

EMMA CLERY: *They were enthusiastic about novels, that was unusual. I think her father even read Gothic novels. It was a very stimulating environment. There were amateur theatricals, there were riddles, games, like in* Emma. *And they were all scribblers, almost all of them did some form of writing, wrote comic poems or essays.*

Jane Austen lived in Bath for a while with her sister and parents, moving to Southampton in 1805, when their father died, to live with a brother who was a sailor. Finally, they had a cottage in Chawton, part of the estate of her brother Edward, and it was at this point that she revised her manuscripts, and away she went with her career.

By the time *Emma* was published in 1815, *Pride and Prejudice*, *Sense and Sensibility* and *Mansfield Park* were quite successful, and she made a little money from some of them. This body of novels became known to the polite reading public, even if the author did not.

JOHN MULLAN: *Most of those people would not have known who Jane Austen was. It was actually with the publication of* Mansfield Park, *the year before* Emma, *that the secret, if that's the right word, began to leak out. Her brother Henry started boasting about it. And it's a famous fact that* Emma, *when it appeared, was dedicated to the Prince Regent, a man whom Jane Austen abhorred, a dissolute gourmand with many mistresses. But he was a fan of her writing.*

It was important, John Mullan added, that Jane Austen was not a member of a literary circle, but was writing in an age when literary circles were the thing. Her work was being read and talked about by friends and family but not other literary figures. There were two other important things about her, he added, one provable and the other something he felt.

JOHN MULLAN: *The provable thing is she cared a great deal about making money. She didn't have much money, she relied on the charity of her brothers. The second thing is that anybody who steeps themselves in Jane Austen, particularly the novels from* Mansfield Park *onwards, cannot doubt that she was an artist with really high ambitions. She was doing completely new things with fiction. She is one of the great experimental writers of European fiction.*

Emma is a fantastic novel, Janet Todd said, before gamely outlining the plot. There are three or four families in a country village, she recapped, and the story is about a community as well as about Emma. She lives in intellectual solitude, although rich, privileged, healthy, only twenty and beautiful, with a sickly, selfish, adoring, elderly father, and she is bored. She seeks Harriet Smith, below her in social status, only seventeen, and she proposes to train her up to be a friend. She treats her rather like a doll, and Mr Knightley, the neighbouring squire who has been advising her since she was a very small child, warns her that she will do Harriet damage. And she does, persuading her not to be interested in the tenant farmer who is in love with her, but to hold out for the handsome new vicar, Mr Elton.

JANET TODD: *It turns out that Mr Elton is more interested in Emma and her £30,000 and, when the mistake is realised in a very, very funny scene, Mr Elton goes off in high dudgeon and comes back with a wife so ridiculous that she is one of the joys of the book. Mrs Elton and her snobbishness and her apparatus of happiness is, I think to me, a great pleasure.*

There is also Jane Fairfax, a beautiful orphan of great accomplishments whom Emma is jealous of, and Mr Knightley feels she is the friend Emma should have had. Emma tries, but Jane is very reserved for some undisclosed reason and, as a result, Emma, who has a great deal of imagination and spirit, invents a backstory for her that is malicious, and is helped in this by the other visitor to the village, Frank Churchill, a rich young man whom Emma had always thought was dedicated to herself. The plot develops and resolves and it ends with marriages, and they all marry the right people.

There is a whiff of Waterloo in the background, Janet Todd suggested, an ironic or maybe absolutely sincere patriotism in the story that is very clear about England, versus France and 'their silly language and their ways'.

JANET TODD: *It's also about what kind of England is coming into being. It's an England where things are changing, where people are coming back from the war. The war is over, there's not going to be another war for a long time. How is it going to work? And the village is close to London; it feels London pushing against it.*

Emma is the only one of Austen's book titles that features the heroine and, in doing that, Emma Clery said, Austen was highlighting her own daring in creating a heroine who is so unusual. Heroines were usually underdogs who were bereaved or had fallen into poverty or had pursuing villains or seducers, whereas the opening paragraph of *Emma* sweeps all that aside. Austen does, though, highlight a danger to her heroine in the first chapter.

EMMA CLERY: *She's facing the 'danger of intellectual solitude', [that's] the phrase that's used there. And Austen takes that really seriously. That is the driving force of the entire novel, this danger of intellectual solitude, which is really based on the very limited horizons that even a very privileged woman had at that time.*

Melvyn emphasised that Emma is also conceited, snobbish, manipulating, classist, spoiled and cruel, which prompted Emma Clery to assert that she was also intelligent, resourceful, imaginative, funny, witty, compassionate and pragmatic, good features that are simply wasted in her narrow circumstances. To John Mullan, all these qualities were there, but her faults were beside the point.

JOHN MULLAN: *The point about the novel is it's almost entirely narrated through Emma's consciousness in incredibly sophisticated and funny ways. We do judge her and we're expected to judge her, but we also inhabit her, we see the world through her eyes.*

A lot of the plot points pass us by on first reading as we are seeing the world as Emma sees it. Jane Austen invented this technique, John Mullan added, later called 'free indirect speech'. Meanwhile, Janet Todd did see cruelty in Emma, to the extent that there were times when she found her intolerable. At one point, Harriet, the simple child who is only seventeen, sees the family of the Martins, whose son courted her and she rejected him, at Emma's prompting, and Harriet narrates this in a very simple straightforward way. Emma is almost moved for a moment and then she says, 'What can you expect from a silly shallow girl like Harriet?' This, Janet Todd stressed, was a girl she had taken into her house as supposedly her friend, which made her behaviour almost unforgivable.

JANET TODD: *There is something about Emma, because we're inside her, that is terribly appealing, as is anybody we're inside. At the same time, I still think there is a cruelty and something quite disturbing in the centre of all that.*

Making a case for Emma, Emma Clery pointed to the way in which it was made very apparent how constraining her circumstances were, and it was because of the lack of options in her life that she was forced into a fantasist role.

EMMA CLERY: *There's a real feminist agenda that can be seen through an array of female characters. We've got Jane Fairfax who, by rights, really should be the heroine of the novel: she's an orphan,*

Jane Austen.

she has no means, she has no dowry, she's doomed to life as a governess, and she has this extraordinary outburst where she says the trade in governesses is like the slave trade. She doesn't say it's got the same cruelty but that there's something involuntary and oppressive about it.

Besides, Melvyn said, readers are sympathetic towards Emma as she is ruled over by a tyrant father who is either sick, or pretends to be sick, and won't let her out of his sight; he even wants her to eat what he wants her to eat. She has never been to London, only 15 miles away, or to the seaside. He is, as John Mullan quoted, a man with 'habits of gentle selfishness'.

JOHN MULLAN: *He's hilarious, but the thing about Mr Woodhouse is that he's the opposite of his daughter. She thinks that she knows what other people are like, and that's what makes her interesting, but most of the time she's wrong. He is incapable of thinking that anybody's different from him.*

Janet Todd suspected that Jane Austen had a soft ironic spot for these 'vegetable people' such as Emma's father, people who can hardly get off the sofa, and she presents Lady Bertram in *Mansfield Park* with a sort of loving concern. Emma's mother died when she was five and she needs to be central to somebody; Mr Woodhouse is the centre, however unfortunate that might be for her.

In Highbury where, as Janet Todd said, 'nothing happens, yet everything's happening', people are always imagining pairings. This, John Mullan added, was the humming heart of Austen's fiction, where everybody unmarried between the ages of fifteen and forty *might* marry somebody. Emma is a matchmaker who is making matches in her mind, and this is nearly disastrous. Some of her errors are more obvious on a second reading of the novel, such as those over Frank Churchill and Jane Fairfax, which is like a detective story.

JOHN MULLAN: *Most people, the first time you read the novel, you absolutely know that Mr Elton is really after Emma and what a fool she is not to see it. And, as he himself says when he proposes and she says, 'But what about Miss Smith?': 'Miss Smith!' He says one of the most truly evil lines in literature. He says, 'Some men might not object ... everyone has his level.' Isn't that fantastic?*

On the first reading, we do not see what Frank Churchill is up to, he is so cunning. Emma has no idea what he is up to and, the first time we read it, nor do we. It is Mr Knightley, Janet Todd said, who is the detective in the book: 'He's the good man, except that he's a bit unimaginative and he doesn't dance when he should and he doesn't necessarily use his carriage.' He has been in love with Emma since she was thirteen, he also knew her as a baby – he is another familial lover in the story. He is looking for clues as he thinks there is something wrong about Frank Churchill.

With marriages in mind, Miss Bates is in some ways a shadow of Emma. There are people who find her boring, as Emma does, but Janet Todd said she enjoyed her thoroughly, partly as, if you listen to her speech, you find out a lot more about Highbury than you would otherwise know, and she gives away a fair number of clues. She also understands when she is being got at by Emma, at the Box Hill picnic, very quickly.

JANET TODD: *In some ways, she shadows her, after all she is stuck there with an elderly mother. She is a spinster, and one of the times Harriet does catch Emma is where she says, 'If you don't marry, as you say you won't because you're first in your father's house and you are everything to your father,' Harriet says, 'but you'll be like Miss Bates.'*

Mrs Elton is another thing altogether, Janet Todd added, with 'her apparatus of happiness and her music and her accomplishments', and she is also a shadow of Emma.

JANET TODD: *She's much stupider and she has no ability, in the way that Emma has, to change and to grow and to learn from her mistakes. At the same time, that snobbishness, that manner of patronising people, of taking them up, of feeling oneself superior, of not understanding that you have to create a community all the time, that is something that is a bit close to the worse side of Emma.*

Returning to Mr Knightley and his love for Emma, John Mullan picked up on the effect that the mention of Frank Churchill's name had on him, which was to generate jealousy. Reading the novel from

Mr Knightley's perspective, we can notice how he subtly changes the way he speaks to Emma and how he replies. She does not see it, or is puzzled by it, asking why he is so cross about this man he has not even met.

JOHN MULLAN: *And Mr Knightley's love (Jane Austen knows exactly what she's doing), his love for Emma, comes right at the end as a surprise to Emma, but it shouldn't be a surprise to the reader, because his love story is there, too.*

Janet Todd noted the cleverness of the novel, where readers can see Emma has been noticing Mr Knightley over and over again, where he stood in a particular time, that he came in his carriage; in mass social scenes, she knows where Mr Knightley is at every moment. He is the best man in the book and Emma says, 'I deserve the best because I never put up with anything else.' They find fault in each other, too, and are not afraid to say it, Emma Clery added, making their relationship relatively egalitarian.

EMMA CLERY: *There's a lovely bit where she teases him about his notion that he's going to look after his young nephews, who she actually has a responsibility for, because he has more time. Of course, he doesn't have more time, Emma's the one with all the time on her hands. And she does it in such a kind of loving but also teasing way, it's like nothing else, I think, in the fiction up to this point.*

For Janet Todd, *Emma* is Jane Austen's masterpiece and it is the last book that she absolutely finished. It is the cleverest, the most subtle, the one in which she thinks about her own artistry, as well as putting artistry into the book. Emma Clery put it first among Austen's works for artistry, preferring *Persuasion* for feeling and plot. For John Mullan, it was Austen's greatest novel, even if lots of her fans find *Persuasion* the most moving and visceral.

JOHN MULLAN: *With* Emma, *it's like reading* Twelfth Night, *you feel the person who wrote this can do anything they want, they are totally in control. And I think, because of that, it's also one of the very greatest of all novels in English.*

JANET TODD: *We all think it's brilliant.*

In the studio afterwards, Janet Todd said she thought that perhaps the humour had not been stressed enough. When she was younger, she said, she wanted the passion that is in *Persuasion* but, now that she is older, *Emma* shows how to carry on and laugh. John Mullan, in support of the humour, mentioned the comedy of Emma's attempt to distract Harriet from the knowledge that Mr Elton never loved her by talking about the poor in Highbury ... only for Harriet to sigh and say, '*Mr Elton* was so kind to the poor,' when he was not kind to the poor in the least but a horrible person. Melvyn found his own concern for Harriet, abused by Emma, outweighed the humour in passages such as that. Emma Clery suggested that other authors were remarkably negative about Austen's work in the nineteenth century, which Janet Todd put down to literary jealousy.

augmented by the Author.

Omne tulit punctum, qui miscuit vtile dulci.

Democritus Junior

Oxford
Printed for
Henry Crijpps
1628

C.le

Blon fe:

Robert Burton.

THE ANATOMY
OF MELANCHOLY

Samuel Johnson, the compiler of his mighty English dictionary,
suffered terribly from depression. 'I inherited a vile melancholy
from my father,' he said, 'which made me mad all my life.'
Reading offered Dr Johnson some respite and one book in particular
helped lift his gloom. Robert Burton's The Anatomy of Melancholy
was, said Dr Johnson, the only book that ever took him out of bed
two hours sooner than he wished to rise. It was first published in 1621.

The Anatomy of Melancholy *is a huge and entertaining work devoted to the causes and treatment of melancholy, a malady that preoccupied many writers of that period. Part medical treatise, part literary anthology, it draws on sources ranging from classical authors to the latest medical authorities, reflecting Burton's astonishingly broad reading. The book captivated contemporary readers and it has influenced later writers including Milton, Keats and Beckett. It is still in print.*

⊷━◆━⊷

With Melvyn to discuss *The Anatomy of Melancholy* were: Julie Sanders, deputy vice-chancellor and professor of English at the University of Newcastle; Mary Ann Lund, associate professor in English at the University of Leicester; and Erin Sullivan, senior lecturer and fellow at the Shakespeare Institute, University of Birmingham.

Opening up the discussion, Melvyn suggested that *The Anatomy of Melancholy* is one of the most unusual books in the English language, which is quite a statement.

JULIE SANDERS: The Anatomy of Melancholy *has been variously described as an encyclopaedia, as a commonplace book, as a mine of quotations, as a medical manual, as a self-help book and, indeed, as one of the messiest books ever written.*

The book is an *anatomy*, an opening-up, a dissecting of what Robert Burton regarded as an epidemic of melancholy in his own time and, Julie Sanders said, he came at this subject by invoking medical, religious, philosophical, ethical, literary and poetic authorities to try to perform that anatomising. The work is full of long citations and interpretations of writing from the ancients, medieval writers and Italian Renaissance humanists.

Burton was born in 1577 to a Leicestershire gentry family and spent his adult life as an Oxford don, a scholar of divinity, attached to the colleges of Brasenose and then Christ Church. He was also working in the library, feeding his voracious appetite for books and he wrote a play, *Philosophaster*, which prefigured some of his satirical attacks on society that he was to include in *The Anatomy of Melancholy*. He was also attached to a rural parish from 1616, but was otherwise, as he put it, a scholar penned up in his study.

JULIE SANDERS: *There are some lost years in the 1590s. Between 1593 and 1599, he seems to temporarily suspend his studies and it's possible that he's the Robert Burton who turns up in London in the notebooks of the physician Simon Forman. This man arrives suffering from a mix of psychological and physical ailments and he's diagnosed with melancholy by Forman. Certainly the age of the patient fits.*

In *The Anatomy*, Burton presents himself as someone who has experienced melancholy. The medical system that gave rise to this term was thousands of years old, starting in the writings of Hippocrates and developed by others such as Galen, a Roman philosopher and surgeon. The idea, Erin Sullivan explained, was that the body was made up of four liquids or humours – blood, phlegm, yellow bile and black bile.

ERIN SULLIVAN: *'Melancholia' is literally 'black bile'. The idea of the system [was] that these different humours in your body are what facilitate the functioning of the organs so, when you put food into your body, the humours help process it, help take the nutrients from the food and take them to the parts of the body that need it. Ideally, these four humours are all in balance.*

The idea was that all people had some kind of imbalance, which, if too great, would lead to disease. There were supposed to be preventative steps such as regulating diet, sleep and exercise, or improving the quality of air available, or socialising, or listening to the right kind of music. For more serious cases, there was bloodletting.

ERIN SULLIVAN: *One of the things that's interesting and perplexing about the humoural system is how long-lasting it is, for 2,000 years almost. There's a really strong investment in the authority of the past but also a sense that, through experience, we find that some of these things are true. Hot and cold make a difference, you can change where you are; if you're feeling very cold, then you eat hot foods to try to clear out the phlegm.*

There was a kind of logic to the system perhaps, but it was one that was already being challenged by Burton's time.

Within this system, Burton described melancholy as a compound mixed malady. Mary Ann Lund explained that this meant it was a disease that was physically rooted, as well as a mental and spiritual disorder. Burton saw it as an anguish of mind, associated with fear and sorrow without a cause, where melancholy was an excess of black bile, of melancholia.

MARY ANN LUND: *You may be just a thoughtful person prone to solitude, and not ill, but, when melancholy in your system becomes too much, becomes excessive, then you become diseased through it and you may be unable to seek the company of other people, unable to do anything, rather crippled by this disease.*

That state was known as natural melancholy. There was also unnatural melancholy, where the other humours became corrupted or burnt. People could also be sanguine melancholics, when their blood became corrupted, which was a different kind of disorder.

MELVYN BRAGG: *What happens then?*

MARY ANN LUND: *You're cheerful, but you laugh at more or less everything ... perhaps a little hysterically at things. If you're a choleric melancholic you pick fights all the time, you get very angry with people, but you're also very brave. They couldn't quite decide whether phlegmatic melancholic really worked as an idea (Galen thought not). But, in those cases, you tended to seek solitary places but near the water, because phlegm was a watery humour.*

It was a core element of this system that there were such things as psychosomatic diseases, and that mental illness should be taken seriously. We heard that Burton said that you might as well tell a melancholy person *not* to be melancholy as to tell someone who was wounded, or someone who was in a fever, not to feel pain, or to stop their physical symptoms.

There was a cult of melancholy around the time of the first publication of Burton's book, in 1621, which could be traced back to ideas in antiquity and arose from a set of problems ascribed to Aristotle, in which he supposedly asked why it was that people who were outstanding in philosophy, poetry and the arts tended to be melancholic. There was also Dürer's *Melencolia*, the famous engraving of female melancholy.

MARY ANN LUND: *In the sixteenth century, it was very attractive to picture yourself as melancholic and, indeed, [in] portraits at this time, courtiers are painted reclining by a riverside, under a tree, wearing black. Melancholy is definitely a pose that people found attractive. Burton's sales were certainly helped by the fact that melancholy was so voguish.*

Burton appears to have written *The Anatomy* to help his own condition, saying, 'I write of melancholy by being busy to avoid melancholy,' Julie Sanders told us. He wrote and rewrote the book for the rest of his life. He also thought that the act of reading was a distraction, a curative, so that the reader, by exploring melancholy, would be attracted away from the actual experience of it. At various points, he says, 'Well, if you have this type of melancholy, this bit of the book might not be so good for you,' or, 'If you've been getting a bit depressed by reading this, this section will be light relief.'

MELVYN BRAGG: *He's quite playful as well. He said, if you're of a jealous disposition, the best thing to do is to marry a prostitute because you'll have no problems, you'll know that she's betraying you, so you can get on with it.*

JULIE SANDERS: *I think he's witty. I think there're lots of literary games going on as well, pushing the possibilities of humour when dealing with a very serious subject.*

The first edition of *The Anatomy* ran to 900 pages and the final one was over twice as long, at 2,000 pages. It is divided into three main partitions: the first with causes and symptoms of melancholy; the second with cures; and the third looks at love melancholy and religious melancholy. Melvyn asked for an example of these melancholies.

ERIN SULLIVAN: *At one point, he's suggesting the different ways in which women suffer from melancholy and how they might need to be married and to have a sexual partner and that will help with things. He does back off and say, 'Oh, I don't really know why I'm talking about this.' You can read it as genuine but also as facetious.*

Moving on to nuns, Burton enters into a critique of Catholicism and how living the celibate life is problematic, which was a contemporary political and religious issue, and he handled this in a light and humorous way.

Mary Ann Lund said this playfulness followed on from Erasmus and *The Praise of Folly*, a paradoxical book in which Folly herself speaks and says how ridiculous everything is. Burton calls himself Democritus and Democritus Junior, another reference to that work of Erasmus in which Folly alludes to Democritus as the laughing philosopher.

MARY ANN LUND: *The story goes that Hippocrates went to see Democritus because the people of his town of Abdera thought that Democritus had gone mad. Hippocrates says, 'Well, why do people think you're mad?' And [Democritus] laughs at worldly anxieties and says 'Why worry about these things?' Hippocrates goes back to the people of Abdera and says, 'Democritus isn't mad at all, he's the wisest man I know.'*

Democritus is also paired with Heraclitus, the weeping philosopher, and those two attitudes to life were ones that Burton oscillated between, lamenting for worldly folly as well as laughing at it.

In the section on love melancholy, Burton turned to authorities that were predominantly literary and poetic, and, for this, he had a large collection of Petrarchan love poetry in his library that he could draw on. These authorities used a set of literary tropes, literary metaphors and clichés that were very standard – 'burning with love' or 'pining away' – only for Burton to say that, in fact, some people *do* stop sleeping or lose their appetite, these are commonplace for a reason, there are real physical manifestations.

Following on from Mary Ann Lund, Erin Sullivan argued that there was a tension between the extents to which some of these tropes were metaphorical or literal.

ERIN SULLIVAN: *If you do take the humoural system seriously, then a burning feeling around your heart could be conceived as the hot humours heating it up or, when you feel very despondent, when melancholy takes hold, you feel cold, you want a blanket around you.*

MARY ANN LUND: *It's also very much based on the individual. Burton says that scarce two of 2,000 concur in the same symptoms. In love melancholy, for instance, some people might have it from not having any sex, from their abstinence. For others, it can be from too much. There's a story of a man who marries a young wife in a hot summer and tires himself out with 'chamber work' and becomes mad as a result.*

What can be the cause of a problem for some can be a cure for others, a matter of Burton having it both ways, as Melvyn put it.

Turning to the long section on religious melancholy, Julie Sanders told us that Burton had little precedent for treating this kind of melancholy separately. Burton was consciously making it a category in its own right, dividing it into religious melancholy in excess, which was superstition, and, in this, he included Catholicism, Judaism and Islam, and melancholy in defect, which was atheism. The Church of England was placed in the middle of these extremes.

JULIE SANDERS: *At the end of the work, he writes about despair as a cause of melancholy. This is where Burton's really at his most serious. The cure of despair is what ends this work, and he adds to it massively in the second edition and it becomes a very straightforward consolatory section, where he's really comforting people who feel that they have been abandoned by God or have been listening to too many strict puritan ministers and reading too many depressing treatises and think that they are destined for hell. And the message is that one shouldn't give in to despair.*

To Melvyn, Burton seemed particularly anxious about the powerful notion put forward, particularly by Calvinists, of predestination – that, even before you were born, you were either elected for salvation or not, and there was nothing you could do about it. This, Erin Sullivan said, was an official part of Church of England theology in Elizabeth's reign and into James's, but it was being called into question increasingly. Burton quotes some who were supportive of the idea, but again has it both ways.

The melancholic landscapes in Keats's poetry, such as 'La Belle Dame sans Merci', may have been influenced by Burton.

ERIN SULLIVAN: *He certainly is concerned about the negative effects that this way of thinking can have. People who really adhere to predestination said that it should be a comforting doctrine because, once you know that you're saved, you really know it. But he says that actually, of course, there are people who are going to think they aren't.*

Burton was responding to the time, Julie Sanders argued, as his anti-Calvinist feelings were starting to grow, and the 1630s were a time of deep religious conflict in England that would lead to civil war, mirrored across mainland Europe in the Thirty Year's War. There was a fierce rise of extremist puritanism, and Burton was saying that this zeal was something that would affect your body and carry you into these states of torment, into religious melancholy.

The work found a ready audience from its first publication, going through so many editions and, as a big folio text, it would have been expensive. Copies from the seventeenth century show lots of underlinings, a mark of how engaged the readers were with the text. Mary Ann Lund told how people in that century reportedly mined *The Anatomy* for quotations and exotic stories to furnish their own learning, and Milton seems to have had Burton's work in mind when he wrote *Il Penseroso*. Erin Sullivan pointed to a rush of plays that came out in 1629, after the third edition, which is the one with a beautiful title page with various versions of melancholy.

ERIN SULLIVAN: *We get plays by Ben Jonson,* The New Inn, *we get Richard Brome's* The Northern Lass, *we get John Ford's* The Lover's Melancholy, *all in 1629 at the Blackfriars Theatre, all quoting and using chunks of Burton. And, interestingly, those plays are all in his own personal library. So Burton purchases the very plays that are responding to him.*

The book continued to be read avidly during the civil war and afterwards. Royalists appeared to find the idea of Democritus attractive, withdrawing from the world and laughing at it.

MARY ANN LUND: *Particularly after the collapse of the monarchy, this sense that one could still observe the world from one remove was attractive. And then, well into the late seventeenth century and, indeed, to Queen Anne's reign, people are still stealing from it. Laurence Sterne takes a large passage from* The Anatomy of Melancholy *and passes it off as his own in* Tristram Shandy.

The Anatomy was not published in the eighteenth century but there were still many copies in circulation for Sterne. Johnson said that, when Burton spoke from his own voice, he had a great spirit and a great power to him, and that is what got him up earlier and seems to have been curative for Johnson in some way. Charles Lamb took the book up in the Romantic period, and Keats based his poem *Lamia* on a story in Burton about an enchantress who convinces a man to marry her, and then it is exposed at the marriage feast by the philosopher Apollonius that she is, in fact, a snake.

Julie Sanders suggested that the bittersweet compound of pleasure and pain in Keats's poetry was coming directly from Burton, such as in the melancholic landscapes of poems like 'La Belle Dame sans Merci'.

Byron apparently used Burton as a mine for quotations to impress women in social situations.

ERIN SULLIVAN: *In the Romantic period, the idea of the sublime is that beauty and awe-inspiring creation is at once positive and also dangerous, or [there's] even a bit of horror about it. You get writers saying things like, 'I can't imagine something beautiful without an undercurrent of pain.' The bittersweet aspect of [melancholy] is really appealing in its complexity.*

The Anatomy of Melancholy is still in print, long after the idea of humours was overtaken by medical science. Julie Sanders thought that there was a reconfiguring of Burton in new theories, post-Freud, through the World Wars, when ideas of depression and trauma and Burton became very relevant.

JULIE SANDERS: *In the past few days, Burton's been cited in the press in an article about information overload and the internet. That's a new version of over-much learning, I suppose. And the value of public libraries. And, I like to think, head on his hand, penned in his study, he would have been quite pleased at that.*

Illumination from the Icelandic manuscript Flateyjarbók *shows King Harald Fairhair cutting the fetters from the giant Dofri.*

ICELANDIC SAGAS

The late Middle Ages was a period when literature flourished across Europe as never before. Italy produced the masterpieces of Dante and Petrarch; English literature began in style with the works of Langland and Geoffrey Chaucer; and the medieval poets of Wales and France laid the foundations of great national literary traditions. But some of the richest and most original writing of the early Middle Ages was produced on a remote island in the North Atlantic, which even today has a population about the size of Leicester. Iceland was first settled in the ninth century by Vikings and the deeds of these first Icelanders and their families are recorded in the Icelandic sagas. Around forty of these sagas, written down between the thirteenth and fourteenth centuries, are known to exist. They are dramatic tales that mix the domestic, the historical and the supernatural as they chart the feuds and love affairs of early Icelandic life.

⊶●⊷

With Melvyn to discuss the Icelandic sagas were: Carolyne Larrington, professor of medieval European literature at the University of Oxford and fellow and tutor in medieval English at St John's College, Oxford; Elizabeth Ashman Rowe, reader in Scandinavian history in the Department of Anglo-Saxon, Norse and Celtic, University of Cambridge; and Emily Lethbridge, research lecturer in the Department of Name Studies at the Árni Magnússon Manuscripts Institute for Icelandic Studies, Reykjavík, Iceland.

According to the Icelanders' own origin myth and histories, Carolyne Larrington said, the Norwegians migrated to the island because King Harald Fairhair was centralising power in Norway and various members of the aristocracy took against this. Added to this was a mixture of Scandinavians in the British Isles who moved to Iceland, particularly women, bringing a Celtic injection to the population. Around the edges of the island, they found a landscape that was not unlike western Norway.

CAROLYNE LARRINGTON: *We're told that there was also forest in Iceland when the Norwegians first arrived there, but, if there was, it seems to have been cut down very quickly. But there was certainly, particularly in the south and in the west, some very good land for farming and, of course, the climate was slightly better in those days.*

The migrants brought their own laws with them, but they did not have a king, and they instituted a system of thirty-six chieftaincies, with local assemblies for local legal matters and, once a year, everybody would meet at the Alþingi, the big general assembly. The settlers had not been there for long when Christianity arrived in 999 or 1000.

CAROLYNE LARRINGTON: *That, at least according to the Icelandic historians, resulted in a more or less overnight conversion to Christianity. Everybody at the Alþingi decided on a vote, more or less, that it would be better for the country to have a single religion, and that* *would be Christianity. It also got the king of Norway off their backs, to some extent, because he was very keen on converting them.*

With Christianity came writings, Latin literature and access to the European culture, which together made the writing of sagas possible, though some texts were being written before then. These sagas, Elizabeth Rowe explained, are now classified according to their subject matter, with groups made up of kings, bishops and saints, other groups with heroes of chivalry, such as King Arthur and Charlemagne, others with heroes of Germanic legend, such as Sigurd the Dragon Slayer, and from the early Viking age, such as Ragnarr Loðbrók, or 'Shaggy Breeks' as he is sometimes known in translation. There are sagas about the other North Atlantic settlements, such as the Orkney Islands, the Faroes, Greenland and North America. Of central importance are the sagas about Iceland itself.

ELIZABETH ROWE: *Critical are the ones that take place in the ninth, tenth, eleventh centuries about the Icelanders' own ancestors. These are often called the family sagas because they're multi-generational and the original epic, sweeping dramas of emotion and violence, such as the saga of Egil, son of Skalla-Grímr, supposed to have been written by one of the leading chieftains of Iceland.*

Some are satirical, poking fun at the chieftains, as power became more concentrated in the hands of half a dozen families rather than the original thirty-six or thirty-nine chieftains. Often there was a historical core of events, and there can be genealogies in the family sagas, making them a way for Icelanders to preserve their history and identity. Emily Lethbridge noted that most Icelanders today can trace their ancestry back to the first settlers, so genealogy has always been extremely important to Icelanders, combined with a very strong sense of local belonging and identity.

There are claims to authenticity in some, and hints at sources. Court poetry was treated as a source since it was held by society at the time that, as the poetry was recited in front of people who took part in the events, they would know if the poems were true or not and would have objected if they were not true.

ELIZABETH ROWE: *[In] Icelandic histories that are not in the form of sagas, such as the* Book of Icelanders, *written by Ari Thorgilsson in the beginning of the twelfth century, he actually talks about his sources and he says, 'I heard this from my foster father who remembered being baptised at the age of three,' something like that. Or, in the king sagas, the author of* Heimskringla, *Snorri Sturluson, talks about his sources as the report of 'men who we consider wise and truthful and they believe these things to be true'.*

There are about 400 or so manuscripts of sagas from the medieval period, Emily Lethbridge said, of which about sixty are sagas of Icelanders or family sagas and a lot of these are fragmentary. The oldest fragment, a single leaf, dates from 1250. The texts would have been produced by scribes or clerics on parchment in religious houses, though, for the most part, it is hard to say who wrote them, or precisely where or when. The golden age of manuscript production was in the fourteenth century.

EMILY LETHBRIDGE: *From then, a manuscript called* Möðruvallabók *is one of the most famous manuscripts, a large heavy volume, and it contains eleven sagas of Icelanders. Seven of these sagas are organised geographically, most of these sagas are very local in character and they focus on a specific local area. And the sagas in this* Möðruvallabók *manuscript chart around the country east to west.*

Generally, lawsuits were critical to sagas and, Carolyne Larrington suggested, the earliest oral forms may have arisen as accounts of particular legal cases. Typically, there would be a feud between two groups of people, and, often, these would be minor figures, but then it would escalate to a power battle between two families. There would be a crisis, somebody very important would be killed and the case would come to the Alþingi where there was a very complex law system, but no executive power to put legal findings into force.

CAROLYNE LARRINGTON: *You have all sorts of extraordinary bits of domestic detail in the middle of them. Like one feud, which kicks off at some level, really, because one woman is a bad housekeeper and she sends her slave to steal cheese from somebody else's pantry. And, when her husband finds out, he slaps her and, a very long way down the line, he pays for that with his life.*

There were traces of other literature in them, with storytellers learning from Latin texts, and there could have been awareness of the Arthurian romances that had travelled from Norway to Iceland of which many are preserved in Icelandic manuscripts. The narrators of the sagas do not have a particularly distinctive voice – they rarely tell what people are thinking and readers have to judge that by their actions and speech. Sometimes the narrator will go further by saying whether others thought that an action was good or bad, but the author does not offer judgements. There can be very dense poetry, perhaps uttered in the middle of a battle, which can give some sense of the violence or the internal turmoil or the joy of battle or the sorrow of the aftermath, but again the author does not express this in his own voice. Generally, the sagas do not talk of emotions or the interior life, but, where there are some with treatments of love, those treatments may have come from the romances.

CAROLYNE LARRINGTON: *[The]* Laxdæla *saga is very interested in love, both love of two foster brothers for one another and the kind of complicated love between one particular woman and the men that she marries. The word 'love' begins to be mentioned quite a lot. So there's a sense in* Laxdæla *saga that something has changed in saga-writing at that point.*

The Bible influenced the sagas, too. Salvation was important to Icelanders, as it was to other medieval Christians. In Scandinavia, which had a long pagan history, the arrival of Christianity was often seen as a historical dividing line between something akin to an Old Testament period and then a Christian era. Sometimes Icelandic

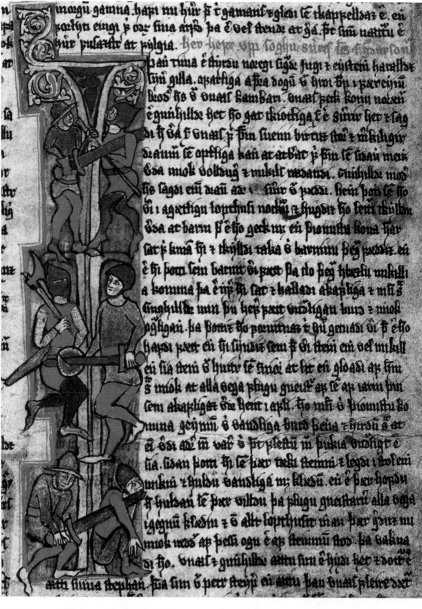

This fourteenth-century copy of the Flateyjarbók *contains a collection of manuscripts of the Icelandic sagas.*

authors would portray their ancestors as virtuous pagans, as they did not like the idea of them burning in hell before they had had the chance to become good Christians. Besides those influences, Elizabeth Rowe continued, there were specific allusions to events in the Bible as well. There is a smaller feud saga of a man called Hrafnkel, which begins with a scene reminiscent of Genesis, where God says to Adam and Eve, 'Of this tree thou shalt not eat.' In this saga, a pagan Icelandic chieftain had devoted his livestock, particularly his favourite stallion, to the fertility god, Freyr, and made a vow that nobody should ride this stallion, punishing anyone who broke that vow with death.

ELIZABETH ROWE: *He hires a shepherd to guard his sheep and he says: 'You can ride any of my horses except this one. If you ride this one horse, you will die.' And so, of course, events transpired that the sheep stray off, the shepherd has to find a horse, the only horse that will stand still for him is this one stallion, he rides it and, of course, the chieftain kills him.*

For a further flavour of a saga, Carolyne Larrington returned to the central story of *Laxdæla*, which is about betrayal. In this saga, Kjartan is about to go on a rite-of-passage trip to Norway and, before that, has become involved with a very spirited young woman called Guðrún. She wants to go to Norway with Kjartan and his foster brother Bolli, but she is left behind as an unmarried woman was not allowed to travel alone in this way. In Norway, Kjartan befriends the king and converts to Christianity, and Bolli, feeling left out, returns to Iceland. He takes no greeting from Kjartan to Guðrún and she, rather hurt, agrees to marry Bolli, something that breaks Kjartan's heart on his return as both the woman he loves and the foster brother he loves have betrayed him.

CAROLYNE LARRINGTON: *It's only a matter of time before either Kjartan kills Bolli or Bolli kills Kjartan. And, in the end, it's Bolli who kills Kjartan, who more or less offers himself to Bolli and says, 'If anyone kills me, I'd rather it was you.' But, of course, once Kjartan is dead, things don't rest there, because Kjartan's brothers will then kill Bolli. And, when Bolli is killed, Guðrún is pregnant. And, as one of the slayers wipes her husband's blood on her apron, she laughs, and the killers ask each other why this is the case, and the one who wiped the blood on the apron says, 'I think my killer is under that apron, still in the womb.'*

Sure enough, eighteen years or so later, Bolli Bollason, the baby that was in the womb, kills the killer and a couple of the others.

CAROLYNE LARRINGTON: *Guðrún, who's really at the heart of the saga, marries four times and we hear about four different husbands, some of whom she loved and some of whom she didn't particularly. And, at the end, Bolli, her son, asks her whom she loved most and she says, very famously, 'The one I loved most was the one to whom I was worst.' And that's all she said, and the assumption, of course, is it's not any of her husbands but it was Kjartan.*

Almost all the places named in the sagas can be visited today. At the spot where Kjartan was said to have been slain, Emily Lethbridge told us, there is a large stone not far from the road, which is mentioned in the saga as the one against which Kjartan set his back as he defended himself from Bolli.

This saga, Elizabeth Rowe added, was a good example of the religious prefiguration outlined earlier. Kjartan, when in Norway, found himself in a swimming contest with a man who turned out to be quite strong and succeeded in ducking him in the water several times. Back on the shore, the man came over and offered Kjartan a cloak as a gift for being such a strong swimmer, and he turned out to be King Olaf Tryggvason, the first missionary king of Norway.

ELIZABETH ROWE: *That contest in the water, and the ducking under, is interpreted as a kind of foreshadowing of the baptism that Kjartan will soon choose, and the gift of the cloak prefigures the baptismal robes that he will receive.*

There is also a Celtic influence in the *Laxdæla* saga, as Kjartan's grandmother was an Irish slave called Melkorka who never spoke to anybody but her son and taught him Irish. It turned out, Carolyne Larrington added, that she was the daughter of the Irish king, which gave Kjartan an even higher opinion of himself.

Among the most popular of the family sagas were those of the outlaws, telling their stories, the events leading up to their outlawry, and how they survived on the run in Iceland. One of the best known featured Grettir, who lived in the very inhospitable central wastes. Grettir dies in a bloody final battle on a bastion fortress island off the north of Iceland, after a combination of witchcraft, curses, sorcery and the carelessness of a slave. Once the outlaws are killed, Emily Lethbridge told us, these deaths are followed up by vengeance chapters in which their family members carry out further killings in order to avenge their deaths.

Over time, the sagas played a significant part in weaving the society of Iceland together, with a very important role as entertainment. Up until the twentieth century, they were read aloud in the communal gatherings of winter evenings.

EMILY LETHBRIDGE: *They were central to the construction of Icelandic identity, one of the key motivations that presumably drove people to write these stories down in the first place. And, right up until the nineteenth century, for example, the sagas – and the Njáls saga in particular – these sagas were used as political propaganda, almost part of the fight for Icelandic independence from Denmark.*

Wherever you go in Iceland, we heard, people will come up and tell you about the sagas that took place in the spot where you are standing and retell you the stories that are still living in the landscape.

One of the first things the Icelanders did when they became an independent republic in 1944 was to call for the return of their sagas from Copenhagen, where they were taken by their Danish rulers. This call was answered in 1971.

CAROLYNE LARRINGTON: *Finally, two absolutely vital manuscript collections, the Poetic Edda, which contains mythological and heroic poetry, and Flateyjarbók, which is a big collection of various texts, including a lot of sagas, came back to Iceland on an Icelandic destroyer, and were welcomed by vast crowds who came down to the docks to see them.*

THE FIGHTING TEMERAIRE

*The Fighting Temeraire from 1839 is one of Turner's greatest works,
the one he called his darling. It shows a famous ship of the age, a
hero of the Battle of Trafalgar, on its final journey, being towed
up the Thames to the breaker's yard. Most of the canvas is sky, an
extraordinary, largely orange sunset reflected in still water. Near the
bottom, left of centre, is a small black fiery tugboat from the new
age of steam, paddles churning. The Temeraire, full masted from
the age of sail, ethereal and white, glides behind to its fate. When
Turner first displayed this masterpiece, the Victorian public was deep
in celebrations of the Temeraire era, with work on Nelson's Column
underway in the new Trafalgar Square, and Thackeray described the
painting as a 'national ode'.*

━━◆━━

With Melvyn to discuss *The Fighting Temeraire* were: Susan Foister,
curator of early Netherlandish, German and British painting at the
National Gallery; David Blayney Brown, senior creator of nineteenth-
century British art and Manton curator at Tate Britain; and James
Davey, lecturer in naval and maritime history at the University of Exeter.

In 1839, Susan Foister told us, Turner was in his early sixties and at the height of his powers. He had achieved success early on, and was appointed a full member of the Royal Academy in 1802 when he was twenty-six. He was commercially successful, had his own gallery and continued to exhibit at the Royal Academy, and this is where he displayed *Temeraire* with three other paintings in 1839.

SUSAN FOISTER: *He had, by that stage, complete command of the powers of painting and he had transformed the genres of paintings. Landscape painting, seascapes, really became something else through Turner, something much more poetic and historic and meaningful. And he was able to use light and colour, and the ways in which he painted, to really transform people's experience of looking at those kinds of scenes.*

Turner had a sense of the great sweep of history and his place in it, and he had already made his will in which he would leave his paintings to the nation and, to that bequest, he would add *The Fighting Temeraire*.

Melvyn mentioned that Turner's father was a barber in Covent Garden, that his mother had been forced to live at Bedlam Hospital for a while, and that the young Turner had been farmed out to relatives for his upbringing. He was, we heard, particularly successful as a watercolour artist, painting subjects like Eton or Oxford or great abbeys, which could be sold as engravings with great commercial success. He was never far from the Thames, moving to Isleworth and then Twickenham, and would sometimes go out in his boat.

SUSAN FOISTER: *The Thames continued to play a really important part in his career and in his paintings, and he was very responsive to the dramas of the Thames. For example, when the Houses of Parliament caught fire, that was an opportunity for a painting of the Thames with this fire blazing around it and reflected in it.* Rain, Steam and Speed, *which he painted after the* Temeraire, *showed the railway bridge over the River Thames at Maidenhead.*

The *Temeraire* was still one of the most famous naval ships in Britain by the time Turner was inspired to paint it. It had been launched in 1798, James Davey said, and really was a wonderful example of British shipbuilding expertise. It was very large – 180ft long, made of oak and armed with ninety-eight guns, a really fearsome armament.

JAMES DAVEY: *It was a large ship, it was a fearsome ship and it took a very active role in the French Revolutionary Wars and then the Napoleonic Wars that followed. On a range of duties around Europe, it was a key part of the Channel fleet that blockaded the French navy in port; it was involved in operations around the Iberian Peninsula, particularly the defence of Cádiz in 1810 and various other operations in the Mediterranean and the Baltic Sea. But, of course, the* Temeraire *is most famously associated with the Battle of Trafalgar.*

Trafalgar was the famous battle in 1805 when a British fleet, commanded by Horatio Nelson, defeated a much larger fleet of French and Spanish ships. Nelson led by example so, as they approached the enemy, he made sure that his ship, the *Victory*, was going to be right at the front of one of the lines approaching the enemy, facing a terrible bombardment. The *Temeraire* was right behind. The *Victory* was locked in a ferocious combat with the French ship the *Redoutable* and it looked for a few moments as though the *Victory* was going to be boarded and taken.

JAMES DAVEY: *Just in the nick of time, the* Temeraire *comes alongside the French ship, launches a number of broadsides into it and then boards and takes it. It then repeats the trick. Later in the battle, another French vessel, the* Fougueux, *attacks the* Temeraire, *but again the* Temeraire *fires a number of broadsides into it, comes alongside, boards and captures the vessel. At the end of the Battle of Trafalgar, Britain has won a great victory, but the* Temeraire *has played a crucial part, capturing two enemy ships but also coming to the rescue of the fleet's flagship.*

When Cuthbert Collingwood, the second in command, sent his dispatches back to the admiralty, he singled out only one ship for mention and that was the *Temeraire*. From that point, the ship had a lasting reputation for audaciousness in battle. After it retired from fighting in 1812, it became a prison hulk, then a receiving ship for new recruits, a store ship and, finally, a guard ship at the entrance of the Medway River.

The time came in the autumn of 1838 for the *Temeraire* to be towed up the river to be broken up in Rotherhithe and, according to David Blayney Brown, it is unlikely that Turner was there to see it or that the journey was publicised at all. It may have been embarrassing to announce the death throes of these once-great ships, or it may have been commonplace as so many were coming to the end of their useful lives at the same time. Once moored, though, she became a great tourist attraction and it could have been then that Turner thought this would be an interesting subject for a painting.

DAVID BLAYNEY BROWN: *He began to realise that he could make that subject a kind of elegy for the Nelson era and for the age of sail and for the heroic age of fighting ships. And he could also introduce the idea of, on the one hand, the ending of an era and then perhaps the movement into a new one, because, after all, the* Temeraire *was towed upriver by steam tugs, so you have the age of sail on the one hand and the new age of steam on the other.*

In this scene, there was the transition from the old to the new, the chance to celebrate a great past and create an image of mortality, because the ship in the picture has an almost human quality, as if that one ship represented the navy and all the sailors, crew and marines who had fought in such ships.

DAVID BLAYNEY BROWN: *Turner, by the 1830s, had taken upon himself the mantle of a national painter who aspired to paint national themes that could speak to the country as a whole. And I think that's what he wanted to do in* The Fighting Temeraire. *He called the picture* The Fighting Temeraire, *which evokes her heroic battle past, her role at Trafalgar and afterwards, and he made her representative of that great age of fighting ships – the wooden walls, the hearts of oak – that in many ways represented Britain.*

For listeners, Susan Foister picked out some of the most striking aspects of the painting. Turner created a fantastic contrast between the great hulk, the bulky, fighting *Temeraire*, which was represented as a ghost, painted in a very pale colour, with some masts and the front broken down.

SUSAN FOISTER: *In contrast with that, and overlapping it, is this black tugboat, and the tugboat is pulling it towards you, the viewer. And, of course, because it's a tug, it's a steam ship, and out of the funnel is coming this burst of fiery smoke. You don't quite know whether this is partly flame coming from its boiler or whether the smoke is partly being coloured by this terrific sunset on the other side of the painting. And that's what, I think, really draws you in.*

Turner, she said, was wonderful at creating the sense of immense skies that disappear over your head and draw your eye to the horizon. There is a very faint sense of the shoreline on either side, just a few buildings, and the sunset is painted in such an immensely powerful and colourful way as to draw your eye down to the horizon and down to the distance. Then, in contrast to the sun on the right-hand side, at the top left of the painting is a white crescent moon.

SUSAN FOISTER: *You get these terrific reflections, the sunset reflected in the water and this golden light. You get the reflections from the boats, although the steamer is churning up the water a little bit. There are these beautiful reflections, it looks very still and calm, and then the moon is also casting this rather beautiful silvery reflection on the water.*

That is Turner's scene, and it might be tempting to treat it as a faithful representation of what happened. The reality would have been very different. The Thames would have been very busy, with tens if not hundreds of ships passing up and down that stretch each day.

JAMES DAVEY: *[There were] ships of all sizes, from great East Indiamen off to the Far East down to small colliermen bringing coal from the north-east into the capital, or even watermen going about their daily business, back and forth across the river, taking passengers back and forth. All of that would have been going on and you don't really get much of a sense of that in Turner's painting, just the sheer density of traffic that would have been on the river.*

Besides, the painting shows the *Temeraire* fully masted and with some furled sails, all of which would have been taken off before it was towed upriver. By the time Turner saw it, he would have been one of many tourists at Beatson's Yard in Rotherhithe buying prints of the ship or collecting mementos. The breakers had paid £5,000 for the *Temeraire*, and it was like an oak mine. The story goes that a lot of houses on both banks of the Thames were built using timber from the *Temeraire*, and just the breaking-up of this ship would have taken years.

JAMES DAVEY: *There's all sorts of things around the country that are made from the wood of the* Temeraire. *I'm afraid there are more things made from the wood of the* Temeraire *than could possibly have originally constructed a 98-gun ship of the line.*

David Blayney Brown told us it took the *Temeraire* two days, working with the tides and moving very, very slowly, to negotiate its way, towed by two tugs rather than one, while Turner makes the passage seem smooth, serene, calm and easy. The setting sun conveys the idea of time, of an ending, of the passing of a day and, through the passing of the day, perhaps the passing of an era.

DAVID BLAYNEY BROWN: *And also, of course, the red tint of the sunset perhaps also suggests blood. Turner later on painted an extremely bloodshot sky over a painting of Napoleon in exile on St Helena. In this painting, perhaps the ruddy glow is there as a beautiful thing but, also, perhaps it evokes the appalling bloodshed that would have taken place on board the* Temeraire *when she was actually in battle. Her decks would have been awash with blood, which would have to be washed off, hosed down and removed. She would have been an absolute bloodbath.*

Turner loved his sunsets, and David Blayney Brown has Turner's sketchbooks at the Tate, entirely devoted to small watercolour studies, following the progress of sunsets or sky effects, so Turner would have had a reserve of imagery in his studio to draw upon to create a sky like this.

The Fighting Temeraire is at Susan Foister's workplace, the National Gallery, where, she said, it is in really quite good condition. The *Temeraire* itself is thinly painted and not in immense detail, with strokes of darker brown against the pale off-white to suggest the form of the ship. There is luminosity and transparency in the reflections in the water, which she thought was something Turner brought from his experience of watercolour painting. Visitors who stand near the painting can still see the marks of Turner, laying his brush on in three dimensions.

SUSAN FOISTER: *If you look at it when the light is falling on it at an angle, you can see exactly the texture of the paint and the marks of the brush. In that patch of brilliant red, vermillion red, above the sun, that's really thickly painted. The moon, although it's small and rather delicately formed, is very thickly painted, and the reflections of moonlight on the water – again he's using paint thickly, rather quickly, with a broad brush to give that effect. He knew exactly what he was doing.*

The Royal Navy, in 1839, was the largest naval force in the world, James Davey said, larger than its next few rivals added together. There was great nostalgia for the navy of yesteryear with its wooden sailing ships, particularly the navy of Nelson's time, and there were many signs of this, not least the naming of Trafalgar Square and, soon after, the building of Nelson's Column. There were great numbers of autobiographies of sailors who were active in the Napoleonic Wars, reminiscing. Warships had already been built with steam power and there was a growing sense of unease about steam, which had the potential to transform the way that navies operated.

Self-portrait by Joseph
Mallord William Turner.

JAMES DAVEY: *On the one hand, there's a lot of excitement about this new technology and how the Royal Navy is in exactly the right place to take advantage of it; but, also, a degree of insecurity and unease because of its potential transformational nature. If one of Britain's rivals, perhaps France or Russia or whoever, gets ahead of the technological game, suddenly the whole Royal Navy could become obsolete.*

To James Davey, the painting is saying that Britain had been dominant on the seas in the past, was dominant at sea right then, but the future was not clear.

There were innovations in the pigments available to Turner at that time, and his pictures were increasingly vividly coloured. David Blayney Brown suggested that a visit to the National Gallery or the Clore Gallery at the Tate would reveal that Turner's early paintings were quite sombre, becoming more and more brilliant over the years. He used new pigments in *The Fighting Temeraire*.

DAVID BLAYNEY BROWN: *In this picture, he uses two vermilions, one of which had been in use for most of his life, but the other, an iodine-based pigment, a particularly vivid scarlet that is sometimes called scarlet lake. That was a new development, recently developed by a friend of Turner, Humphry Davy. And the yellow, an intense lemon yellow (which, of course, is softened out in the painting because it's working in conjunction with other colours), it's a new colour, a barium-based chromate yellow, and something that Turner used really more than any other artist at the time, and was criticised for, and joked about, because he said once, 'I've taken all the yellow unto myself this year, there's none left for you.'*

Turner was also using a new cobalt blue that we can see in the picture and, controversially for artists then, he used black, which, according to the standards of the time, was supposed to be created by mixing other colours.

The Fighting Temeraire was not Turner's first painting related to Trafalgar. George IV commissioned him to create an immense battle painting, Susan Foister told us, which was absolutely full of sailors, and the *Temeraire* is a ghostly reminiscence of that.

SUSAN FOISTER: *In the commission that he painted for, in the first place, St James's Palace, you see sailors swarming over these boats and you see their suffering thrust in front of you not only with the blood, but there's one particular sailor who looks almost as though he's being crucified in front of you. Turner certainly felt great empathy for the suffering of the sailors in these battles.*

While *The Fighting Temeraire* is a work of imagination rather than an accurate depiction, this has not stopped people pointing out the ways in which it departs from reality. David Blayney Brown mentioned some of these, such as the height of the sun in the sky, which was shown as lower than it would have been when the *Temeraire* arrived at Rotherhithe, and the sun being in the wrong part of the sky altogether, as it appears to be setting in the east, where the ship had come from, rather than in the west, where it was heading. It would be bizarre, he said, to expect a picture like this to be absolutely literal in those sorts of details.

DAVID BLAYNEY BROWN: *The other thing that's really quite spectacularly wrong, and Turner would have known this because he travelled on steamboats all the time – he went up and down the Thames to Margate, he went across the Channel – he knew exactly where a steamboat's funnel would have been positioned in relation to its boiler, i.e. over it. It would not have been up towards the bows and a long way away from the boiler and the paddles. It would have been centre. But Turner's moved it so that, of course, the funnel doesn't conflict with the bow of the* Temeraire *itself.*

This, Melvyn understood, was 'corrected' by a printer who made a copy of the painting, and Turner was absolutely furious. It was corrected back to the wrong position in the next edition.

The painting was well received by critics. Thackeray, Susan Foister said, was really inspired by this painting, he really responded to what Turner was trying to do with colour and with the story of the ship. He was particularly taken by the tug, which he called a spiteful tugboat that was dragging the *Temeraire* to its end. He described the painting as a national ode.

DAVID BLAYNEY BROWN: *Thackeray also called the tug the* Temeraire's *executioner, which I think is wonderful because, of course, it humanises the tug as well. If the* Temeraire *is representing Nelson's entire navy, all the people that had served in it, in the form of one ship, so the tug was this creature that is actually killing all that off.*

The Fighting Temeraire was, said Susan Foister, the culmination of a certain type of experimentation with paint, and Turner went on to paint even more extraordinary pictures.

Afterwards, there was talk of Turner's love for *The Fighting Temeraire*, his 'darling', which he loaned out once and vowed not to do so again, or ever to sell it. He was apparently offered £5,000 for it, which he refused, and that was, coincidentally, the sum the breakers had paid for the ship itself.

SUSAN FOISTER: *After his death in 1851, there was this terrific fight about his will, but eventually his paintings came to the National Gallery. And one thing that perhaps people don't appreciate is that, when the National Gallery was first built, the Royal Academy, where Turner showed the* Temeraire *in 1839, was in the National Gallery, the right-hand side of the building that we know today. That painting was shown in Trafalgar Square, moved to his gallery, then came back to Trafalgar Square and was put on display in 1857.*

Which is where it is today, in Room 34.

RELIGION

+⟫━◆━⟪+

It's the hot subject. Just as there was matter and anti-matter in confrontation soon after the Big Bang, so the forces of religion and anti-religion stand toe to toe slugging it out. The antis – the atheists – would most likely say that there is nothing there. Religions are fairy tales, controlling mechanisms, comfort blankets, the survivalist magic of other ages, and we really must stop giving them the credit they have demanded – and often received – through millennia. Religion is dead. There were two famous slogans daubed on walls in the 1968 Paris students' revolution. The top one said, 'God is dead. Nietzsche.' The lower one read, 'Nietzsche is dead. God.'

Because God, in many parts of the world, in various guises, is still alive – in the Islamic states, in evangelical North America, in Hinduism, among followers of the Buddha, in Israel, in Catholic South America, in extreme Protestant conclaves all over the English-speaking world. But not much in the UK, where the Church of England decays in influence by the year and intellectuals don't even want to waste their energy discussing it. And anti-religion has its champions, most influential of whom is Richard Dawkins, whose brilliant scientific scholarship and inflexible belief in non-belief has become a world force in arguments on this subject.

What cannot be denied is the massive importance of religion to so many of our formative civilisations and their development. To stick with Christianity, for example: since, say, the fifth century ad, Christianity has been intertwined with European and then world history, mythology, art, music, architecture, ceremony, war, conquest, education, tyranny, like no other force. None is comparable. It has,of course, been assumed by many for their own non-religious purposes: by conquerors to sanction and glorify their slaughters; by an organisation such as the Vatican to justify its astonishingly effective and long-lived control system. Its weapons include the Inquisitions and inventions like purgatory, confessions, penitence and pilgrimages, as well as the glamour and allure of sacred festivals and pageants, music and spectacular art and architecture. It's been argued that the Roman Catholic Church has been the most effective control system in human history.

And so, to understand why we are what we are, it is often indispensable to be at least aware of the shaping force of religion.

I was brought up in the north-west of England in a town called Wigton. It had a population of about 5,000 people and ten active churches in my childhood. Let's say the late 1940s, early '50s. These churches ran the town.

I went to the Anglican church and accepted all of it – the resurrection, the miracles, eternal life … all that can be forgiven.

Yet it is hard for me to forgive the Church for the 'gift' of sin. It's a blight. It's entirely destructive; at best, it was supposed to be a brake, but it is rarely at its best. And, in its history, the Anglican Church, like so many other institutions, has done terrible things to people.

Most civilisations took in forms of religion from the start. In a sense, it is as much history as faith. And it is often impossible to gauge whether it is purely a fig leaf, a convenient cloak for the powerful to sweeten their colonisations, or whether it truly is an essential drive in itself.

From the ways it is entangled with politics, often cruelly, we are left puzzled. What of the crusades against the Cathars? The Cathars were a devout sect in the south of France whose Christianity was thoroughly at odds with the prevailing Catholicism. This led to their mass extermination. And, again and again, religion has been on the side of the 'bad'. Brutal force, sanctified by prayers, themselves propagated as essential to the 'good' life, but also essential to the obedience demanded by an imperial Church.

Yet, again and again, religion has spurred on the arts, examples of self-sacrifice and magnificent philanthropy. The most curious thing of all, I think, is that, despite the fury of logic and unbearable examples of iniquity being brought against it, religion refuses to go away. For billions of people, in the age of artificial intelligence, there are still gods and goddesses, saints and martyrs, and a better life to come. In the variety of the subject we choose, there are always those underlying tensions. Is it plausible? Is it more of an instrument of authoritarianism – the 'opium of the people'? Or is it an essential mystery that we cannot yet explain through reason?

I realise that, in this foreword, I have been much more personal than previously. That is perhaps because it is such a contentious issue and, although I can no longer be categorised as 'a believer', we on the programme are keen to keep religion in our sweep around the globe of 5,000 years. All the subjects chosen by Simon here contain one of the aspects of faith at work. At the Big Bang, there was matter and anti-matter. The latter seems to have gone away, but physicists still puzzle about it. For many, religion is anti-matter, but it won't go away.

THE SIEGE
OF MÜNSTER

*In the early sixteenth century, the Protestant Reformation
revolutionised Christian belief. One radical group of believers was
the Anabaptists, who rejected infant baptism and formal clergy and
believed that all goods should be held in common. They were also
convinced, as were others, that the Second Coming was imminent.
In 1534, in the German city of Münster, a group of Anabaptists
attempted to establish a new Jerusalem, ready for the last days before
the apocalypse. But the city was besieged and descended into tyranny.
Books were burnt and women were forced to marry. As starvation
spread, the city's ruler lived in insane luxury. The horrors of the
Anabaptists of Münster have resonated through European memory
ever since.*

With Melvyn to discuss the siege of Münster and its impact were: Diarmaid MacCulloch, professor of the history of the Church at the University of Oxford; Charlotte Methuen, professor of Church history at the University of Glasgow; and Lucy Wooding, Langford fellow and tutor in history at Lincoln College, Oxford.

Diarmaid MacCulloch began by explaining that the Anabaptists emerged out of the early years of the Protestant Reformation in which Luther and his supporters wanted to make Christianity truly biblical again and to look at the New Testament and try to line up the Church to make it look like the New Testament. All the Anabaptists were doing was trying to take the Bible seriously.

DIARMAID MACCULLOCH: *The word Anabaptist is a term of abuse, it means re-baptiser, because what they did was to make people baptise themselves again or be baptised again as adults, having been baptised as infants by the Old Church. And the reason they did that was a biblical one. They looked at the New Testament and said, 'You can't find infant baptism in the New Testament therefore, if we're going to be serious about the Bible, we've got to make baptism for believers, for adults.'*

They were discovering lots of other things in the Bible because it was a very remote, alien book that the Church had domesticated in various ways and, Diarmaid MacCulloch continued, 'Even Martin Luther was horrified by the sheer logic of what they were doing.' He and reformers like him thought they were going to overturn the world and they had a very powerful vision of themselves as prophets of the world. It could be said that the first Anabaptists were simply developing that idea, announcing that the world was going to come to an end soon.

DIARMAID MACCULLOCH: *There are lots of reasons you should think that, in the early sixteenth century. The Turks are pressing in on Christendom, they appear to be about to destroy it, surely that's part of God's plan? It's taking the logic of what Luther and other great reformers thought and just applying it and being very excited by it. The trouble was that Luther, by now, was beginning to see that things were a little more complicated than that.*

There were plagues and famines, there was the fall of Islamic Granada and the expulsion of the Jews from Spain, there was a sense that society was in a crisis that had to be God's purpose, not simply a series of political accidents.

The Anabaptists were drawing from Zwingli in Zurich and Luther in Wittenberg, Charlotte Methuen added. According to them, sacraments only worked if you believed, and they could not say that a child believed, in which case, you cannot baptise people until they are adults, when they can show that they believe.

CHARLOTTE METHUEN: *The reason baptism becomes such an issue is precisely because plagues, infant mortality, were enormous, and so, for parents of children who had been taught for generations that, if their children weren't baptised, they wouldn't be saved, to say that you couldn't baptise children was actually saying something really terrible about the fate of their children if they died unbaptised. And it becomes such an issue that, in the [Holy Roman] Empire, adult baptism is actually made illegal.*

The Anabaptists thought the Church was just for the elect, whereas Zwingli, Luther and Calvin went on to say that the Church, the visible Church, was for everybody and all should be drawn in, living their lives according to the laws of the land. Anabaptists had a totally different understanding of the way that Church and state related to one another, and were challenging the Catholic and Lutheran sense of a united Christendom.

For the Anabaptists, the apocalypse and the Second Coming of Christ were one and the same thing. One of great differences between their way of interpreting the Reformation message and the one that Luther had in mind, Lucy Wooding explained, related to their inexperience in theology.

LUCY WOODING: *Luther was a radical, no doubt, but he's a theological radical. Now a lot of the people we're looking at in this story today are very ordinary people. Hoffman is a travelling fur trader, one's a baker, one's an apprentice tailor – they don't have the kind of intellectual framework to fit their reading of scripture into. They are taking it at face value, they're tremendously excited, they take it very, very literally.*

They also expected change much more immediately than perhaps some of the more educated reformers did. Luther was proving more conservative than they might have expected, not supporting the popular revolt of the German Peasants' War in the 1520s, in which 100,000 people died. Persecution, violence and disaster followed that conflict, which might have been expected to discourage unrest.

LUCY WOODING: *For the Anabaptists, it was entirely the opposite, because, if you look into the Bible, the true prophets of God, the early Church, the early apostles, they're all persecuted. For the Anabaptists, the more people persecuted them, the harsher the treatment that was meted out to them, the more they were convinced that they were the chosen people and that they were pursuing the right path.*

The Anabaptists were a disparate selection of different communities found in Switzerland, in the central southern German regions and in northern Germany and the Netherlands, with different people following different prophets. Melchior Hoffman started as a Lutheran lay preacher and then became more and more radical, preaching in marketplaces, whipping up excitement in cities in particular with parallels, Lucy Wooding suggested, to the way Christianity was spread in the first place, with the letters of St Paul to different cities, to Corinth, to Thessalonica, to small groups of beleaguered Christians in different city communities, and the Anabaptists identified with that.

At the heart of this concentration on cities was the idea of finding or building the new Jerusalem.

DIARMAID MACCULLOCH: *Melchior Hoffman, this furrier who travels, gets the idea in his head that it's not Münster actually to start with, it's Strasburg, one of the biggest cities in Europe, a very tolerant city. Hoffman was just so impressed by that, he thought this must be the new Jerusalem. Hoffman preached Strasburg in the very early 1530s and, unfortunately, the city authorities weren't that impressed by being cast as the new Jerusalem, so they chucked him in jail.*

Münster had been a prince-bishopric, a city of the Holy Roman Empire run by its bishop as a secular ruler until he had been thrown out by a reformation inspired by Luther. There were many factions in that city, Charlotte Methuen explained, following the unrest of the Peasants' War. There were tensions between the guilds and the higher priests around the bishop who, until 1532, had not been ordained, and the lower clergy and citizens. The Lutheran faction was gaining the upper hand in 1532–3.

Situated in the north-west of Germany and near the Netherlands, a long way from Melchior Hoffman's Strasburg, a lot of preachers were passing through Münster.

DIARMAID MACCULLOCH: *It's very natural for them to look at this great wealthy city, with its great cathedral, its walls, and think, 'Well, actually this is likely to be the new Jerusalem.' And it's one Dutchman who actually had that idea, not Strasburg, as Melchior had said, but Münster, the local big city. And his name was Jan Matthys.*

There was one preacher in particular who set the scene, Charlotte Methuen explained, and this was Bernhard Rothmann, who emerged initially as a Lutheran with Zwinglian interests, and he became the city preacher in Münster in 1532. He did not agree with Luther over the sacraments, as became obvious when the city council said it wanted a Lutheran liturgy.

CHARLOTTE METHUEN: *Bernhard Rothmann says, 'Well, I don't want to give you Lutheran liturgy.' He doesn't approve of infant baptism any more, he wants to give them an Anabaptist liturgy. And that causes enormous tensions within the city, but it also provides the moment for Jan Matthys, who was looking for places to preach. He sends emissaries into Münster in early 1534 and baptises Bernhard Rothmann.*

Within two years, Münster had changed from being run as a Roman Catholic prince-bishopric to somewhere the Anabaptists could seize power.

Jan Matthys, Diarmaid MacCulloch suggested, was someone whose charisma was more evident than his theological scholarship. He was a traveller who could draw people to him with an arresting simple message: 'Come to the new Jerusalem.' When people had been disappointed by the mainstream Protestants, here was someone saying he could show them the way forwards, that the last days were going to happen and together they could make them happen.

DIARMAID MACCULLOCH: *What you're doing, of course, is empowering ordinary people in a world where they don't feel they have any power. And people have been driven into a state of*

Jan Matthys.

excitement by the fact they've seen the powers of this world being thrown down, the pope's power going, the prince-bishop's power going, those Lutheran councillors being pushed aside by more radical figures. And, in that situation, any leader with charisma can step in, and that's what Jan did.

What Matthys managed to do, Charlotte Methuen said, was get Rothmann converted, who then started to proclaim the coming of the new Jerusalem, the coming of a community in which all people would be equal. In 1534, they declared that all things belonged to all people.

CHARLOTTE METHUEN: *And they burn the city archives so that all records of ownership, of land ownership, for instance, disappear. What we're getting from Rothmann, and then with him from Matthys's emissaries, is a sense that the divisions of society (we have* *to think of this as a very, very hierarchical society – we have a clerical hierarchy, we have a secular or temporal hierarchy) are being wiped away and all people are going to be equal.*

When Luther wanted to dress down, Lucy Wooding added, he liked to dress in courtly garb, very much part of the establishment. People like Matthys were much more down to earth, and the idea of having goods in common was much more appealing to the poor than it was to the rich. These people were taking Luther's freedom of Christianity very seriously in a way Luther did not anticipate them taking it, Charlotte Methuen continued, where they were not just removing the difference between spiritual and temporal but also getting rid of the differences within temporal hierarchies.

In 1534, in February, the ousted prince-bishop of Münster, Franz von Waldeck, laid siege to the city and continued for eighteen months. The Lutherans were alongside him as they were panic-stricken that the Reformation was getting away from them, and they wanted to win Münster back. Jan Matthys predicted the Second Coming would happen at Easter in 1534, but he had to reassess that once Easter had passed. He had a new revelation, which was that he should go out to face the bishop's forces with twelve chosen apostles.

LUCY WOODING: *He saw himself as David going out to encounter Goliath and he said that this would unleash an apocalyptic confrontation and that the last days would start to unfold from this. It's actually quite a pathetic scene in many ways. By the standards of the time, he's quite old, he's in his fifties, on a lone horse riding out. And he must have had in his heart the conviction that this is what God wanted him to do.*

MELVYN BRAGG: *Were the twelve behind him?*

LUCY WOODING: *They must have been terrified, or perhaps they, too, were carried forwards by their godly zeal. They were hacked to pieces. Münster had lost its prophet.*

There was consternation, but then another charismatic young man stepped forth, Jan Bockelson, who came from Leiden and whose name was to strike terror in Europe. He was twenty-five, born the same year as Calvin, and he ran Münster under the siege for another fourteen months or so. He was a tyrant, Charlotte Methuen said, and in charge of a city that now had three times as many women as men. He introduced polygamy and forcible marriage for the women, some of whom had been left behind by their husbands to look after the property in Münster and some of whom were Anabaptist sympathisers who had come to be part of the new Jerusalem.

CHARLOTTE METHUEN: *He sets himself up in Matthys's house with a great palace next door for his own sixteen wives, all of whom, except one, were under twenty, interestingly. He keeps a very, very strong, strict discipline within the city. He stops torture happening but he's quite capable of summarily executing anybody who stands against his leadership. And the situation in the city really starts to deteriorate.*

He was a very charismatic tyrant with an extraordinary sense of theatre and, Lucy Wooding said, reportedly dabbled in theatricals before this stage of his career. There are two eyewitness accounts of what happened in the city during the siege, and they may well have been biased as the writers were trying to distance themselves from events, but, on one day, it seems, John of Leiden appeared stark naked in the marketplace.

LUCY WOODING: *Nakedness, of course, is a sign of purity, going back to Adam and Eve before the Fall, but it's going to get anyone's attention. And he then went into a trance for three days, during which time he couldn't speak, so he claimed. And [he] then emerged from that to say, 'Well, we're going to have a new system.' They get rid of the council, they bring in twelve elders. But he had a chilling way of trying to get people ready for the latest revelation and then unleash it upon them.*

He also issued gold coins, which he distributed all through Europe, with his head on, proclaiming the message of the last days with a statement that he was a king for all Europe, for all Christendom, for all the world. Yet, in Münster, there was an insane lack of proportion. The city was starving but the court of John of Leiden and his wives was not starving, there was enormous luxury at the centre of it.

DIARMAID MACCULLOCH: *They gather together, the court, to honour God, because this is God's representative on earth. But, around them, people are just dying of hunger and thirst. People are being executed if they stand up, if they express their despair. It's a nightmare world. It reminds one of Kampuchea in the 1970s.*

CHARLOTTE METHUEN: *And they say that they washed the whitewash off the walls of the churches and sold it to people as milk. The level of starvation among the people themselves was just horrendous.*

They held out partly because they were very well organised, they had a charismatic leader and they had to defend the city or surrender and face a very unpleasant death. In the end, the city fell, as they were betrayed and the bishop's men were let in.

LUCY WOODING: *There was horrible carnage – thousands of people probably died. And the ringleaders were kept back for a very unpleasant execution, in January of 1536, where they were, effectively, tortured to death, because that point had to be made.*

DIARMAID MACCULLOCH: *It is really chilling going to Münster, because you can still see the irons that were heated to red hot with which their flesh was torn and pinched.*

CHARLOTTE METHUEN: *And you can still see the cages in which their bodies were then hung on St Lambert's Church. As you walk up the main shopping street in Münster, there are three cages in which the bodies were hung on the church tower.*

The Anabaptists were left with a reputation for crazed barbarity, Diarmaid MacCulloch said, which was completely different from the nature of most Anabaptists. There was a certain terrorising aftermath in the Netherlands, where an organisation called the Batenburgers went on attacking clergy. Largely, Anabaptists were appalled by what some of their number had done.

DIARMAID MACCULLOCH: *A priest from Friesland, called Menno Simons, gathered the shocked remnants and committed them to pacifism. The future of Anabaptism and all the radical strands of religion around it was a commission for pacifism for the future, which is still there. They're passionately committed against violence and that's the result of this particular trauma.*

The siege of Münster left Protestants terrified of disorder. Calvin made it clear that his followers were not that sort of Protestant and would respect the order of government, and that became significant for the status of Protestantism for the rest of the century.

HILDEGARD OF BINGEN

If you had walked into the abbey of the monastery at Disibodenberg in Germany 850 years ago, it is quite possible that you would have heard a solo chanting voice singing a piece of sacred music by the twelfth-century composer Hildegard of Bingen. Little known until thirty years ago, the music of Hildegard is now regarded as among the best of the Middle Ages. But, remarkably, the music is only a small aspect of her overall achievement. Hildegard was a twelfth-century nun and a scholar of impressive breadth. Sometimes known as the 'Sibyl of the Rhine', she wrote a series of works documenting prophetic visions she had experienced. She was an accomplished theologian and also wrote about science, medicine and the natural world. Held in high regard by royalty and religious figures alike, she has long been revered as a saint, although it was not until 2012 that she was officially canonised by Pope Benedict.

With Melvyn to discuss Hildegard of Bingen were: Miri Rubin, professor of medieval and early modern history at Queen Mary University of London; William Flynn, lecturer in medieval Latin at the University of Leeds; and Almut Suerbaum, associate professor of German at Somerville College, Oxford.

Hildegard was born around 1098 in the Rhineland, which, as Miri Rubin explained, was part of the Holy Roman Empire, a vast political entity covering most of today's Germany but also Italy and parts of eastern France.

MIRI RUBIN: *This is a vast continental bloc that was ruled, from the year 800 on, by an emperor. What makes an emperor different from a mere king is that this is an emperor crowned and endorsed by the pope. In the Middle Ages, and until 1802, in fact, the Holy Roman Empire is a confederation of large parts of Europe, and this obviously creates a tremendous political challenge.*

The emperor did not have a standing army and could not tax everywhere and, during most of Hildegard's life, there was civil war to establish which family should hold the imperial crown and also, most importantly for Hildegard, what the emperor owed to the pope. Throughout this restless period, there were thriving monasteries and nunneries that were extremely important as centres of religious life.

MIRI RUBIN: *These institutions are founded by the elite – indeed, by emperors and empresses themselves – but are also inhabited and run, on the whole, by elite persons. You have to bring a sort of dowry if you are a nun. You have to have some property to contribute, so this is a way of life that is deeply privileged and has tremendous impact.*

Hildegard came from this kind of elite background, William Flynn continued, and her family were landowners. She was born in Bermersheim, her father was Hildebert, her mother was Mechtild, and, from the age of five, she reported that she had visions. She was given into the care of another noblewoman, Jutta of Sponheim, from the age of eight, when Jutta was only fourteen. Her biographer, Guibert of Gembloux, said that she was the tenth child of Hildebert and Mechtild, though Guibert was an unreliable witness who tried to make her into a perfect Benedictine saint.

WILLIAM FLYNN: *The Sponheim family was regionally one of the more powerful families. It was a good move on the part of a noble family that didn't have as much capital, really. Also, Jutta had insisted, against the will of her family, that she was going into a religious life. Jutta seems to have resisted her family quite a bit; she wanted to go on pilgrimage, but they manoeuvred her into deciding to become part of a monastery.*

Together, in 1112, they entered the male Benedictine monastery of Disibodenberg, which had only started being built in 1108. According to Guibert, Hildegard and Jutta were 'completely inured as if they were dead'. They received food and water through a window, and their priest might have lived in a cell next door and contacted them through a window. This was an intense religious life.

WILLIAM FLYNN: *Jutta would have been quite reasonably educated at home; she would have known how to read Latin. She taught Hildegard how to read, certainly, and recite the psalms, and that is about the extent of what Hildegard acknowledges as her education, because she does call herself, later on, 'an unlearned woman'. It seems that Hildegard, who is obviously a bright star intellectually, feels somewhat constrained by the life that she has been put into.*

According to Guibert, Hildegard learned to play the ten-stringed cythera, but that may have been meant allegorically, an allusion to the Ten Commandments and the virtuous life. It is more likely that she learned to sing by way of the normal monastic instrument of the monochord.

The Benedictine monasteries were very important politically and for theological learning, as well as being places of intellectual learning, with libraries for the monks and, at Disibodenberg, for the women associating with them.

ALMUT SUERBAUM: *The day is structured by a variety of activities; they pray regularly, but, in between those spaces, they also listen to readings of texts by the Church Fathers, they listen to gospels that are explained through the commentaries of the Church Fathers, and, in almost all Benedictine monasteries, we know they also spend time writing, creating the books that they will then read and study.*

Unlike those in the scholastic tradition, Hildegard did not use quotations when she wrote. Almut Suerbaum challenged the description of her as *indoctus*, or 'unlearned', which, she argued, did not mean that she was uneducated but that she was not writing in the Benedictine format, which was imbued with the range of texts the monks had read. Supporting her in this work for sixty years was a male confessor, Volmar, who acted as her secretary, companion, aide and perhaps tutor.

ALMUT SUERBAUM: *It is clearly a relationship of dialogue between them – he is her secretary. Bernard of Clairvaux had at least three secretaries simultaneously, so it is a common practice, that's not just something for women who themselves can't write. It is a relationship that is clearly about theological discussions, he is her confessor and her spiritual guide.*

MELVYN BRAGG: *Why do you think it lasted so long?*

ALMUT SUERBAUM: *They clearly worked together very well. She comments on the fact that he advises in the composition of the* Scivias, *but so does one of her nuns, so it is a group of people with whom she talks.*

In 1136, or thereabouts, Jutta died and, quite soon afterwards, Hildegard founded her own establishment near Bingen. It was a bold step and required a lot of political negotiation as well as theological determination, something that seemed to have been one of her strengths. She met a lot of resistance not only as it was an unusual thing for a woman to do but also for economic reasons. As Almut

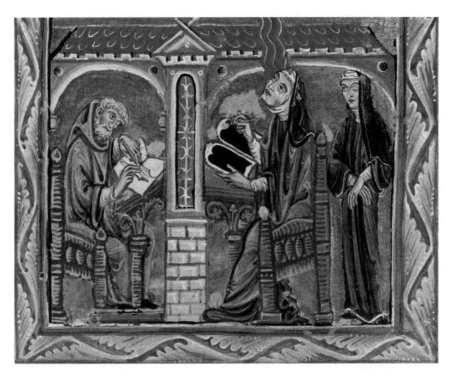

*Hildegard receives a
vision in the presence
of her secretary Volmar.*

Suerbaum explained, the aristocratic women who had come to join
the convent at Disibodenberg had come with very large dowries,
so the monks were not keen on losing either their main spiritual
attraction, by that time, or those dowries.

Earlier, Miri Rubin mentioned the civil wars in the Holy Roman
Empire and the tension between the emperor and the pope. The
Church had an idea from the mid-eleventh century that it should
be free from interference from secular authorities. The popes had
increasingly demanded that they, not the emperors, should appoint
the bishops, as they were meant to be spiritual leaders and not
political ones. The emperors wanted to appoint them, owing to their
political significance. This could lead to schism between the emperor
and the pope.

MIRI RUBIN: *Sometimes the emperor goes and appoints his own
pope, an anti-pope, and then what do you do? Who is a bishop
in Germany to be loyal to? Who, indeed, is an abbess to be loyal
to? Which pope? The local one appointed by her emperor, or the
one appointed by the pope in Rome? Who is the head of the whole
Church organisation? And Hildegard finds this extremely vexing.*

Hildegard wanted to see the pope ruling religious appointments.
She also wanted to see a really strong reforming spirit within

monasticism itself, and her letters were all about raising consciousness and getting people as engaged in this work as she was.

Hildegard's first visions came in 1141 and were the basis of her first book, *Scivias* ('Know the Ways'). She described her manner of seeing, several times during her life, William Flynn said, and she tried to differentiate hers from the way that others had visions, which came in ecstasy, in trances or in dreams.

WILLIAM FLYNN: *Hildegard insisted that all her visions, except for one, came while she was completely awake. They seem to me to be related to listening to things read to you, absorbing a lot of material, and then a sudden flash where all of that makes sense, all of her memorised material comes to her as a picture. That is actually related to memory techniques that are taught to Benedictines and taught since classical times.*

She said everything made sense to her at once, and it came to her in a series of pictures that she then wrote a book for, to explain every element of each picture in a very detailed manner that would be teaching for the rest of her nuns. *Scivias* was a huge work, 600 pages long, and it took Hildegard ten years or more to complete.

Almut Suerbaum translated the fuller meaning of *Scivias* as 'Know the Ways of the Lord'. It contains three books, with twenty-six visions divided between them, where the first book is about the creation and the creator God, the second about salvation, and the third about salvation history, using some quite abstract images.

ALMUT SUERBAUM: *It starts with a vision of light emanating from the peak of a mountain, and these images, in the manuscripts that are probably composed very close to her lifetime and perhaps with some input by her, also have illuminations. All the central moments, the key images of most of these visions, are illuminated.*

These images are then elucidated and explained. The visions are prophetic, allegorical, symbolist, they are images given to her by divine inspiration to communicate with others. Most of the images used spectacular amounts of gold leaf and silver, so they reflect light. What is often foregrounded is the apocalyptic, the warning to watch out, for the sake of the Church, and to reform.

Some of the images that William Flynn has studied are of the angelic host, and are done in a series of nine concentric circles with the normal nine of the angelic hosts being two angels or archangels, then five powers and then two cherubim and seraphim. They are placed around what could be interpreted as a mirror, where the angels are light, reflecting God's light.

WILLIAM FLYNN: *That image is related to two other images – one of the Trinity, which has also concentric circles, but it has a sapphire figure, a human figure, in the middle of it, and then colours of gold and silver, to make a trinitarian one. Another one is about the sacraments of the Church, especially baptism, where that trinitarian figure dissolves into a blue pool, sapphire again, and gold and silver around, and then it becomes a baptismal font.*

Hildegard claimed she did not write like the philosophers wrote, William Flynn added. That could mean she wrote like a divinely inspired person, not like somebody who has been schooled the 'right' way.

What Hildegard was also doing, Miri Rubin emphasised, was treading the very fine line of communicating her ideas with everyone while in a position of total subordination to divine will.

MIRI RUBIN: *She is always emphasising: 'This isn't my idea, God tells me this. I am as nothing, I am a channel, I am an aqueduct, I am merely conveying this.' People will listen to her because she is not claiming to be a wise woman, a clever woman. She is just the chosen woman, perhaps for her unlearnedness, she says, therefore she is a pure vehicle. Because there is no place for a woman to get up and talk in the Church in the twelfth century.*

When Hildegard did preach, she travelled to other convents for this, offering sermon commentaries during mealtimes rather than addressing laypeople.

ALMUT SUERBAUM: *She takes parts of the gospel, explains them, referring to the commentaries, and she takes on the voice of a preacher, except she usually stresses that she has been invited to speak. There is a double legitimisation: she is authorised because she speaks through God and she speaks that which God has inspired her to say; and she speaks because others have asked her and they seek her advice.*

The extraordinary thing, to Melvyn, was that her visions made Hildegard famous throughout the western Christian world. She was famous everywhere, Miri Rubin agreed. A letter survives from John of Salisbury, one of the great intellectuals of the twelfth century, to another important monk who was travelling in Germany, in which he asked him to get his hands on some copies of the amazing visions of Hildegard. He wanted to read them as she may have had solutions for the troubles of the Church. She was taken very seriously and wrote some very effective, powerful and passionate letters in support of her aims.

Many of Hildegard's letters survive, 400 or so, and the only writer of that time with so much surviving correspondence was Bernard of Clairvaux. In some cases, there is a two-way correspondence, both her letters and the replies, and these were collected in her lifetime and probably redacted.

ALMUT SUERBAUM: *It really ranges from letters to Bernard of Clairvaux – where she consults him about whether she should carry on writing down her visions, and he encourages her very firmly to do that – to letters to the emperor, letters of criticism to her fellow bishops. But, also, letters where she is asked for advice by a woman whose husband is terminally ill and to whom she replies about how to prepare for a good death, or letters from fellow abbesses who clearly have trouble running their own convents and to whom she gives advice.*

Turning to Hildegard's music, William Flynn stressed that the main thing to understand was her accommodation of music and words, her completely fresh, brilliant poetry with unusual but regionally recognisable music. The works, only rediscovered after 800 years, condensed her visions, as the words often related to visions and then the music perfected them. She was working out of a regional tradition.

WILLIAM FLYNN: *It is of largely south German, translated through Hirsau reform monastery networks, so William of Hirsau and Theogerus of Metz, but the fundamental people are Hermannus Contractus and Berno of Reichenau. They created a chant theory that also influenced the actual compositional style. It doesn't sound like a Gregorian chant, but it sounds much more modern, even modern in our terms, because it has a very strong, fundamental note and a strong note at the fifth, that's the regional style. She is different, though.*

Not only did Hildegard write the music, Miri Rubin added, but she allowed her nuns to perform it in extraordinary ways. People complained that she allowed them to wear glorious white shimmering garments with beautiful crowns, so when they performed they were living this liturgy, it was very real.

Hildegard also wrote scientific and medical texts, works on nature, flora, fauna, and stones and their qualities.

MIRI RUBIN: *Throughout the early Middle Ages, since late antiquity, every monastery had a full collection of herbals, medical books and so on. These are institutions that have to care for themselves, and also offer care for others. So medical books are galore. Anyone who has access to a monastic library and is able to read Latin, as clearly she could, would be able to access this material and, in her case, bring them to a tremendous synthesis. She talks about sexuality, conception, things she did not experience herself in an active way.*

Hildegard was talking about sexuality, Miri Rubin suggested, as she believed in marriage and procreation and worked from her imagination and these medical writings. Her texts were in demand, and there was a copy in York in the fourteenth century. William Flynn noted that there were widows in the monastery and there may have been married lay sisters there, too, with at least one reporting that Hildegard had helped her through problematic pregnancies in her youth.

Some of Hildegard's language in her medicinal texts is taken from vernacular words, which Almut Suerbaum thought was an indication that she had seen the medicinal herbs in the gardens and had talked to people about them. Some of her cures were a mix of benediction, incantation and charm, probably through practices she encountered, and she is known in Germany today for her herbalism.

MIRI RUBIN: *Her sense of authorship was overwhelming. And that is why, even today, she is the patron saint of Die Grünen, the Greens (Green Party) in Germany. She is considered to be someone who has impacted on thinking about the environment. You can go to any worthy bakery in Germany and get Hildegard Brot, which is wholemeal and healthy.*

Volmar died in 1173, which was a huge loss for Hildegard, and she wrote movingly about his life. In her final years, Hildegard was still fighting. She had allowed the burial of someone in her graveyard who turned out to have been excommunicated by the Archbishop of Mainz, who then put the convent under an interdict, which meant that they could not receive sacraments or sing. She went to two competing archbishops and succeeded in lifting the interdict, only to die six months later.

ALMUT SUERBAUM: *[Her] legacy at the time, as the manuscripts show, is that of a visionary, of a prophetess, of an apocalyptic prophet who criticised the Church, who looked at the end of the world and the need to reform. The musician is a modern rediscovery.*

In the studio afterwards, there was discussion of the way that Hildegard interests Protestants and Catholics today for the common themes she raised. Melvyn asked if the relationship between Hildegard and Volmar was not unlike that of Abelard and Hélöise, only to hear that it was better than that, as Volmar suppressed his own ego and did not interfere.

THE SALEM
WITCH TRIALS

*In 1692, in the New England colony of Massachusetts, two young
girls, Abigail Williams and Betty Parris, had fits, started twitching
and would not wake up. They and their families blamed their
behaviour on witchcraft and the hunt was on for the supposed
witches responsible. This was in Salem village. The puritans living
there and in the surrounding Essex County started to find witches
wherever they looked, with neighbour accusing neighbour and many
confessing in the hope of avoiding the noose. It was no use onlookers
arguing there was no such thing as witchcraft as this was taken as
proof that they themselves were witches. Once the trials were over,
there were justifications, reparations, but over 100 innocent women,
men and children had been accused and held in jail by then. Twenty
had been put to death, most of them women.*

━┿━◆━┿━

With Melvyn to discuss what became known as the Salem witch trials
were: Susan Castillo-Street, emerita Harriet Beecher Stowe professor
of American studies at King's College London; Simon Middleton,
associate professor of early American history at the College of William
and Mary, Virginia; and Marion Gibson, professor of Renaissance
and magical literatures at Exeter University's Penryn Campus.

An engraving depicting
a witchcraft trial.

Salem village was settled in 1626, Simon Middleton told us, becoming absorbed into a larger puritan colony. The settlers were mainly farmers, all associated with the puritan migration. By the time of the witchcraft trials, the village had become a rural hinterland to a more successful Salem town, which was trading with the West Indian plantations.

SIMON MIDDLETON: *[The puritans] left England to try to build pure churches in the New World. They worry greatly that the Anglican Church retains too many corruptions and Catholic practices. The importance of establishing a pure church is because the puritans are also Calvinists, they believe in predestination, meaning that some are bound to go to heaven. Most are bound to go to hell.*

The only way to learn what your fate would be was to study the Bible and the self, while being part of a pure church, led by a minister who was trustworthy and well informed. You could then look out for signs that you may be one of the saved. There was a split in Salem village between those who lived further away from Salem town, who wanted a church in the village to serve them better, and those nearer Salem town, who were content to travel there.

The people who had emigrated to Massachusetts were Congregationalists who, unlike the Presbyterians, believed very strongly that the congregation should be in charge of its own church.

SIMON MIDDLETON: *This is one of the reasons you see, in New England, a fragmentation as groups break away from the early settlement and settle around the colony, each with their own particular variation and view of how the religious practice should be ordered. When they're all fighting against Anglicans in England, they're joined together, but, when they get to the New World, they part and fall out with each other, very famously in the Antinomian Controversy of the 1630s.*

There were about 600 people in Salem village. One of the many splits within it was between the Putnam family, who supported the new church, and the Porters, who opposed it. These families had arrived at the same time, at the founding of the village, and, since then, the Porters had flourished through trade and the Putnams had declined, and they were feuding.

The puritans believed in a world of invisible spirits, a world of devils and witches, none of whom could be seen. They also believed in the importance of confession, which would prove very important in the trials. What was paramount was the integrity of the community.

SUSAN CASTILLO-STREET: *They did have the idea that they were the inheritors of the Israelites, as the chosen people of God. But the difference was that they believed that they could create the perfect society not in heaven but here on earth and, specifically, in America. Their rhetoric is very much in terms of biblical typology; the persecution from the Stuart kings was rather like the Israelites and pharaoh in Egypt. The crossing of the Atlantic was like the crossing of the Red Sea.*

For these settlers, any kind of difficulty was a badge of honour, because this showed that the devil considered them a threat and they were being tested. They believed that the devil could work through someone's spectre, an invisible presence that could carry out malefic witchcraft, which some people said they could see through.

SUSAN CASTILLO-STREET: *The afflicted girls, the young women who began all of this, claimed that they could see spectres tormenting others. The problem there is that there're no external corroboration so someone can allege that someone's spectre is tormenting them, even if that very person has a perfectly good alibi and is physically present somewhere else.*

Salem was also on a frontier. The colonists had burnt Native American villages to the ground, something that Melvyn recalled the puritans thought was a 'sweet blessing of the Lord', and the Native Americans had made raids and taken away prisoners, so the threat was ever-present.

SUSAN CASTILLO-STREET: *There was a kind of invasion psychosis, really. So many of the people who were the accusers in the witch trials had very direct experience of the battles. For example, Mercy Short was taken captive by the Wabanaki. While she was there, she was made to witness the dismemberment of one of the captives as a lesson to other captives not to flee. Another, Mercy Lewis, was orphaned and lost her family. She then was a servant with the Putnams.*

The first accusers were two girls, Abigail Williams and Betty Parris, who fell ill and started to accuse people of bewitching them. Betty was about nine years old and Abigail was about eleven or twelve.

MARION GIBSON: *We know [how old they were] because John Hale, one of the preachers who was called to try to find out what was wrong with them, tells us their ages. These are changed by later writers, but we know that they were actually quite young girls. They start being afflicted. They think that demonic creatures are pinching them, they start twitching and writhing and their bodies are contorted in strange ways, so their hands are turned backwards and their limbs are twisted.*

MELVYN BRAGG: *Do they show these backward-turned hands or are we expected to believe that?*

MARION GIBSON: *We're expected to believe that.*

It is not clear what was going on, whether the children were consciously putting their bodies into strange shapes, or whether it even happened at all. The girls were living in the house of Samuel Parris, the minister who was causing much dissent in Salem village. Betty was his daughter and Abigail was said to be his niece, and the first person they accused was his slave, Tituba. There was tremendous pressure on this household to be godly and on the girls to be silent, to be submissive, to respect the adults around. Also, importantly, Abigail probably had no father and mother. It may have been that Samuel Parris listened to them as they were saying things he wanted to hear.

MARION GIBSON: *He wants to hear that he is a godly man and that therefore the devil hates him and wants to attack his family. And he feels persecuted anyway because, in the wider community, he's not well liked and there are dissensions and problems in the community surrounding the minister. He already feels under threat and this confirms his sense that the devil is after him.*

It is possible that he put the girls up to all this, but there is no evidence for this other than that they were living in his household.

Samuel Parris was in the centre of a really vicious fight between the factions in Salem village. The Porter faction had gained control of the church government the previous October and stopped giving him his salary.

Cotton Mather, a Conregationalist minister whose writings include a commentary on the witchcraft trials in Salem, Massachusetts.

SIMON MIDDLETON: *There's also Cotton Mather, this brilliant intellectual minister, and, in 1689, he publishes a book called* Memorable Providences of Witchcraft and Possession, *in which he describes the case of the bewitchment of some children in Boston, the Goodwin children, and it describes exactly the kind of behaviour and afflictions that then appear in Salem. And it's not too much of a stretch to see Parris (everybody would have been aware of Mather's publication) reading that, and then highly suggestible children in the household picking up on that.*

Once the accusations were made, there were arrest warrants and people were brought in for questioning, and the cases went to grand jury and then to trial. The legal process was very deliberative and very bureaucratic, although, unusually, the court did not take a bond from the accusers to stand up for their accusation and confirm that they would be in court. The next people accused, Sarah Osborne and Sarah Good, were vulnerable; they were older and poor and had a reputation for arguing with neighbours.

It was remarkably difficult for the accused to defend themselves, on account of the issue of spectral evidence. As the accusations increased, many defended themselves by simply proclaiming their innocence and, almost without exception, those who did were later hanged. This was linked to the idea that confession was good for the soul, and there was also a presumption of guilt.

SUSAN CASTILLO-STREET: *Tituba probably understood from the beginning that, if she confessed, she might be freed, as ultimately happened after a long period of imprisonment, so her confession was remarkably florid and evocative, and that instance touched off the outpouring of confessions that followed.*

Tituba, accused, had, in turn, accused other people, including Sarah Good and Sarah Osborne. She talked about how they had demonic spirits, familiars in the shape of animals, about how they pinched and attacked the children and made her sign the devil's book and had drawn her into their witches' coven. But, Marion Gibson emphasised, she survived the trials, whereas Sarah Osborne died in prison and Sarah Good was hanged, so Tituba's strategy was the right one for her.

In all of the original documents, Tituba was described as an Indian woman. In the 1860s, with the civil war and the American politics of slavery, there was interest in people of African-American descent and, around that time, Tituba somehow began to be described differently.

MARION GIBSON: *It's very likely that she was a Native American woman, and research done in the 1990s threw up a record in Barbados from the 1670s of a girl called Tatuba, who was being sold, who was part of an inventory of an estate owned by a man called Samuel Thompson in Bridgetown, Barbados. And this may be our Tituba. She's listed among child slaves, so, by the time of the Salem trials, if this is our girl, she's probably twenty-five to thirty years old.*

It made absolute sense for the accused to confess, Simon Middleton continued. Those who confessed were kept in jail in the expectation that they would implicate more people, rather than moved swiftly to execution, and there was a chance that time would allow them to weather out the storm of accusations, and then they could be treated differently. As the number of accusers widened, the case of Rebecca Nurse illustrated the value of confession even for those with impeccable reputations.

SIMON MIDDLETON: *Rebecca Nurse is a member of the church in good standing, a member of the elect, and it's her trial and execution that really is a turning point in the trials, and her case is worthy of remembering because, of all of them, she's the truly principled puritan. And when she's told under questioning, 'Just confess and we can sort something out,' she says, 'I cannot confess to something I do not believe I've done, I can't tell a lie.' So it is her adherence to principles that takes her ultimately to the noose.*

There was also the case of Elizabeth and John Proctor, who ran a tavern and owned a farm. He was genial but blunt, Susan Castillo-Street told us, and Elizabeth was his much younger third wife. She was accused by John Indian, another slave of Samuel Parris. It started when some girls at Ingersoll's Tavern said that Elizabeth Proctor's spectre was in the room. The wife of the tavern owner said they really shouldn't say that sort of thing, and one of the girls said, 'Oh, it was for sport.' That then subsided, but people began to accuse Elizabeth Proctor of witchcraft, citing in support that she had allegedly offered someone some herbal medicine and, when it was refused, had made that person ill. John Proctor came to the hearing to protest his wife's innocence, which left him open to accusation, too. He was imprisoned and denied all guilt to the end.

SUSAN CASTILLO-STREET: *He tried to write an appeal to some clerics in Boston, saying that this was a bit of a nonsense, that some of the accusations were simply specious, they were false – probably the very worst thing that he could have done. If he had confessed, they would have let him off. Elizabeth Proctor managed to avoid hanging because she was pregnant. When he was eventually hanged, he died very bravely, he forgave his accusers.*

One of the other aspects of the Parris household was that John Indian, a slave living there and perhaps the husband of Tituba, was also accused of practising magical medicine.

MARION GIBSON: *John was asked by a white female colonist, Mary Sibley, to bake a thing called a witch cake, which is something that you do by getting together cornmeal and the urine of the bewitched people, a lovely thing, and baking it and feeding it to a dog who will then take the witchcraft or the infection out of the household.*

Accusations started to spread across the wider Essex County. Simon Middleton noted that Andover, a nearby village, ultimately had more accusations than Salem. George Burroughs had been a minister in Salem earlier and had been preaching up on the north-eastern coast, towards where the Wabanaki Indians were, and he became a key figure. These village communities were on the front line, facing the French and really terrifying Native American allies, so attacks become quite common and the threats of attack even more so. Burroughs came to be seen as the orchestrator of every incident.

SIMON MIDDLETON: *People testify to seeing hundreds of witches flying around with Burroughs as this black man in the lead. And what we see then developing is the trials start to happen and the whole thing snowballs because, once you've got jails with twenty-five or thirty people confessing to be witches, if you believe in witchcraft as a real force, then you have to proceed legally.*

The governor of Massachusetts, William Phips, returned from London in May and established a court of oyer and terminer to hear the cases, and the court proceeded with its work. Cotton Mather, the leading thinker in the state, was a really powerful force in the trials as he justified the acceptance of spectral evidence, whereas, in English legal tradition, that was one thing to count against the accused, but there needed to be other supporting evidence.

SUSAN CASTILLO-STREET: *Cotton Mather's favourite word was 'nevertheless'. In one statement, he says that one should proceed with extreme caution and be very careful not to incriminate innocents. 'Nevertheless', one should eliminate all witches. He liked to play it both ways. In 1702, when he was attempting to spin the witch trials according to his own perspectives, he describes the devil as rather like an Indian sagamore or as a French dragoon, which I think supports the hypothesis of the Indian frontier as a very, very crucial factor.*

There has been another theory for the state of the accusers' minds, which relates to diet and suggested that these people were experiencing ergot poisoning.

SUSAN CASTILLO-STREET: *Ergot is a kind of fungus that can infect grain and, when it breaks down, one of the components is lysergic acid, or LSD, as we know it. They could have been having a really remarkably bad trip of some sort. The symptoms would be hallucinations and fits. This, however, has been convincingly debunked, because the girls, between the hearings, were hale and hearty, there were no symptoms at all.*

People in Salem were being hanged right up until the end of September 1692. By the close of the trials, according to Robert Calef, a Baptist writer and opponent of Mather, at least 300 people had been suspected in Essex County and about 150 were in jail. Then the colonists began to realise that something terrible had happened and that surely not all these people could be witches.

MARION GIBSON: *There is a story, also, that the wife of the governor William Phips was herself accused. That's a story that comes out about a decade later, but it may well be that there is truth in it. And that would tend to turn people's attention to the idea that some of those who were accused might indeed be innocent. It may be that the story starts to change its direction when the elite get involved and people important to them are accused.*

What Melvyn wanted to know was why, when other parts of the colony were quite well run, did the wiser heads not step in here? That, to Simon Middleton, was the key question. Why did men of power listen to teenagers and women when they normally never did?

The colony was facing war, there had been a series of epidemics, and they had lost their charter in 1685 when James II established the dominion of New England.

SIMON MIDDLETON: *There is social anxiety at work here, and the fact that the devil is abroad in Massachusetts appeals to people in leadership positions as a possible explanation for why everything is going wrong, and it's not their fault so much. The other thing is that, although it's a very big deal for historians later, Salem actually wasn't that big a deal for William Phips and the council at the time. If you read the provincial council minutes, they're much more worried about the French and the Indian attacks from the north. They're about as worried about Salem as they are about the problem of wolves taking livestock.*

The trials came to an end when the court of oyer and terminer was wound up, Marion Gibson continued, as part of the problems with the charter and the politics of governing the colony. There was a new court and it did continue to convict people and sentence them to death, but Governor Phips stepped in to pardon them. The elite tried to put an end to it, and succeeded in 1693. The trials came to be seen as the great example of a terrible American mistake, a moment when they got it badly wrong. These were late examples of trials for witchcraft, and these sorts of trial were petering out. By the 1730s, in England, there was a law to say that, if anyone claimed to be a witch, they could be tried not for being a witch, but on grounds they were fraudulent.

In the studio afterwards, there was discussion of Robert Calef's character assassination of Cotton Mather and his beliefs, which led to Mather having Calef's book burnt in Princeton Yard. Arthur Miller's *The Crucible* was praised, even if he did raise Abigail Williams' age and lower John Proctor's so that they could be romantically linked. Simon Middleton quoted the historian Keith Thomas, who said that witchcraft was about explaining things, dreadful things that were happening when other explanations no longer served. And Susan Castillo-Street picked up on a theme in Salem and in *The Crucible* – 'what a toxic emotion fear could be'.

MAIMONIDES

One of the most visited sites in the city of Tiberias on the western shore of the Sea of Galilee is a simple marble tomb. This is the final resting place of the medieval philosopher, theologian and lawyer Moses Maimonides. You get some idea of his importance to the history of Jewish scholarship from the Hebrew inscription, which reads: 'From Moses to Moses, there arose none like Moses.' Today Maimonides is widely regarded as one of the greatest scholars of the Middle Ages. He spent much of his life in Egypt and was influenced by a rich mix of Jewish, Islamic and ancient Greek thinkers. His authoritative magnum opus on Jewish law remains central to the subject more than eight centuries on. And his book The Guide for the Perplexed *is one of the masterpieces of medieval philosophy.*

With Melvyn to discuss the life and work of Maimonides were: John Haldane, professor of philosophy at the University of St Andrews and J. Newton Rayzor distinguished professor of philosophy at Baylor University, Texas; Sarah Stroumsa, Alice and Jack Ormut professor of Arabic studies and currently rector at the Hebrew University of Jerusalem; and Peter Adamson, professor for late ancient Arabic philosophy, LMU Munich.

Maimonides was born in Córdoba in Andalusia in Muslim Spain, around 1135, where his father was both a rabbinical leader and a doctor. John Haldane described Córdoba as a cultured, affluent city of merchants and learned people and a place that was relatively tolerant. When Maimonides was about nine years old, a more aggressive form of Islam became dominant in Morocco, Andalusia was invaded by the Almohads, and Córdoba was taken

JOHN HALDANE: *This Almohad movement doesn't want to see either Jews or Christians living freely, and they have the slogan, 'No synagogue, no church.' And, at that point, he and his family are faced with a choice that actually others had in other circumstances: whether to flee, whether to suffer martyrdom or whether to convert. And his family flee.*

It would be fair to say, John Haldane added, that Jews had found it easier under Islam in this period than under Christianity. The history of Jewish philosophy in its first phase was conducted essentially in the Islamic lands, and later in Christian lands. Maimonides was writing in Judaeo-Arabic, which was Arabic but in Hebrew lettering and, as far as John Haldane recalled, only one of his works was written in Hebrew.

JOHN HALDANE: *He's growing up in a very cultured environment. His father's a doctor, he's studying science, which, at that point, is astronomy, optics, logic, some medicine. Later, he's going to study medicine more, he's going to practise as a doctor. It's said that the one thing he didn't like was poetry.*

His family fled Córdoba, moving around the Iberian peninsula, travelling to Fez, to the Levant and then to Fustat, outside Cairo. What had happened to them in Spain with the Almohads was unusual, Peter Adamson said, and they would have found toleration in Egypt, if not stability. The Fatimid Caliphate, which was Shiite and had founded Cairo in the tenth century, was on its last legs. There were crusaders up in Palestine and, in the wider region, there was a Sunni force, the Ayyubids. In the 1160s, the Fatimid Caliphate was under pressure.

PETER ADAMSON: *The Fatimids invite the Ayyubids into Egypt to help them stave off an invasion from the crusaders, and this leads to good news and bad news for the Fatimids. The good news is that they managed to stave off the crusaders, and the bad news is that the Ayyubids decide that they don't really want to leave.*

The invading general died shortly after the battle, and his nephew was Salah ad-Din, also known as Saladin, who became the vizier of this nominal Fatimid Caliphate and then sultan of Egypt.

The Fatimid Caliphate had created a really impressive intellectual metropolis, with the Al-Azhar Mosque and the connected Al-Azhar University. There was a community of Jews living in Cairo at this time, numbered in the thousands rather than tens of thousands, and, in this group, Peter Adamson suggested, Maimonides would have been a big fish in a small pond. His command of the legal tradition and texts was probably greater than that of any other scholar who was there at the time.

PETER ADAMSON: *It's possible that he was influenced by some of the ideas that come through the Shiite Fatimid tradition, this kind of Shi'ism called Ismailism. But, I think, equally important is that being in Cairo puts Maimonides in the centre of Mediterranean culture. He exchanged correspondence with people all over the Muslim world and beyond, so Baghdad, Yemen, also in southern France, all over Egypt, sometimes on legal issues but also on a wide range of other issues, including philosophy.*

We do not know exactly what happened to Maimonides and his family before they reached Cairo, Sarah Stroumsa said. We know they had taken the opportunity to flee from Córdoba and spent time in north Africa.

SARAH STROUMSA: *Our assumption must be that they outwardly behaved as Muslims, everyone, all the Jewish community including Maimonides' family. And, when they managed to flee, I think we have to assume a traumatic experience in the background. The first few years in Egypt allowed Maimonides some years of peace and quiet to establish himself in the Jewish community and to write.*

Before long, though, his brother was lost at sea and, with him, the family's treasure that he was looking after. Maimonides fell into a year of real depression. He now had debts to cover, he had his brother's widow and small child to support and he had to find a way to support himself. This was when he moved into the court of Saladin to work as one of the court's physicians. This may well be when he also moved from the precincts of the Jewish community and got into theological debates and conversations with Muslims.

We know more of the life of Maimonides than we do of many of his contemporaries. The reason for that, Sarah Stroumsa said, is that we are lucky. We have something that is the closest we have to an archive. In synagogues, Jews do not discard documents on which they expect to have written the name of God, the tetragrammaton, the four letters YHWH or JHVH.

SARAH STROUMSA: *They collect all papers written in Hebrew and put them aside for decent burial. In Cairo, because of the climate and because of the continuity of the community, we have a treasure trove of documents called the* Genizah, *which was found in the synagogue in the nineteenth century and contains Maimonides' correspondence, Maimonides' deeds, his writings, everything about him. And this gives us a wonderful opportunity to see his life and to see his emotions.*

Maimonides became a rabbinical leader of Egyptian Jewry, John Haldane said, and had a reputation for brilliance, and he had practical wisdom. He addressed the question of whether it was ever right to adopt the modes of dress and other behaviours of Muslims in order to survive.

JOHN HALDANE: *There's a debate about this, whether it's a proper thing to do, and he says it is better that than martyrdom, though better still for the purity of the law to go into exile, to flee. But what is interesting is that he sees the purity of Jewish observance as residing in this world, the condition of the interior soul. What emerges is this purity of intellect.*

His first important work was his *Commentary on the Mishnah*, the written form of Jewish oral traditions. John Haldane explained that the Torah can be understood in a narrow sense as the first five books of the Hebrew Bible. There is also the broader sense, which is the entire Hebrew Bible (what Christians call the Old Testament) plus the Talmud, which is the oral tradition, codified, written down, plus commentary.

JOHN HALDANE: *In his role as a legal scholar, he works on the oral commentary, at one point producing an edition, as it were, of this, but then also producing commentary on this. This is a very rich source of both rabbinical teaching and guidance, but it also is going to lead into some of the philosophical ideas that will become the subject and treatment of* The Guide, *which is the work we're going to come to.*

Before reaching *The Guide*, Melvyn asked Peter Adamson to outline some of the influences on Maimonides. There was Aristotle, who would have been known to him to some extent thanks to the Greek–Arabic translations that were done in the ninth century. He was also deeply influenced by philosophers writing in Arabic who were influenced by Aristotle, such as Al-Farabi, a tenth-century Platonist and Aristotelian, and Avicenna and his contemporary Averroes. There was also the strong influence on him from the rabbinical tradition.

PETER ADAMSON: *This giant of Jewish philosophy and legal scholarship is also influenced in various ways by Islamic theology. He talks extensively about the schools of speculative theology in Islam, which are known as* Kalam, *which means 'word', or Ilm al-Kalām, 'science of the word'; he's actually very critical of them. He doesn't like the fact that they present this world that is not amenable to rational analysis, because God can, effectively, do whatever he wants. God can turn you into a frog and then turn you back again, there's nothing impossible about that.*

Like Averroes, Maimonides thought that was a very unsettling kind of doctrine because it limited human ability to find the world intelligible and to explain the world using philosophy.

It is clear that, from his attempt to write his *Commentary on the Mishnah*, Maimonides already had his life work planned for him. It was a preparation for distilling all the oral law, as found in the Mishnah in the Talmud, and putting it together into one code, the *Mishnah Torah*, literally the second law or the second to the written law.

*A draft of Maimonides'
legal code, the* Mishnah
Torah, *in his own hand.*

SARAH STROUMSA: *And, as he himself tells us in the introduction
to Mishnah Torah, his intention was to write a concise code, not
really a vade mecum but something that would be concise enough,
which will put together all the traditions, cut through all the
accumulated debates and disagreements and diversity of opinions,
and present, in Hebrew, in Mishnaic Hebrew, the end result: what is
the law regarding every single matter?*

These laws covered such things as the first prayer in the morning
to the prayer to be said over the dead, the laws of what would
happen when the third temple was built, and 'laws of sacrifices that
were as relevant then as they are today, which means completely
irrelevant'. In Jewish tradition, as in Islamic tradition, before getting
to a legal decision, rabbis would first go through all the literature,
starting from the Bible, then the commentaries, the Mishnah, the
Talmud, which would offer various opinions and then perhaps they
would come to a decision.

SARAH STROUMSA: *Maimonides says this is a waste of time. You
can learn it in order to sharpen your brain, but this is not what
you are made to be. As a person, as a Jew, you were made to get to
behave correctly, which is what the law is for, and then to think and
to sharpen your brain in order to get to intellectual achievements.*

Really Maimonides was looking in two directions, John Haldane
thought, one to Judaism and one to philosophy. With regard to

Judaism, he shared the idea that this people uniquely possess a revelation from God and they stand in this special relationship to God, and Maimonides is very respectful of that. With regard to Jewish philosophical thought, he is looking for a way of understanding reality, not just the question of what has been given in revelation, but in the broader sense.

JOHN HALDANE: *And there he's looking to Greek philosophy in one way or another. Some of the great Christian writers, such as Augustine, are commonly influenced by this Neoplatonic tradition, which is a very strong intellectual tradition. Aristotelianism is very naturalistic; Neoplatonism is very speculative.*

This issue about philosophy and the law was really embodied in the *Mishnah Torah*, Peter Adamson suggested, in a section called 'The Book of Knowledge'. A lot of this is a résumé of Aristotelian philosophy, in which Maimonides goes through Aristotle's cosmology, his theory of the four elements, his ethics. He presents the virtues as the golden mean, where courage is the mean between cowardice and recklessness.

PETER ADAMSON: *He doesn't slavishly follow Aristotle by any means. For example, he says that, on some points, you want to adopt the extreme rather than the mean, so a good Jew should always be meek, for example, and you should not just be the right amount meek, but as meek as possible. He's not a thoroughgoing Aristotelian, but it's really significant that he sees Aristotelian philosophy as a basis for which you could study Jewish law.*

It was important to distinguish the two tracks that Maimonides tried to present. One was for the nation – the question of how to build a righteous nation – and, for that, the *Mishnah Torah* presented the code.

SARAH STROUMSA: *There is also the way that the individual can take and, for the individuals, there might be other ways. We can see that he had two ideals for two models for human perfection. One was obviously Moses, who had it all, who had revelation, who had knowledge and who understood as much as a person can understand. And the other model for human perfection was Aristotle.*

An individual could reach the ideal without going through the *Mishnah Torah* and all the Halakhot or laws, and, for that, you had to be an exceptional individual. Maimonides thought of the Jewish law as the perfect setting for a group of people, as this would prepare as many as possible.

Maimonides' masterpiece is thought to be *The Guide for the Perplexed*, which he wrote *c.* 1190. While it is a very complex work, John Haldane found it relatively easy to say who the *perplexed* were. *The Guide* was not for the person who was simply observing the law and whose conduct was straightforward and who was untroubled.

JOHN HALDANE: *Nor is it for the philosopher who's thought matters through in their own way. The perplexed is much more like somebody in the present day who's a well-educated person but feels a tension between what they're learning from science, what they're learning from philosophy and what they're hearing in a church or in a synagogue or in a mosque. They're perplexed: 'How can you reconcile the learning of the day with the religious teachings of the day?'*

The perplexed was the honest doubter, Melvyn suggested. What Maimonides was trying to do, John Haldane continued, was to provide a reconciliation and this was going to get Maimonides into trouble with some people. He was going to treat a lot of scripture as allegorical.

JOHN HALDANE: *He's going to say, 'Look, you have to understand that this was produced for people at a certain stage in development. The first thing that Moses had to do was get the people to believe in a single God. The imagery of that is talk to God as if God were a lordly master somewhere, in another place. That's a stage you go through but what you're proceeding to is the more philosophical understanding.'*

God, Maimonides argued, was beyond any category of language or sense of a thing; God is not a being in that sense, God *is* being.

In Sarah Stroumsa's view, Maimonides' assumption was that you could not be a true believer if you were an ignoramus.

SARAH STROUMSA: *In order not to be an ignoramus, you have to understand the reality as it is. Which means that you have to know logic in order to think correctly and you have to study the reality, and take it for what it is and not force the truth on the reality – the truth should be what is reflected in reality.*

One of the things that was important to see in *The Guide*, she said, was that it was not just a reconciliation of the law of Moses with philosophy, it was also the reconciliation of the law of Abraham with philosophy. Maimonides tried to show that, if you studied the reality of the world, you would get away from pagan superstitious beliefs and get to understand that there is a single God, which you cannot really perceive, you can only get closer by understanding what he is not.

This negative theology, Peter Adamson explained, was the view that it was not possible to say anything about God, and perhaps not think anything about God either. This tradition ran back to the Neoplatonists and was also something the Almohads said, which raised interesting questions about possible influences. Maimonides took this in a new direction, with an unusually rigorous line.

PETER ADAMSON: *He really thinks you can't say anything true about God, you cannot say anything positively about God and have it come out true. The reason it would be misleading is that it would put God on a par with us or other created things. So, for example, Sarah and John know a lot about Maimonides, so they're knowing, but you cannot say that God is knowing, because then you'd be putting God on a par with John and Sarah.*

Peter Adamson explained that Maimonides says therefore that you should interpret everything in scripture about God either just allegorically or symbolically as a concealed negation. If it says that God is knowing, you should take that to mean he does not lack knowledge that we might have. Alternatively, it is what Maimonides calls an attributive action. For example, to say God is providential sounds like a comment about God, but actually it is talking about the world, that it is providentially ordered, and not a statement about God.

One point that John Haldane wanted to emphasise was the monotheism of Judaism.

JOHN HALDANE: *The whole richness of the Jewish people is that they passed from the phase of polytheism of the people that surrounded them to a belief in a single deity and an all-powerful transcendent deity. Christianity, for example, introduces Trinity; it looks like it's breaking up the unity of God.*

The question was, John Haldane continued, what were people to do to perfect themselves? If we believe we are made as images of God, we have intellect, we have will, then we are to engage in this imitation of the divine by becoming, to the extent that we can, godlike, transforming the world that God has expressed out of his nature back into mind through our knowledge of it. The world is a creation out of mind and it is a reception into mind, and that idea, John Haldane thought, was a fantastic and enduring contribution, although it left a question about the humble, who were incapable of that, which was a problem.

The mind is the soul for Maimonides, but only, Sarah Stroumsa said, when he spoke to the multitudes. When he spoke to the initiate, he always distinguished between the soul and the upper part of the soul, which was the intellect.

SARAH STROUMSA: *For him, the whole purpose of human existence is the perfection of the intellect not just the soul. The soul is a complicated entity, it has baser parts and these are the parts that we have to feed and that we have to take care of, but these are not the parts of which we, as human beings, should be proud. The part of the soul that makes us really what we are, humans, is the intellect.*

The Guide was translated into Hebrew around the end of Maimonides' life, and it proved controversial for some. Peter Adamson mentioned that, while there were those who liked the rationalist approach and wanted to take it further, others thought it had gone too far. In France in 1230, rabbis asked the Dominicans to burn Maimonides' works because they thought he was being too radical, too Aristotelian.

When he called his *Mishnah Torah* 'second to the law', Maimonides wanted to canonise his book, Sarah Stroumsa said, and she thought he achieved that.

SARAH STROUMSA: *You can interpret it away, but you cannot discard it. People read the* Mishnah Torah *as if it really is the second to the law. People, as mentioned in the beginning, come up to Tiberias; if he is buried there, he would turn in his grave. People think of him as the topmost Jewish thinker.*

THE BALTIC CRUSADES

From the twelfth century, the popes approved a series of crusades on the Baltic lands, principally Prussia and regions now covered by Lithuania, Latvia, Poland and Estonia. The Teutonic Order led the fight to convert so-called pagans to Christianity and, if the pagans refused, it was no sin to kill them. Over the next 100 years, the Teutonic Knights ran their own state based in Prussia. Many German speakers settled these lands claimed for Christendom, and they built ports on the newly secured Baltic Sea, which, through the Hanseatic League, transformed trade in northern Europe. There was rarely peace during these crusades, and the changes in who lived in the region and how they lived had great significance for the history of Europe.

—•—

A wall mural from a cathedral in Poland depicting leaders of the Teutonic Knights.

With Melvyn to discuss the Baltic crusades were: Aleks Pluskowski, associate professor of medieval archaeology at the University of Reading; Nora Berend, reader in European history at the Faculty of History at the University of Cambridge; and Martin Palmer, visiting professor of religion, history and nature at the University of Winchester.

Martin Palmer began this history with events in the first half of the twelfth century, when the Church in Rome wanted to establish that Europe was now the land of Christ, that the pope was his appointed representative, and that secular and religious authority should reside within the papacy.

MARTIN PALMER: *This was coming out of a period where it was quite dubious whether Christianity would actually make it to the twelfth century. You had the Vikings and the northern invasions of pagan communities that devastated Christianity in England, Scotland, Ireland, across the northern parts of France and Spain, and you also had the Muslim rise coming up from north Africa, the conquest of Spain, Sardinia, Corsica, Sicily, and also the fact that piracy and slave trading meant that the Mediterranean, or the northern part of it, was extremely dangerous – in fact, many cities ceased to function on the coastline.*

This immense trial had lasted for about 300 years and the Church was now establishing itself. The papacy had also brought in the Peace of God, which was an attempt to control the feuding that was going on, by saying that the Church would now determine what was a just war.

MARTIN PALMER: *You also had a sense of a real threat that was coming into this Christendom, because you then had the heresies. You had the Bogomils coming in from eastern Europe, spreading their notion of a sort of Manichean dualistic religion, that this world was essentially evil, that only the spiritual world was true and was godly, which led to the Albigensians, a famous heretical sect in the twelfth century down in the south of France.*

There was also a sudden sense that paganism was dangerous, and there was a fear of the Orthodox Church because there had been a schism between the western and eastern churches in 1054. There was then an incentive to claim the Baltic before the Orthodox Church did. Crusade was called against the Baltic pagans in 1147 as part of the momentum behind the Second Crusade and the preaching of Bernard of Clairvaux. Bernard argued that there were lands in the Baltic that could be taxed for the papacy. He also broke a rule of the Catholic Church at that time by saying that the pagans could not be left to live in peace.

There was a series of tribal societies dominating the eastern Baltic who were about to be attacked, and these were subdivided broadly into two linguistic groups, Balts and Finno-Ugric, which meant Estonians and Livs.

ALEKS PLUSKOWSKI: *They are relatively small-scale in terms of their territories, except for Lithuania, which has formed the Grand Duchy by this point. But the others are small-scale, extended-kinship* *groups based on an aristocratic hierarchy, male-dominated and militarised and focused on powerful families, based in strongholds that litter the landscapes of the eastern Baltic.*

There had long been inter-tribal feuding, which the crusaders were to take advantage of, especially in Livonia. There had been Prussian tribal expansion to the south and west at the borders of Pomerania and the kingdom of Poland, with raids across the border on monasteries, on towns like Gdańsk, and this caused a lot of tension on the Polish frontier, but, overall, the land was thinly populated.

The targets of the crusades were to be pagans, people who invested spirituality in the natural environment such as in trees, rocks, prominent boulders, lakes or rivers. These places were the focus of cultic activity with the leaving of offerings, and cemeteries were also important sites connected to ancestor worship. Something that marked out the Balts particularly from the first century to the thirteenth, was a ritual that developed in north-eastern Poland in the region of Masuria associated with a Prussian Galindian group later on.

ALEKS PLUSKOWSKI: *Here we have the living burial of horses, developing as a specific ritual within a funerary context. It is most likely associated with a cult of the sun or some solar symbolism, particularly in terms of how the horses are aligned across the entire region. By the Viking age, we see huge numbers of horses being sacrificed and buried, hundreds and hundreds in some cases.*

Even before the crusades were called, there was warfare in the region. In 1108, a Flemish cleric in the Baltic region wrote a letter asking Germans to come to the aid of this land.

NORA BEREND: *Very specifically, [he] said, 'Follow the example of your brothers from Gaul, the French, who went to Jerusalem to liberate Jerusalem, and come here to liberate this land.' So, pre-crusade, there is justification that is very similar: that the pagans are killing Christians in particularly cruel ways. They talk about disembowelling Christians and very gruesome images in this letter.*

The crusade on the Baltic people might then be a way of helping Christians who were already there. There was also the idea of conversion behind the crusade, and it was fairly novel to tie the cause of a crusade very specifically to converting the local populations. That was the context for the idea of 'converting or exterminating' that came in from Bernard of Clairvaux. There was also another idea, borrowed from the Holy Land.

NORA BEREND: *By the very early thirteenth century, Livonia is seen as the land of the Virgin Mary. Bishop Albert of Riga writes to Pope Innocent III asking him not to abandon the land of the mother when he cares for the land of the son. Jerusalem, the Holy Land, is the patrimony of Christ, and Livonia is the patrimony of the Virgin Mary, his mother. [That] is a complete invention.*

There was absolutely no historical background for placing the Virgin Mary in Livonia, and initially there were no holy sites or places of pilgrimage in the Baltic at all.

People on the ground had been waging war between themselves for quite a while in the Baltic, and there were German merchants there who had long-standing interests and who were appealing to Bernard and the pope to espouse their cause. There were already people on the ground who were very happy to attack and to receive justification for their attacks in the name of crusade. Besides, even before Bernard of Clairvaux, the Church was very much espousing violence in certain cases, and the right kind of violence was actually meritorious.

NORA BEREND: *We have many sources, from all over Europe, even extolling taking booty as a sign of divine favour, killing people and taking their possessions as a sign that God was on your side. Bernard of Clairvaux did not come out of the blue, he very much was building on this existing tradition.*

The Teutonic Knights were most closely associated with crusading in the Baltics. Martin Palmer told how they emerged from the hospital for Germans in Jerusalem and, after that city fell, they moved to Acre and became an order in 1189. They became a military force, supporting King Andrew in Hungary, later moving their headquarters to Venice in 1291 after the fall of Acre, and then on to Marienberg in 1309. The understanding initially was that they would keep what they conquered in the Baltics.

MARTIN PALMER: *It was now extremely difficult to go crusading in the Holy Land. You'd taken your vow, you'd got all the tax relief that you got if you went on pilgrimage and, if you were a German or a Dane or indeed English, it was a jolly sight easier to go to the Baltic on crusade than it was to go all the way to the Holy Land. You were far more likely to get land and a fiefdom.*

The Teutonic Knights were monastic, so the land they won was claimed for the order, not divided up among families. Later, as bishops began to move in and parishes were established, the bishops called for funding and they were given a third of the seized land. There was also a different order in Riga, supporting the bishop, made up of people who were, Martin Palmer said, 'a horrendous crowd called the Sword Brothers, who were founded around about 1300, and they just were thugs of the most appalling kind'. There was another group in Old Prussia that was reputedly worse. These orders were dissolved by the pope and responsibility for the military monastic crusade was passed to the Teutonic Knights.

The Teutonic Order drew its recruits mostly from German-speaking aristocratic families in the eastern parts of the Holy Roman Empire, Aleks Pluskowski said. The recruits joined the military order as crusaders, dedicated to the promotion of Christian holy war and directly obedient to the papacy. They were the fighting arm of the papacy and the lands that were conquered in the eastern Baltic were held by the order as papal fiefs.

ALEKS PLUSKOWSKI: *Violence has a role within Christian ideology at this time, especially with a crusading ideology, and the fighting is built into the lifestyle of the military orders. So you pray, you fast,*

A wall mural from a cathedral in Poland depicting leaders of the Teutonic Knights.

but you fight as well. The idea behind these institutions was to create a permanent garrison in areas where Christendom had expanded, because most crusaders would go home after completing their period of penitential warfare.

The Teutonic Knights had amazing reputations as fighters and they were probably the most professional mercenaries of their time. The Kingdom of Poland was really where everything started for the order's Prussian crusade because Duke Konrad I of Masovia invited them to secure his frontier. Following a short internal civil war, the Poles joined the crusade and helped take Prussian territory.

Despite the crusades, there was not total war throughout the Baltics. There was collaboration between the parties who might have been expected to be vigorously opposed to each other.

NORA BEREND: *You find a lot of chronicle accounts saying things like, 'The snow turned red with the blood in a battle, so many people were killed.' You have accounts of people being massacred. You could get this sense of a total war. But then, at the same time, there was trade going on – for example, the Teutonic Order was partly financing its own wars in the Baltic region through trade with Lithuania.*

There were trade treaties, allowing Lithuanian merchants and merchants from the Teutonic Order estate to cross regions, even though these two states were at war. There were also internal wars between the tribes, such as when the Lats tried to side with the order against the Estonians, or when Riga was allied with pagan Lithuania against the order. The trade and alliances did not necessarily follow Christian versus pagan.

Over several centuries, there was a broad Christianisation. Some of the conversions may have been willing and permanent.

NORA BEREND: *There are other accounts that actually claim forced conversion. There are accounts from missionaries thinking that they managed to convert but, the minute they turn their back, the population just shrugs off Christianity. We have accounts in the early period of people washing themselves in their local river to wash away baptism. They do a kind of un-baptism to return to their previous customs.*

All the while, there was so much potential for trade as well as for fighting. One of the earliest accounts of this is from the eleventh century, Martin Palmer said, and it was written by Adam of Bremen who wrote, 'Men cared as much for fur as they did for the salvation of their souls.' It was a complicated picture. On the one hand, there were accounts by the likes of Henry, a priest in Livonia, writing around 1230, who said they all had to preach to the people and be pastors to them, not slaughter them, to be kind to them unless they rose up (in which case it was acceptable to kill them).

MARTIN PALMER: *Then we have this extraordinary book called the* Livonian Rhymed Chronicle, *written almost certainly by a Teutonic Knight, and, in this rather nice rhyming way, he talks about how wonderful it is to slaughter pagans. He also praises them for being noble warriors, but he has no qualms about wiping them out. He portrays the mother of God, the Virgin Mary, as a war goddess, and these are sacrifices to her.*

The war was so closely entangled with trade, Aleks Pluskowski said, that merchants would accompany the crusades, take part in crusades and fund them, while taking advantage of the opportunities. There could be kinship groups, where one brother was fighting and another was trading. Trade and war were inseparable.

The constant fighting and feuding created antagonism and the firming-up of borders between opposing sides. The new Catholic states pushed up against the Slavic principality of Novgorod, which was Orthodox. The borders became more fixed once the Teutonic Order tried to launch crusades into this region in the 1240s and were defeated by Alexander Nevsky of Novgorod in the famous Battle on the Ice in 1242. The orders then stopped attacking Russian territories until the turn of sixteenth century when the Livonian master sought crusading bulls again.

NORA BEREND: *The Teutonic Order actually created a state in Prussia, which was one of the most efficient and modern states of the time. The Hanseatic League started exploiting the local economy, taking grain from Mecklenburg, Pomerania, to western Europe. It became one of the main grain-producing areas.*

Prussia was a fairly successful venture in itself, so there was less value in expanding the boundaries into Russia. The border tension did provide grounds for the Teutonic Orders to justify their presence there, Aleks Pluskowski said, as they argued they were providing security for Christendom against Russian territories, against eastern Orthodoxy and against pagan Lithuania, and this was also a justification for holding the territories.

To this, Nora Berend added that again the tensions between the Livonians and Novgorod were commercial, and that may have been a reason behind the crusade against the Rus.

NORA BEREND: *Whether Alexander Nevsky really had this big victory, scholarship is a bit more divided, because Alexander rose to power and stayed in power with Mongol backing. He was an ally of the Mongols and, after his death, the life that was written about him, which is a resource, tried to turn him into this hero, and it seems that this text really presented this western danger as much more serious than it actually was. It attributes to Alexander this fantastic victory on the ice.*

The same Livonian Rhymed Chronicle *that was already mentioned suggests that there were only about twenty knights, so it may not have been a huge battle.*

The movement, settlement, conquest and trading interests were still very much intertwined, she said. For example, there was some kind of trading port in Riga before the crusades, and then Albert turned it into his bishopric, thanks to the conquests, and, in the thirteenth century, it became part of the Hanseatic League. Swelling the population of the increasingly German-speaking lands were artisans from the Netherlands, Belgium and northern France, Martin Palmer added, where there had been a sharp rise in population, and this skilled migration was transforming the economy.

The migrants from the west kept coming, but not without resistance. Aleks Pluskowski mentioned the Estonians, who rebelled in the mid-fourteenth century in what became known as the St George's Night Uprising. It came almost a century after the crusades there had apparently ended, the area was owned by the Danish crown and the Estonians might have been expected to settle down.

ALEKS PLUSKOWSKI: *Then you have this massive organised Estonian uprising that attacks Christianity specifically, but also, of course, the Danish and German colonists, or rather, by this point, we're talking about later generations. And it's unprecedented in terms of its scale. But it is suppressed and, at that point, the Teutonic Order buys Estonia from the Danish crown.*

There was cultural resilience among rural communities at the edges of control under the new Christian regime. In Estonia, certain practices, such as funerary rites, continued into the nineteenth century.

The Teutonic Order started to lose its power once it confronted the combined forces of Poland and Lithuania. The order had kept using the justification that they were fighting against the pagan Lithuanians but, in the meantime, the Lithuanians had converted to Christianity in 1386 and had formed a dynastic union with Poland. Poland even made a challenge at the papal court over whether the Teutonic Order still had a right to be fighting or not.

NORA BEREND: *More importantly, [the Teutonic Knights] were defeated in 1410 at the battle of Tannenberg or Grunwald. After that, it still took about a century and a half, two centuries, for the Prussian Teutonic state to disintegrate, but that was the major turning point. And it was the military might of Poland and Lithuania that led to that.*

MARTIN PALMER: *The Teutonic Knights end, effectively, as a force, as a governing force, because the grand master of the Teutonic Knights converts to Lutheranism in 1525. You can't have monks in Lutheranism. You have a huge shift away from the medieval Catholic model because, frankly, it's beginning to creak.*

The Teutons lost territories, they had to move their headquarters, the state started to secularise and eventually it became part of the wider Germany. They created a German-speaking heritage in the region for 800 years, and their crusades changed the map of Europe.

ALEKS PLUSKOWSKI: *They created basically the (roughly) modern border area between Estonia, Latvia and Russia and also northern Lithuania and southern Latvia. In Prussia, it was a little different because you have major political shifts in the post-medieval period with the expansion of the kingdom of Prussia. And then, of course, what happens afterwards, with the Yalta Agreement in 1945, you have Prussia being dissolved and separated between Lithuania, Russia and Poland. There the geographical boundaries have shifted dramatically.*

In the studio afterwards, there was discussion of the English dimension. Initially, this took the form of missionaries, and Martin Palmer mentioned Henry the Englishman, who was martyred in Finland *c.* 1147 and is the patron saint of that country today. There was also Henry Bolingbroke, who went on to be Henry IV and who went crusading in the Baltic region in 1390.

ALEKS PLUSKOWSKI: *He is probably the most famous and reaches Vilnius with a huge contingent of English archers before attempting to go down to Jerusalem. This crusading ideal lives on. But the English component is very interesting. We have lots of English merchants present as well; in fact, in Gdańsk, we have a whole English merchant quarter that's established because of trading connections.*

Nora Berend pointed out the multiplicity of the peoples who participated not just the English but also the Scandinavians and the Danes, and there were rivalries between these groups. The Lithuanians, she said, developed a 'fantastic diplomatic procedure' to deal with the Christians, so they kept promising baptism at crucial moments when it seemed that they were going to be defeated in war.

RUMI'S POETRY

The Sufi writer and teacher Rumi is so important in the Islamic world that four modern countries claim him for their own: Afghanistan, as he was born in that area in the town of Balkh in 1207; Uzbekistan, as he lived in Samarkand as a child; Turkey, as he lived, worked and died in the Anatolian city of Konya; and Iran, as he wrote in Persian. Rumi is treasured throughout Islam and beyond for his poetry: his Masnavi *and* Divan. *His output was extraordinary, around four times greater than Homer's* Odyssey. *The* Divan *is a massive collection of lyrical poems; the* Masnavi *are spiritual verses of enormous complexity, described controversially in the fourteenth century as the 'Persian Qur'an'. His followers founded the Mevlevi Order of Sufis, known outside Turkey for their whirling dervishes.*

With Melvyn to discuss the poems of Rumi were: Alan Williams, Leverhulme Trust research professor at the University of Manchester; Carole Hillenbrand, professor of Islamic history at the University of St Andrews and professor emerita of the University of Edinburgh; and Lloyd Ridgeon, reader in Islamic studies at the University of Glasgow.

While Rumi was very much of the Persian world, Carole Hillenbrand explained that he and his family lived originally in what is now Afghanistan and his father was a reputed teacher and scholar with a group of disciples around him. At one point, around 1212, they were living in Samarkand and Rumi's father had a dispute with the ruler and left the area. That may or may not have been prompted by rumours of terrible activities by the Mongols, further east.

CAROLE HILLENBRAND: *The family, lock, stock and barrel, moved, and they travelled first to Baghdad and then Mecca and Damascus before, finally, having come from the extreme eastern part of the Islamic world, ending up on the western periphery in the Sultanate of Rûm, hence Rumi's name, which is the Arabic word for Byzantium. They settled in the area of the Seljuk sultanate and, finally, the father of Rumi was invited to Konya, which is where Rumi was destined to remain.*

Rumi's father, Bahā ud-Dīn Walad, helped make Konya into an important place of learning, teaching Islamic law and the Sufi doctrine, even before Rumi built on that himself, and the *Maaref* of his father, 'intimations of the mystic path', was an important text for him. Another influence on Rumi, Alan Williams added, was the head of the Madrassa in Konya, who was called Burhan ud-Din Muhaqqiq. He was perhaps the first visionary of some mystical attainment that Rumi had met.

ALAN WILLIAMS: *There is a non-human influence on him, which is the elephant in the room, if you like. It's the Qur'an itself and the Hadith tradition. This is perhaps the greatest influence on Rumi and it runs through his life like a golden thread, and one must remember that before one speaks about human influences.*

One of the main influences on Rumi was Shams-e Tabrizi, who came into Rumi's life around 1244 when Rumi would have been thirty-seven and Shams-e Tabrizi would have been fifty-five. He was a very mysterious and charismatic figure who was thought of as a mad wandering Qalandariyyah.

MELVYN BRAGG: *Mad wandering what?*

ALAN WILLIAMS: *An antinomian wandering dervish, sometimes they were even naked – like naked fakirs. These are the wild-haired men of Islamic mysticism, Qalandaris, as they're called, or Kalandars. Now we know now that Shams-e Tabrizi was actually a very learned man and we can see from his writings that he was both a man of immense kindness but, at the same time, of great severity. And his name, Shams, means 'the sun'.*

Their meeting was seen as the transformation point in Rumi's life. It was said that Rumi was raw that he became cooked when he met Shams-e Tabrizi that when Shams-e Tabrizi disappeared, that he was burnt by the experience. For two years, with a brief period of separation, they had the most intense mystical relationship.

ALAN WILLIAMS: *Rumi's own pupils were so jealous of that close liaison that [Shams] was hounded out of town, or he left of his own accord, we don't know quite which. It seems, if we sift the evidence, that Shams left town and didn't say where he was going and Rumi pined after him and wrote to him and begged him to come back. He came back soon but, within a year, he disappeared for ever, and there was a great controversy in the literature about whether or not he was bumped off by Rumi's disciples.*

It is difficult to tell what Shams-e Tabrizi taught Rumi, Alan Williams continued, as we do not know enough about him, but it was probably the case that 'he unlocked the poet in Rumi'. In the period after they met, there was a massive outpouring of poetry until his death in 1273. Theirs was not a sober relationship, but it was a chaste relationship of mystical companionship and communication.

Sufism did not appear in the Qur'an, Lloyd Ridgeon observed, but emerged as a social phenomenon in the ninth and tenth centuries, and it was part of a movement and representative of 'normative Islam' that related to the performing of prayers, going on pilgrimage, fasting and other matters.

LLOYD RIDGEON: *Despite this, there were some individuals who perhaps took the emergence of the movement a little bit further. In particular, there was one Sufi called Hallaj and he was executed in 922 because of his supposed statement, 'I am the truth,' or 'I am God.' Many people thought he was blurring the distinctions between creator and created, between man and God.*

After that, Sufism became a little more conservative and this idea of mysticism, of some kind of unitive experience of man and God, was pushed into the background. Nevertheless, the Sufi tradition remained incredibly popular among the masses. For people like Rumi, mysticism was about the understanding of witnessing God, however that may be. Theologians and clerics wanted to preserve an ontological distinction between the human being and God, whereas the Sufis tended to blur these distinctions. There were also many interpretations of what Sufism was. There were the Kalandars, the wild dervishes, who were regarded by many Sufis as beyond the pale. There was also the more intellectual variety provided by Sufis such as Ibn Al-'Arabi, a famous Spanish mystic who ended up in Damascus, who had a famous disciple, Sadr al-Din al-Qunawi, who was a very close friend of Rumi as well.

LLOYD RIDGEON: *Rumi occupies a stable middle ground, in the respect that he's not intellectual, he's not wild or untrammelled. He represents a form of Sufism that does emphasise that degree of mysticism whereby people can really understand what God is all about, become near to God.*

381

Carole Hillenbrand turned to the poetry, starting with the *Divan*, an enormous work of some 3,500 poems or more, with lyrical poems called ghazals, as well as quatrains and odes. Most of the time, the poems are about love, the passionate yearning both for God and also for a human beloved, and many are written in the first-person singular.

CAROLE HILLENBRAND: *There's a wonderful line in the* Divan: *'We were once in heaven, we were friends of the angels, let us all return there, that is our city.' In other words, there's yearning to be re-joined to where we were in eternity before we were born. It's an echo of the Qur'an, which says, 'We belong to God and to God we are returning,' and, in the meantime, the human soul is yearning to be reunited.*

The poems are quite short, Alan Williams said, like sonnets, about fifteen to twenty lines, and they seem to have been composed almost by improvisation, experimenting with some fifty-five different meters across the collection. He read first from the original Persian, before giving his own translation of one of the most famous lines of the *Divan*, using a meter similar to the original.

ALAN WILLIAMS:

> *Dead was I then*
> *I came to life*
> *Weeping I then*
> *Started to laugh*
> *The kingdom of love came*
> *I became kingdom of perpetual love*

This then goes on for another twenty verses, that's one single verse I've just quoted. They're quite long by English sonnet standards, but they're very discrete, each one of them is like a jewel of many facets to contemplate.

There is great variety in the imagery among the complex set of ideas, and they are flashed through with brilliant insights.

CAROLE HILLENBRAND: *They come like comets from outside in the darkness and shed light on us. Or, alternatively, like fireworks that spread sparks in wide directions or, indeed, sometimes the inspiration coming from the imagery is like an electric current, sometimes on and sometimes off. But all these images have an incredibly powerful effect on the listener. And the listener is the word, because they're musical as well.*

The *Masnavi* is Rumi's second masterwork. There is a distinction between his two major works, Lloyd Ridgeon said, the *Masnavi* and the *Dīwān-e Shams*, in that the *Masnavi* is didactic, teaching the specifics of what the dervish would do, what the Sufis were doing, whereas the *Dīwān-e Shams* is very different and has Rumi's own personal experiences.

LLOYD RIDGEON: *When you read the* Divan, *you can actually get to understand what Rumi personally is experiencing in terms of his separation from Shams, in terms of his love for Shams, and so forth. In the* Masnavi, *you get very short stories and sometimes they're short and then he digresses and comes back to that short story again; it's something that really hooks the reader.*

One of the themes in Rumi's work is mercy, one of the predominant features of Sufism, and it is expressed in the very first line of the *Dīwān-e Shams*, which Lloyd Ridgeon translated as 'sudden resurrection, endless mercy'. It is an idea of mercy, fed into an ecumenical perspective in Rumi. He engaged both men and women, which may help explain why Sufism was popular in the medieval period, and he touched on experiences that related to Muslims, Christians, Jews and Zoroastrians.

MELVYN BRAGG: *He converted, we are told, (besides Muslims) Christians and Jews as well?*

LLOYD RIDGEON: *Well, that's what we're told by the hagiographies, now whether that's true or not is another question. But it's certainly possible to read those kinds of stories into the* Masnavi. *There's a very famous story about Rumi and the blind men, when, of course, the blind men go into the room and each touches a part of the elephant, one person touches the tail, one person touches the elephant's ear, another the leg, and they all have an aspect of the truth.*

Carole Hillenbrand mentioned another line attributed to Rumi, which suggested he was respectful of all faiths: 'I am not a worshipper of the cross or the crescent / I am not a Zoroastrian or a Jew.' While not found in Rumi's original works, this captured the spirit of what he was saying and, 'as Voltaire would say, if it didn't exist, then it ought to have done'.

The ghazals of the *Divan* can be translated beautifully into rhythmic verses, but the *Masnavi* is much more demanding. Persian has no indefinite or definite article that is separate from the word and no pronouns that are commonly used, so trying to cram the syllables into an iambic line, Alan Williams said, was like fitting a quart in a pint pot. The *Masnavi* is written more fully as *Masnavi-i Ma'navi*, which Alan Williams told us meant the spiritual *Masnavi* or the *Masnavi* of meaning, the couplets of meaning. The text is vast and contains over 200 stories.

ALAN WILLIAMS: *Sometimes they're extremely short, I mean two lines, and they can be in the mouths of animals, birds, flies even, people, of course, heroes from scripture, and so on, but all of these stories are just the husk, as Rumi calls it, they're the husk because what he's trying to get to is the meaning. And so the* Masnavi *is an ocean of meaning, and reading it is like being drowned, it's like being plunged into a vast ocean.*

All of the images are ways to give the imagination food for thought. Alan Williams read the first of the thirty-five lines of 'The Song of the Reed', in Persian, and then gave his own translation.

Rumi's followers founded the Mevlevi
Order of Sufis, known outside Turkey
for their whirling dervishes.

ALAN WILLIAMS:

> Listen to this reed as it is grieving;
> It's telling of the tale of separations.
> 'Since I was severed from the bed of reeds,
> In my cry men and women have lamented.
> I need the breast that's torn to shreds by parting
> To give expression to the pain of heartache.
> Whoever finds himself left far from home
> Looks forward to the day of his reunion.'

One of the most engaging things about Rumi's poetry in the *Masnavi*,
according to Lloyd Ridgeon, and his storytelling is that he used very
simple language that everyone could understand. In Tehran today,
people would be able to recite his poetry and find it comprehensible,
whereas in the UK, Melvyn noted, 'we can't recite Chaucer back to
each other'.

One of these *Masnavi* stories, Alan Williams continued, looks like a romance when it starts, but it turns very dark. A king falls in love with a slave girl, only for her to fall sick and for him to discover that this is love sickness; she was already in love with someone else, a goldsmith far away in Samarkand.

ALAN WILLIAMS: *He then hauls this goldsmith all the way back to, presumably, Konya and poisons him, he poisons him slowly, so he turns ugly, the girl falls out of love with her lover and she dies. The whole thing ends badly but, in the meantime, there has been a divine messenger who comes down from heaven and tells the king what's really wrong with the slave girl. And the king has fallen in love with the divine messenger because he knows that his love for the slave girl was just a love of form.*

One of Lloyd Ridgeon's favourite stories in the *Masnavi* is about Moses and the shepherd. The shepherd is making a prayer to God, saying, 'Oh, God, I'll do anything for you, I'll give you some milk, I'll give you shoes.' Moses, as a theologian, castigates him because he believes that he should not be using such inappropriate language, and the shepherd has to go away and feels downcast. God then chastises Moses for using such language to a poor shepherd, who was praising God in the way that he saw best.

LLOYD RIDGEON: *What's most interesting about Rumi, of course, are his images. In his works, he talks, for example, about the 'effervescence of the chickpea bubbling away in the water', which is a metaphor for the individual and the experience of God. And it's these kinds of images that make Rumi's message really get across.*

While Rumi was writing, he was surrounded by political turmoil. He had travelled thousands of miles from the eastern extremity of the Islamic world, Carole Hillenbrand said, from Afghanistan to the western extremity, thinking that he was escaping from the Mongols. He was in exile, which added a dimension to his 'Reed' stories, severed from his original home. Then the Mongols came to Konya quite early on, in 1243, and they took over.

CAROLE HILLENBRAND: *Yet Rumi manages to evoke admiration in the Mongol protector, who is Persian. And apparently Rumi was very much welcomed by the Mongol agent and even did spiritual concerts in this man's house. It's a really difficult time for the whole of the Muslim world, dreadful bloodshed, demographic movements and so on. It's just the worst possible thing to have happened, and yet he produces this sublime work.*

The kind of poetry that Rumi was writing in the *Masnavi* was on an altogether different scale from the ghazal. He took on the voices of many different registers in the poem, Alan Williams said, speaking as the author, the sheik, a grandfather, the old man, telling stories as though talking to a child, interrupting himself with analogies that are quite intellectual. He segues from speeches into discourses that become quite mystical or become moral discourses.

ALAN WILLIAMS: *Then they turn into ecstasies. And then he stops the whole proceedings and says, 'Silence.' And there's a behaviour, a procedure that the reader becomes used to, almost as if learning the ropes of how to swim in this ocean. And it's really an experience of going through the stages of mystical elevation. The reader himself, herself, feels raised up inside, raised up in the imagination. It's a cathartic experience reading it, an uplifting experience reading it.*

It can be difficult to assess how popular Rumi was in his own lifetime. There was a history written at the time by an individual called Ibn Bibi, Lloyd Ridgeon said, and he did not mention Rumi at all in this history of Seljuqs in Konya. In the generation after his death, there were aspects of veneration of Rumi and there were hagiographies written about him. Rumi's son, Sultân Walad, composed poetry about the *Masnavi*.

LLOYD RIDGEON: *Other Sufi orders are composing their own commentaries on the 'Song of the Reed'. And, by the sixteenth century, we have a very famous Persian poet called Jami who says that, although [Rumi] was not a prophet, he had a book, i.e. he's comparing the* Masnavi *to the Qur'an – that's an incredible compliment to Rumi.*

Rumi is extremely popular still in the former Persian Empire, the countries ending in 'stan', as Carole Hillenbrand put it, and in Turkey as well as Iran. There is a wide Iranian diaspora sharing his work, with 250,000 Iranians living in Los Angeles alone. There has been a 'Rumi boom' in the modern age, Lloyd Ridgeon noted, where everyone wanted 'a piece of Rumi'.

LLOYD RIDGEON: *Even massive popstars: like Bob Dylan released an album of Christmas carols in 2009 and he did a video to 'The Little Drummer Boy' and, halfway through the video, you get images of whirling dervishes. We also have Madonna reciting poetry from Rumi. Philip Glass has been involved in a massive project related to Rumi. And it's all part of this huge project, which has perhaps been spearheaded by people like Coleman Barks and Robert Bly. It just goes on and on and on.*

TITUS OATES AND HIS 'POPISH PLOT'

In 1678, Titus Oates claimed he had discovered a Catholic conspiracy to shoot Charles II. He knew all the details, as he had invented every one of them himself; it was one of the great works of historical fiction. For three years, his fabricated 'Popish Plot' inflamed fears that there were secret Catholics in power, conspiring to return England to Catholicism under the king's brother James, Duke of York. Soon Charles banned Catholics from London; crowds paraded, burning effigies of the pope through the city; vigilantes hunted for signs of supposed sympathisers, throwing them in prison. There were executions of innocent priests, lords, even archbishops, and Titus Oates basked in the adulation of a grateful public. Though he was eventually caught out, the fear of plots and of the mob left a deep mark on politics and religious tolerance for decades.

⊰——◆——⊱

With Melvyn to discuss Titus Oates and his 'Popish Plot' were: Clare Jackson, senior tutor and director of studies in history at Trinity Hall, Cambridge; Mark Knights, professor of history at the University of Warwick; and Peter Hinds, associate professor of English at the University of Plymouth.

Titus Oates in the pillory.

In Great Britain in the 1670s, there was a perception among the Protestant majority that Catholics, in general, were a problem. There was a distinction, though, between those perceptions and the experiences that Protestants had of Catholics they knew.

CLARE JACKSON: *The day-to-day reality is that Catholics are a very small minority, the underground nature of Catholic devotion makes it quite difficult to know exactly how many, but maybe 60,000 out of a population of 5–5.5 million. So just over 1 per cent or, even in a densely cosmopolitan city like London, not more than 2 per cent, but disproportionately perceived to be a much greater threat than that.*

There was a whole edifice of penal laws, dating back to the Elizabethan and Jacobean periods, that made attendance at Church of England services on a weekly basis compulsory for all adult men and women, with an obligation to take communion at least three times a year. Some of the penalties for recusancy would be standing fines of £20 a month, which may equate to £2,000 a month in today's terms, so really quite ruinous. For all that, most Catholics aimed to observe their faith unobtrusively and, when it came to people in their locality, neighbours and friends, Protestants might be much more nervous about reporting on Catholics who would then face financial ruin.

History cast a very long shadow over this period, Clare Jackson continued. In the Elizabethan period, there had been conspiracies associated with Mary, Queen of Scots, and there was the threat of the Spanish Armada, then there was the Gunpowder Plot under King James and then the Irish Rebellion of 1641, which was aimed at annihilating Protestants in Ireland.

CLARE JACKSON: *One of the themes that we hear in the Popish Plot is '41 is come again'. Also, geographically, Protestantism is not doing that well at this stage in European geopolitics, it's been consigned to the northern peripheries. The big European superpowers, France and Spain, are Catholic, and Protestantism is flourishing, but very much on the fringes of Holland, northern Germany, Scandinavia, Scotland and England. But there's always Ireland out to the west.*

This fear of potential encirclement, geographically, together with a history of popish plots was a toxic mix. Added to this was a fear of post-Reformation orders like the Society of Jesus, the Jesuits, who had international finance and backing for their mission to bring England back into the fold of the Catholic Church and would loom larger in popular imagination than the quiet majority of Catholics.

There was also suspicion of Charles II from before his Restoration in 1660, when he had been courting the favour of Catholic powers to regain his throne. Once restored, Mark Knights said, Charles sought to moderate the rather punitive religious settlement that parliament wanted to impose on Catholics and on Protestant dissenters, and that created a lot of suspicion about his real intentions.

MARK KNIGHTS: *Coupled to that was the fact that his brother James, Duke of York, had also shown evidence of his distancing from the Church of England and embracing the Catholic faith. Charles's problem really was about perceptions of Catholicism at court. And those are also exacerbated by the fact that, from 1670, his mistress, the Duchess of Portsmouth, was both Catholic and French and therefore personified the two fears that Englishmen at the time had about the threat from popery.*

In 1672, England went to war against the Dutch, the only other major Protestant power in Europe at the time, in alliance with Catholic France. That was one of the big turning points in popular opinion.

MARK KNIGHTS: *Why was the king taking Protestant England to war against Protestant Holland in alliance with Catholic France? And that, retrospectively, seems a turning point; Edward Dering, for example, who keeps a diary in this period, records in 1681 that that's one of the major points in this anxiety about 'the growth of popery and arbitrary government', as Andrew Marvell was to put it.*

Titus Oates was something of a rogue, with a history of disappointment and humiliation. That was how Peter Hinds began to describe him, and those were some of his better qualities. He was born in 1649, the son of a Baptist preacher, and his life went from bad to worse.

PETER HINDS: *He was sent to a couple of schools and he was expelled, usually for reasons to do with money; he got into disputes about money. He went up to Cambridge, he was sent to Gonville & Caius College. He was transferred to St John's College and then he was kicked out of Cambridge, again over a dispute about money, so he left Cambridge without a degree.*

MELVYN BRAGG: *He wouldn't pay for a coat that somebody had made for him.*

PETER HINDS: *Exactly, a dispute over a bill with a tailor.*

By 1670, Titus Oates managed to get a licence to preach and took holy orders. In 1673, he found a living in the village of Bobbing in Kent, but this went badly and his parishioners accused him of drunkenness, lewd behaviour, unorthodox views, blasphemous views, even and stealing. He was dismissed from this living and became a curate in Hastings for a while, where his father had a living.

PETER HINDS: *At this moment, he did something very extraordinary, which has resonances later (it seems like a prefabricated scheme to get himself a job in a school). He accuses a schoolmaster of sodomy with a pupil, which is a total fabrication, and this is discovered and he's bound over pending trial. But he flees to London. It's a catalogue of disgrace really that's emerging.*

MELVYN BRAGG: *And then he becomes a naval chaplain and gets chucked out of there for sodomy.*

Then, in 1677, he converted to Catholicism. When first asked about this, he claimed that he did it to go undercover, to discover a plot, putting his body and soul in danger for king and country. Later, he changed that story and said that it was a genuine conversion, claiming he 'was seduced by the popish sirens into a belief'. He had been taken under the wing of Father Richard Strange, the head of the Jesuit order in England, for reasons that were unclear, perhaps as Strange wanted to save a soul. He sent him off to an English college in Spain and, when Oates left there in disgrace, Father Strange had faith in him again and sent him off to Saint-Omer in northern France, but again he left there in disgrace and returned to England, where he was to meet Israel Tonge.

Tonge, born 1621, was in his late fifties, while Oates was in his late twenties. Tonge, Clare Jackson said, was an academic with various degrees and a life of serial disappointments and failures that had engendered a seething resentment.

CLARE JACKSON: *He's elected a fellow of a college in the 1650s, the short-lived Cromwellian college in Durham, but then it closes. He's an Anglican chaplain to a garrison in Dunkirk, but then it's sold to the French. But then, worst of all, he's given a really ambitious opportunity to take a living in the city of London, St Mary Staining, in June 1666, but, less than three months later, there's the Great Fire of London and his whole church and parish go up in flames.*

MELVN BRAGG: *And he blames the Catholics.*

CLARE JACKSON: *And he blames the Catholics, as many people did. And it seems to breed in him a persecution complex, a belief that this Popish Plot is out there.*

Somehow, while in conversation with Oates, Tonge expressed his belief in a plot, and Oates saw an opportunity to make money from Tonge. Oates flattered him and even claimed that the Jesuits had offered him £50 to assassinate Tonge for some of his (apparently unread) anti-Jesuitical writings. They decided to work together to expose the plot Tonge believed existed for which Oates could fabricate as much proof as anyone might need.

PETER HINDS: *Oates was destitute, in poverty, he was in London and he needed to take up with somebody. He'd met Israel Tonge briefly before and he falls back on his company because here's some access back into London society. And he strings Tonge along. He claims he's still undercover as an informer on the Jesuits, and Tonge buys this story completely. There's not a close alliance between the two of them, he's using Tonge.*

Oates embellished his evidence over a long period of time. Initially, Mark Knights said, the core of it was that there was a Jesuit plot to reconvert England forcibly to Catholicism, which involved assassinating Charles II (the 'black bastard', as the Jesuits called him).

MARK KNIGHTS: *Oates revealed quite graphic details about how this was to be accomplished, named individuals who were alleged to have attempted to shoot the king, their locks on their muskets jamming at the crucial moment, or Jesuits being sent with foot-long daggers, which were 6 inches wide, to plunge into the king.*

Titus Oates tells Charles II of the Popish Plot, from a playing card designed by the English painter and engraver William Faithorne in 1684.

Oates peppered his plots with snippets of detail that were hard to assess quickly. He said, for example, that, on 24 April 1678, there was a big council of all the Jesuits in London, fifty of them, who were all in this plot. It had a ring of credibility about it and he had a fantastic memory about all the inventions that he had made, and he was very bullish about them all.

Somehow, his stories gained traction. The details seemed to make his story more credible, such as when he 'revealed' a silver bullet was to be used to shoot Charles.

PETER HINDS: *Oates accuses John Grove and Thomas Pickering of attempting to assassinate the king in St James's Park on his regular walk by shooting him, but this has failed on a number of occasions. The flint was loose in the rifle, the gunpowder was wet. Lots of lurid details, like they chose to chew the bullets to make them jagged in order that they'd do more damage and make it more possible to kill Charles II. It's not simply a plot that is going to happen. Here is a plot that's ongoing, we've been damn lucky that Charles isn't dead already, because people are trying to assassinate him right now.*

Oates made lots of grander but vaguer claims about invasion forces and rebellion, supposedly revealed to him by his contacts at Jesuit seminaries. Apparently 20,000 Scots were prepared to rise in rebellion, joined by 20,000 infantry men and 5,000 cavalry ready to rise in Ireland. France was ready to provide troops and arms and ship them over to Ireland, bolstering the idea of Catholic encirclement.

Then, in 1678, there was a major development that was taken as corroboration of mischief. Oates had twice given sworn depositions of the truth of his claims and, about two weeks later, the magistrate who had heard his evidence was found dead. This was Sir Edmund Berry Godfrey, often described as quite a querulous individual, who took his responsibilities as a magistrate very seriously when suppressing vice.

CLARE JACKSON: *He disappears out on Saturday 12 October and then, on Thursday 17 October, his body is discovered in a ditch near Primrose Hill. Later, it's shown that there are strangulation marks around his neck and his own sword has been very viciously driven through him, emerging out his back. This is the event, the catalyst, that electrifies or transforms what's been a lingering alarm and anxiety and perhaps scepticism into (for those who were looking for it) concrete evidence that there must be a plot out there.*

If people believed that Sir Edmund Berry Godfrey had been murdered by papists, then they believed it was because he knew too much and that there were bloodthirsty Jesuits at large, and it would only be a matter of time before somebody else was killed.

The success of Oates's stories was not inevitable. The disbelievers initially included the king as, when Oates was initially revealing his information, he gave some details that Charles II knew to be false.

MARK KNIGHTS: *Charles was listening to all this so, at one point, Titus Oates describes Don John of Austria, who he claimed to have met, as a tall, fair man, and Charles II knew him as a short, dark man. There were some clear problems with some of the evidence. But it's not really until, I think, the summer of 1679, some time after these initial revelations, that real scepticism starts to kick in. And that's largely because Oates and his cronies pushed the story too far.*

Oates made an accusation that Charles's queen, Catherine of Braganza, had been involved in the plot and had paid her physician, Wakeman, to poison the king. The presiding judge, Sir William Scroggs, went out of his way to question Oates's evidence because there was a lot riding on this case. If Wakeman were convicted, then the queen would be implicated, which would have led to a crisis. Scroggs steered a very neat path between trying to expose the faults of Oates's testimony and maintaining a belief in the plot as a whole. Wakeman got off, but others were far less fortunate.

With Berry Godfrey's death, a new range of informers claimed to be able to solve this mystery and introduce other evidence against different people. There was a huge amount of money available from secret service funds for informers.

CLARE JACKSON: *There's a whole cast of people who begin to enter. It's also coincidental that, a few days after Berry Godfrey's body is found, parliament meets and immediately sets up its own enquiry. What was really quite a limited knowledge of this plot, and Oates's claims, suddenly becomes much wider.*

Then the court of public opinion decided that somebody needed to be found guilty. And, although Wakeman was acquitted, lesser people on the political scale were convicted on the testimony of these informers, particularly in relation to Berry Godfrey's death.

CLARE JACKSON: *And the other interesting thing, culturally, is the extent to which Berry Godfrey becomes this Protestant martyr very quickly for the whole plot. And that's the point also at which disbelief in the plot almost becomes, as people describe it, its own form of heresy, that the minute you start saying, 'I'm not so sure about this,' then there's a heresy going on.*

The lack of evidence did not seem to matter, Melvyn observed, the frenzy had its own head of steam and, if someone disbelieved, that proved something was being concealed and the heretic's house would be searched and wrecked.

CLARE JACKSON: *In the end, there're probably about twenty-three individuals executed directly related to the plot, and then about another seven die in prison. Scroggs does explain the sheer seriousness of what is going on, at the very first trial of Edward Coleman, and says to Oates, 'To take away a man's life on a false oath is murder,' and that's precisely why perjury punishments are so vicious. But, whenever a great event happens, there's enormous pressure on the authorities to find those responsible and bring them to justice.*

Berry Godfrey appeared on medals, on playing cards and in processions, and his death became central to the plot's credibility. The processions themselves played a part in maintaining the mood.

MELVYN BRAGG: *We had the popish marches with the effigy of the pope. At one stage, the effigy was filled with live cats, so, when they burned him, the cats squealed, and that was supposed to be the pope in hell, is that right?*

PETER HINDS: *That's right. There must have been some serious financial support for these processions. They happen on 17 November, the accession day of Queen Elizabeth, the Protestant queen, people clambering to get the best positions. There were places being sold near Temple Bar, where this effigy of the pope was tipped into the fire. The window places were being sold for vast sums of money.*

Amid the frenzy, Oates found time to put out a very expensively produced book, *The True Narrative of the Horrid Plot*.

There were politicians for whom the plot was useful, whether true or false. There were forces in parliament who wanted to bring down two big beasts, Mark Knights said. The first was Charles II's prime minister, the Earl of Danby, who was impeached and had a formal parliamentary trial process. The bigger target was James, Duke of York, the king's brother, because he was the heir to the throne as the king had no children.

MARK KNIGHTS: *The king had no legitimate children anyway. And many MPs in parliament were petrified of the prospect of a popish successor, to use the language of the day. And they used the Popish Plot as a way of bringing the succession issue into parliament and to bring in legislation that would exclude James from the succession.*

With the mood of panic and hysteria becoming all the more acute, James was increasingly vulnerable. People had been talking about the possibility that Charles could be induced to divorce his Catholic queen and marry a Protestant, Clare Jackson said, or that he might retrospectively legitimise his eldest illegitimate son, the Duke of Monmouth, or that limitations might be placed on James and a regent put in place. Now there was an air of urgency to this talk.

CLARE JACKSON: *If Charles really is liable to be assassinated in the park any day, we don't have time to wait for him to get divorced and marry someone else and have children. It does place James and his position under the spotlight, and there's a lot of debate in parliament about whether the restrictions on Catholics, that they should be placed in an exclusion zone 20 miles around London, should apply to James as well.*

There were those advising Charles to keep James near, and not send him into the arms of people like Louis XIV. Eventually, Charles decided to banish James, first to Brussels and The Hague and then to Scotland, as well as to banish his eldest illegitimate son, the Duke of Monmouth.

CLARE JACKSON: *Monmouth becomes the Protestant saviour to the question of the succession. If only it could be found that, really, Charles had married Monmouth's mother, Lucy Walter. And just as there's the people's readiness to believe in Titus Oates's plot, you can see the desire of people to believe in a black box that would show that Charles and Lucy had been married. And it's Charles who comes out and says publicly, many times, 'I've only ever been married to Queen Catherine. This isn't going to work.'*

Gradually, after all the executions, the energy behind the idea of the plot started to peter out. The more unsavoury the characters who were drawn in, the less credible the evidence became. And, as Melvyn pointed out, the king was *not* assassinated. It was not until 1684 that the wheels really came off for Titus Oates, when James, Duke of York, took an action against Oates for having been called a traitor by him, and a huge fine of £100,000 was imposed on Oates and he was sent to prison.

Mark Knights: *There are two further trials later in 1684 for perjury. And Oates is put in the pillory, lots of stuff thrown at him, he's whipped through London on two occasions, he says his back has got thousands of lashes on it, and he's slung into prison, where he languishes for the entire reign of James II from 1685 to 1688. Come the [Glorious] Revolution of 1688, with the invasion of William, the displacement of James, Oates is released from prison, he's rehabilitated a little bit, he's given back a small pension, he re-enters the limelight, but he never quite recaptures his earlier glory.*

But he did live until 1727, Melvyn observed, which was not a bad life.

In the studio afterwards, there was discussion of Ireland being the dog that didn't bark in the panic, for all Oates's suggesting that it would. Clare Jackson mentioned one of Oates's strokes of luck, when letters were found relating to Edward Coleman, the former secretary to the Duchess of York, Richard's wife. They did contain damaging details, although, as Coleman said, they were not treasonable. Peter Hinds drew attention to the mood on the streets of London, as people would have noticed the doubling of the militia, the tightening of security around Whitehall and Westminster, the searches and arrests and calls for information. Besides that, Mark Knights added, the government lost control of the press at this time, which led to an enormous explosion in the amount of printed propaganda that was available on the streets, and this fed the public appetite for news about the plot and stimulated it. Even Samuel Pepys was caught up in the frenzy. Clare Jackson noted that he wound up in prison for six weeks, largely for being too close to James, Duke of York, while at the admiralty, and it was harrowing for Pepys as he faced capital charges.

ZOROASTRIANISM

*'Now have I seen him with my own eyes, knowing him in truth to
be the wise lord of the good mind and of good deeds and words.'
Thus spake the real Zarathustra, the prophet and founder of the
ancient religion of Zoroastrianism. It has claims, though these are
contentious in some people's eyes, to be the world's first ethical
monotheistic creed. And, perhaps as long ago as 1200 BC, Zarathustra
also said, 'I point out the way, it is the truth, it is for all living.' Truth
is the central tenet of the religion that holds that people must, above
all, do good things, hear good things and see good things. How was
the religion so powerfully established in the influential civilisations
of ancient Persia, what is its body of beliefs and how have they been
developed and disseminated?*

⊹•⊹

With Melvyn to discuss the history and philosophies of
Zoroastrianism were: the late Farrokh Vajifdar, fellow of the Royal
Asiatic Society and a lifelong student of Zoroastrianism; Alan
Williams, Leverhulme Trust research professor at the University of
Manchester; and Vesta Sarkhosh Curtis, curator of Middle Eastern
coins at the British Museum.

Zarathustra probably lived around 1200–1000 BC, Vesta Sarkhosh
Curtis began, although certain scholars date him much later.

He is also known as Zoroaster. He came from a priestly background somewhere in the north of central Asia, north-east of the Caspian Sea. His father's name was Pourušaspa and his mother's name was Dugdōw. It is said, in later texts, that, when he was conceived by his mother, an enormous light shone around her, a sign of divine glory, and that he was born smiling and talking. The Avesta, the holy book of the Zoroastrians, tells that he was a high priest.

VESTA SARKHOSH CURTIS: *He had several revelations during his life, but his first revelation came to him at the age of about thirty, when he was taking part in a special ceremony (and these again are later descriptions) and he went down to the river to cleanse himself, and, when he came back, he was carried by light to a certain place and this was when he saw Ahura Mazda, or the Wise Lord. And it was then that he decided to follow the path of righteousness and also to teach the truth to people.*

The many deities that Zarathustra had been brought up with, Melvyn suggested, tended to be very muscly and seeking victory, so the replacement by one god, Ahura Mazda, the Wise Lord, was a radical step. It was also a very dangerous thing for him to do.

VESTA SARKHOSH CURTIS: *There was an awful lot of opposition to him. A lot of the priests, the magi, were very much against his reforms, and his ideas were not welcome. The other problem was that, in his teachings, he saw people as equals; he did not see, for example, a difference between rich people and poor people, and everybody on the last day of judgement came to salvation. This was a very new idea.*

The legends say Zarathustra enjoyed the support of the king of the time, Vishtaspa, who then agreed to accept this good religion and introduce it at his court.

The precedents for his religious or spiritual teachings were already to hand in the Rigveda, Farrokh Vajifdar continued, except Zarathustra reduced to the rank of demons or *daevas* many of the gods whom the Indians had elevated to *devas*, the shining ones.

FARROKH VAJIFDAR: *He kept two, at least, behind – one was Mithra and the other was Varuna. Varuna was the creator god, the king of the gods; Mithra was the enforcer of the solemnly given word, the contract, also the god therefore of friendship. Zarathustra incorporated these functions into this new Ahura, the sole Ahura called Mazda, which, as you quite rightly say, means wisdom. And that is the essence of Mazda.*

The idea was that wisdom was everywhere, if only followers could seek it, reach for it and use it. He could have easily said 'all powerful, all seeing', Farrokh Vajifdar added, which Zarathustra conveyed in his Gathas, the sixteen or seventeen hymns in the Avesta that were his own compositions. There was no conflict between the material and the mental or spiritual worlds, described as two opposite poles of a unitary whole, where man is a product of the physical form and the spirit.

This relationship between the material and the spiritual is a complex one for westerners to understand, Alan Williams said, as they have a theological background in western monotheism. Ahura Mazda is the figurehead, the focus, but surrounded by a pantheon of six other spiritual beings, or entities in some sense.

ALAN WILLIAMS: *If you're a monotheist, you think of these as aspects of God. But, in fact, they work with God, they collaborate. One of them, a very important one, is the idea of Kshatra Vairya, which means the best governance. This is symbolised by the sky, each of these divine beings has a physical correspondent. The sky looks after the earth, which is the next Amesha Spenta, or blessed immortal. And the Spenta Ārmaiti is the earth and represents holy piety, translated as 'benevolent piety'.*

Water is spiritualised in the concept of Haurvatāt, which means perfection or wholeness. The next divine being is represented in plant life as Ameretat, immortality. The next very important divine being in this heptad, or group of immortal beings, is the good mind, Vohu Manah, represented by the beneficent animal that is tended by mankind. Humanity itself is the representative of God, Ahura Mazda; the Wise Lord is also known as the Spenta Mainyu, the most holy spirit, and it is man who is the physical embodiment of that most holy spirit. Lastly, there is the notion of supreme truth, Asha Vahishta, embodied in the physical creation of fire, which is a very important religious symbol of Zoroastrianism. These are the realities through which mankind could approach God, embodiments in the physical universe. Ahura Mazda is known primarily as the creator: he created the universe in order to contain the evil spirit and to defeat him ultimately so the world has a purpose.

ALAN WILLIAMS: *This is very difficult to understand, but I can make it clear in this way. This is not ditheism, this is not two gods. Plutarch understood this in first century BC very clearly and he says, the 'Zoroastrians have one god and one demon.' And this is how Zarathustra understood the universe, that there were two spirits or two wills and that they're in conflict with one another. These are not two beings, not two gods, but one monotheistic god and one force of total negativity, which is resisted by man on earth.*

As Zoroastrianism developed, it became more complicated, Melvyn suggested, and, as it was adopted by leaders with military ambitions, it may have become corrupted. That was the way it unfolded in history.

FARROKH VAJIFDAR: *Alan has mentioned Plutarch, for example; Plutarch, for goodness sake, was situated well in the west. He may have visited Persia, I'm not sure, but the religion originated in the east in a society of pastoralists. The military aspects of the religion were really minimised. In other words, [Zarathustra] used force only to counteract deceit and certainly in self-defence. But there is no militarism involved in it.*

Returning to the compelling nature of Zarathustra's revelation, Alan Williams preferred to call it a reformation, as Zarathustra was reacting and he was a radical reformer. Zarathustra's real contribution was that he introduced the idea of an ethical and a soteriological plan, an eschatological plan.

ALAN WILLIAMS: *That's a long word that simply means a whole line of history that ends in a judgement, a judgement that, he explains, is in terms of our own choice. And it's this idea that we build our own destiny by making choices for good or choices for evil, in following the good spirit or the evil spirit, and there is a soteriology here, which is extremely attractive, that we can actually build our future and that we'll be judged on that. And then there's the promise of heaven or paradise or hell, damnation.*

By the time Zoroastrianism became a state religion, Vesta Sarkhosh Curtis continued, the Persian or Iranian tribes had moved into the highlands of Iran. By the time of the first Persian Empire under Cyrus the Great, the Persians were well established in what we call now Iran. Depending on the dates for Zoroaster's life, that would allow perhaps 400 or 500 years for the religion to develop before Cyrus the Great.

VESTA SARKHOSH CURTIS: *We think that the Achaemenids, the ancient Persians, were Zoroastrians. They do not mention Zarathustra in their inscription, but that is neither here nor there – they don't need to mention the name of the prophet. They certainly mention again and again Ahura Mazda. All the inscriptions open, 'By the wish of Ahura Mazda ... '*

The Persians found in Zoroastrianism a religion that was a friend of the person who told the truth and an enemy of the person who told a lie. This was said again and again by Darius in his Behistun Inscription, created in his reign at some point between 522 and 486 BC.

VESTA SARKHOSH CURTIS: *They follow the righteous path, they introduce a religion that is good. Also, if you look at the figure of Cyrus the Great, he followed a religion that also enabled other people to follow freedom. The Jews were allowed to go back to their homeland and take their cult statues with them. It was a very open religion.*

If someone went to a Zoroastrian temple, they would have seen fire; Zarathustra introduced the worship of fire as a symbol, where the spiritual fire is strengthened through truth. According to Herodotus, the Persians initially had no fire temples.

FARROKH VAJIFDAR: *The magus, who was a freelance priest, not necessarily a Zoroastrian at the time, would (presumably for a consideration) pray to any god of your choice. And later, when they embraced Zoroastrianism, then, of course, they took over [the practices] in a big way, and we're very grateful to them because they were the ones responsible for the faithful transmission of Zarathustra's words.*

Regarding the practices around fire, there was always ritual purity within the person as well, within the worshipper and the priest. The priest had to isolate himself at such times through a very complex ritual.

FARROKH VAJIFDAR: *In a fire temple, the fire is maintained by priests in the sanctum sanctorum. The worshippers can view it from outside; they say their own prayers in conformity with set prayers, which had been taught to them since childhood. There is no congregational worship in that sense, you do your own thing and pray to whichever aspect of the divinity you wish for.*

In the highest grade temples, the fire burned permanently, constantly maintained by priests who wore a veil over their mouths so that they would not pollute the idea of fire, which had to be kept free of anything extraneous to the wood itself.

The funeral ceremonies were also distinctive and arose out of the problem of what to do with a body when it was no longer animated, no longer alive.

ALAN WILLIAMS: *In Zoroastrian terms, the body, when the person is alive, is a sacred thing; as we say, the body's a temple. It's not considered to be something filthy or something to be spurned. But when the spirit leaves the body, then the body itself is shed like a shell.*

The spirit as it comes out of the body is the person, and this was another of Zarathustra's insights – that the soul lives on and therefore the soul is judged on the life it has led. The problem remained of what to do with a dead body.

ALAN WILLIAMS: *On the central Asian steppes, in the Iranian desert and, even to this day, in the city of Mumbai, Zoroastrians have to confront the problem of what to do with a corpse. And so we have the idea of the Tower of Silence, which is a form that's crystallised out of the idea of putting a body on top of a hill and allowing wild animals to dispose of it. This sounds unhygienic to modern western ears but, in fact, it's a relatively hygienic way of disposing of the dead.*

FARROKH VAJIFDAR: *If I may interrupt, not wild animals, I must stress this – these have to be raptors because the bodies are exposed on open towers, animals cannot get in, not wild dogs nor wolves.*

ALAN WILLIAMS: *You're absolutely right to correct me on that and the modern practice. But in ancient times …*

FARROKH VAJIFDAR: *Then the body was actually weighted down so the wild creatures could not drag it to a nearby stream or on to arable land. This was one of the reasons, in fact, we had Towers of Silence.*

The principle of this, Alan Williams said, was that the body should not pollute the earth, it should be raised above the earth, it should not pollute the waters and, above all, it should be distinct from the way that Indians disposed of the dead – for example, the cremation of the corpse was totally forbidden because it would pollute the fire.

Much of the ideas of Zoroastrianism were, for a long period, transmitted orally rather than written down, a tradition that may be alien in the west but still exists in countries like Iran, for example, and many parts of the Middle East, where people learn to recite stories and poetry, again and again, and keep oral traditions alive.

VESTA SARKHOSH CURTIS: *We know that it was very important, according to later texts, to recite the Avesta in the original language. This is the holy book of the Zoroastrian, which is the words of the prophet himself. It was very important for these priests to preserve this tradition and they also recited these prayers in the original language, which is exactly like the language of the Gathas and Zoroaster.*

Crucially, added Alan Williams, in ancient oral cultures, orality was accompanied by ritual action; every word of the Yasna, the sacred liturgy of the Zoroastrian rite, was accompanied by sacramental actions.

As for why the Gathas and the Yasna were committed to writing, Farrokh Vajifdar suggested that those who transcribed them were losing touch with the original language and they had to fix it down.

FARROKH VAJIFDAR: *Also, there is a question of why this alphabet was invented, based on an earlier consonantal alphabet, and the answer must be (this is conjecture perhaps) [that] the religion came from the east, where the pronunciation of the original Gathic words was rather different to the south-west, where it emigrated as a state religion. Before they lost touch, they felt they had to commit this to writing. And this is around about the sixth century perhaps.*

Turning to the influence of Zoroastrianism, Farrokh Vajifdar noted the big names in Greek culture who wanted to find out about it. Pythagoras was supposed to have visited or wanted to visit Persia. Plato might have been to Syria, where he met some of the magi, and, as a kind of honorary consul, he did meet the magi in Athens.

FARROKH VAJIFDAR: *A magus is supposed to have visited Plato on the last evening of his life and, of course, before then there were interchanges with them. Now the curious thing is why did they all wish to go to Iran? Right up to the times of Plotinus, the Neoplatonist, the founder of Neoplatonists, Porphyry, all these people. Why Iran? Again, they tell you it was either to meet the successors of Zarathustra or, in the earliest cases, perhaps to meet with Zarathustra himself.*

Regarding the influence of Zoroastrianism on Judaism and Christianity (or which came first, Judaism or Zoroastrianism), Melvyn observed that people were going to argue about that outside the studio for a very long time. There were apparently interconnections between Judaism and Zoroastrianism, perhaps from a time when Nebuchadnezzar took the leading members of the Jews to Babylon where they stayed until Cyrus let them to go back.

ALAN WILLIAMS: *We're talking about a milieu in the ancient world when the Jews were tremendously grateful to Cyrus and to the Achaemenians for liberating them and allowing them to go to Jerusalem to build a temple. In a nutshell, the postexilic books of the Bible show signs of having incorporated many ideas. I think now it's generally accepted that the way in which the postexilic books have changed is that they're distinct. This idea of eschatology, ideas of judgement, ideas of future life, these then take on a much larger role in both Judaism and Christianity.*

There was also the idea of the saviour in the Gathas, in the sense that Zarathustra talked about himself as one who came to heal the world. The saviour is there in most ancient texts and, of course, in Christianity.

VESTA SARKHOSH CURTIS: *Zarathustra's teachings talk about the Saoshyant, the saviour of the world, who rules at the end of the world and, according to Zarathustra's doctrine, the world comes to an end – there are 3,000 years and the last 1,000 years are ruled by Saoshyant, he's the saviour. He's the one who raises the bones of the dead, and he is the one who helps Ahura Mazda give them back their life.*

This great religion, Melvyn observed, which went through so many centuries and three Persian empires, was heavily challenged by the Muslim invasions of the seventh century, after which about 95 per cent of Zoroastrians converted to Islam and a few of the others went to Gujarat, where the Parsis still practise Zoroastrianism. To this day, Vesta Sarkhosh Curtis added, there is a very small minority in southern Iran who follow this faith. But what she found most fascinating was the way Shia Islam created a branch of Islam that, to her, shows strong parallels with Zoroastrianism.

Painting depicting Zarathustra speaking with Goshtasb, the king of Persia, from a Zoroastrian temple in Isfahan, Iran.

VESTA SARKHOSH CURTIS: *The greatest influence of Zoroastrianism or the Iranian religion came to Shia Islam. This is the branch of Islam that believes that, after the prophet Mohammad, there are twelve imams, and the twelfth imam is the saviour. He disappears and he reappears on the last day of judgement. I think this whole idea of Shia Islam has very Zoroastrian nuances, the whole idea of creating this line. Also, in Shia Islam, legend has it, and we believe, that the wife of Imam Husayn, the daughter-in-law of Imam Ali, was an Iranian princess.*

A good number of Zoroastrians went from the Persian Empire into Gujarat and settled there, where the religion developed.

FARROKH VAJIFDAR: *It would be safer to call it Parsiism, which has certain Zoroastrian roots, but they were certainly heavily influenced by Hindu ideas, Hindu customs, which is inevitable with their long stay.*

He and Alan Williams concluded with a remark on the Sasanian Empire, which was a very repressive regime and did no favours to Zoroastrianism, which may have been an additional reason Islam caught on, even if it did take centuries before the 95 per cent of Zoroastrians converted to Islam, as Melvyn mentioned earlier.

THE PUTNEY DEBATES

*St Mary's Church, Putney, stands on the south bank of the Thames about
6 miles upriver from central London. Inside, a slate plaque commemorates
a seismic event that started here during the English Civil War and
went on to influence politics in England and abroad for centuries.
The possibility of modern democracy could be said to have emerged
here. On 28 October 1647, Oliver Cromwell and other members of
the New Model Army met in St Mary's Church, as it turned out, to
discuss a new constitution for England. Charles I had been defeated
and imprisoned, and it seemed a new future beckoned. There were
still religious and political differences to be overcome and, over many
days of discussions, the participants tried to resolve them. But, within
a month, the king had escaped and the talks ended without agreement.
Nevertheless, the Putney Debates are commonly regarded as a major
advance in our idea of what democracy is and how it can be realised.*

With Melvyn to discuss the Putney Debates were: Justin Champion, emeritus professor of the history of early modern ideas and honorary fellow at Royal Holloway, University of London; Ann Hughes, emerita professor of early modern history at Keele University; and Kate Peters, fellow in history at Murray Edwards College, Cambridge.

The English Civil War had started about five years before the Putney Debates. By 1640, Charles I had alienated most of the local elites who were represented in parliament; the underlying tensions between the king and parliament were over principles of religion and principles of politics.

JUSTIN CHAMPION: *This king believed he was appointed by God and could pretty much do what he wanted, he didn't need the counsel of parliamentarians. Most of the political nation believed they had some role in governing the kingdom, even if only to give counsel for the king. By 1640, these two political factions were fighting in Westminster. By 1642, because of an atmosphere of conspiracy, where Charles I was regarded as ultimately being in league with the Antichrist, compromising true religion, parliamentarians thought it necessary to fight a war.*

That war was bloody, brutal and protracted, with a first and then a second civil war, which included great set pieces as well as assassinations and murderous conflicts in villages. It was thought that God's providence would decide who was wrong and who was right through what happened on the battlefields. As the war progressed, a revolutionary spirit was at large and the king's opponents moved from wanting to negotiate with him to finding it impossible to hold talks, as so much blood had, by then, been spilt. There was still expected to be a peaceable resolution, though, and, in the early stages, nobody wanted to kill the king.

Parliament established a New Model Army of 20,000 in 1645 to fight the king's forces and, in time, some of these soldiers would turn into statesmen with a role in the Putney Debates.

JUSTIN CHAMPION: *One of the huge problems was: 'How do we negotiate a peace settlement with somebody who's clearly behaving badly, maybe corrupted by the Antichrist, but is still appointed by God?' And one of the problems is parliament doesn't quite know what to do. Presbyterians in parliament want to negotiate a peace. Those soldiers who fought, and had seen their comrades die, realised that really parliament wasn't driving them forwards.*

The English, with the help of a Scottish army, had decisively defeated the king. The New Model Army had a series of stunning victories, Ann Hughes said, and God had shown his providence in their support, but there was still no clear way to a settled peace. Perhaps the majority wanted a settlement with the king and the expensive army to be disbanded so they could go back to the old ways. There was a significant opposing view among the New Model Army.

ANN HUGHES: *Here's this very, very powerful thing that you see at Putney: 'We have fought for God's cause, we've fought for the people's cause, we're not an army that's just been paid, many people are volunteers, we want things to change. There must be some recompense for all the suffering that there has been.'*

Religion, Melvyn observed, was woven into this history, sometimes as an excuse for war and sometimes a cause. Religion *was* crucial to this war, Ann Hughes agreed, as were very powerful instincts towards obedience and hierarchy.

ANN HUGHES: *But if, as significant groups of people felt in England, the king is not on the side of true religion, he's too close to Catholicism, he's going back on central tenets of English Protestantism, then the notion that you're fighting for true religion, for God's cause, is absolutely central. The trouble for parliamentarians was that, by 1646–7, there's absolutely no agreement on the actual content of the true religion that you're fighting for.*

The Presbyterians were fighting for a reformed, national, comprehensive, compulsory Church, to complete an English reformation. In the course of the war, though, and, very significantly, in the New Model Army, there emerged a belief in religious liberty for Protestants. Often the experience of making choices about religion inspired individuals to think they could have choices over politics as well.

The New Model Army started petitioning parliament with grievances in 1647. Initially, Kate Peters said, they were standard military grievances. Parliament wanted to disband the army now that peace had broken out, as it was so expensive and the cost in taxation was unpopular. Also, the Presbyterians in parliament did not like the New Model Army.

KATE PETERS: *There's been a very impressive smear campaign going on in the press in 1646 about how dangerous the army is, how it is the harbinger of radical religious ideas. Parliament needs to disband the New Model Army and it starts discussing this in February. One of the problems with disbanding the army is that there are very strong arrears of pay, about £3 million.*

The soldiers did not want to be disbanded until their arrears of pay had been settled, and they wanted indemnity against any acts of war they had committed. Parliament's plan was to disband them without paying the arrears in full and, if the soldiers did not like that idea, they would be redeployed to Ireland.

These petitions became a way of gathering political power as more and more people put their names to them. Parliament, wanting to control the army, ordered its leader, Thomas Fairfax, to stop the petitioning, and he tried to obey but was powerless. Still the petitioning continued.

KATE PETERS: *Out of that comes a very famous declaration of dislike by an MP called Denzil Holles, who attacks the army, attacks their petitioning, calls them 'enemies of the state' and 'disturbers of the public peace' by continuing their petitioning work. And this opens up a clear fissure between the interests of parliament and the interests of the army.*

Into this fissure stepped a junior cavalry officer, Cornet Joyce. In June 1647, when parliament was very worried about the New Model

Army regiments coming close to London, the troops were camped out at Newmarket, gradually getting closer to the capital. Then, on 2 June, Cornet Joyce turned up with 500 men at nearby Holdenby House, where the captive Charles I was playing bowls.

JUSTIN CHAMPION: *His mission is to protect Charles from a plot. He doesn't precisely talk about the plot, it may be Scottish, it may be Presbyterian. And, in essence, the exchange is between Joyce, a very lowly cavalry officer, and Charles I, who reminds him, 'I am your king, I'm appointed by God, what are you doing here?' There's this very delicate exchange, first the commissioners keep him apart, eventually he does talk to him.*

Charles I noticed that Joyce was armed, saying, 'I see you have a sword and you may kill me.' Joyce was very respectful, stating he had no bad intentions to Charles at all.

JUSTIN CHAMPION: *When Charles is encouraged to leave with Joyce the following morning, he again asks him for his commission and Joyce simply looks over his shoulder, where there are 500 troops, and says, 'This is my commission.' That's a moment where the sword of the army becomes an incredibly powerful political force. It doesn't convince Charles I, of course, because he agrees to everything and has his fingers crossed all the time, and he is clearly still plotting to escape.*

Charles was taken from Holdenby House to Newmarket, where he was under the power of the New Model Army.

Another voice being raised was that of the Levellers, a radical democratic movement based mostly in London, which emerged from the radical religious congregations. Ann Hughes explained that, from 1645 to 1647, the Levellers had developed the criticism that parliament had let them down; parliament was the representative of the people, it had called the people out to fight against the king, and yet the condition of the people had not changed. Accordingly, if parliament was not acting in trust for the people, it should be disbanded and replaced with another assembly.

ANN HUGHES: *As one very famous Leveller pamphlet by one of their very important leaders, Richard Overton, said, what happens in the end is 'a change of our bondage is the uttermost is intended us.' Through pamphleteering, they get into trouble with parliament. Two of the most important Leveller leaders, John Lilburn and Richard Overton, are imprisoned by the House of Lords for illegal pamphleteering. They're very adept at making their individual suffering emblematic of a general cause.*

The New Model Army had developed a formal political structure in 1647 – a general council. Out of that came a declaration, Kate Peters told us, that the army would not disband until its grievances had been addressed. At Reading, they came up with the Heads of Proposals, probably put together by Henry Ireton, who was Oliver Cromwell's son-in-law and commissioner-general of the army, and also a lawyer, working with John Lambert, who was another army man, and with Lord Wharton and Lord Saye-and-Sele, who were sympathetic members of the House of Lords. They came up with proposals for a settlement for peace with the king, which Ireton put forward for debate at Putney.

KATE PETERS: *These are genius, these are a very, very plausible set of proposals that could have led to a settlement; what parliament has been offering to the king has been going nowhere. They're suggesting biannual parliaments, to get rid of the parliament that we've got and start again, a redistribution of seats within parliament, that parliament should have a lot of control over the army for about ten years, that parliament should have control over the king's choice of key ministers of state.*

They were looking for ways to limit the king's power but, Kate Peters stressed, these proposals were much more lenient than those parliament had been offering previously. The most important proposal was for religious toleration. They said the Book of Common Prayer and the bishops could stay, but that people should be free not to worship with them.

At Putney, the headquarters of the New Model Army, the different proposals were put forward for debate. To these, the Levellers added 'The Case of the Army Truly Stated' and the briefer 'Agreement of the People', which was first articulated on 28 October, Justin Champion said, and printed a few days later. Argued by Leveller officers Rainsborough and Sexby, these pamphlets made a case for the sovereignty of the people, where the consent of the people was the source of legitimate government and where every male over twenty-one should have the vote.

JUSTIN CHAMPION: *Of course, Henry Ireton, as a lawyer and as a man of property, says straightaway [of the Levellers' proposals], 'This is madness, this is the route to absolute anarchy, confusion, this is too new.' [In reply,] Rainsborough and Sexby say, 'My god, if I'm going to consent to legitimacy, I need to be able to vote. I've spilt my blood so I need a voice.'*

ANN HUGHES: *Rainsborough's the one who says this very moving phrase that echoes down the ages: 'The poorest he that is in England has a life to live as the greatest he.' And there's also this burning sense of betrayal where Sexby says, 'If we had not a right to the kingdom, we were a mere mercenary army.' We're fighting for other people not for our own rights.*

Religion, Kate Peters said, was again very important implicitly and explicitly because, if they were to get a settlement, they were going to have to get a settlement on religion. There was a fundamental distinction between what the Levellers and the agitators were trying to argue about religion and what Ireton and Cromwell were trying to argue. For the Levellers, individual conscience was a very important principle.

KATE PETERS: *Conscience is the thing that you get from God, so you must follow your conscience. Essentially, what they're saying is that, although the people can give political power to parliament, they*

The New Model Army at the Battle of Naseby, 1645.

cannot give religious power to parliament because religious power comes from God not from man. Parliament must have no say at all over any religious policy.

That was the opposite of what people like Henry Ireton and Oliver Cromwell wanted, which was much more linked to political order, with an inclusive Church where everybody could belong and their differences tolerated.

These constitutional matters were discussed in Putney over two weeks, initially at St Mary's Church and then nearby. They were brought to an unexpected and abrupt conclusion, Melvyn noted, by Charles I escaping from Hampton Court and setting up his own army, so to begin the second civil war.

KATE PETERS: *One of the impacts of the fissures between Cromwell and Ireton and the agitators is a deep distrust that grows between the agitators and the grandees of the army. Although in many ways Ireton and Cromwell concede an awful lot towards the Agreement of the People, by the end they kick it into the long grass and send the soldiers back to their regiments to keep the peace.*

With the Putney Debates interrupted, there was a radical road that was not taken, Justin Champion added. The key moment was after Charles had escaped and some radical figures in the army tried to mutiny at Corkbush Field in Hertfordshire on 15 November, with the 'Agreement of the People' pamphlet in their hats and with green Leveller ribbons. Rainsborough, at the end of the Putney Debates, was unhappy with the compromising and wanted a rendezvous of all the regiments to vote for the 'Agreement of the People'. Against that, Cromwell and Fairfax wanted military discipline.

JUSTIN CHAMPION: *Rainsborough and other troops turn up uninvited and try to agitate among the soldiers. At least one person is shot; Richard Arnold, a lowly foot soldier, is sacrificed to their cause. That's really the end of that very radical tradition. They try again in May 1649. The tradition of the freeborn liberties (although most of the people after the civil wars don't know about the Putney Debates) does survive into a radical Whig tradition in the later seventeenth century and into the eighteenth.*

Some historians see the failure of the Leveller agenda as a missed opportunity, a failure of revolution, Kate Peters said. More liberal historians would see it as the start of a statement of human rights, of civil rights, a statement of the importance of democracy and representation. It is possible to trace both a very radical tradition and a very liberal tradition from the Putney Debates.

Awareness of the debates only really re-emerged in the twentieth century after the records had been rediscovered in 1890 in the library of Worcester College and published. Ann Hughes pointed to their role in radical thought and inspiration, particularly around the Second World War, with the notion that the army had fought for a cause and was expecting things to change because of the sacrifices made in that cause.

Justin Champion, meanwhile, urged everybody to read the Putney Debates. It was not social class that was the basis of citizenship for the Levellers and for these ordinary men at Putney, it was who you were as a human being.

JUSTIN CHAMPION: *The language and the power of ordinary buff-coated soldiers, poor men, debating about and imagining what their rights and their duties and responsibilities might be is still very, very powerful. And the debates around why consent makes government legitimate still have huge purchase for us today, especially the arguments around poverty.*

MARGERY KEMPE AND ENGLISH MYSTICISM

The English mystic Margery Kempe led a remarkable life at a turbulent time, from 1373 to 1438. After the birth of the first of her fourteen children, and again from her forties and for the rest of her life, she had visions of Jesus Christ that were so intense she wept profusely to the amazement of many and annoyance of some. She felt the pain of the crucifixion and she imagined herself married to Christ, living as man and wife. This was a time when England was on high alert for heretics and Margery Kempe was threatened with burning at the stake, interrogated as she travelled from her home in Norfolk across the country, by land and sea, to Jerusalem, Rome, Norway, Poland, Germany and Santiago de Compostela. We only know of her now because she dictated her story to scribes towards the end of her life. That book disappeared until the 1930s, when it tumbled from a cupboard at a country house, as guests were looking for a spare ping-pong ball.

⊷※⊶

With Melvyn to discuss Margery Kempe and English mysticism were: Miri Rubin, professor of medieval and early modern history at Queen Mary University of London; Katherine Lewis, senior lecturer in history at the University of Huddersfield; and Anthony Bale, executive dean of arts and professor of medieval studies at Birkbeck, University of London.

   Miri Rubin started out with Margery Kempe's early life. She was probably born around 1373, to a distinguished family in what was then Bishop's Lynn, now King's Lynn, an important port in Norfolk, trading with the Hanseatic ports of the Baltic. Her father was five times mayor of Lynn.

A fourteenth-century carving from King's Lynn Minster depicting a woman who would have been a contemporary of Margery Kempe.

MIRI RUBIN: *Around twenty, she married John Kempe, a merchant family not as distinguished as her own but also part of the elite. She gets pregnant soon after and, in that first pregnancy, clearly she suffered a lot, both physically and personal, spiritual, mental anguish. In the course of that, she has the first of her visions of Christ.*

Her vision was of a physical Christ who comforted and encouraged her when she feared that her pain was a punishment for sin. She had been scarring herself with constant scratching.

MIRI RUBIN: *Terrible scratching of herself that leaves scars for a lifetime, as she says. And really the description in the book of the anguish is extremely moving. But she still goes on and she has fourteen children. We don't know if these are fourteen births or fourteen children. If fourteen live children, it may well have been more births, given the child mortality at the time.*

She would have had some numeracy and literacy, some religious education, access to the sacraments including confession, and the chance to hear preachers and monks and friars around Lynn, but she could have no official place in the hierarchy of the Church.

Church authorities were on the lookout for heretics at this time and Margery was to be accused of heresy at stages of her life. There were Wycliffite, pre-Protestant heresies, Anthony Bale explained, based on the thoughts of the Oxford theologian and cleric, John Wycliffe, whose position became known as Lollardy.

ANTHONY BALE: *The distillation of what we might think of as Lollard thought arrives in 1395 in the twelve Lollard Conclusions, which are presented to parliament and pinned on the doors of St Paul's Cathedral and Westminster Abbey. These include statements such as that worship of the bread and wine of the sacrament is a kind of idolatry, that confession to priests is illegitimate because only God has the right to absolve human beings of sin, that clerical celibacy leads to sodomy, that pilgrimage and devotion to relics is a kind of idolatry.*

These Wycliffite heretics called for the Bible to be in English and for a move towards a congregational religion as opposed to a clerical one, and they were extremely hostile towards the established church and the clergy.

ANTHONY BALE: *Heresy is essentially a thought crime, it's a crime that exists in people's minds, in people's devotional selves. Identifying it, finding it, actually involves a degree of surveillance and drilling down to what normal people are doing. In the early fifteenth century, you get this incredible culture of surveillance and censorship.*

Margery Kempe's first visions came around the time of her pregnancy, about six months after she gave birth, Katherine Lewis said, which had been a very difficult experience for her with physical illness, as well as mental anguish over an unconfessed and unspecified sin, which may have been some kind of sexual sin.

KATHERINE LEWIS: *She's absolutely preoccupied with sexuality and with the fact that she lost her virginity, and, many times in the book,* *she tells us she wished she'd never married and never had sex. She goes to her confessor; she wants to confess this sin because she thinks she's going to die. And the confessor is very sharp with her, and she can't get the sin out. Then she goes into this frenzy, and the first visions that she has are terrifying visions of demons breathing fire and attacking her and pulling her about.*

This was when she started to self-harm, because the demons were supposedly encouraging her to try to kill herself so that she would go to hell and be damned. Then, in the middle of all of this, just when it seemed as though she really had lost her mind, Christ appeared to her.

KATHERINE LEWIS: *It's a wonderful vision. He appears, he's a very handsome man, he's clad in purple and he just sits on the side of her bed and he says, 'Daughter, why have you forsaken me when I never forsook you?' And then he disappears, elegantly (as Anthony says in his translation) off up into heaven again. And that's it. But it restores her senses, it brings her back to herself.*

Nothing then seems to change in her life for about another fifteen years, and she carries on living as she was and having more children. She believed that Christ physically appeared to her and that he was concrete. In later visions, she touched him and felt him. In modern terms, it might be described as some kind of mental illness or psychosis, but that was not at all how she saw it. The book is clear that the visions came from God, but one of the main themes of the book is that Margery Kempe questions the source.

KATHERINE LEWIS: *She believed they came from God, but sometimes she very properly doubted this because even the most learned theologian could have difficulty discerning whether they had come from God or from the devil, let alone a woman. This is what makes women's visions problematic, because of all the stereotypical ideas about their intellectual and moral failings, and this sense that they really would not be capable of discerning the origins of the vision.*

There had been some significant instances of women in northern Europe having visions and recording them, before Margery Kempe. Miri Rubin pointed to Hildegard of Bingen from the twelfth century, who had the intellectual skills to command her own writing project within her monastery. From the thirteenth century, there were women who were not in religious houses but who developed a spirituality that was noticed and written down by priests, who were fascinated by them. Marie of Oignies, from the diocese of Liège in modern Belgium, was a major intellectual figure, and Jacques de Vitry wrote down her visions. These were translated widely throughout Europe, and Marie wrote about crying and how she found her way to a chaste marriage.

MIRI RUBIN: *Above-all important, to my mind, is Bridget of Sweden. Felicitously, the year she dies in is the year we think Margery was born, in 1373, an extraordinary Swedish aristocrat who moves from marriage and bearing eight children to a life of chaste marriage* *and, after the death of her husband, pilgrimage throughout Europe. Margery mentions her, Margery's inspired by her and, particularly, by her devotion to the Virgin Mary.*

We know of Margery Kempe's life from the book she dictated, which was apparently finished in her last years. The first person she asked to write it down was a man who had lived in Prussia for some time and was almost certainly her eldest son. That version was so ill written that nobody could understand it.

ANTHONY BALE: *The text that we now have says, this is so misshapen in Deutsch letters, in German letters. Then the book is given to another man, who had been a friend of this man from Prussia, and he can't understand it either. It's then given to a priest who tries to read it and can't do anything with it and then, somewhat later, miraculously, this priest is able to work on it.*

The text makes obvious this difficult route to completion, an account of collaborative authorship that was very much in keeping with how medieval texts were written. Texts would have a listener, a reader, a writer, a scribe and these were all parts of what it was to be an author in the Middle Ages. The account of Margery Kempe's life is reliable, up to a point.

ANTHONY BALE: *This is not an impartial document, this book is designed to show Kempe in a particular way. It's modelled on sacred precursors, particularly Bridget of Sweden and Marie of Oignies, and it looks like a saint's life in some ways, it looks like a confession in other ways. And, of course, one of the famous generic tags that's given to it is that it's the first autobiography in the English language. And, to some extent, that's true – it's the story of Kempe's life – but it's not the whole story.*

That uncertainty is the case in so many medieval documents, Melvyn observed, you just have to take a deep breath and say, 'Well, we'll go with it.'

About fifteen years after the first vision of Christ sitting on her bed, Margery Kempe started to have conversations with Christ, Katherine Lewis continued, and he reassured her again about her sin and told her he had now forgiven all of her sins. She would never go to hell, she would not even go to purgatory. This took the form of direct speech from Christ, after he ravished her soul.

KATHERINE LEWIS: *This is where he also starts outlining for her aspects of what go on to be her vocation, what we might describe as the public ministry she creates for herself. Really importantly, one of the things that he says is that she's to go and see a local anchorite (again, it comes back to this issue of discernment of spirits) and the local anchorite will be able to reassure her. And, indeed, when he hears about the revelations that she's already had, he's moved to tears by them and says that she's sucking at the breast of Christ.*

The anchorite told her she was to come back whenever she had other visions and he would be able to reassure her about their origins. She was to travel around the country and tell people of her visions.

When she went on to ask Christ why he had not shown these visions to professional religious people, Christ talked about the fact that a lot of sin hid under the habits of holiness. Her role then was to go out to correct what she saw as problems.

Her travelling away from Bishop's Lynn and telling of her visions put her on really dangerous ground.

ANTHONY BALE: *It's something that she has to make very clear, that she's not preaching. Obviously it's forbidden by St Paul for women to preach and it's forbidden in the medieval Church, and she makes that very clear that she's not preaching. But she does. Particularly when she's at the Bishop of York's house in Cawood, it's very clear that she is, effectively, preaching, she's telling a parable and she's getting herself in very dangerous territory there.*

When she was about forty, Margery Kempe went on pilgrimage to Jerusalem, an event that had a lasting impact on her. It was important for her to find people to travel with, at a time when travelling in groups was the safe thing to do. She dressed in white, a sign of purity and probably virginity. She had a servant with her at first, but then her servant abandoned her, part of a series of trials. One of the most symbolic rejections of her was when her fellow pilgrims refused to eat with her, an exclusion from a Christian group that she found very painful. She also said they stole her money, and they dressed her in a ridiculous cloak made of badger fur.

MIRI RUBIN: *The groups find her irksome because she does go about correcting people, constantly inveighing when people want to settle down and have a good time, like the Canterbury pilgrims of Chaucer, and she's always there reminding them, 'Don't mention God's name in vain,' or don't behave this way or the other. But, when she reaches Jerusalem, everything comes together in the most extraordinary fashion – and remember that Jerusalem at this time is under Mamluk control but, nonetheless, Christians have access to the holy places, the Franciscans have created a trail of pilgrimage that allows people to walk in the footsteps of Christ, the Via Dolorosa. And you can imagine, for a woman who's been communicating regularly with Christ, what this means.*

One of the things to bear in mind, Anthony Bale added, about this account of her persecution was that this authorised her in a way, this was her Via Crucis, she was like Christ. Being a renegade, being someone who saw the truth that others did not see, then became a very authorising position for her.

Back in England, in Leicester, Margery Kempe was investigated for Lollardy and was examined for her opinion on the articles of the faith. The authorities were hoping to catch her out, Katherine Lewis said, focusing on the Mass and her opinion on the true presence in the Mass. It was not only her potential heresy that attracted attention; the mayor of Leicester had noticed her white clothing.

KATHERINE LEWIS: *He asks her why she goes about in white and then he says to her, 'I think you've come to lead all our wives away.'*

Portrait of Bridget of Sweden.

And there is this fear that she is setting a very subversive example because yes, she's still married, but she's taken a vow of chastity and her husband has authorised her pilgrimage, but he's not there, and she's earning a living for herself as a holy woman, she has a purse of money that she carries around with her. The Bishop of York asks her where she gets the money from and she says, 'Well, people pay for me to pray for them.'

She also came to the attention of the most powerful man in England at the time, John, Duke of Bedford, who was governing England in the absence of Henry V. He sent his men to arrest her, fearing Lollardy, and the men told her they would have a £100 reward for that work, which was a lot of money. Also, Margery Kempe had been in the household of the Duke of Bedford's aunt, Joan Beaufort, whose daughter she allegedly counselled to leave her husband. She denied that claim, but that was the kind of accusation she faced.

The thing about Margery Kempe, Miri Rubin said, was that she was abroad and visible and audible. A woman could be a bride of Christ if she was in a monastery, or she could be out of the way like Julian of Norwich, the anchorite she visited, but Margery was out and about.

When she was sixty or so, Margery Kempe set off for Gdańsk on the journey that appears at the end of the book.

ANTHONY BALE: *She sets off for Gdańsk as a renegade. She is accompanying her daughter-in-law, who was from Gdańsk, to Ipswich. Her son had died and she was going to put her daughter-in-law on a boat to send her back to her own family in Prussia. And then Kempe, who's been told not to go, gets on the boat and she goes off to the Baltic. The boat is blown off course and ends up in Norway over Easter, and then they make their way to Gdańsk. Then she undertakes an incredible journey.*

She had an injured foot, yet travelled something like 800–1,000 miles, partly on wagons, partly walking. Margery went to see the Holy Blood at Wilsnack, which was a famous pilgrimage location, and then went on to Aachen and then to Calais and then back home. She struggled, and the text is very detailed about how difficult this journey was.

Some people may have thought she was a hypocrite who wanted to draw attention to herself, Miri Rubin suggested, but, just as many would have found her exemplary. People thought she might be a prophetess and she had a constant stream of patronage and support. Very respectable monks in the course of the fifteenth century wanted to have a copy of her book, and, thanks to them, there is a surviving manuscript.

MIRI RUBIN: *Her story also fits into the biblical story and, indeed,* The Book of Marjory Kempe *is full of citations from the Bible, of suffering, of prophecy, a lot from the Hebrew prophets. She's also building really importantly on the deep carnality of the religion of incarnation; the body is a vehicle, Christ offered his body after all. She's making something quite unique (and, being a woman, it's troublesome) out of the resources of Christianity.*

She felt compelled by Christ to do what she did – he gave her a sense of mission. She was also very aware of earlier female mystics, and the potential that she, too, might earn a reputation for holiness.

KATHERINE LEWIS: *There is no English counterpart (with the exception of Julian of Norwich, who wasn't known as a visionary at the time). I think one of the things that we've got going on here is an attempt, collaboratively with Kempe and her scribe, to provide the English answer, if you like, to Bridget of Sweden, to provide a home-grown manifestation of holiness within that urban setting.*

The manuscript that we have was held by the Carthusian monastery of Mount Grace in Yorkshire in the late fifteenth, early sixteenth centuries, when the monks read it very sincerely, very piously as evidence of devotional practices, and we can tell from their marginalia that they were taking the spiritual message from it. Later on, there were early printed versions in 1500 and then again in 1521, but they were heavily edited.

ANTHONY BALE: *They take most of her life out and they just give us a few bits of her visions and they call her a devout anchoress of Lynn, which she wasn't. An anchoress is someone who's withdrawn; she was someone very much in the world. Her reputation does endure but in a quite small way. She certainly didn't become a saint. And then, really between the English Reformation in the sixteenth century and 1934, she more or less disappears.*

She was exactly the kind of figure who was so much connected to the old religion, he added, with her faith in the sacrament, her faith in pilgrimage, her love of indulgences, which were really not appreciated by the Church of England. Yet, in her lifetime, she was also suspected of being a Lollard.

MIRI RUBIN: *[When the book] is discovered in the 1930s and is then published, both in modern English and in middle English, what's fascinating is that Catholics like Graham Greene are enthusiastic about it as well as the Church of England, because, for Catholics, she talks about the old religion and, for Anglicans, she's just a wonderfully colourful English religious character.*

In the studio afterwards, there was more discussion of Margery Kempe's husband, who was described as forbearing in many ways, even if, while in Canterbury together, he apparently left her alone as she embarrassed him. When she first suggested they live chastely, Katherine Lewis said, he was like St Augustine, saying that's a really good idea but just not yet.

KATHERINE LEWIS: *Yet he does enable her to follow that lifestyle and, later on in life, when he has this terrible accident and he gets brain damage and she has to look after him, she says she doesn't want to look after him, but Christ reminds her that really her husband has enabled her to follow the vocation because he was prepared to let her live this different form of life.*

ANTHONY BALE: *And she points out that they'd had so much enjoyment of each other's bodies when they were young that it was now fitting that she should look after him when he's fouling his own linen by the fireplace and the table.*

While there is a certain type of criticism that makes him into a villain, Miri Rubin noted, where she maybe would have wanted to start her chaste life earlier but they produced fourteen children, their marriage was also a framework of respectability, a household, a safe haven. And the book itself is a revelation.

MIRI RUBIN: *Virginia Woolf writes in* A Room of One's Own, *'Ah, if only some historian here in Girton would write a book about, say, a Tudor woman, just a normal woman.' To me, this is the book.*

LIST OF PROGRAMMES TO DATE

13 July 2006
Greek Comedy

28 September 2006
Alexander von
Humboldt

5 October 2006
Averroes

12 October 2006
The Diet of Worms

19 October 2006
The Needham
Question

26 October 2006
The Encyclopédie

2 November 2006
The Poincaré
Conjecture

9 November 2006
Alexander Pope

16 November 2006
The Peasants' Revolt

23 November 2006
Altruism

30 November 2006
The Speed of Light

7 December 2006
Anarchism

14 December 2006
Indian Maths

21 December 2006
Hell

28 December 2006
The Siege of
Constantinople

4 January 2007
Jorge Luis Borges

11 January 2007
Mars

18 January 2007
The Jesuits

25 January 2007
Archimedes

1 February 2007
Genghis Khan

8 February 2007
Karl Popper

15 February 2007
Heart of Darkness

22 February 2007
William Wilberforce

1 March 2007
The History of
Optics

8 March 2007
Microbiology

15 March 2007
Epistolary Literature

22 March 2007
Bismarck

29 March 2007
Anaesthetics

5 April 2007
St Hilda

12 April 2007
The Opium Wars

19 April 2007
Symmetry

26 April 2007
Greek and Roman
Love Poetry

3 May 2007
Spinoza

10 May 2007
Victorian Pessimism

17 May 2007
Gravitational Waves

24 May 2007
The Siege of Orléans

31 May 2007
Occam's Razor

7 June 2007
Siegfried Sassoon

14 June 2007
Renaissance
Astrology

21 June 2007
Common Sense
Philosophy

28 June 2007
Permian–Triassic
Boundary

5 July 2007
The Pilgrim Fathers

12 July 2007
Madame Bovary

27 September 2007
Socrates

4 October 2007
Antimatter

11 October 2007
Divine Right of Kings

18 October 2007
The Arabian Nights

25 October 2007
Taste

1 November 2007
Guilt

8 November 2007
Avicenna

15 November 2007
The Discovery of
Oxygen

22 November 2007
The Prelude

29 November 2007
The Fibonacci
Sequence

6 December 2007
Genetic Mutation

13 December 2007
The Sassanian
Empire

20 December 2007
The Four Humours

27 December 2007
The Nicene Creed

3 January 2008
Albert Camus

10 January 2008
The Charge of the
Light Brigade

17 January 2008
The Fisher King

24 January 2008
Plate Tectonics

31 January 2008
The Court of
Rudolf II

7 February 2008
The Social Contract

14 February 2008
The Statue of Liberty

21 February 2008
The Multiverse

28 February 2008
King Lear

6 March 2008
Ada Lovelace

13 March 2008
The Greek Myths

20 March 2008
Søren Kierkegaard

27 March 2008
The Dissolution of
the Monasteries

3 April 2008
Newton's Laws
of Motion

10 April 2008
The Norman Yoke

17 April 2008
Yeats and Irish
Politics

24 April 2008
Materialism

1 May 2008
The Enclosures

8 May 2008
The Brain: A History

15 May 2008
The Library at
Nineveh

22 May 2008
The Black Death

29 May 2008
Probability

5 June 2008
Lysenkoism

12 June 2008
The Riddle of the
Sands

19 June 2008
The Music of the
Spheres

26 June 2008
The Arab Conquests

3 July 2008
The Metaphysical
Poets

10 July 2008
Tacitus – The
Decadence of Rome

25 September 2008
Miracles

2 October 2008
The Translation
Movement

9 October 2008
Gödel's
Incompleteness
Theorems

16 October 2008
Vitalism

23 October 2008
Dante's *Inferno*

30 October 2008
Simón Bolívar

6 November 2008
Aristotle's *Politics*

13 November 2008
Neuroscience

20 November 2008
The Baroque

27 November 2008
The Great Reform
Act

4 December 2008
Heat: A History

11 December 2008
The Great Fire of
London

18 December 2008
The Physics of Time

1 January 2009
The Consolation of
Philosophy

5 January 2009
Darwin: On the
Origins of Charles
Darwin

6 January 2009
Darwin: *The Voyage
of the Beagle*

7 January 2009
Darwin: *On the
Origin of Species*

8 January 2009
Darwin: Life After
Origins

15 January 2009
Thoreau and the
American Idyll

22 January 2009
A History of History

29 January 2009
A Modest Proposal
by Jonathan Swift

5 February 2009
The Brothers Grimm

12 February 2009
The Destruction of
Carthage

19 February 2009
The Observatory at
Jaipur

26 February 2009
The Waste Land and
Modernity

5 March 2009
The Measurement
Problem in Physics

12 March 2009
The Library of
Alexandria

19 March 2009
The Boxer Rebellion

26 March 2009
The School of Athens

2 April 2009
Baconian Science

9 April 2009
Brave New World

16 April 2009
Suffragism

23 April 2009
The Building of St
Petersburg

30 April 2009
The Vacuum of Space

7 May 2009
Magna Carta

14 May 2009
The Siege of Vienna

21 May 2009
The Whale

28 May 2009
Saint Paul

4 June 2009
The Trial of Charles I

11 June 2009
The Augustan Age

18 June 2009
Elizabethan Revenge
Tragedy

25 June 2009
The Sunni-Shia Split

2 July 2009
Logical Positivism

9 July 2009
Ediacara Biota

17 September 2009
St Thomas Aquinas

24 September 2009
Leibniz vs Newton

1 October 2009
Akhenaten

8 October 2009
The Dreyfuss Affair

15 October 2009
The Death of
Elizabeth I

22 October 2009
The Geological
Formation of Britain

29 October 2009
Schopenhauer

5 November 2009
The Siege of Münster

12 November 2009
The Discovery of
Radiation

19 November 2009
Sparta

26 November 2009
*A Portrait of the
Artist as a Young
Man*

3 December 2009
The Silk Road

10 December 2009
Pythagoras and the
Pythagoreans

24 December 2009
The Samurai

31 December 2009
Mary Wollstonecraft

14 January 2010
The Frankfurt School

21 January 2010
The Glencoe
Massacre

28 January 2010
Silas Marner

4 February 2010
Ibn Khaldun

11 February 2010
The Unintended
Consequences of
Mathematics

18 February 2010
The Indian Rebellion

25 February 2010
Calvinism

4 March 2010
The Infant Brain

11 March 2010
Boudica

18 March 2010
The Scream and
Edvard Munch

7 November 2013
Ordinary Language
Philosophy

14 November 2013
The Tempest

21 November 2013
Pocahontas

28 November 2013
The Microscope

5 December 2013
Hindu Ideas of
Creation

12 December 2013
Pliny the Younger

19 December 2013
Complexity

26 December 2013
The Medici

3 January 2014
Plato's *Symposium*

16 January 2014
The Battle of Tours

23 January 2014
Sources of Early
Chinese History

30 January 2014
Catastrophism

6 February 2014
The Phoenicians

13 February 2014
Chivalry

20 February 2014
Social Darwinism

27 February 2014
The Eye

6 March 2014
Spartacus

13 March 2014
The Trinity

20 March 2014
Bishop Berkeley

27 March 2014
Weber's *The
Protestant Ethic*

3 April 2014
States of Matter

10 April 2014
Strabo's *Geographica*

17 April 2014
The Domesday Book

24 April 2014
Tristram Shandy

1 May 2014
The Tale of Sinuhe

8 May 2014
Second Sino-Japanese
War

15 May 2014
Photosynthesis

22 May 2014
*The Rubaiyat of
Omar Khayyam*

29 May 2014
The Talmud

5 June 2014
The Bluestockings

12 June 2014
Robert Boyle

19 June 2014
The Philosophy of
Solitude

26 June 2014
Hildegard of Bingen

3 July 2014
Mrs Dalloway

10 July 2014
The Sun

25 September 2014
Julius Caesar

2 October 2014
Julius Caesar

9 October 2014
The Battle of Talas

16 October 2014
Rudyard Kipling

23 October 2014
The Haitian
Revolution

30 October 2014
Nuclear Fusion

6 November 2014
Hatshepsut

13 November 2014
Brunel

20 November 2014
Aesop

27 November 2014
Kafka's *The Trial*

4 December 2014
Zen

11 December 2014
Behavioural Ecology

18 December 2014
Truth

15 January 2015
Bruegel's *The Fight
Between*

22 January 2015
Phenomenology

29 January 2015
Thucydides

5 February 2015
Ashoka the Great

12 February 2015
The Photon

19 February 2015
*The Wealth of
Nations*

26 February 2015
The Eunuch

5 March 2015
Beowulf

12 March 2015
Dark Matter

19 March 2015
Al-Ghazali

26 March 2015
The Curies

2 April 2015
The California Gold
Rush

9 April 2015
Sappho

16 April 2015
Matteo Ricci and the
Ming Dynasty

23 April 2015
Fanny Burney

30 April 2015
The Earth's Core

7 May 2015
Rabindranath Tagore

14 May 2015
The Lancashire
Cotton Famine

21 May 2015
Josephus

28 May 2015
The Science of Glass

4 June 2015
Prester John

11 June 2015
Utilitarianism

18 June 2015
Jane Eyre

25 June 2015
Extremophiles

2 July 2015
Frederick the Great

9 July 2015
Frida Kahlo

24 September 2015
Perpetual Motion

1 October 2015
Alexander the Great

15 October 2015
Holbein at the Tudor
Court

22 October 2015
Simone de Beauvoir

29 October 2015
The Empire of Mali

5 November 2015
P vs NP

12 November 2015
Battle of Lepanto

19 November 2015
Emma

29 November 2015
The Salem Witch
Trials

3 December 2015
Voyages of James
Cook

10 December 2015
Chinese Legalism

17 December 2015
Circadian Rhythms

25 December 2015
Michael Faraday

31 December 2015
Tristan and Iseult

14 January 2016
Saturn

21 January 2016
Thomas Paine's
Common Sense

28 January 2016
Eleanor of Aquitaine

4 February 2016
Chromatography

11 February 2016
Rumi's Poetry

18 February 2016
Robert Hooke

25 February 2016
Mary Magdalene

3 March 2016
The Dutch East India
Company

10 March 2016
The Maya
Civilisation

17 March 2016
Bedlam

24 March 2016
Aurora Leigh

31 March 2016
Agrippina the
Younger

7 April 2016
The Sikh Empire

14 April 2016
The Neutron

21 April 2016
1816, the Year
Without a Summer

28 April 2016
Euclid's Elements

5 May 2016
*Tess of the
d'Urbervilles*

12 May 2016
Titus Oates and His
'Popish Plot'

19 May 2016
The Muses

26 May 2016
The Gettysburg
Address

2 June 2016
Margery Kempe and
English Mysticism

9 June 2016
Penicillin

16 June 2016
The Bronze Age
Collapse

23 June 2016
*Songs of Innocence
and of Experience*

30 June 2016
Sovereignty

7 July 2016
The Invention of
Photography

22 September 2016
Zeno's Paradoxes

29 September 2016
Animal Farm

6 October 2016
Lakshmi

13 October 2016
Plasma

20 October 2016
The Twelfth-Century
Renaissance

27 October 2016
John Dalton

3 November 2016
Epic of Gilgamesh

10 November 2016
*The Fighting
Temeraire*

17 November 2016
Justinian's Legal
Code

24 November 2016
The Baltic Crusades

1 December 2016
Garibaldi and the
Risorgimento

8 December 2016
Harriet Martineau

15 December 2016
The Gin Craze

21 December 2016
Four Quartets

29 December 2016
Johannes Kepler

12 January 2017
Nietzsche's *On
the Genealogy of
Morality*

19 January 2017
Mary, Queen of Scots

26 January 2017
Parasitism

2 February 2017
Hannah Arendt

9 February 2017
John Clare

16 February 2017
Maths in the Early
Islamic World

23 February 2017
Seneca the Younger

2 March 2017
Kuiper Belt

9 March 2017
Elizabeth Gaskell's
novel *North and
South*

16 March 2017
Palaeocene–Eocene
Thermal Maximum

23 March 2017
Battle of Salamis

30 March 2017
Hokusai

6 April 2017
Pauli's Exclusion
Principle

13 April 2017
Rosa Luxemburg

20 April 2017
Roger Bacon

27 April 2017
Egyptian *Book of the
Dead*

4 May 2017
Battle of Lincoln
(1217)

11 May 2017
Emily Dickinson

18 May 2017
Louis Pasteur

25 May 2017
Purgatory

1 June 2017
Enzymes

8 June 2017
Christine de Pizan

15 June 2017
American Populists
and the Gilded Age

22 June 2017
Eugene Onegin

29 June 2017
Plato's *Republic*

6 July 2017
Bird Migration

21 September 2017
Kant's Categorical
Imperative

28 SEPTEMBER 2017
Wuthering Heights

5 OCTOBER 2017
Constantine the
Great

12 OCTOBER 2017
Aphra Behn

19 OCTOBER 2017
Congress of Vienna

26 OCTOBER 2017
Feathered Dinosaurs

2 NOVEMBER 2017
Picasso's *Guernica*

9 NOVEMBER 2017
The Picts

16 NOVEMBER 2017
Germaine de Staël

23 NOVEMBER 2017
Thebes

30 NOVEMBER 2017
Carl Friedrich Gauss

7 DECEMBER 2017
Moby Dick

15 DECEMBER 2017
Thomas Becket

22 DECEMBER 2017
Ludwig van
Beethoven

28 DECEMBER 2017
Hamlet

11 JANUARY 2018
The Siege of Malta,
1565

18 JANUARY 2018
Anna Akhmatova

25 JANUARY 2018
Cicero

1 FEBRUARY 2018
Cephalopods

9 FEBRUARY 2018
Frederick Douglass

15 FEBRUARY 2018
Fungi

22 FEBRUARY 2018
Rosalind Franklin

1 MARCH 2018
Sun Tzu and *The Art
of War*

8 MARCH 2018
Highland Clearances

15 MARCH 2018
Augustine's
Confessions

22 MARCH 2018
Tocqueville:
*Democracy in
America*

5 APRIL 2018
Roman Slavery

11 APRIL 2018
George and Robert
Stephenson

18 APRIL 2018
Middlemarch

26 APRIL 2018
Proton

3 MAY 2018
Almoravid Empire

10 MAY 2018
The Mabinogion

17 MAY 2018
Emancipation of
the Serfs

PRODUCERS TO DATE

Olivia Seligman, Ariane Koek, Sarah Peters, Natasha Maw, Elaine
Lester, Alice Feinstein, Charlie Taylor, Phil Tinline, James Cook,
Thomas Morris, Simon Tillotson

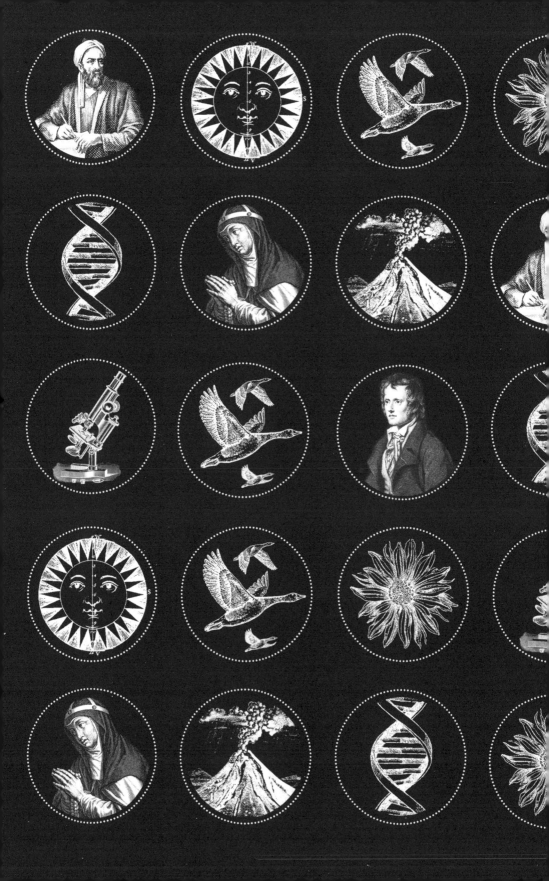